*The Catholics
and German Unity
1866–1871*

GEORGE G. WINDELL

THE CATHOLICS
AND GERMAN UNITY
1866–1871

UNIVERSITY OF MINNESOTA PRESS · MINNEAPOLIS

Library of Congress Catalog Card Number: 54-13011

PUBLISHED IN GREAT BRITAIN, INDIA, AND PAKISTAN BY
GEOFFREY CUMBERLEGE: OXFORD UNIVERSITY PRESS, LONDON, BOMBAY, AND KARACHI

To Marie

Preface

THE following pages present the results of an investigation into the role of Catholicism in the political history of Germany during the critical interval between the destruction of the German Confederation in 1866 and the formal establishment of the Bismarckian *Reich* in 1871. Particularly the book attempts to trace the origins and development of Catholic political movements, and to explore their relationship to other parties and to the major events of the period.

In pre-1866 Germany the political center of gravity had been Catholic Austria; the new Empire was to revolve about Prussia, long regarded as the shield of Protestantism in Central Europe. The intervening years saw a bitter struggle throughout Germany which brought about a profound shift in the balance of political forces within the country as a whole and within many of the individual states — a shift which obviously affected the status of the Catholic Church and, in turn, the attitudes and actions of its German members. But, specifically, how did Catholics react to the sweeping changes ushered in by the War of 1866? And what influence did they exercise on the complex events of the following years?

Superficially, it appeared that the answer to the second of these questions was "Very little." In comparison with the well-known importance of the Prussian *Zentrumsfraktion* before, and the even greater fame of the imperial *Zentrumspartei* after, this period, it seemed that Catholics were relatively apathetic politically. Investigation revealed, however, that this impression of passivity was a result of the erroneous assumption that the absence of a large-scale organization denoted lack of activity. It became apparent that Catholics, organized or unorganized, exercised a tremendous influence upon the political life of several German states during these years, and on a number of critical occasions dominated policy decisions of governments which, in most cases, they did not control. Moreover, in the Reichstag of the North German Confederation, individual Catholics wielded an influence far out of proportion to their rather meager numbers. And further, these facts had a profound effect on Bismarck's foreign and domestic policy.

Relatively complete, if scattered, information about the political activity of Catholics in most of the individual states is found without great difficulty. Only once, however, has there been a substantial attempt to treat these separate developments as a comprehensive whole — in volumes two and three of Karl Bachem's *Vorgeschichte, Geschichte, und Politik der Zentrumspartei*. This work, excellent in many ways, succeeds in creating a unified picture only in the sense that it brings together in one place much of the relevant information. It makes little attempt to analyze, or to relate its material to other political developments. Moreover, since the work is an official party history, it deals with the period before 1871 only as the background out of which the *Zentrumspartei* arose. And, since Bachem was closely associated with that party, the work cannot be regarded as that of an independent scholar.

Thus the problem of creating a synthesis of the various streams of Catholic political action, and of relating them to the larger questions of German history, remained. The present work is an attempt to solve that problem. It makes no claim to have employed hitherto unknown or unused materials. All the sources which have been utilized are published; many of them appeared long ago, although a number of the most important were not available to Bachem. It does, however, seek to approach the evidence from a fresh point of view. The author believes that some new insights have been gained, and some conclusions reached which suggest the necessity of considerable modification in conventional accounts of the *Reichsgründung*. Bismarck's two most recent biographers, Erich Eyck and Arnold Oskar Meyer, for example, scarcely more than mention the influence of the great statesman's relations with the Church and with south German Catholicism on his policy between 1868 and 1870, although they seem to have been the determining factor in some of his most important decisions. Particularly, there is nowhere adequate recognition of the connection between the rapid growth of political Catholicism in south Germany and the origins of the Franco-Prussian War. Ludwig Bergsträsser, in his comprehensive collection, *Der politische Katholizismus: Dokumente seiner Entwicklung,* covers the years 1866 to 1870 in an essay, including only a few documents at the beginning and at the end. Such examples could be multiplied.

The author is under no illusion that the final word has been said in this book on any of the problems which it treats. He hopes, however, that it will open the way to further study of this short but vitally important period in German history, which has been so often dealt with only from the viewpoint of high politics. A large number of later German domestic problems have their origin not in the events of 1871 and after, but in those of 1866 through 1870, yet most histories treat domestic affairs between those dates merely as part of a dreary interlude separating two decisive wars. Much remains to be done before a reasonably complete picture of the influence of domestic politics on Bismarck's foreign policy emerges. Such a picture, to which it is hoped the following pages make a contribution, is vital to a better understanding of nineteenth-century and, perhaps, twentieth-century German history.

Of the many individuals to whom I am obligated, space permits acknowledgment of only a few. I am deeply indebted to Professor Lawrence D. Steefel, who, in addition to directing the research upon which this book is based, unselfishly made available the results of his own investigations. To Professor and Mrs. John B. Wolf, who have been a source of constant encouragement for more than a decade, I can now express appreciation. This book owes more to them than perhaps either realizes. Thanks are due my colleagues, Professors H. Clay Reed, John A. Munroe, and Walther Kirchner, each of whom read parts of the manuscript while the work was in progress. I am especially grateful for the criticisms offered by my good friend and colleague, Professor Evelyn H. Clift, who, going far beyond the call of duty, read the entire manuscript in its original form. My wife, Marie Elizabeth Windell, prepared the index. Without her constant sacrifices and sympathetic understanding the book could never have been completed. 　　　　　　　　　　　　　　　　　　G. G. W.

Newark, Delaware
August 1954

Table of Contents

*The Catholics
and German Unity
1866–1871*

Chapter 1

Catholic Germany and the Crisis of 1866

On July 3, 1866, Prussian arms defeated those of the Habsburg Empire at Königgrätz in what proved to be the decisive battle of the Seven Weeks War. Like many other victories on the battlefield, Königgrätz came to have political and psychological significance which far overshadowed the actual military results. For, although Austrian ability to wage war was far from destroyed, Prussian superiority in combat had been demonstrated. Rather than tempt fate by striving to bring troops from the Italian front in Venetia, and rather than face the possibility of more serious disasters within the Empire proper, including the ever-present possibility of a Hungarian revolt, Vienna requested Napoleon III's armed mediation. Austria's acknowledgment of defeat meant that the destiny of Germany was, barring some unforeseeable catastrophe, committed into the hands of the north German great power, and that the dualism which had heretofore balked all attempts to solve "the German Question," as the nineteenth century understood the term, had ceased to exist.

The ensuing negotiations, during which Bismarck finally converted the King to a policy of moderation toward the defeated enemy, in order to preserve the possibility of future amicable relations, and to forestall French military intervention, culminated in the Preliminary Peace of Nikolsburg on July 26, and in a definitive settlement at Prague on August 23. The terms, softened though they were in comparison with the King's original demands, set the seal on the destruction of the old Germany. The German Confederation of 1815 was dissolved, and Prussia acquired the right to organize all Germany north of the Main into a new confederation without participation or interference by Austria. The four states south of the Main were granted

3

permission to form a second confederation, also without Austrian participation.[1]

Although the ultimate creation of a united Germany[2] under Prussian leadership was implicit in the results of Königgrätz, the final form of the union existed only in the visions or the half-formulated plans of several parties and many individuals. The German Empire, which came into formal existence on January 18, 1871, was largely the product of the conflict between these viewpoints and policies. Certainly not the least important group — one whose outlook must be understood to make clear the struggles of the complex period between 1866 and 1871 — was formed by Germans who belonged to the Roman Catholic Church. As a religious and philosophical system, Catholicism was fundamentally opposed to many of the prevailing social and political ideologies of the third quarter of the century, and, as an institution of traditional authority and influence, it claimed the loyalty of millions of Germans.[3] In the years between 1866 and 1871 German Catholics

[1] No study of this period can ignore the provocative, if somewhat doctrinaire, work of Robert C. Binkley, *Realism and Nationalism, 1852–1871,* which treats the period from the end of the revolutionary epoch to the completion of Bismarck's edifice in terms of a crisis between federalism and centralism within individual countries and on a continental scale. For Germany the thesis is particularly enlightening. Catholics represented the extreme wing of federalism; the doctrinaire liberals stood at the other limit. On the Austro-Prussian conflict the best detailed work is still Heinrich Friedjung, *Der Kampf um die Vorherrschaft in Deutschland, 1859 bis 1866.* For a brilliant recent treatment of the "German problem" up to 1866 from a non-Prussian viewpoint, see H. Ritter von Srbik, *Deutsche Einheit, Idee und Wirklichkeit vom Heiligen Reich bis Königgrätz.* On the German Confederation and attempts to reform it after 1851, see E. E. Kraehe, "A History of the German Confederation, 1851–1866" (unpublished doctoral dissertation, University of Minnesota, 1948).

[2] Because of the possibilities of confusion arising out of changes in political boundaries, the term "Germany," when used without qualification, should be taken in its current conventional sense, *i.e.,* excluding Austria.

[3] A study which would continue Srbik's monumental work past 1866 is badly needed. Perhaps even more desirable would be the completion of Franz Schnabel's magnificent *Deutsche Geschichte im neunzehnten Jahrhundert,* as yet covering only the period up to 1848. Of the extensive literature dealing with the *Reichsgründung* only a few examples can be cited here. The two best known general discussions are Heinrich von Sybel, *Die Begründung des deutschen Reiches durch Wilhelm I,* and Erich Brandenburg, *Die Reichsgründung.* Sybel's work has been used extensively in the present study because, although outdated, it does contain a wealth of factual information, and because its author was a participant in many of the events described. Brandenburg's book is the work of one of Germany's outstanding twentieth-century scholars. Other general works of use for this period are the following: Sir Adolphus Ward, *Germany, 1815–1890*; William H. Dawson, *The German Empire, 1867–1914*; Friedrich Darmstaedter, *Bismarck and the Creation of the Second Reich*; and, especially, volumes 8–10 of Alfred Stern, *Geschichte Europas seit den Verträgen von 1815 bis zum Frankfurter Frieden von 1871.* These have also been used in the present work, but, except in special cases, they will not be cited individually

4

exercised a much greater influence on the nation's history than has generally been recognized. In almost all important decisions their weight was in some way felt; in several, it appears to have been decisive.

The immediate reaction of articulate Catholics to Königgrätz was one of deepest pessimism, for they saw in the exclusion of Austria from their country a catastrophe of almost unimaginable proportions. From North and South came expressions of shock, abhorrence, despair, and resignation. Perhaps the most vivid example of the general feeling is found in the utter revulsion which Hermann von Mallinckrodt, one of the outstanding leaders of the Prussian *Zentrumsfraktion,* or Catholic party, expressed in a letter written under the immediate stimulus of the news of the battle: "The world stinks." Two months later, in September, Mallinckrodt branded Prussia as "the camp of dishonor," and, for a time, he seriously considered emigrating to Habsburg territory.[5] August Reichensperger, artist and art historian, and also a leader of the Prussian Catholic fraction, found it so difficult to accept a Germany without Austria that he abandoned politics altogether to find solace in his art.[6] The young Hessian, Georg von Hertling, later chancellor of the Empire, would never forget the "misery and shame" which his family felt upon the arrival of Prussian troops in Darmstadt: "I can still see the Prussian Hussars with loaded carbines stop on the corner, a battalion of the fifty-third infantry regiment march into the street where we lived in order to enter individual houses to demand quarters."[7] What impressed Hertling most was the complacency with which some of his Prussian relatives regarded these events, in contrast to his own "passionate bitterness."[8] Two years later the young man, then a *Privatdozent* at Bonn University, was still unable to reconcile himself, and refused to join in the cheers for the Prussian monarch and his consort when they visited the university for the celebration of its bicentennial.[9] From Mainz, Bishop Wilhelm Emanuel

hereafter. Only the two latest of the innumerable Bismarck biographies need be mentioned: Erich Eyck, *Bismarck, Leben und Werk,* and Arnold Oskar Meyer, *Bismarck, der Mensch und der Staatsmann.* There is a summary in English of Eyck's work under the title *Bismarck and the German Empire.*

[4] Johannes Ziekursch, *Politische Geschichte des neuen deutschen Kaiserreiches,* 1:193.
[5] *Ibid.*
[6] Ludwig Pastor, *August Reichensperger, 1808–1895. Sein Leben und sein Wirken auf dem Gebiet der Politik, der Kunst, und der Wissenschaft,* 1:578–86.
[7] Georg von Hertling, *Erinnerungen aus meinem Leben,* 1:160–61.
[8] *Ibid.,* 161.
[9] Hertling to his mother, Bonn, Aug. 9, 1868, *ibid.,* 195–96.

Freiherr von Ketteler, Germany's outstanding Catholic prelate, wrote that he saw in the war the destruction of all that had been won by the Wars of Liberation.[10] It was several weeks before he was capable of separating in his mind the will of God and the purposes of man as they had manifested themselves that summer. Although he found the latter "so painful that it is better not to look at them at all," he did eventually discern the hand of Providence in the outcome of the war.[11]

In some places the war resulted in civil disturbance and outright violence of Catholic against Protestant. In some areas of the Prussian Rhineland, for instance, Catholics for a time forcibly resisted the order for mobilization against Austria. At the town of Lampheim, in Württemberg, the news of Königgrätz set off an attempt by a Catholic mob to destroy the recently constructed Lutheran church, along with the home of its pastor.[12]

In order to explain the impassioned reaction of responsible individuals, it is necessary to review some of the political relationships that existed in mid-nineteenth-century Germany, and some of the intellectual currents that helped to keep those relationships in a state of constant agitation. The most important single fact is that statistically the exclusion of Austria reduced the Catholic part of the population to a minority. In 1855 Catholics numbered about twenty-three million of the forty-three million inhabitants of the German Confederation. Of this total, about twelve million lived in the German sections of Austria.[13] If we allow for the growth of population in the ensuing eleven years, it is apparent that Catholic Germany was almost exactly halved by the Treaty of Prague. On the basis of the census of 1871, the first accurate accounting for all Germany that seems to be available, Catholics numbered a little under fifteen million, contrasted with twenty-five and one half million Protestants. These figures include the overwhelmingly Catholic Alsace-Lorraine, which must, of course, be excluded from consideration for the period from 1866 to 1871.[14]

[10] Ketteler to his sister Sophie, Mainz, July 13, 1866, in W. E. Freiherr von Ketteler, *Briefe von und zu Wilhelm Emanuel Freiherr von Ketteler, Bischof von Mainz*, edited by J. M. Raich, 338–39. Hereafter this collection of Ketteler's correspondence will be cited as *Ketteler Briefe.*

[11] Ketteler to his brother Wildrich, Mainz, July 26, 1866, *ibid.,* 339.

[12] Adolph Rapp, *Die Württemberger und die nationale Frage, 1863–1871*, 78, note; Joseph Hansen *et al., Die Rheinprovinz, 1815–1915: Hundert Jahre preussischer Herrschaft am Rhein*, 1:782–84.

[13] Srbik, 2:326.

[14] For the pertinent census figures for 1871, see Appendix.

6

Catholic Germany and the Crisis of 1866

Of the twelve to thirteen million Catholics in Germany between 1866 and 1871, over half dwelt in Prussia,[15] traditionally regarded by Germans of both confessions as a "Protestant state," just as Austria had always been looked upon as a "Catholic power."[16] Although Prussian Catholics at that time had no grounds for complaint about the treatment of their Church by the government,[17] they could still find no cause to be jubilant about the future, particularly since extreme Lutheran elements chose to interpret the war as a "Protestant crusade."[18]

In the eyes of the majority of German Catholics, however, Prussia's victory assumed a significance far too great to be explained in terms of relative numbers alone. Of more importance was the fact that the Church represented a variety of conservatism that was coming to be more and more out of harmony with the prevailing spirit of the age. Traditionally, German Catholics had looked both to Rome and to Vienna, viewing them as the twin pillars which supported their ideal of a "Christian-Germanic" society, a federal union of princes and peoples under the leadership of the Habsburg Emperor. That conception, although a pale afterglow of the old imperial idea, still retained some validity even following the destruction of the Empire by Napoleon and the establishment of the German Confederation by the Congress of Vienna.[19]

On the other hand, German Catholics were no more immune to the

[15] Prussia in 1864, *i.e.*, before the annexations of 1866, included 7,201,911 Catholics. After the annexations the figure was 7,808,991. See *Historisch-politische Blätter für das katholische Deutschland*, edited by Joseph Edmund Jörg and Franz Binder, 59:679–90; 66:3–4. (Hereafter this journal will be cited as *HPB*.) The article cited contains a complete discussion of Prussian religious statistics for the period from 1861 to 1865.

[16] See *HPB*, 58:655, 781–83.

[17] The Prussian constitution guaranteed freedom of worship. Since the Catholic section of the Prussian *Kultusministerium* had for a number of years been headed by a Catholic, Prussian members of the Church were in a much more favorable position than were their fellows in some of the south German states, where they had to face the anticlericalism of liberal ministries.

[18] The Lutheran rector of the University of Greifswald spoke of a *"Gustav Adolphs-ritt in katholisches Land,"* *HPB*, 58:783. Ludwig Windthorst, the leader of the imperial *Zentrumspartei*, later dated the beginning of the *Kulturkampf* from the battle of Königgrätz. See Eduard Hüsgen, *Ludwig Windthorst, sein Leben, sein Wirker*, 78.

[19] See Karl Bachem, *Vorgeschichte, Geschichte und Politik der deutschen Zentrumspartei*, 2:230. This long work, by a member of the Cologne Catholic publishing firm, J. P. Bachem and Sons, contains the complete or partial texts of many documents unavailable elsewhere in this country. It must be used cautiously, since it is an official history of the Center party by a man whose family was long associated with the party. See also Hansen, 1:796–97; *Augsburger Allgemeine Zeitung*, Nov. 30, 1866, 5494 (hereafter cited as *AAZ*); Hertling, 1:66, 160, 226; *HPB*, 59:1.

emotional appeal of nationalism than any other group in the nineteenth century. Therefore, the national and the imperial principles had to find some sort of a reconciliation in their minds and hearts. The two did reach an uneasy equilibrium in the ideal of *Grossdeutschland,* a hoped-for federal union of all the German states, with a national parliament, under the Habsburg Crown. Thereby, Germany would be again united, would become again a nation, but at the same time continuity with the past would be preserved. In the period beginning with the revolutionary upheavals of 1848, most German Catholics sought a *grossdeutsch* solution of the German problem. That solution, however, became progressively more and more difficult to achieve because of the bitter conflict between the two German great powers. Most Catholics outside Prussia, and many within, found themselves, therefore, unable to forgive the Hohenzollern monarchy for what they considered its anti-German policy, particularly after 1851.[20] Prussia effectively sabotaged an all-German policy toward France during the Crimean War; she refused in the War of 1859 to go any further than ordering mobilization of her army on the Rhine, and, perhaps even more significantly, she watched complacently Italy's absorption of the major part of the Papal State in 1860.

Moreover, from the middle of the century on, Catholics in all countries found their position ever more seriously threatened by the multiplication of secular doctrines which undermined traditional religious, intellectual, and social concepts. The vast proliferation of scientific discoveries, the spread of scientific techniques and attitudes into disciplines, such as history and economics, which had heretofore been considered as somehow involving moral qualities, were changing basic assumptions about man's nature and purpose. Industrial expansion was at the same time beginning to transform the physical basis of life in continental Europe. Both were helping to create a secular, positivistic, and agnostic temper, which the Church and its adherents could regard only with extreme misgivings.[21]

In Germany, these trends were most apparent in the development of post-1848 liberalism, secular in its aims, hostile to the international Church, demanding civil marriage and state control of education,[22]

[20] Ziekursch, 1:242; Hertling, 1:160.
[21] Hansen, 1:796–97; *AAZ,* Nov. 30, 1866, 5494; Hertling, 1:66.
[22] The issue of secular versus ecclesiastical control of education was one of the most agitated of the period. During the 1860's, especially in Baden and Bavaria, measures spon-

striving for a highly centralized political authority to be exercised through a parliament and a responsible ministry, all in the interest of individual freedom. The beginning of the new era in Prussia in 1858 brought an end to the period of reaction which had succeeded Olmütz, and gave new heart to all German liberals. A year later, the *Deutscher Nationalverein* came into existence, under the leadership of the Hanoverian politician, Rudolf von Bennigsen. It openly espoused exclusion of Austria from the Confederation, and creation of a *Kleindeutschland* under Prussian hegemony.[23]

The beginnings of Catholic political organization in Germany likewise are to be found in the upheaval of 1848. At that time there was still no unbridgeable gap between Catholicism and the liberal movement. The relatively small clerical fraction which appeared in the National Assembly at Frankfurt reflected the liberal spirit that had come to characterize Catholicism in most western European countries during the 1840's, and its members, like most other Germans, were buoyed up by the dream of "unity through freedom" which played such a large role in the early months of the assembly. The Clericals of the *Paulskirche* sought generally to advance the interests of their Church within the framework of the constitutional state which the revolution sought to create. They were willing to accept the principle of liberty of conscience, and did not oppose severing the bond between throne and altar, provided that the Church was guaranteed the right to control its own affairs. Specifically they insisted that the Church be allowed to maintain its own schools, its own press, and its lay organizations without restriction. Catholic delegates had a considerable voice in the ultimate wording of articles five and six of the *Grundrechte*, which was perhaps the assembly's most significant achievement.[24]

sored by the liberals, providing for secular control of all schools, provoked serious crises. See *HPB*, 53:93; Bachem, 2:233–37, 304–5. Concern for the problem of Catholic higher education is apparent as early as 1862 when the demand was raised at the Aachen meeting of the *Generalversammlung der Katholikenvereine Deutschlands* (annual meeting of delegates from various Catholic lay organizations) for a "free Catholic university for Germany." Both Archbishop Geissel of Cologne and his successor, Melchers, frequently advocated the establishment of such a university. The latter referred to it (1869) as "a question of life and death for Catholic Germany." See Hansen, 1:797.

[23] See Hermann Oncken, *Rudolf von Bennigsen, ein deutscher liberaler Politiker, nach seinen Briefen und hinterlassenen Papieren,* 1:315–62.

[24] Srbik, 1:452–53; Theobald Ziegler, *Die geistigen und socialen Strömungen des neunzehnten Jahrhunderts,* 286–89; Richard Lempp, *Die Frage der Trennung von Kirche und Staat im Frankfurter Parlament,* 37–39, 41, 50; Georges Goyau, *L'Allemagne religieuse: le catholicisme, 1800–1870,* 3:xxvi–xxvii.

Even the hierarchy, strongly influenced by the liberal Catholic movement in France and Belgium, showed broad sympathies for the political objectives of the revolution. Many bishops, in Germany as elsewhere, were coming to feel that the future welfare of the Church could best be guaranteed by regaining the loyalty of the masses, not in close ties with authoritarian governments. A conference of German bishops, held at Würzburg in Bavaria, October 22 to November 16, 1848, issued a declaration that "however decisively and strongly the Church abhors and rejects anarchical movements of all kinds, it has a vital interest in securing [for itself] everything that is inherent in the general demand for freedom from administrative supervision and control over truth, and it cannot fail to seek its rightful share in the pledges that the princes have made to their peoples." [25] The bishops indicated their willingness to accept separation of Church and state under certain specified conditions, which included freedom of the Church to carry on its educational work without governmental restriction, particularly the right to establish and operate educational institutions; freedom of the clergy from state examination and supervision; unrestricted liberty to establish lay religious organizations; and the right to administer, without accounting to political authorities, the Church's own ecclesiastical and charitable funds.[26]

On the all-important issue of political unity, German Catholics in 1848 thought along the lines of a federal union including Austria. Their liberal viewpoint at that time cannot be dissociated from their assumption, then shared by the majority of Germans, that such a state would emerge from the revolution. But when it became clear by December 1848 that the union of all Germany had miscarried, and that the only hope remaining was a Prussian-dominated *Kleindeutschland,* German Catholics rapidly lost their enthusiasm for unity. In the ensuing years they gradually returned for the most part to their former imperial outlook, although, paradoxically, in practice they usually supported a narrow particularism.[27]

Thus, between 1851 and the founding of the Empire there could be no Catholic political party functioning in Germany as a whole. During most of that period, from 1851 to 1866, only in Prussia was there

[25] Ziegler, 289.
[26] *Ibid.*
[27] Srbik, 1:454–55.

10

a party that can specifically be called "Clerical" or "Catholic," although in other states with large Catholic populations, such as Bavaria and Baden, the viewpoint of the Church had considerable influence on the policy of conservative parties generally. In Prussia there was a combination of circumstances which made a formal Catholic party useful. The Hohenzollern kingdom was predominantly Protestant; therefore, Catholics, as the largest religious minority, had special interests to defend.[28] The Prussian constitution, even though it may have been a travesty of the liberal conception of a charter, particularly after its revision in 1850, was sufficiently liberal to permit a political opposition to operate effectively. During the period of reaction after Olmütz, the Catholic fraction generally cooperated with the liberal opposition, constantly protesting the emasculation of the constitution by the Camarilla. This action was, on the whole, logical, since the fraction still retained something of the liberalism of 1848. Moreover, as indicated above, the Church, under the Prussian constitution, had a status much more favorable than it had, for instance, in Catholic Bavaria. In the latter the mere fact of its being the official state church made it subject to considerable governmental interference. In practice the position of the Church in Prussia was further improved during the reaction because the several ministries failed to make use of their constitutional rights of supervision over ecclesiastical affairs.[29]

Meanwhile, from Rome, Pius IX, after his own flirtation with liberalism in 1848, was steadily maneuvering the Holy See step by step into open opposition to the entire liberal trend of the nineteenth century. Ably abetted by the Jesuits, whose influence over the Papacy continually grew, he pressed onward toward official rejection of any possibility of compromise between the Church and contemporary secular doctrines. That rejection was implicit in his promulgation of the Dogma of the Immaculate Conception in 1854, and became open in the Encyclical *Quanta Cura,* with its attached Syllabus of Errors, ten years later.[30]

The increasingly reactionary attitude of the Holy See had an impor-

[28] The Catholic fraction was particularly interested in thwarting the attempts of radical liberals to secularize the schools. Unsuccessful efforts were made in the *Landtag* in 1862 to end completely the confessional character of the higher schools, and to deconfessionalize religious instruction in the *Volksschulen.* See Hansen, 1:798.

[29] Ziekursch, 1:192; Sybel, 2:108; Brandenburg, *Reichsgründung,* 2:269–70.

[30] Binkley, 60; Hansen, 1:797–98.

tant bearing on the political scene north of the Alps. It contributed, on the one hand, to the breakdown of the above-mentioned working alliance between Catholics and liberals, particularly in Prussia, but also in the South. The open hostility of the Pope toward "progressive" ideas placed a useful weapon in the hands of the orthodox anticlerical liberal, for, by attacking "ultramontanism," he was able to contrast his own "advanced" ideas with the "obscurantist" doctrines of a faith that, from his point of view, was determined to force the world back into the Middle Ages.[31] On the other hand, it set up critical tensions within the ranks of Catholics themselves. More and more they were faced with the distasteful choice between loyalty to their Church and adherence to their political principles. The conflict was especially acute for Catholic intellectuals, such as the Prussian August Reichensperger and the great Bavarian ecclesiastical historian, Ignaz von Döllinger, who had long advocated that the Church adapt itself to the modern world.[32]

These tensions ultimately destroyed the Prussian Catholic fraction. With the beginning of the new era in 1858, it abandoned its ecclesiastical designation in order to indicate its acceptance of the new régime, and became the *Fraktion des Zentrums.* This title it derived actually from the central position of its seats in the Chamber of Deputies, but it also hoped thereby to symbolize its role as a mediator between conflicting interests. Its members expected that the new régime would bring to an end Prussia's policy of obstructionism in the Federal Diet at Frankfurt, and that she would henceforth pursue again a "German" rather than a selfishly Prussian policy. These hopes were, however, deceived. The failure of Prussia to aid the Habsburg Empire in the War of 1859, which contributed to the Austrian defeat, and to the succeeding unification of Italy, meant, on the one hand, the loss of most of the Pope's temporal sovereignty and, on the other, the victory of anticlerical liberalism on the peninsula. Nevertheless, in spite of the inevitable disillusionment of the fraction, and of Prussian Catholics generally, with the government's foreign policy, the subsequent ap-

[31] *HPB*, 58:784–85, 790.

[32] See Pastor, *Reichensperger*, 1, *passim.* In Döllinger's case the personal conflict was so severe that it drove him, after the promulgation of the Dogma of Papal Infallibility in 1870, to open denial of the spiritual primacy of the Pope. See Fritz Vigener, *Drei Gestalten aus dem modernen Katholizismus: Möhler, Diepenbrock, Döllinger* (published as Beiheft No. VII of the *Historische Zeitschrift*).

pearance of the *Nationalverein* left them with little choice other than to support it on internal issues.[33]

The difficulty of the party's position is apparent from the program it published in 1861. Following an introduction which criticized party programs in general as attempts to mislead the voters, and after denying that the Center had a specific program, the document proceeded, in the style of platforms everywhere, to list and discuss the general principles for which the party claimed to stand. The disclaimer of a specific program indicates, of course, only the failure of the Center to find a group of positive doctrines that would appeal to all its voters. On only one or two points does the program bear the stamp of deep conviction. The party announced itself to be *grossdeutsch,* that is:

It wants the whole of Germany *to remain united* [italics supplied]; it demands that Austria not be separated from us, because national feeling and the duty of self-preservation demand it. It does not want a [form of] unity in Germany which can be achieved only by revolution and civil war; it does desire, above all, a unification of Germany on the basis of the further development of existing legal relationships, which will lead much sooner to freedom and power for the fatherland than [will] the forcible overthrow of legitimate authority which the so-called *Kleindeutschen* have in mind.[34]

There follows a list of the usual demands for freedom of the Church within the state. The list included, specifically, a clause supporting equality for all confessions, and one demanding legal provision for the "corporative independence" of both the working class and the peasants. In short, it upheld the idea of "self-government in all areas of civil life." The program, however, opposed unlimited freedom for individuals to enter all occupations, on the grounds that *Gewerbefreiheit* was not demanded by the working class, and that it was thus a chimera, put forth by "capitalists and demagogues" for their own profit. The hope was expressed that in time a golden mean would be discovered. On these social questions the party stated that it agreed fundamentally with the *Kreuzzeitungpartei, i.e.,* the extreme conservatives. But on other issues it supported the general liberal trend, favoring,

[33] Ziekursch, 1:192–93; Ludwig Bergsträsser, *Geschichte der politischen Parteien in Deutschland,* 50; *AAZ,* Nov. 30, 1866, *Beilage,* 5494; Brandenburg, *Reichsgründung,* 2:269–70.

[34] "Eine programmatische Kundgebung der preussischen Zentrumspartei, 1861," in Felix Salomon, *Die deutschen Parteiprogramme,* 1:84–85.

for example, equalization of the land tax, elimination of "unjustified" privileges, inauguration of a "rule of law," and the consequent ending of arbitrary rule by the bureaucracy. Finally, it advocated establishment of "a free communal, district, and provincial constitution." [35] The contradictions in the platform seem not to have been apparent to its authors, who brought it to a close with a ringing appeal for Catholic voters to elect men who would announce in advance their intention to join the *Zentrumsfraktion* if elected.[36]

Thus, after 1859, the Center underwent increasingly severe stresses, gradually succumbing to the fate of most moderate parties in time of crisis. During the constitutional conflict it halfheartedly supported the opposition to Bismarck on domestic questions, but, on the other hand, it constantly hoped for a compromise, for it could not accept the probable results of a clear-cut liberal victory. On questions of foreign policy it combated vigorously the minister-president's refusal to recognize the rights of the German Confederation during the Schleswig-Holstein crisis, and it fought bitterly to prevent his constant sabotage of all attempts to reform the Confederation. There were no crucial religious issues at the time, issues which could hold the party together in spite of its vacillation and political instability. In each succeeding election after the beginning of the new era, it lost seats to one extreme or the other, until, in the election of July 3, 1866, its representation fell to such an extent that it could no longer maintain its independent existence, and was forced to disband.[37]

For the purpose of this study, the other states north of the Main can legitimately be ignored in the period before 1866, since Catholicism played an utterly insignificant political role in all of them. South Germany, on the other hand, considered as a whole, was Catholic, although in only two of the states, Bavaria and Baden, did Catholics form a majority of the population. On the question of Germany's future, south German Catholics were, before the war, as indicated above, mainly of *grossdeutsch* persuasion. Traditionally, the South had felt closer to the Habsburgs than to the Hohenzollerns. Prussian order and efficiency were often admired, but seldom loved, and the average southerner had a healthy distrust of the military tradition of

[35] *Ibid.*, 85.
[36] *Ibid.*, 86–87.
[37] Ziekursch, 1:193; Bergsträsser, *Politische Parteien*, 50; Hermann Wendorf, *Die Fraktion des Zentrums im preussischen Abgeordnetenhause, 1859–67*, 106–22, 127–28.

the Prussian state. The events of 1848 did nothing to lessen that distrust; nor did Prussia's behavior at Frankfurt, while Bismarck represented her in the restored Federal Diet, help to allay the misgivings. On the whole, during the fifties, south Germans, Protestant and Catholic alike, whether liberal or conservative, remained true to their traditional allegiances.[38]

The beginning of the new era in Prussia, the War of 1859, and the subsequent rebirth of a strong *kleindeutsch* movement reacted with considerable force on south Germany. Between 1859 and 1863, there developed in each of the states a significant division of public opinion on the question of national unity. The process was closely connected with the growth of the *Nationalverein*, and with the fact that the liberal movement, therefore, became more and more closely identified with the idea of Prussian hegemony. Nevertheless, the *kleindeutsch* liberals in no case represented more than an extremely vocal minority in the total population of any of the four southern states. Only in Baden, where the obvious danger from France tended to counteract the historic particularism, did they actually come to dominate the government before the War of 1866. But everywhere south of the Main they were strong enough as early as 1861 to precipitate a general crystallization of views, and to stimulate the organization of political parties to defend either the *grossdeutsch,* or the particularist attitude. For the most part, the people of south Germany still felt that the nation could not dispense with either great power. Many of them were convinced that the conflict between the two was all that prevented one or the other from swallowing up the smaller states. Therefore, when the *grossdeutscher Reformverein* was founded in 1862, dedicated to German unity through reform of the existing Confederation, it found that the majority of south Germans wished it well, and that a large number would actively support it as a counterweight against the *Nationalverein.*[39]

In Bavaria, the most populous of the four states, the events described above resulted in a political situation of considerable complexity. The minority of the population that was politically active, with its hard core in the bureaucracy, had long professed moderately liberal views on internal policy. As late as the early sixties, there was no for-

[38] Sybel, 6:78; Srbik, 2:246–47; Hertling, 1:226; Ziekursch, 1:242.
[39] Ziekursch, 1:242; Bachem, 2:230.

mally organized Conservative party. The Bavarian constitution provided for a system of indirect election to the lower chamber, and this arrangement naturally favored the well-organized professional politicians. Before 1867, the rural population, almost entirely Catholic, seems not to have exercised the franchise to any considerable degree. During these years also, the clergy, whose political influence on the rural voter was later decisive, appears to have remained aloof from political activity. The ministers of the popular King Max II and, after his death in 1864, the succeeding ministry of Baron Ludwig von der Pfordten under the young Ludwig II attempted to preserve Bavaria's independence from either great power by exploiting the quarrels between them.[40]

However, as more Bavarian liberals succumbed to the lure of the *Nationalverein,* and moved into the *kleindeutsch* camp, conservative and *grossdeutsch* Bavarians found themselves forced more and more into an extreme particularist and anti-Prussian attitude. That was particularly true after the founding in 1863 of the Bavarian Progressive party (*Bayrische Fortschrittspartei*), which worked as an open ally of the Prussian Progressives. The strength of particularistic sentiment among groups hostile to Prussia was considerably increased as a result of the policies pursued at Berlin by Bismarck's "fighting ministry." Those policies likewise proved highly embarrassing to Prussia's would-be friends in the South, for Bismarck's ruthless subversion of the constitution made him appear the negation of all they wanted the Prussian government to stand for. During the early stages of this polarization of Bavarian opinion, confessional issues were scarcely present at all, except in so far as they may have subconsciously influenced viewpoints. For example, many liberal Catholics showed no qualms at joining the Progressives. Nevertheless, gradually the terms "liberal" and "conservative" came to be associated with "Protestant" and "Catholic," for few people in south Germany were able to avoid associating *kleindeutsch* liberalism with the Protestant tradition of Prussia, however tenuous the link may have been in fact. By 1865 the *grossdeutsch-*conservative elements were either being swept up in the rising tide of what the liberals called "ultramontanism," or were being forced into the *kleindeutsch* camp to avoid it. Thus the division came more and

---

[40] Chester W. Clark, *Franz Joseph and Bismarck, The Diplomacy of Austria before the War of 1866,* 17, 187; Bachem, 2: 230–231; *HPB,* 64: 648–52.

more to represent a religious cleavage, as well as a deep-seated difference of political opinion.[41]

In the Bavarian lower chamber elected in 1865, the Catholic-Conservative party, however, could still depend on only twelve to fourteen
votes.[42] Hence, at the outbreak of the war, which Bavaria fought and
lost in alliance with Austria, political Catholicism was as yet relatively
undeveloped, in spite of the increasing tendency of liberal circles to
blame all evils on "ultramontane" influence.[43]

The influence of the Holy See cannot be ignored as a factor in the
injection of confessionalism into Bavarian political controversies. It
seems certain that the clergy, following the spirit of the Syllabus of
1864, did not fail to point out to the faithful the evils and errors of
liberalism. The postwar liberal minister-president, Prince Hohenlohe-
Schillingsfürst, found the widespread interest aroused by the Syllabus
worthy of comment in 1865,[44] and certainly the *Historisch-politische
Blätter,* through its capable editor, Joseph Edmund Jörg, later one of
the leaders of the Bavarian Patriot party, was, as early as 1864, thun-
dering its denunciations of liberalism in terms that the Pope could
scarcely have disapproved.[45]

In contrast to Bavaria, the Grand Duchy of Baden, which had
shown itself to be the most radical section of Germany in the upheaval
of 1848–49, was troubled by clerical issues in a virulent form during
the entire period between the end of the revolution and the German
War. The suppression of the republican and quasi-socialist uprising by
Prussian arms in 1849 had resulted in the restoration of the authority
of the Grand Duke. The prerevolutionary constitution was reintro-

[41] Bachem, 2:230–31; Clark, 18–19. Bavarian Protestants were only slightly less hostile
to Prussia than Catholics just before the War of 1866. See Karl A. von Müller, *Bayern im
Jahre 1866 und die Berufung des Fürsten Hohenlohe,* 47, note 3.

[42] Bachem, 2:238–39.

[43] Prince Hohenlohe, who became head of the ministry on the last day of 1866, frequently expressed in his diary the belief that the "ultramontanes" or the "ultramontane
party" was responsible for Bavaria's disastrous policy before, during, and immediately
after the war. Hohenlohe himself came from a Catholic family, and his brother was a
Cardinal. See Prince Chlodwig zu Hohenlohe-Schillingsfürst, *Memoirs,* 1: *passim.*

[44] Hohenlohe to Queen Victoria, Munich, April 15, 1865, *ibid.,* 1:138.

[45] For example, on the school conflict in Hesse-Darmstadt, he wrote: "The school has
nowhere in the world the overwhelming importance that it possesses in Germany. . . .
Modern liberalism is well aware of this. If it succeeds only in separating completely the
schools from the Church, then the existence of the latter will cause it little concern in the
future. The Church will then be a building with four walls, whose interior, as the liberals
count on, will become emptier with every decade." "Die Kammer in Darmstadt und der
Dom zu Mainz," *HPB,* 53:93.

duced, and a brief period of reaction followed. However, in 1852, Prince Friedrich succeeded to the throne as regent for his mentally incompetent brother, Grand Duke Ludwig. The Regent, whose sympathies were liberal, soon demonstrated a desire to inaugurate substantial reforms in the administration of the Duchy. His natural inclinations were strengthened by his marriage, in 1856, to Princess Louise, daughter of the Prince of Prussia, later King William I. The Princess had absorbed early in life something of the highly progressive views of her mother, Augusta of Weimar. In 1858, Friedrich succeeded his brother as Grand Duke, contemporaneously with the inauguration of the new era in Prussia.

The presence on the throne, during a period of general reaction in Germany, of a prince inclined toward reform gave rise to a series of bitter conflicts between the Baden government and the Catholic hierarchy. At the head of the latter was the aged and contentious Archbishop Vicari of Freiburg, an outspoken opponent of the state's right to exercise any control over the Church. The conflict actually began in March 1851, when a convocation of bishops from the whole Rhineland area met at Freiburg under the presidency of Vicari, and issued a memoir to the German governments which repeated most of the demands made by the Würzburg convocation of 1848.[46] The Baden government refused to accept these demands, both in 1851 and when they were repeated two years later. These refusals occasioned a campaign carried on from the pulpits to force the government to change its policy. Since political use of the clerical office was in violation of a standing government regulation, a considerable number of priests were arrested. The climax came in 1852, when Vicari personally prohibited a funeral service for the deceased Protestant Grand Duke, and was, therefore, himself placed under house arrest. Although the episcopate did not abandon its demands, the acerbity of the conflict abated somewhat after 1854, and in 1859 a reasonably satisfactory concordat was negotiated between the Papacy and the government. The moderate success of the Church was, however, only temporary, for it came at the very time that Friedrich I was beginning his sweeping liberalization of the state, aided by several leading Progressive politicians. The concordat failed to secure the approval of the *Landtag* when it was pre-

---

[46] For a general discussion of the development of the Church-state conflict in Baden, see Franz Dor, *Jakob Lindau, ein badischer Politiker und Volksmann*, 16–33.

sented in March 1860, although later substantially the same rights were conferred upon the Church by ordinary legislation. Since acceptance of this solution of the problem would have been a tacit admission of the right of the state to legislate in ecclesiastical affairs, the hierarchy, and particularly the Archbishop, continued to regard the situation as completely unsatisfactory.[47]

This conflict, which, for the most part, concerned the control of ecclesiastical appointments, did not arouse great excitement among the mass of Catholic laymen. What did touch them deeply was the Grand Duke's open espousal of *Kleindeutschland*. This was signaled by his naming, in 1861, of Franz von Roggenbach as minister of foreign affairs. From the moment of his appointment, Roggenbach dominated the ministry. He came from a Catholic family, but was himself emancipated, and was, in fact, an intimate of Princess Augusta of Prussia, and a friend of the future emperor Friedrich III. At least in part as a result of these associations, Roggenbach had become convinced of the necessity of German unity under the leadership of a liberal Prussia.

The sympathy of the Grand Duke and Roggenbach for Prussian hegemony in Germany did not extend to approval of Bismarck's policy after his advent in 1862. As liberals who had inaugurated reforms which in some ways made Baden constitutionally the most advanced of the German states, they abhorred Bismarck's defiance of constitutional limitations on his power. Equally unsatisfactory to them was Prussia's, and, as a matter of fact, Austria's, treatment of the *Bund*'s wishes in the Schleswig-Holstein affair; for Roggenbach's conception of a united Germany involved reform of the German Confederation. On these points, at least, the government was at one with the majority of its Catholic subjects.

In the early sixties, following the appointment of Roggenbach, there developed gradually among Catholic laymen an increasing interest in combating both the government's liberalism and its *kleindeutsch* tendencies. The men most closely associated with arousing this concern were Jakob Lindau, a Heidelberg merchant, and Dr. Ferdinand Bissing, a *Privatdozent* at Heidelberg University.[48] It was from widely

---

[47] Hermann Baumgarten and Ludwig Jolly, *Staatsminister Jolly, ein Lebensbild*, 102–3.

[48] Josef Weber, *Die katholische Presse Südwestdeutschlands und die Begründung des deutschen Reiches, 1866–72*, 5–6. Lindau and Bissing, along with the jurist Reinhold Baumstark and the priest F. X. Lender, later formed the "Quadrilateral" in the Baden *Landtag*.

differing motives that these men entered the political arena. Lindau seems to have been activated almost entirely by religious fervor. Until he became concerned, as a result of his attendance at the Aachen meeting of the Catholic Laymen's Organizations in 1862, with the problem of defending traditional moral concepts against the onslaught of liberalism, he had had no connection with politics. Only very slowly did he develop deep convictions on the question of the political future of Germany. Although he used the *grossdeutsch* arguments, he did so apparently more because of tradition than because he was deeply convinced of their wisdom. Lindau's constant goal was to combat the growing materialism and secularism which were beginning to infect the masses. To him, political action furnished only one method of accomplishing that goal. He sought the same end through his work with the "Casinos," the Catholic clubs that he and others organized for the purpose of stimulating interest among young people in important questions of the age.[49]

Bissing, on the other hand, was a freethinker, who though nominally a Catholic, was interested primarily in politics, and who saw in Catholicism a tool that could be used to combat Prussian domination of Germany. To him, *Grossdeutschland* was the supreme objective, and had it not been for the growing identification of liberalism with Prussian hegemony, he might well have remained sympathetic with the liberal program.[50] The contrasting motivation of these two outstanding Catholic politicians has a certain amount of general significance, for it demonstrates two diametrically opposed types of impulses that led Catholics, not only in Baden, but elsewhere in Germany as well, to make politics a career.

It was the internal problem of relations between Church and state, never settled to the satisfaction of either, rather than the larger question of German unity, which finally precipitated the first actual crystallization of political Catholicism in Baden. On July 29, 1864, the *Landtag* approved a law designed to reform the administration of the schools. The measure was intended as a compromise between complete secular control of education and the Church's traditional position. It provided for an elected interconfessional board in each district to su-

---

[49] *Ibid.*, 6; Bachem, 2:306–7. Lindau also began in 1865 the publication of a newspaper, of which he served for many years as the guiding spirit.

[50] Weber, 7.

pervise the school system. The law was, of course, unacceptable to the Archbishop. Ten days before its final passage, Vicari had issued a strongly worded pastoral letter denouncing it, and after it went into effect, he led the bitter agitation against its enforcement. Not only did the clergy, as might be expected, support the Archbishop, but also, within a short time, a large number of laymen came to the aid of their spiritual leaders. When protests availed nothing, Vicari instructed Catholics to boycott the forthcoming elections for the local boards, and likewise forbade the clergy to take part in these interconfessional bodies. By no means did all Catholics follow the advice of their prelate. About twenty-eight per cent of them voted, compared with a figure of about thirty-six per cent for the Lutherans and a little more than fifty per cent of the small Jewish population. In some solidly Catholic areas the boycott did prevent the election of a board. However, it appears that most of those Catholics who cast their ballots were liberals or, in some cases, individuals with little political experience who yielded to official pressure.[51]

Although the boycott proved relatively ineffective, the school question was far more important in arousing political interest among Catholic laymen than the former struggle over the bestowal of Church offices had been. The question of the schools touched the average man in a way the other issue did not. It involved local interests directly, and thus served to introduce many Catholics more or less painlessly to the complexities of political action.[52]

In 1865, during the campaign which preceded elections for district assemblies and for the *Landtag*, Archbishop Vicari again saw fit to intervene. This time he addressed a pastoral letter to all members of his diocese, asking voters to cast their ballots only for men known to be "loyal to the Church." "Elect those who know your Catholic convictions and your needs, and those who have the courage to practice their faith openly." [53]

Despite Vicari's ubiquitous activity, and also despite the growing resistance among Catholics to the government's policies, nothing that can properly be called a Catholic party existed before the founding of the North German Confederation in 1867. The Catholic delegates in

[51] Bachem, 2:304–5; Baumgarten and Jolly, 104–5.
[52] Bachem, 2:305–6.
[53] *Ibid.*, 308.

both chambers were still unorganized. As in Bavaria, the Catholic population was largely rural, and lacked as yet both sophistication and sufficient political experience to make possible a party capable of successfully opposing the liberals who dominated the government.[54] Tactics of Catholic politicians had perforce to be designed to impress the ordinary Catholic citizen with the seriousness of the issues, as when, for example, on May 12, 1866, the four Catholic members of the upper chamber resigned their seats in protest over a declaration of the Minister of Justice, Lamey, that law is a formal statement of public conscience. This doctrine, implying the typically liberal, secular conception of organized society, had already aroused Bishop von Ketteler of Mainz to write a pamphlet entitled *Ist das Gesetz öffentliches Gewissen?* In it he had denounced the principle as contradictory to the teachings of the Church and as subversive of moral order.[55]

However little to their liking Catholics in Baden found the course pursued by their government, it required the shock of defeat in 1866 and the succeeding destruction of the old order in Germany to convert their opposition into an important political force. During the crisis of early summer in 1866, the people and the government alike were swept up in the anti-Prussian "south German passion" which overwhelmed the entire area.[56] It was only on the bleak morning after the disaster, with the German Confederation lying in ruins about them, that the Catholics of Baden felt themselves obliged to attempt concerted political action to save themselves from Prussianization. Even so, it took two years for that action to become at all effective.

Unlike Baden, the Kingdom of Württemberg, next to Bavaria the most populous state south of the Main, was, like Prussia, a Protestant state with a large Catholic minority. Before 1866 there was no specifically Catholic party, and the government pursued generally a *grossdeutsch* and particularistic policy which was satisfactory to Catholics. Moreover, there appears likewise to have been no organized pro-Prussian party until after the end of the war, when, on August 7, 1866, the *Deutsche Partei* was established.[57]

Relations between Church and state in Württemberg had followed

[54] *Ibid.*, 313, 316, 324; "Die badischen Wahlen zum Zollparlament," *HPB*, 61:777–78.
[55] Bachem, 2:310.
[56] Adolph Rapp, *Die öffentliche Meinung in Württemberg von 1866 bis zu den Zollparlamentswahlen, März, 1868*, 44.
[57] *Ibid.*, 23, 68.

something of the same pattern as in Baden, without, however, evoking the same violence or passion. The liberal minister of public worship, Rümelin, a Protestant, negotiated a concordat with the Papacy in 1857, which, as in the case of the Baden agreement, was rejected by the *Landtag*. Again, as in the Grand Duchy to the west, the *Landtag* proceeded in 1862 to grant by legislative enactment a large measure of freedom to the Church.

The Catholic third of the population, of course, supported Austria in her conflict with Prussia, and, in the absence of a Catholic party, tended to divide into *grossdeutsch*-conservative and *grossdeutsch*-democratic factions. The existence of the latter is evidence that there was in Württemberg, as well as in Baden, a considerable republican and egalitarian tradition dating from 1848. Liberal groups, on the other hand, tended to recruit most of their members from Protestants. Curiously enough, Catholics, a minority in the population as a whole, permanently dominated the hereditary upper house, because at the time of the mediatization of the bulk of the princes in 1806, there had been in Catholic Upper Swabia a disproportionate number of *reichsunmittelbar* [58] nobles, who automatically achieved for themselves and their descendants the status of hereditary peers. Some of the most capable conservative Catholic leaders came from the nobility.[59]

The most important politician in Württemberg was the nominal leader of the *Grossdeutsch*-Democratic party, Rudolph Probst, perennially the representative of Biberach in the lower chamber, and later one of the founders of the German Center. Probst, like many of his fellow Catholics, began his career as a liberal. In 1848, for example, he favored separation of Church and state. Subsequently, however, he gradually abandoned his orthodox liberal views, and emerged in the *Landtag* as a defender of the interests of the Church, while, at the same time, he was developing more and more into the leader of the popular democratic movement.[60] As a whole, politics in Swabia showed much less tendency to polarize around religious or ecclesiastical issues than in either Bavaria or Baden. Neither the War of 1866 nor its aftermath produced a concerted Catholic political movement. Although

[58] *I.e.*, owing feudal homage directly to the Emperor with no intervening lord. There is, unfortunately, no translation.

[59] Rapp, *Öffentliche Meinung*, 23; Weber, 4; Bachem, 2:249.

[60] Bachem, 2:252, note; Weber, 4.

Catholics entered more vigorously into politics after 1866 than before, they did so under other than religious banners, at least until Probst became the first Württemberg member of the Center in 1871.[61]

The last of the south German states which requires consideration here is the diminutive Grand Duchy of Hesse-Darmstadt, for it played a role in the German problem far more significant than its size would indicate. Hesse-Darmstadt consisted of two physically separated areas. The northern portion, Upper Hesse, belonged to north Germany, and the more important section south of the Main, bordering on Baden and Bavaria, was associated historically with south Germany. Thus the state served politically and culturally as a bridge between North and South. In the hands of the régime favorable to Berlin, Hesse-Darmstadt inevitably betokened extension of Prussian influence far to the south, while, conversely, a *grossdeutsch*-particularistic government at Darmstadt served as a barrier to the expansion of Prussian hegemony on either side of the Main.[62] The latter situation prevailed fully until 1866, and, in part, until 1871.

After the end of the tumultuous revolutionary period, the government of the Grand Duchy was conducted by a warm friend of Austria, and one of Bismarck's bitterest enemies, Baron Reinhard von Dalwigk zu Lichtenfels, who, with the support of the Grand Duke, Ludwig III, followed consistently a *grossdeutsch* policy in German affairs, and a rigidly conservative one at home.[63]

The Catholic population of the Duchy, less than a third of the total, found, in general, that its interests were well served by the Dalwigk régime. For Catholics, however, in the long run, it was far more significant that, in Bishop von Ketteler of Mainz, Hesse possessed the outstanding prelate of Germany. Ketteler, a man of exceptional ability, an aristocrat by birth, with political experience dating from 1848, when he sat in the National Assembly, had early become interested in the problems of the working class, as industry developed in the Rhine valley. By the early 1860's, he had become convinced that only the moral teachings of Christianity could mitigate the increasingly bitter class struggle. He regarded as immoral the economic doctrines of the Man-

[61] Rapp, *Öffentliche Meinung*, 33; Weber, 4.
[62] Srbik, 2:50.
[63] See Wilhelm Schüssler (ed.), *Die Tagebücher des Freiherrn Reinhard von Dalwigk zu Lichtenfels aus den Jahren 1860–1871* (hereafter cited as *Dalwigk Tagebücher*), *passim*.

chester School, which German liberals upheld, because these doctrines signified to him the destruction of man's soul. He was equally certain of the immorality of the secular socialism of Marx and Lassalle, for essentially the same reason. Thus motivated, Ketteler sought to stimulate interest in social problems among the clergy under his jurisdiction, and, through his writings, in the Church generally.[64] He was capably assisted in this work by Dr. Christian Moufang, the Canon at Mainz, and head of the city's large seminary.[65]

Ketteler's personality and his waxing interest in the social question drew him inevitably into politics. His relations with Dalwigk were so excellent that, as early as 1854, he was able to negotiate with the Hessian government a very favorable agreement, which gave the Church practically complete independence from secular control. Moreover, both he and the minister had, at least after the burgeoning of *kleindeutsch* liberalism which followed the War of 1859, a powerful enemy in common.[66]

The first test of Catholic strength came in the *Landtag* elections of 1862. During the campaign the newly organized Hessian Progressive party demanded the revocation of the 1854 agreement with the Bishop, establishment by law of freedom of conscience, and subjection of the Catholic Church to the same regulations that applied to Protestant sects. The party's anti-Catholicism, and its known preference for Prussian hegemony, stimulated Catholics to attempt the formation of a political party to contest the election. The guiding spirit of the resulting *Grossdeutsch-konservative Partei* was Dr. Moufang, who already represented Catholic interests in the upper chamber. Apparently loath to raise the religious issue directly, he maintained that the party was not confessional, and stressed German rather than internal Hessian issues. On the position of the Church, his party asked, along the lines of the Frankfurt constitution, that each sect be allowed to regulate its own affairs independent of state control, and, interestingly

[64] The chief scholarly biography of Ketteler is Fritz Vigener, *Ketteler, ein deutsches Bischofsleben des neunzehnten Jahrhunderts.* See also the eulogy by the late nineteenth-century scholar, Otto Pfülf, S. J., *Bischof von Ketteler.* Also Johannes Mundwiller, S. J., *Bischof von Ketteler als Vorkämpfer der christlichen Sozialreform. Seine soziale Arbeit und sein soziales Programm.* In English there is George Metlake (pseud. for John J. Laux), *Christian Social Reform: Program Outlined by Its Pioneer, Wilhelm Emanuel Freiherr von Ketteler, Bishop of Mainz.* See also his *Briefe* cited above.
[65] Ralph H. Bowen, *German Theories of the Corporative State,* 86.
[66] Bachem, 2:351; Weber, 3; Vigener, *Ketteler,* 273ff; Oncken, *Bennigsen,* 1:463.

enough, in view of the party's general attitude toward Prussia, it offered the Prussian constitution as a prime example of satisfactory regulation of the Church-state issue.[67]

This first venture of Hessian Catholics in party formation proved disastrous. While there had formerly been eight Catholics in the second chamber — of whom, however, only two had stood forth as active defenders of the Church — the *Grossdeutsch-konservative Partei* managed in 1862 to capture only two seats out of a total of fifty, against thirty-eight for the Progressives. Since the members were elected, as in Prussia, on a three-class system, the new party had actually succeeded in electing only one member by popular vote, for the other won his seat as landowner. Even the long-term Catholic member, Seitz, was defeated, and Mainz itself went to the Progressives. The party did not survive the election.[68]

Despite the hostility of the *Landtag*, Dalwigk retained the confidence of the Grand Duke, and remained in office. When, two years later, the threat of war in Germany arose, Hesse-Darmstadt, exposed to easy conquest by Prussia, had the unenviable choice of capitulating to Bismarck or of gambling on a Habsburg victory. For Dalwigk, there was actually no choice; his well-known hatred of the Prussian minister-president, and all he stood for, made the former alternative impossible. Hesse-Darmstadt was one of the first states definitely to commit herself to the Austrian cause, and, although opposition to this policy was strong, Hessian troops fought loyally beside those of the other south German states during the Seven Weeks War. The opposition included even the nephew of the Grand Duke, a supporter of the *Nationalverein*, who was much concerned over Ketteler's alleged influence on the government. Even Hesse's defeat was insufficient, however, to dislodge Dalwigk from office.[69]

The peace treaties which ended the war created, in regard to Hesse-Darmstadt, a situation almost as anomalous as the status of the Schleswig-Holstein duchies had been up to 1864. Upper Hesse was required to join the North German Confederation, while the rest of the Duchy south of the Main was not. Thus, even more than before,

---

[67] Bachem, 2:351–52.
[68] *Ibid.*
[69] See *Dalwigk Tagebücher*, 270 and *passim*; Clark, 270; Ernst Vogt, *Die hessische Politik in der Zeit der Reichsgründung, 1863–1871*, 137.

Hesse-Darmstadt was to be a bridge between north and south Germany. Although Moufang's *Grossdeutsch-konservative Partei* had failed, and although Hesse's geographical position and her political status made next to impossible the founding of a successful Catholic party in the years between 1866 and 1871, the commanding influence of Bishop von Ketteler was sufficient to make Mainz one of the chief centers of German Catholicism. Even against the bitter opposition of some of his own associates, Ketteler after 1866 became more and more the leader of the branch of Catholic opinion which held that the past could not be disinterred, and that, since *Kleindeutschland* had become a reality, it had to be accepted.[70]

It is clear, then, that 1866 was a year of severe crisis for German Catholics. The final exclusion of Austria from any share in the affairs of Germany destroyed at one blow the foundation upon which they had so long built their way of life politically. The ensuing four and one half years meant for them a painful readjustment to new and always changing circumstances. The Catholic historian, Karl Bachem, has concluded that German Catholics were the victims of their own *Gefühlspolitik* during those years.[71] Nevertheless, beneath their surface emotionalism, there was a hard core of realism, perhaps born out of the despair caused by the war, which sought to enlighten the faithful about the changed world, and which ultimately made it possible for them to influence greatly what they could no longer prevent, the unification of Germany under Prussia.

[70] This idea of Ketteler's first appeared in print early in 1867 in his book, *Deutschland nach dem Kriege von 1866*. See Chapter Four, below.

[71] *Zentrumspartei*, 3:10.

Chapter 2

The Foundations of Catholic Strength

Despite the chagrin that German Catholics felt in the summer of 1866 over the outcome of the war, and despite the apparent weakness of organized political Catholicism, the situation was scarcely as desperate as they believed. Throughout the period between 1866 and 1871 Catholics were able to exercise considerable influence on the affairs of several of the states, and on those of the North German Confederation as well. Although one searches in vain for *a* Catholic political movement during these years, political activity of Catholics was actually widespread, and it was from these activities that later leaders of the Center gained the experience which made that party so formidable from the very moment of its creation in 1871.

The political liabilities of Catholic Germany which have been discussed in the preceding chapter were to a degree balanced by certain assets of estimable value. The most obvious, and probably the most important of these, although the most difficult to analyze, was the hierarchy itself. Potentially, as the core of a political organization, it had power which could scarcely be matched by any other group inside or outside the Church. This was most obviously true in solidly Catholic Bavaria, where traditionally the bishops had wielded great influence on public opinion,[1] but it applied to a lesser degree even in the more highly urbanized areas, such as the Prussian Rhineland. Several attempts of the clergy to influence Catholic voters before 1866 have

---

[1] In Bavaria also the extraordinarily large number of persons in holy orders helped to produce a particularly close link between the clergy and the Catholic population. In 1863 there were nearly a thousand monks and almost four thousand nuns in the kingdom. During the succeeding ten years, while the number of monks increased only slightly, the number of nuns grew to more than five thousand. See Julien Rovère, *La Bavière et l'empire allemand: histoire d'un particularisme*, 99.

already been noted, although those examples are scattered and in no way represent an established policy. However, in the years following the war, the clergy was increasingly active politically in several states, attempting to secure the election to the several *Landtage* of delegates favorable to the interests of the Church. The reasons are not difficult to comprehend. Formerly, the Church had generally been able to secure most of what it demanded through direct relations with governments. That had been true even in predominantly Protestant states, where the influence of the Church in upholding conservative traditions had been, in the main, both welcomed and appreciated.[2] Moreover, the close link between the Church and Vienna had served Catholic interests well, not only in Austria, but in Germany as a whole. The latter advantage disappeared, of course, with Königgrätz, but, in any case, the rise of liberalism, with its demand for parliamentary government, and the increasing political importance of the masses were undermining the effectiveness of traditional ties between throne and altar. When the arch-conservative Bismarck emerged in 1866 as the advocate of universal manhood suffrage, it was clear that times had changed, and that new techniques were necessary. Should not the Church also strive to organize the masses against secularism, against the anticlericalism of the bourgeois liberals, in order to attain its objectives, as Bismarck was doing to achieve his?[3] The nerve center of this development was the Cathedral at Mainz, whence Ketteler exercised an ever-growing influence on Catholic thought, through a constant stream of pamphlets and books on nearly all the major social and political issues which affected the interests of the Church, as well as on purely doctrinal questions.[4]

A second source of Catholic strength can be seen in the growth of the movement that by 1866 was already coming to be called Social Catholicism or Catholic Socialism. Here again the influence of Ketteler is paramount, both because of his writings and because he

[2] In 1851 Bismarck had referred to Catholics in Prussia, for example, as the best subjects of the King. See Ziekursch, 1:108.

[3] Bismarck, in a speech of April 19, 1866, expressed the conviction that "in a country with monarchical traditions and loyal sentiments, universal suffrage will strengthen the monarchy, since it will counteract the influence of the liberal bourgeoisie." *Ibid.*

[4] Ketteler's personal influence on other prominent Catholics, both within and without the hierarchy, should not be ignored. He had studied under Döllinger at Munich, where he had been a classmate of Melchers, who became Archbishop of Cologne in 1869, and had, during his student days, been a protégé of Archbishop (later Cardinal) Breisach.

successfully communicated his interest in social welfare to young candidates for the priesthood who studied in the seminary at Mainz. Later, these men, as scholars, writers, and priests, propagated his doctrines throughout Germany.[5] The core of this movement was the large number of laymen's organizations which had begun to appear in Germany under clerical sponsorship in the middle of the century. These were created to deal with the critical social problems produced by industrialism and the increasing proletarianization of the working classes. The first of these *Vereine,*[6] a *Katholischer Gesellenverein,* was established at Elberfeld (Rhineland) in 1847 by a priest who was himself of working-class origin, Father Adolph Kölping, a fellow student of Ketteler at Munich. Father Kölping sought to bring together journeyman workers from various trades in order to give them opportunities to supplement their education, to secure healthful relaxation in a religious environment, and to increase their awareness of moral and civic obligations. His ultimate goal was to produce "a virtuous and honorable group of masters."[7] From Elberfeld the *Gesellenvereine* spread to Cologne in 1849, and thence rapidly to most German cities which had large Catholic populations. Each of them had a regular meeting place, usually an inn, which, by arrangement, furnished accommodations for traveling members of related organizations from other cities. Each was headed by a priest, assisted by a committee of lay members, and was usually under the supervision of a group of prominent local citizens.[8]

It would be profitless to trace in detail the mushrooming of the *Gesellenvereine* and other similar organizations. The Catholic-Socialist publicist Rudolph Meyer, writing in the 1870's, described fourteen major varieties of Catholic social organizations, as well as at least an equal number of derivatives and offshoots, which by that time embraced many thousands of members.[9] Of those that were concerned

[5] Bowen, 79, 86.

[6] Unfortunately, the English word "union," which translates *Verein* literally, does not convey the true meaning here. These groups, at least in the beginning, were more social clubs and educational societies than labor unions of the late nineteenth- and twentieth-century variety.

[7] Arnold Bongartz, *Das katholisch-soziale Vereinswesen in Deutschland,* 58–59. A complete discussion of the growth of these organizations, with a wealth of statistical material, may be found in the work cited and in Rudolph Meyer, *Der Emancipationskampf des vierten Standes.*

[8] Hansen, 1:794; Bowen, 87; Francesco S. Nitti, *Catholic Socialism,* 116.

[9] *Emancipationskampf des vierten Standes,* 338–42.

primarily with the working classes, mention may be made of the *Lehrlingvereine*, clubs of apprentices, modeled on the *Gesellenvereine*, as were also the *Meistervereine* and the *Knappenvereine*. The last were, for the most part, established in mining districts of the Ruhr to care for the interests of the young men just beginning their hard life in the pits. For older workingmen the similarly organized *Arbeitervereine* served much the same purpose. All these societies, with the possible exception of the original *Gesellenvereine*, were in a sense attempts of churchmen to counteract the socialist organizations which began, shortly after the middle of the century, to compete seriously for the loyalty of the workers. Conversely, these Catholic groups may be said to have influenced to a degree the direction of socialist development in Germany, since Lassalle, for example, was impressed by Ketteler's practical social views, if not by his religious approach to the question.[10]

In numerous communities parallel societies were created for young women, and in the course of the two decades after the Revolution of 1848 there were established by, or in conjunction with, the abovementioned organizations a series of auxiliary units for specific purposes. Among these were the various savings and loan associations and insurance societies which appeared in industrial towns, and the *Akademie des Gesellenvereins*, founded in Berlin in 1859 to serve as a continuation school for workingmen. The development of these lay organizations was by no means complete by 1866, or even by 1871, but even by the former date prototypes of all of them were in existence, and many of them had achieved widespread influence.[11]

During the same period efforts were also being made to provide organizations among Catholics of higher social strata. In the fifties and sixties, several groups known as *Marianische Congregationen junger Kaufleute* were founded. These were social clubs designed to accomplish among the more highly educated youth of the bourgeoisie objectives similar to those of the previously mentioned proletarian societies. In some of these, priests took a leading role; others were more secular in character, although still under the sponsorship of the Church. The "Casinos" which developed in the southern states after 1862, especially in Bavaria under the sponsorship of Émile Ringseis, a Munich

[10] *Allgemeine deutsche Biographie*, 15:673.
[11] Meyer, 338–42; Bongartz, 58, 62, 65–68, 82–83, 98–100, 102–4, 107–13, 149, 151–54, 156–58; Hertling, 1:57.

schoolmaster, and in Baden through the cooperation of Jakob Lindau, had similar objectives and functioned in approximately the same fashion.[12]

In terms of direct political significance the most important of these Catholic lay organizations were the farmers' unions, the *Bauernvereine*, which sprang up rapidly during the sixties. As German agriculture, particularly in the West, in keeping with the trend in most European countries during the second half of the nineteenth century, became increasingly capitalistic, farmers found themselves progressively more at the mercy of the national and international market. The small farmer in western Germany, like his counterpart in America, was faced with the problem of rising land prices, increasing costs of production, high interest rates, and disadvantageous terms for mortgages. During the late 1850's in Westphalia, where the problem was particularly acute, Baron Burghard von Schorlemer-Alst, a conservative Catholic landowner who was deeply concerned with preserving the traditional social pattern of the area, became interested in the problems of the peasant farmer. In 1860 he founded at Burgsteinfurt the first *Westfalischer Bauernverein*, which became the prototype for others.[13]

As conceived by its founder, the purpose of the organization was, in general, to create a cooperative society which would "elevate its members religiously, morally, intellectually, socially, and materially." Specifically, Schorlemer-Alst sought to create among the peasants a consciousness of what he believed were their real interests, so that "a strong, moral, self-confident, free, and independent peasant class" might be preserved. In that way he felt that the peasants would be able to satisfy their legitimate demands, and that this in turn would "contribute to the solution of the social question in so far as it concerns the rural population." [14]

Among the first concrete achievements of the baron's parent organization was the negotiation of a contract with an insurance company providing for low-cost fire insurance on peasant holdings. Soon other individuals and groups, impressed by the success of Schorlemer-Alst's venture, established similar societies in other Westphalian districts,

[12] Bongartz, 50–57; Bachem, 2:306–8; Anton Doeberl, "Graf Konrad Preysing und das Erwachen der katholisch-konservativen Partei in Bayern," *Gelbe Hefte*, 2:843.

[13] Bongartz, 117.

[14] *Ibid.*, 118.

and, in 1867, several of them merged into a larger body under the presidency of the indefatigable Baron. This organization bore the same name as its parent club, the *Westfalischer Bauernverein*. The membership, at first restricted to Catholics, was in 1869 opened to anyone who belonged to "one of the two Christian confessions." [15]

Acting in the main as a bargaining agent for its members in their dealings with banks and insurance companies, by 1870 the *Westfalischer Bauernverein* had achieved a position of considerable power locally. It possessed a reasonably well-filled treasury, and was publishing its own newspaper, the *Westfalischer Bauer*, edited by Schorlemer-Alst's first collaborator and chief lieutenant, J. Breuker. The Baron himself had achieved significance not only in political circles — by 1870 he was a member both of the Prussian chamber and of the North German Reichstag, and was on intimate terms with the chief Catholic politicians — but in the Catholic intellectual sphere as well. His two long pamphlets, *The Situation of the Peasant Class in Westphalia* (1864) and *The Status of Rural Landholding in Westphalia* (1868), brought him into the public eye everywhere in Germany as a defender of the traditional peasant way of life against the inroads of capitalism.[16]

Almost all of the above-mentioned organizations professed to have no political objectives; almost universally their charters contained provisions which specifically forbade discussion of political questions at their meetings.[17] Such prohibitions were at best unrealistic, and seem mostly to have been devices to insure technical compliance with laws that forbade religious societies to engage in politics. The problems which the various *Vereine* were attempting to solve, the issues with which they perforce dealt, had political implications even when they did not directly revolve about a political axis. Hence, isolation proved in practice impossible. This is most obvious in the case of the farmers' organizations. The *Westfalischer Bauernverein*, for example, acted as sponsor for a petition presented to both chambers of the Prussian *Landtag* on November 16, 1869, protesting a tax measure. The

---

[15] *Ibid.*, 117; Nitti, 189, 192.

[16] Bongartz, 117–18, 120; Bowen, 88; H. Hüffer, "Die Soester Konferenzen," *Festschrift Felix Porsch zum siebzigsten Geburtstag, passim.*

[17] E.g., the *Gesellenvereine*: "Politics and religious polemic are . . . completely excluded." Bongartz, 61. The *Meister-* and *Knappenvereine* had similar prohibitions, as did the *Westfalischer Bauernverein*. *Ibid.*, 61, 65, 98, 124.

petition was signed by slightly more than two thousand peasant land-holders. Two years later, at the beginning of the *Kulturkampf,* the Prussian government ordered the *Verein* dissolved because of alleged illegal political activity. The dissolution was not permanent, for the *Verein* simply reconstituted itself on a slightly different basis in order to comply with the law.[18] Intentionally or unintentionally, through these lay organizations political Catholicism was building a reservoir of strength.

While the political significance achieved by the organizations dis-cussed above may have been the result of circumstance rather than intent, however unlikely that may appear, the War of 1866 and the founding of the North German Confederation stimulated the forma-tion of Catholic associations which, while obviously related in form to the earlier types, were openly political in character. Mention may be made of the *Neuer Bürgerverein,* established at Cologne in 1867 "to secure the broadest popular basis for continuing work in the service of the Catholic cause, especially in elections."[19] This group was exclu-sively bourgeois in membership, in spite of the fact that it soon changed its name to *Katholischer Volksverein.* The clergy had no part in its founding or direction, although later some young clergymen were permitted to join. A number of Rhenish Catholics who became impor-tant figures in the Center, including both Julius Bachem and Dr. Her-mann Cardauns, successive editors of the *Kölnische Volkszeitung,* Germany's leading Catholic daily, were associated with this, the first specifically Catholic political club founded in the Rhineland after 1848.[20]

The same year witnessed the founding of a similarly named club at Breslau in Silesia. This second *Katholischer Volksverein* was conceived and organized by the theologian, Dr. Joseph Wick, for the purpose of "discussion and advancement of the rights and interests of the Cath-olic population in state and community." It immediately adopted a set of definite proposals which it hoped to see carried out by the North German Reichstag. Among other things, it sought continued "develop-ment of Prussian constitutional monarchy," readoption of the *Reichs-verfassung* of 1848, the reconciliation and unification of "our entire

---

[18] Nitti, 191–92; Bongartz, 120–21, 124–25.
[19] K. Bachem, 3:26.
[20] *Ibid.,* 26–27; Julius Bachem, *Erinnerungen eines alten Publizisten und Politikers,* 41.

fatherland," and extension to all states of the North German Confederation of the rights and privileges which belonged to the Catholic Church in Prussia.[21] This program resembles closely the one offered by Catholic delegates in the Constituent Reichstag of 1867, and one which they were still reiterating in 1871.

For the sake of completeness, a final example of a social-political organization which had unconcealed political objectives must be mentioned, the *Bayrisch-patriotische Bauernverein.* This powerful farmers' organization was established in 1868 by Count F. X. von Hafenbrädl, a Bavarian landowner, on the model of the Westphalian society of Schorlemer-Alst. Since the problems of the rural cultivator in Bavaria bore some resemblance to those of the peasant in northwestern Germany, something of the type might well have developed without external stimulus. While the two organizations had largely similar objectives, the Bavarian *Bauernverein,* as indicated above, made no pretense of political nonpartisanship. As is apparent from its name, it served as an arm of the Patriot party, the title which the powerful clerical-democratic coalition in Bavaria took for itself in 1868–69.[22] Acceptance of the party's principles was a prerequisite for membership in the *Verein,* which served as one of the party's chief agencies in delivering the vote of the rural population.[23]

The social tensions resulting from the steady progress of industrialism, and the dawning political crisis, not only affected the working classes, the urban bourgeoisie, and the peasants, but also forced upon Catholic intellectuals a concern with the implications of apparent historical trends. The demand, made first in 1862 but constantly reiterated later, for a "free" [24] Catholic university, has already been mentioned. It arose largely from fear of the increasingly secular attitude of existing universities and distrust of what Peter Reichensperger called "arrogant German science." [25] Catholic university students found themselves troubled more seriously than before with the age-old conflict between the tenets of their faith and the new viewpoints which they inevitably met in their academic training. For example, Count Georg von Hertling, following the traditional course of the European

[21] K. Bachem, 3:27–28.
[22] See below, Chapter Six.
[23] Bongartz, 130–34; *HPB*, 64:654–56. See also Chapters Six and Eight, below.
[24] *I.e.,* free of governmental control or influence.
[25] Hansen, 1:797.

student, was a resident in several universities during the first half of the 1860's, and in all of them he found others who, like him, were trying to assuage this turmoil within themselves. Upon his matriculation at the University of Munich in the fall of 1861, Hertling began to attend meetings of the then two-year-old Catholic student society, *Aenania,* and, a few months later, decided to join it. The club had been founded, in Hertling's words "to counteract the widespread misuse of academic freedom by [demonstrating] its proper use." He described the twin bases underlying the group as "firm religious conviction" and "sincere intellectual effort." [26] The Count was modest about his own contributions to the organization, but they must have been significant, since, when in 1862, *Aenania* set out to establish liaison with some Catholic student associations in Switzerland, it was Hertling and one of his close friends who were selected to make the journey as official representatives of the Munich group.[27]

Hertling, upon his transfer to Berlin in the fall of 1862, became associated with a similar organization in the Prussian capital, the *Katholische Leseverein.* This group embraced not only students at the university, but also alumni and former students. In this more sophisticated company, the Count missed the intensity and zeal which he had found at Munich. Although several prominent Berlin Catholics were associated with it — among them both the first counselor and the director of the Catholic section of the *Kultusministerium*; the Hessian Ambassador, Arnold Biegeleben; and Prince Boguslaw Radziwill, whom Bismarck later described as the evil genius of political Catholicism — it was Hertling and his friends who, with the enthusiasm of youth, determined in 1863 to infuse new vigor into the organization.[28]

Hertling hoped to accomplish his goal by sponsoring the establishment of a national organization of Catholic student clubs. Initially the three existing societies, the Berlin *Leseverein,* the Munich *Aenania,* and the *Winfridia* of Breslau, were to form the core. It was planned that the new organization would send representatives to the forthcoming *Generalversammlung der Katholikenvereine* at Frankfurt, where, speaking in the name of the Catholic students of the entire country,

[26] Hertling, 1:41–42.
[27] *Ibid.,* 51.
[28] Prince Otto von Bismarck-Schönhausen, *Gedanken und Erinnerungen,* 2:154–55; Hertling, 1:55–57.

they would pledge cooperation with the other lay groups.[29] The Count had thus come to visualize the student societies as one segment of a general Catholic movement in the social and political sphere, of which the working-class organizations would form the major part.[30] As was to be expected, Hertling was nominated to speak in behalf of the allied student groups at Frankfurt. According to a friend, the young man made a stirring appeal, asking the assembly to support the student groups, begging students to join existing organizations and to found new ones at all German universities. His peroration is indicative of the spirit of the whole:

There was a time — and this year we celebrate its fiftieth anniversary — when the German youth ceased to tarry in the quiet chambers of his home, or in the halls of learning, for there was a fatherland to be saved from the hand of a powerful oppressor. Today the fatherland is free, yet many minds still are shamefully bound by the chains which the enemy of truth, the spirit of negation, has created for them. Truly the prize to be won is no small one, and if all Catholic sons of Germany go forth with conviction and with strength, joyful and inspired, victory must be ours, because then the blessing from above cannot fail.[31]

The speech, though apparently well received in Frankfurt, did not, as its author wryly admitted later, signal the dawn of a new era. It did not even cost him the friendship of any of his Protestant friends in Berlin. Hertling later expressed the belief that scarcely any of his professors were aware that he had made it, for there was practically no coverage of this or any other of the Catholic assemblies in the general press. Nevertheless, partly as a result of Hertling's speech, Catholic student associations were founded at other universities, and Hertling himself was later associated with one of the newer ones at Würzburg during his sojourn there in 1866. A little later, as *Privat-*

---

[29] Hertling, 1:65–66.

[30] "We young people were being carried along, without being aware of the connection, by the current which — one can take the year 1848 as the point of departure — had taken hold in wider and wider circles, and had found its powerful supporters in outstanding men such as Bishop von Ketteler. Everywhere Catholics were beginning to be aware of the oppressive bonds which state governments had placed upon the Church; in many places they were coming to experience them for themselves, and to demand their abolition. People of like mind would meet together in groups of many different kinds. . . . In the annual general meetings of the Catholic societies . . . this feeling, growing ever more powerful, found solemn expression. There, the Catholic student societies were to find their place." *Ibid.*, 1:66.

[31] *Ibid.*, 66–67.

dozent, he was indirectly connected with the *Arminia* at Bonn, which proved to be one of the most active. By 1867 Catholic student organizations had become sufficiently numerous to make possible the holding of the first *Generalversammlung sämmtlicher katholischen Studentenvereine Deutschlands* at Berlin. Similar meetings followed at Münster in 1868 and at Würzburg in 1869. Every year more groups were represented.[32]

Although it is difficult to assess the degree to which these student organizations were significant in molding the views of young Catholic intellectuals, it appears safe to conclude that, by introducing a considerable number of young men to political and social issues which were of importance to Catholics generally, they did contribute to building the reservoir of strength upon which political leaders later were able to draw. Since university graduates usually achieved positions of some public importance ultimately, it is reasonable to suppose that these clubs indirectly had a considerable effect on many individuals at a later date.

Among mature scholars as well, the sixties saw increasing anxiety over critical problems which were looming in Germany. In this connection, too, Bishop von Ketteler stood out. His influential pamphlet *Die Arbeiterfrage und das Christenthum*, published in 1864, forms one of the chief piers on which later Catholic social philosophy rested. Even before its appearance, however, other Catholic scholars were growing apprehensive over the effects of industrialism on the moral fiber of society, and, particularly, over the effects of the growing power of the middle class in politics. The historian Ignaz von Döllinger had in 1863 taken the initiative in convening a meeting of German Catholic scholars at Munich to discuss the relationship of scholarship to the great issues of the age.[33] While Döllinger himself was primarily concerned with combating papal antagonism to all modern attitudes and beliefs,[34] he personally recommended to the assembly that scholars

---

[32] *Ibid.*, 68, 166; Hansen, 1:797; *HPB*, 68:409–10.

[33] Bongartz, 29, 149.

[34] His major address on "The Past and Present of Catholic Theology" argued that the teaching of the Church on many points of doctrine had changed drastically in the course of its history. Therefore, he concluded, research in Church history had two fundamental tasks: first, to investigate what it had taught at various times in the past, and, second, since any dogma might be opposed to the tradition of the Church, to test whether or not any doctrine could be defined dogmatically. Hertling, 1:204–5; Emil Michael, *Ignaz von Döllinger*, 17–20.

concern themselves with the increasingly important social questions. He suggested likewise that existing Catholic societies undertake, in a more direct and positive fashion, to find solutions for those problems, instead of merely trying to mitigate their evil consequences. In his view all the Catholic societies had a duty to counteract the demoralizing influences of a rapidly changing environment upon a population that was, perhaps, being liberated too rapidly from the restraints of the older way of life. He appealed especially to the *Gesellenvereine* to take steps in that direction. Since he believed that the proper approach was through education, he strongly opposed the entry of Catholic associations into political agitation.[35]

This question of what was the proper function of the Catholic *Vereine* was obviously of pivotal importance to the Catholic social movement, and it provoked, both at the *Gelehrtenversammlung* and later, much extremely bitter controversy. Döllinger's conception, representing the most conservative view, was opposed by the increasingly political approach of Ketteler, although the latter's views had not yet fully matured. Moreover, the conflict over whether the Catholic masses were to be pushed into the political arena under the banners of the Church contributed much to the final break between Döllinger and Joseph Edmund Jörg, his able secretary. Jörg, who had been the historian's amanuensis for six years, believed that it would be foolish not to use the political strength which could be generated by the Catholic associations. He insisted that they furnished the best means for educating the Catholic masses politically, particularly in Bavaria, where the peasants, if organized, would hold the balance of power. The crisis which developed in 1866 within the Munich Casino over whether it should seek to become more "democratic" — *i.e.*, attempt to enroll the masses — represents another phase of the same conflict.[36]

Jörg, after 1862, when he began his career as editor of the *Historisch-politische Blätter*, used the columns of that journal to propagate his views. Year after year he devoted an increasing amount of space to discussions of the social question, and began in 1865 to publish a series of his own articles entitled "Aphorisms on the Social-Political

[35] Nitti, 115; Hans Martin, "Die Stellung der 'Historisch-politischen Blätter' zur Reichsgründung, 1870–71," *Zeitschrift für bayrische Landesgeschichte*, 6 (1933):65.

[36] Fritz Wöhler, *Joseph Edmund Jörg und die sozial-politische Richtung im deutschen Katholizismus*, 12–13; Martin, *Zeitschrift für bayrische Landesgeschichte*, 6:64–65; Doeberl, *Gelbe Hefte*, 2:844.

Movement." These gave, in reality, a detailed historical analysis of economic liberalism and the various ideas which had arisen in opposition to it. His motive was primarily to disseminate among conservative Catholics detailed information about problems which he felt transcended in importance party quarrels in Germany, or even major international conflicts. Jörg planned to issue a revised version of the ten articles as a book in 1866, but publication was delayed by the war, and his *Geschichte der sozial-politischen Parteien in Deutschland* did not appear until the following year. Reception was mixed. The *Neue Freie Presse,* the Viennese liberal organ, accused the author of attempting to incite a revolution against property, while democratic and Catholic groups generally expressed approval.[37]

Of the results which can be attributed to the intellectual labors of Jörg, Döllinger, Ketteler, and others, the most striking was the founding, in the summer of 1868, of the journal *Christlich-soziale Blätter* by Rector Joseph Schings of Aachen. This journal was the first Catholic publication devoted entirely to exploration of social problems. A few months later three of the Catholic societies met at Crefeld in the Prussian Rhineland and established the *Christlich-soziale Partei.* The program which it adopted reveals its nature and its contradictions. It advocated economic doctrines that appear to be a blend of Lassallean socialism and the medieval ideal of a corporative society. While it desired a thoroughgoing reconstruction of the social order, the impetus for that reform was to come from the Church, not the working class. Through a moral transformation of social relationships the looming revolutionary solution of the world crisis would be avoided. The new party adopted the *Christlich-soziale Blätter* as its official organ.[38]

As a political party, the *Christlich-soziale* never achieved any real importance; most of its membership was absorbed into the Center after 1871. Nevertheless, as an intellectual influence on Catholicism, its significance was far-reaching. Its relationship to the ideas of Pope Leo XIII is too obvious to require comment. In Germany it formed an axis around which gathered a group of scholars and writers, and thus became an important agency for preserving and increasing the influence of the Church on the working classes. Associated with it, in one capacity or another, were Moufang; Count Lösewitz, an economist

[37] Wöhler, 18–20.
[38] Bongartz, 24, 29; Nitti, 132; Bowen, 86–87; Laux, 157–58; Vigener, *Ketteler,* 545–48.

who had abandoned Protestantism under the influence of Ketteler's ideas; the historians, Rudolph Meyer and Arnold Bongartz, both of whom became chroniclers of Catholic Socialism; as well as Hertling and Jörg.[39]

One important source of Catholic strength remains to be considered — the press. The nineteenth century was the age in which the newspaper and the weekly or monthly periodical reached their peak as influences on public opinion. The quarter century from, roughly, 1850 to 1875 was a period in which the individual editor, through the cogency of his arguments or the brilliance of his style, could still command a wide circle of readers. This was true, of course, only in countries like Great Britain, the United States, and Germany, which possessed relative freedom of the press. In Germany, of the many basic rights of the citizen that had been so hotly debated at Frankfurt in 1848, *Pressefreiheit* alone had survived the collapse of the revolution more or less intact in most of the states.[40]

In the 1860's the popular press in Germany was almost exclusively political in character. Every organized party, and almost every informal group which possessed any discernible political opinion, had one or more organs which nominally represented it. Nevertheless, the views which appeared in these publications bore the personal stamp of the editor, and seldom was there any rigid adherence to official doctrines. Among the several papers that were generally regarded as Catholic in outlook there was, within the expected conservative frame of reference, the widest possible divergence in specific points of view. This situation, which applied equally to the journals of other groups, is evidence that the press was still decentralized, that parties still possessed only rudimentary organization, that party discipline was weak or nonexistent, and that, of course, the press was free.[41]

During those years Catholic interests were not unrepresented on any level of journalistic activity. In the *Historisch-politische Blätter* Catholic Germany had a journal that for integrity and quality of writing ranks high among nineteenth-century periodicals. It was founded in 1838 by Guido Görres, son of the scholar and editor, Joseph

[39] Nitti, 142–43.

[40] Otto Bandmann, *Die deutsche Presse und die nationale Frage, 1864–1866,* 164. The care that Bismarck exercised in "feeding" news to newspapers in all sections of Germany is evidence of the importance that he ascribed to the press.

[41] *Ibid.,* 163–64.

Görres, and was directed by him until his death. In 1866 the magazine had already been for a number of years under the guidance of Jörg, during whose long tenure it reached its full stature. It could in no way be described as a "typical" Catholic organ, for Jörg never hesitated to adopt a position that was highly unpopular with the bulk of his readers whenever he felt justified by facts, logic, and the interests of his faith and his country.

From the beginning of the Schleswig-Holstein crisis the *Historisch-politische Blätter* took, for example, a position which was radically different from that of the rest of the Catholic press. Jörg's arguments, revealed in his commentaries on the current scene which appeared in nearly every issue under the running title "Zeitläufe," are impossible to classify definitely as either pro-Prussian or pro-Austrian. Certainly, however, they leaned toward the former. At a time when most Catholics, even in Prussia, were extremely angry at Bismarck's Schleswig-Holstein policy, Jörg advocated Prussian annexation of both duchies. To him they were simply two more middle-sized states, in which Jörg saw the chief stronghold of liberalism. Were they to be admitted to the confederation as states, they would add to the strength of a political philosophy that he considered to be the heart of nearly all contemporary evils. His dislike for liberalism was not unrelated to an even more bitter hatred he felt toward France, which under Napoleon III (whom he regarded as a typical liberal without the "customary mask") had reached what seemed to him the inevitable consummation of liberalism — dictatorship devoid of morality. His attitude toward France was strengthened by his fear of revolution in general, and by his resentment over the revolutionary settlement of the Italian question at the expense of the Pope, for which Napoleon III had been largely responsible. He was terrified that the German conflict would produce a situation in which Napoleon could, and would, intervene. In order to prevent that catastrophe, Jörg was convinced that the middle states had to consent to Prussian annexation of the duchies, for Prussia's pride would never permit her to accept coercion by Austria, or by the German Confederation. The crucial problem, as he saw it, was not the disposition of the duchies, but preservation of a common policy by the German states in face of the threat from the west.[42] Further-

[42] The creation and preservation of a common German policy toward France was Jörg's major objective from the beginning of the Schleswig-Holstein crisis. His belief that Prus-

more, Prussia, he believed, would find all her energies absorbed for a long time in incorporating Schleswig and Holstein into the monarchy. During that period she would cease to be a disruptive factor in Germany. This complex chain of reasoning led Jörg likewise to criticize Austrian policy bitterly, for the Vienna government, he wrote, had, under the pressure of the *grossdeutsch*-liberal party, abandoned her traditional role as defender of the world-wide interests of the Church in order to play the sordid game of power politics. It was this immoral renunciation not only of the principles of justice, but of her own interests as well, that was responsible for her loss of Venetia in the War of 1866, he concluded shortly after its termination.[43]

On the surface, Jörg's arguments contain many apparent inconsistencies. If, however, they are judged always in terms of his basic hypothesis, a constant thread is visible in all his writings. He believed that the great crisis of the age was not to be found in the political turmoil, but in the social revolution that must come as a result of the triumph of liberalism, and that, therefore, at all costs the unity of the German great powers had to be preserved to prevent Napoleonic and thus, to him, liberal, domination of Germany. From this viewpoint there was no real inconsistency between his *grossdeutsch* outlook and his grudging admiration for Bismarck. For he knew that Bismarck's "fighting ministry" could give way only to a liberal one. Thus, too, can be explained his criticism of Austria for becoming involved in Schleswig-Holstein as Prussia's ally, for thereby the great powers became separated from the middle states. And finally it also explains his approval of the Gastein Convention of 1865. "They are secretly grind-

sian annexation was the only means of accomplishing it came later. Cf. his view early in 1864: "We must have a unified German policy at any cost. It would have been better to leave ten Schleswig-Holsteins under the scepter of Denmark than to follow a course that must lead to a hostile division between the German middle states and the great powers, and especially one that will inevitably result in German hostility to Austria. The cow is being killed to save the calf. The German right to Schleswig and Holstein has not been lost during the duchies' four-hundred-year-long connection with Denmark, as present events prove; through division in Germany, however, only too easily can *all* [italics in the original] German rights and *all* German honor be lost. Let Germany be prepared both today and tomorrow to use either kindness or force; any division among the German states will throw her into the arms of France, and whatever we lose to France is lost forever. No one really denies this terrifying prospect; everyone is content to place the responsibility for it on Austria and Prussia. Even if that were true, however, how would it help our poor fatherland?" *HPB*, 53:231. See also *ibid.*, 59:13–15.

[43] Hans Spielhofer, "Zur Vorgeschichte der bayrischen Zentrumspartei," *Historisch-politische Blätter*, 165 (1920):155; Bandmann, 36, 116; *HPB*, 58:215–16, 796; 65:21, 323.

ing their teeth in Paris," wrote the Bavarian journalist, "and that is music to our ears." [44]

A viewpoint far more representative of most German Catholics was that of the leading Catholic daily of western Germany, the *Kölnische Blätter*,[45] published by J. P. Bachem, the important Rhineland book publisher. During the Schleswig-Holstein crisis, while Jörg showed at least an understanding of Prussia's problem, the *Kölnische Blätter* repeatedly issued violent denunciations of both great powers because of their disregard of the German Confederation and of the interests of the small and middle states individually. On the ground that the duchies did not in any case belong to Denmark, but were in fact German states, it denied categorically either Prussia's or Austria's right to them without the agreement of the other members of the *Bund*. After the end of the Danish War, the *Blätter* was also worried over the possibility of French intervention in Germany, a possibility which it considered to have arisen because of the blow which Prussia and Austria had struck at the prestige of the confederation by their bilateral action, but unlike Jörg, it denounced any solution of the problem that would hand the duchies over to Prussia.[46] For, wrote its editor, if Prussia gained Schleswig and Holstein, she would become powerful enough to make any federal union of the German states impossible. "If Schleswig-Holstein becomes Prussian, then Germany will become Prussian; if Schleswig-Holstein remains German, then Prussia must also remain German." [47]

The *Kölnische Blätter*, in company with the overwhelming majority of the *grossdeutsch* and Catholic press, failed to comprehend the revolutionary implications of Prussian policy. While Jörg, almost alone of Catholic editors, regarded the burgeoning propaganda about the "Prussian mission" as sufficiently serious to justify bitter denunciation on many occasions, the Bachem paper persisted in calling it a meaningless and empty slogan. Concerning Bismarck himself the misconceptions at Cologne and at Munich appear to have been equal, although quite dissimilar. While Jörg saw in the Prussian statesman a bulwark against the growth of revolutionary liberalism, and thus failed completely to appreciate that Bismarck was fully capable of reversing his course if

[44] Bandmann, 74, 115–16.
[45] On Jan. 1, 1869, it was renamed the *Kölnische Volkszeitung*.
[46] Bandmann, 19–20.
[47] Oct. 11, 1864. Quoted by Bandmann, 36.

thereby his ends could be served, the Cologne *Blätter* constantly agitated for his dismissal because of his alleged narrow Prussian particularism.[48] On only a few occasions did the *Kölnische Blätter* give evidence of even mild enthusiasm for any aspect of Prussian policy. It did, for example, greet the Gastein Convention of 1865 in a fashion that was quite at variance with its usual character, calling the agreement a Prussian victory and rejoicing that Olmütz had finally been wiped from the record, and that Schwarzenberg had at last been repaid in kind by Bismarck.[49]

As events in Germany moved toward the point of explosion during the first half of 1866, each of these outstanding representatives of the Catholic press continued to deal with the problems and their possible solutions in its own characteristic fashion. Even in face of the threat of war between the two German great powers, the *Kölnische Blätter* persisted in its uncompromisingly hostile attitude toward Bismarck, maintaining on March 26 that the question of the duchies was one of law and, therefore, that it could not be settled by force! The paper argued that neither Austria nor Prussia should be predominant in Germany. Each should submit *to* Germany; *i.e.*, each should regard itself simply as first among equals in the community of German states. When, on March 28, the newspaper asked Austria to submit its quarrel with Prussia to the Federal Diet, it clearly sought only to bring pressure on Berlin to abandon the policy of annexation.[50]

When Bismarck's project for reform of the confederation was dropped like a bombshell into the Diet on April 9, the Cologne paper's reaction bore witness to its confusion. Like most of the Catholic and *grossdeutsch* press, it could not, because of its loathing for Bismarck, accept the proposal at face value. The immediate reaction of "wait and see" quickly gave way to a strong opposition.[51] The propaganda campaign in the government press, which began in May and included an obviously planted article in the *Norddeutsche Allgemeine Zeitung* attempting to inject a confessional issue into the struggle, convinced the *Kölnische Blätter* at last that Prussia was bent on war. It denounced the above-mentioned article for "unchaining religious fanaticism for political purposes," and characterized the attempt as "worthy of the

[48] *Ibid.*, 116.
[49] *Ibid.*, 73.
[50] *Ibid.*, 113–14.
[51] *Ibid.*, 154–55.

days of the Thirty Years War."[52] By the middle of the month it had lost all but the most tenuous hope that war could be avoided, and commented bitterly, "What power can prevent Napoleon III from achieving the Rhine frontier if Prussia and Austria fall upon one another?"[53]

Although this attitude resembles closely Jörg's former point of view, he himself had already abandoned any hope of a common Austro-Prussian policy immediately after Bismarck presented the reform proposal. His shock over Bismarck's abrupt about-face did not blind him to the fact that Prussia's adoption of the *Nationalverein* program as its own was decisive. As he pointed out, once Prussia had taken this step, others must follow inevitably; Prussia could not turn back. She had now staked her honor on creating a German parliament, and had, therefore, to destroy the old confederation, even at the cost of civil war. Jörg regarded the exclusion of Austria from Germany, therefore, as unavoidable, unless Vienna immediately accepted the Prussian proposals, or unless Austria won the war. He was under no illusions, of course, that the Habsburgs could, or would, accept, and since he never seems to have considered the possibility of an Austrian military victory, his only solution for the dilemma was to propose the revival of the old idea of a confederation within a confederation. Prussian hegemony would be recognized over all Germany except the Habsburg lands, but the Danubian monarchy would be granted a position of honor equal to that of Prussia. This solution, while it would have avoided the total exclusion of Austria from Germany, would have meant certainly the destruction in fact of any real Austrian influence. It approximated, at all events, the maximum position which the *kleindeutsch* faction was willing to allow Vienna. Thus Jörg, though he embraced this plan without enthusiasm, stood far closer to the *kleindeutsch* position than any other major Catholic figure. It may be claimed with considerable justification that, before the outbreak of the war, he anticipated views which Ketteler adopted only after the catastrophe.[54] He was, however, motivated almost entirely by a desperate hope of preserving a united front against France.[55]

Jörg, then, almost to the day of the outbreak of war was relatively

[52] *HPB,* 58 : 655–56.
[53] Hansen, 1 : 783.
[54] In *Deutschland nach dem Kriege von 1866,* published Jan. 1867.
[55] Bandmann, 156–58; *HPB,* 57 : 753, 826ff., 833.

friendly toward Prussia. Furthermore, it was not the war itself, but the Prussian alliance with Italy, and the postwar absorption of Hanover, Nassau, and other defeated states which ultimately converted him into perhaps the most bitter enemy of Bismarck in Germany. Only twice, apparently, during the war, despite the pressures on him, did he succumb to political passion. The first instance came at the beginning of hostilities, when, infuriated by the Prussian-Italian alliance, he reprinted from an Austrian publication an appeal "To German Catholics," which particularly charged Prussian Catholics with the duty of refusing to fight because of the heinous alliance between their King and the despoiler of the Pope.[56] A modern scholar has called this an incitement to high treason.[57] The second, and more easily understood, instance of the failure of his usually exceptional powers of judgment came when he predicted that either France would emerge from the war as the master of Central Europe, or that, more probably, it would result in a general European war, with unforeseeable, but certainly, for Germany, disastrous consequences.[58] On July 12, when the war was all but over, he still was convinced that France would be the real victor.[59] Within a few weeks, however, his rage had subsided, and he was able to analyze the new situation with his wonted penetration.

In the monthly *Historisch-politische Blätter*, which bears the stamp of greatness (even when it was wrong, it was wrong in the grand manner and with impeccable style), and in the daily *Kölnische Blätter*, Catholic Germany possessed two powerful voices which were heard throughout the country. Moreover, these two were abetted by a host of smaller newspapers and magazines with a more restricted circulation, which also made their presence felt, although in more limited areas.

[56] In this curious article, Prussian Catholics were urged to tell their King: "We cannot, we may not; God, rather than man, must be obeyed, let come to us what will." *HPB*, 57:1010ff.

[57] Bandmann, 117.

[58] *HPB*, 58:55–68.

[59] "For thirteen years I have referred to him [Napoleon] by circumlocutions [for example, *Imperator*] because I was willing to bestow the title *Kaiser* on no one except him who bore it in descent from the old sovereigns of the *Reich*. Now I will concede [it] to him before he mounts to a still higher title, and before the political police teach me a better one. I say, therefore, in conclusion: later there will appear a stronger one, namely the revolution; but for now, however, the great German reformer is — His Majesty the Emperor of the French [*der Kaiser der Franzosen*]." *HPB*, 58:160.

In the middle Rhine valley, for instance, Catholic interests were served by two newspapers, both published at Mainz. The more important of the two, the *Mainzer Journal,* dated from 1848, when Canon Lenig established it as an "independent" newspaper. Reacting against the violence which characterized the revolution in that region, the *Journal* rapidly gravitated into the conservative camp, and became one of the stanchest defenders of the Dalwigk ministry. In Hesse-Darmstadt itself the paper achieved considerable influence because of its determined support of "conservative interests in Church and state," as its masthead proclaimed in December 1853, but for Germany as a whole its main importance arose from the fact that both Moufang and Ketteler often used its columns for their pronouncements on socio-political issues.

Under its first editor, Franz Sausen, the *Journal* did not concentrate alone on local affairs, but set its sights on the larger questions of Germany and of Europe. In that way it managed to achieve circulation in Baden, Württemberg, Bavaria, and even in Alsace and Lorraine, as well as in Hesse itself. Even after Sausen's death in 1866, the tradition was continued. So small was its interest in local matters that, for example, its columns during the late summer of 1866 contained no comment on the implications of the Nikolsburg Peace for the Grand Duchy, despite the fact that by its terms the northern half of the state was to enter the North German Confederation. Moreover, the paper ignored completely the 1867 discussions of the Hessian *Landtag* on the future relationship of the truncated Duchy to North Germany. These startling omissions are perhaps in part attributable to the paper's desire to avoid making Dalwigk's situation more difficult, since the minister was under heavy fire from those who desired incorporation of the entire Hessian state in the new confederation.[60]

The second Catholic newspaper of Mainz, the *Katholisches Volksblatt,* was founded in 1857. A Sunday newspaper, known popularly as the *Mainzer Blättchen,* it appealed to a less sophisticated public than the *Journal,* and acquired a wide circle of readers in Hesse, Baden, and in the Catholic regions of Württemberg. It seems never to have achieved any national significance.[61]

Farther up the Rhine, Catholics of Baden were less well represented

[60] Bachem, 2:354–56; Weber, 1–3, 10.
[61] Weber, 3, 18–19.

in the journalistic field. The prevailing liberalism of the Roggenbach régime produced a difficult environment for conservative newspapers of any stamp. After the demise of the short-lived *Süddeutsche Zeitung* of 1848, Catholics did not succeed in establishing a permanent press outlet until 1860, when a group of them purchased the then insignificant *Karlsruher Anzeiger*. After several years of financial difficulties, the *Anzeiger* gradually achieved a status of respectability and some importance. It was renamed the *Badischer Beobachter* in 1863, and by 1866 it had become the chief organ of Catholicism in southwestern Germany. It was assisted, not very ably, by several smaller newspapers that made their appearance during the mid-sixties. Among these were the *Pfalzer Bote,* founded by Jakob Lindau in 1865, and the *Freiburger Bote,* established the same year. Both appeared three times a week. In addition, the *Christlicher Pilger* supplemented them on Sunday. None of these, except the *Beobachter,* had more than a meager circulation, and none of them had any importance outside Baden.[62]

Württemberg likewise possessed only one Catholic daily of any note, the *Deutsches Volksblatt,* which first appeared in Stuttgart in 1848. The founder was Dr. Florian Riess, who, some years later, entered the Society of Jesus. The *Volksblatt* was designed to appeal to educated Catholics, and, consequently, exercised comparatively little influence on the masses. Politically, it spoke with the voice of the clergy, which in Württemberg was allied with the democratic wing of the *grossdeutsch* party. Its viewpoint was generally close to that of Rudolph Probst.[63] Like Probst, and like Jörg in Bavaria, the *Volksblatt* avoided the nearly fatal weakness of most Catholics during the period: the tendency to oversimplify political issues. Thus, while generally favoring Austria, it maintained consistently up to 1866 that the position of the Church, and of Catholics, was more desirable in Protestant Prussia than in the Habsburg Monarchy. The only other Catholic organ in Württemberg was the popularly written weekly, the *Katholisches Sonntagsblatt,* which was unimportant and conventionally conservative.[64]

In Bavaria the Catholic daily press was surprisingly weak, considering the fact that the kingdom was one of the two Catholic strongholds

---

[62] *Ibid.,* 6–8; Bachem, 2:324–25; Vogt, 153–58.
[63] See Chapter One.
[64] Bachem, 2:250; Weber, 5; Rapp, *Öffentliche Meinung,* 32–33, 78.

in Germany. In the sixties there were a number of small newspapers of limited importance, but none which could be compared with the *Kölnische Blätter* or the *Mainzer Journal*. Part of the difficulty arose from the fact that the bulk of Catholic strength was found in the rural population, which was relatively immune to the press, while the cities, particularly Munich, were generally liberal. The most important Catholic newspaper was the *Augsburger Postzeitung*, which, however, found great difficulty in competing with the *grossdeutsch*-liberal *Augsburger Allgemeine Zeitung*, one of the truly great newspapers of the nineteenth century. In the capital there were several papers which were either openly or covertly Catholic in emphasis. The two more important ones were the *Neuer Bayrische Kurier*, dating from 1857, although in the sixties still nominally independent, and the *Münchener Volksbote*. The latter, under its fiery editor, von Zander, led the campaign to oust Richard Wagner from the affections of King Ludwig II, and it was to a great extent responsible for creating the public scandal over the composer's liaison with Cosima von Bülow. The Wagner-Bülow triangle was sufficiently outrageous in itself to offend the moral and religious sensitivities of Bavarian Catholics, but, in addition, Wagner was regarded as pro-Prussian and as dangerously liberal in his political, as well as in his personal and artistic, life. Besides these two papers there were a number of others of minor import in the provincial towns, all of which had, of course, a limited circle of readers. In all there were by 1871 in the whole of Germany one hundred and twenty-six daily newspapers with a specifically Catholic viewpoint.[65]

Besides these examples of the Catholic press which had, or aspired to have, general circulation, there were a number of publications with varying degrees of significance dedicated to special areas. Among them were such journals as the *Katholisches Literaturblatt*, founded in the Rhineland in 1865, and many organs published by the various *Vereine* for their members, including the already mentioned *Westfalischer Bauer*, and, after 1868, the *Christlich-soziale Blätter*.[66]

With the exception, then, of a few outstanding publications such as the *Historisch-politische Blätter*, the *Kölnische Blätter*, and the *Main-*

[65] Heinrich Bornkamm, "Die Staatsidee im Kulturkampf," *Historische Zeitschrift*, 170 (1950):54; Bachem, 2:246; Journal, Sept. 1, 1866, Hohenlohe, *Memoirs*, 1:164; Spielhofer, *Historisch-politische Blätter*, 165:155; Ernest Newman, *The Life of Richard Wagner*, 3:48–50, 97–99; Rovère, 99.

[66] Bongartz, 64; Hertling, 1:181; Nitti, 186, note; Bachem, 3:28.

zer Journal, Catholic Germany did not possess a periodical press of outstanding importance before 1871. In this field, as in others, the sinews of power were in an early stage of development. Bachem maintains, in retrospect, that the major stumbling block in the development of Catholic political strength during the sixties was the lack of an effective press.[67] With due reservation concerning the views of a man who was for all his life associated with the publishing business, this judgment appears to be in the main justified. It finds corroboration from no less a person than Bishop von Ketteler, who, as early as 1862, confided to a friend his concern that "by far the greatest part of the press in Germany, serving the cause of evil, is now the main power which fights against the realm of God," and prayed that the evil might be countered by a press which would "serve the cause of truth to an equal extent." [68] In a world which was changing with unprecedented rapidity, he felt it vitally necessary to find "new ways to fight evil." [69]

Nevertheless, despite the embryonic character of political and social Catholicism at the time of the collapse of the old Germany in 1866, the raw materials for the construction of future power were at hand; they needed only to be developed and used. It was the realization of Ketteler and others that new tactics had to be devised to deal with new situations which gave the Church in Germany its best hope for the future. Though the shock of the crisis and the war prevented most Catholic leaders from realizing it, the prospect was not nearly so dismal as it appeared to them in the fall of 1866.

[67] Bachem, 2:246.
[68] Ketteler to Countess Hahn-Hahn, Mainz, Feb. 20, 1862, *Ketteler Briefe,* 273.
[69] *Ibid.*

Chapter 3

The North German Confederation

Nowhere does Sybel's dictum that the German Empire was founded in the fall of 1866 [1] seemingly find more striking confirmation than in the shift of political forces and the resulting metamorphosis of political parties which took place throughout Germany immediately following the war. During those months many of the features which were to characterize the political pattern of the Empire during the first decade after 1871 originated. Among the most significant of them were the National Liberal and Free Conservative parties in Prussia, which gave Bismarck, for the first time, consistent parliamentary support for his national policy. Moreover, with the drafting of the constitution of the North German Confederation, its adoption by the governments, and its approval by the Constituent Reichstag in the spring of 1867, the future *Reich* acquired its basic constitutional structure.

Nevertheless, Sybel's judgment appears, upon closer analysis, to be more striking than valid, particularly if it is considered from the viewpoint of Germany as a whole, rather than that of Prussia, and in the light of 1866–67, rather than that of the period in which Sybel wrote. In fact, from the end of the war in 1866 until the proclamation of the new Empire in January 1871, there was no Germany at all in the constitutional sense of the word. Prussia's victory abrogated those sections of the 1815 treaty which had established the German Confederation, and left all the German states technically sovereign. While the Treaty of Prague, of August 23, 1866, authorized Prussia to form a new confederation of the states north of the Main, it also required her to recognize the sovereignty of the four south of that river. Actually two Germanies were envisaged by the treaty, for the southern states were

[1] Sybel, 5:460.

granted the privilege of forming their own confederation if they chose. Since the *Südbund* was abortive from the beginning, there were in reality, between 1866 and 1871, at least five sovereign political units within the limits of what was to become the *Reich*.[2] Although the ties of nationality and language of course remained, and although new links were forged during these five years, it is impossible to deal either with political developments in general, or with political Catholicism specifically, within a national frame of reference. North was North, and South was South, and, at least so argued most southern Catholics, never the twain should meet.

If one confines his attention to north Germany, or, on the basis of later knowledge, assumes that the absorption of the South was inevitable, Sybel's argument has much to recommend it. In Prussia the outbreak of the war had coincided with a bitter political campaign preparatory to *Landtag* elections. The elections took place at the height of the military conflict, on June 25 and July 3, and thus the final balloting occurred on the very day that Prussian arms were destroying the old Germany at Königgrätz. The chronological relationship between events on the battlefield and the campaign within Prussia was of major importance in molding the future party structure of north Germany, for it was the most significant single factor in the collapse of the liberal opposition to Bismarck. Before the fighting broke out, the minister-president had, on May 28, appealed for the election of pro-government deputies, arguing that it would further the accomplishment of Prussia's "German mission." At the same time he promised that if the support he requested were forthcoming, the constitutional conflict which had rent the country for four years could easily be resolved. The fortuitous juxtaposition of the final balloting and the decisive battle of the war convinced many voters that opposition to Bismarck was now tantamount to betrayal of sons and brothers fighting in Bohemia. As a result, the opposition parties lost more than a hundred seats, most of which were won by conservative candidates.[3] However, the Conservatives, despite their control of approximately a hundred and fifty seats in the new chamber, did not form a majority. But their gains did make it possible for Bismarck to secure the King's

[2] *Ibid.*, 5:399–400.

[3] It was, of course, knowledge that the battle was impending, rather than its occurrence or its result, that was influential.

consent to a compromise with the *Landtag* on the constitutional question. Accordingly, the King, in his speech from the throne, requested passage of a law appropriating funds *ex post facto* to cover the expenditures of the preceding four years. Bismarck, who was well aware that he could not hope to carry out his plans against a hostile *Landtag,* saw in the indemnity the only practicable means of harvesting the political fruits of the military victory.

Although the *Fortschrittspartei* and the Left Center, the two most important liberal groups, stood firm *as parties* against the indemnity, a significant number of deputies from each broke ranks. Fearing that continued opposition would rob the victory of its consequences, and might cost them their political future, they organized, in conjunction with the Old Liberals, who had always been willing to compromise with the monarchy in the interests of German unity, the National Liberal party, which pledged itself to support Bismarck in building a new Germany.

The Conservative party itself, defender of the feudal and Protestant tradition, although it was finally induced to support the indemnity legislation, also found itself shortly afterward torn by dissension. Many Conservatives were indignant at Bismarck's appeal to the masses, considering it a betrayal of their interests and even of the monarchical principle itself. Some, indeed, had opposed the war as "unchristian." Those Conservatives who preferred to follow the ministry in its new course found the reactionary attitude of their colleagues little to their liking, and, therefore, they seceded from the Conservative party to organize a new group, the *Freikonservative Partei*, which, like the National Liberals, openly committed itself to support of Bismarck's German policy. It was these new parties which, first in the Prussian *Landtag,* later in the North German Reichstag, and finally in the Imperial Reichstag, served as the parliamentary base for Bismarck's régime down to 1878.[4]

On the other hand, the party which was to form the most important opposition group in the first years of the Empire, the Catholic Center, was noticeably missing from this first postwar *Landtag.* As has been indicated above, the strength of the *Zentrumsfraktion* had been steadily declining for a number of years before the war.[5] In the last prewar

[4] Hansen, 1:784–85; Ziekursch, 1:192; *AAZ,* Nov. 8, 1866, 5121–22; Oncken, *Bennigsen,* 2:10–11.

[5] See Chapter One.

chamber it had numbered only twenty-six, and had been able to place only one member on a standing committee.[6] The already tenuous hold which it had on the loyalty of voters was severely shaken by the war, particularly by the equivocal position taken before and during the fighting by many Catholic laymen, and even by some of the hierarchy. The opposition of many Catholics had been outspoken. In the Rhineland, during the weeks immediately before the outbreak of hostilities, numerous mass meetings had been held to protest the government's warlike policy; petitions had been circulated demanding that peace be maintained. The Archbishop of Cologne had dispatched a letter to the King begging him to prevent the outbreak of war. In some Rhenish districts there had been considerable active resistance to mobilization. Nevertheless, after the war began, the Cologne Archbishop had responded to the King's request for prayers from all clergymen for the success of Prussian arms. The *Kölnische Blätter* criticized the Archbishop for his action, pointing out that the prayers might better have been said in behalf of the triumph of justice. To compound the confusion, many members of the clergy, despite the public stand of the Archbishop, continued to voice their disinclination for the war.[7]

In the revolutionary realignment of forces which followed the victory, Prussian Catholics found themselves in an exceptionally unenviable position. As Prussians they might feel elation; as Catholics they were subject to a deep depression. Their confusion was apparent in the results of the election. Fifteen members of the old Center won seats in the new chamber, but among the fifteen were only four from Prussia's most important Catholic region, the Rhineland. Although the *Fraktion* survived long enough to vote *en bloc* against the indemnity and against the extraordinary appropriation to pay for the costs of the war, the old divisions which dated from the beginning of the constitutional conflict, now sharpened vastly by the inevitable despair

[6] Ziekursch, 1:192; *AAZ*, Jan. 29, 1866, 455. The approaching demise of the party had been apparent to its members for several years before 1866. Hertling (1:73–74) mentions attending a dinner given by the *Fraktion* in 1863, at which time it was already so rent by dissension that one of the members present at the dinner spoke of the affair as a *Henkersmahl*, or, in an American idiom, "The condemned men ate a hearty meal."

[7] Hansen, 1:782–84; Pastor, *Reichensperger*, 1:579–80; H. von Sybel to Hermann Baumgarten, Bonn, May 14, 1866, Julius Heyderhoff (ed.), *Deutscher Liberalismus im Zeitalter Bismarcks*, 1:284–85; Friedjung, 1:300. According to contemporary rumor, priests in Silesia sent considerable sums of money across the frontier to aid the Habsburg Monarchy. See Goyau, *L'Allemagne religieuse*, 3:65.

over the future, soon led the remnant to disband. Its members then attempted to find shelter where they could. Nearly every one of the other parties, from Conservative to National Liberal, absorbed some of them.[8]

It may be superfluous to point out that those Catholic politicians for whom their faith served as a guide to political action found no solution to their dilemma in these *mariages de convenance*. None of the parties that they perforce joined were genuinely interested in satisfying the particular politico-religious concepts of these unwilling adherents. Catholics were now forced to pay the penalty for their inability in former years to agree upon a common policy. Particularly they suffered the consequences of their inconsistency during the years of the constitutional crisis, when their attitude toward the government had vacillated between halfhearted opposition and fainthearted support. The voters had now largely abandoned them, and time alone could rescue them from the limbo in which they found themselves.[9]

For the small Catholic minorities in the other north German states, whether annexed by Prussia or entering the new Confederation as separate entities, the new circumstances posed extremely serious problems, unlike those faced either by old Prussian or south German Catholics. For the former, the new order in north Germany meant only the sharpening of hitherto existing conflicts, since the internal structure of their state was little affected; for the south Germans, whose governments were still independent despite military defeat, some freedom of choice remained. But in Hanover, Saxony, and the other states which lost their independence, persons who had been hostile to Prussia had to adjust to a completely new situation: to decide whether to resist Bismarck's new order as far as possible or to cooperate. As one would expect, Catholic politicians, of whom the Hanoverian, Ludwig Windthorst, is the outstanding example, immediately allied themselves with particularistic groups of whatever religious persuasion and sought to salvage as much local power and prestige as they could. In general their success was negligible. Hanover, for example, was for some

---

[8] One member voted in favor of the indemnity, and Peter Reichensperger, who was ill, missed the roll call. On the extraordinary appropriation two members voted with the majority. On the question of the annexation of Hanover and Electoral Hesse the group split; five voted for it and eight against. Reichensperger again was not recorded because of illness. Wendorf, 125–26. See also Ziekursch, 1:194.

[9] Hansen, 1:785, 796; Sybel, 5:428; Wendorf, 122–23, 127–28.

months under Prussian military occupation as a conquered territory, and there, as elsewhere, important liberal leaders, who had formerly condemned Bismarck as the destroyer of liberty, faced about and joined the National Liberals for the sake of German unity.[10]

The outline of the new Confederation had been contained in the Prussian proposal for reform of the Federal Diet of June 10, 1866, although at that time the inclusion of all members of the old *Bund,* except Austria, was at least nominally contemplated. This maximum objective had proved impossible to achieve, despite Austria's military defeat, because of the complex international issues involved, particularly France's unwillingness to see Prussia dominate the whole of Germany. Accordingly, shortly after the conclusion of the final peace with Austria, Prussia had negotiated a series of treaties with the states north of the Main which had supported her during the war, providing for the establishment of a confederation along the lines of the June 10 proposal. Most of these treaties were signed on August 18, although a few reluctant governments, such as those of the two Mecklenburgs and Saxe-Meiningen, did not capitulate until a few weeks later, under the threat or actual use of force. The inclusion of Upper Hesse and Saxony was finally assured by the conclusion of peace treaties with the Darmstadt and the Dresden governments respectively. The new *Bund* was to include twenty-two states, with a total population of about thirty million people. Of these, roughly twenty-five million were inhabitants of Prussia, which had been enlarged by about four and a half million through the annexation of Schleswig-Holstein, Hanover, Electoral Hesse, Nassau, and the free city of Frankfurt.[11]

The four south German states, all of which had fought against Prussia, although allowed to retain their sovereignty by the Treaty of Prague, emerged from the war somewhat less than completely independent. Three of them, Württemberg, Baden, and Bavaria, were required to accept, as part of the peace settlement, offensive and defensive alliances which committed them to place their total military strength under Prussian command in case of war. The existence of these treaties was kept secret for the time being, and none of them defined specifically what constituted a *casus foederis.* In particular, it was not clear

[10] Oncken, *Bennigsen,* 2:11–13. Two of the major figures in the National Liberal party were the Hanoverians, Johannes von Miquel and Rudolf von Bennigsen. Both had been instrumental in the founding of the *Nationalverein.*

[11] Sybel, 5:350–51.

whether the decision rested with the southern states, individually or collectively, or with Prussia.[12]

Largely because of Bismarck's illness, brought on by the exertions of the summer, it was not until December that delegates from the various states met at Berlin to discuss details of the projected constitution for the new *Bund*. Consequently the draft which had been prepared by Bismarck did not receive approval by the governments until early February 1867. The draft constitution represented Bismarck's attempt to effect a compromise between liberal and democratic demands for a parliamentary régime, on the one hand, and the necessity of preserving military independence for the Prussian crown and local autonomy for the states, on the other. Its most significant and controversial provisions were, first, the collective sovereignty of the states in the *Bundesrath*, and, second, universal, direct manhood suffrage for election of the new Reichstag. Like most compromises it was completely satisfactory to no one. Bismarck, who had originally intended that approval of the constitution by a Reichstag elected for that purpose, after it had been adopted by the state governments, would suffice to place it in effect, was forced to compromise with the Prussian liberals, and to agree that subsequent ratification by the state diets would be required.[13] Elections for the Constituent Reichstag took place on February 12, 1867, under the provisions of the not yet officially adopted constitution. Each constituency comprised approximately a hundred thousand persons. Voting was public, since the constitution, as drafted, did not provide for the secret ballot.

In a preelection campaign, which was short but spirited, Catholics of north Germany again gave ample evidence that events of the preceding year had shattered whatever political cohesion they had once possessed. At first Catholics in the Rhineland took little part in the campaign. Their chief press organ, the *Kölnische Blätter,* formerly the spokesman for the Catholic Fraction, supported candidates of the *Fortschrittspartei, i.e.,* those liberals who had *not* made peace with Bismarck. The *Blätter,* desiring to salvage whatever was possible from the disaster of 1866, apparently had concluded that Bismarck could thus most effectively be fought.[14] The Rhenish clergy — following a

---

[12] *Ibid.,* 5 : 383–97.

[13] *Ibid.,* 5 : 437–38.

[14] *AAZ, Beilage,* Jan. 22, 1867, 356; Klemens Löffler, *Geschichte der katholischen Presse Deutschlands,* 40; Hansen, 1 : 786. The *Kölnische Blätter* explained its position as follows:

pronouncement by Archbishop Melchers on February 1, 1867, that he would "remain independent of the efforts of all political parties" — declined to take any active part in the election.[15]

The Archbishop's reticence is an indication that the hierarchy had warmed noticeably toward Berlin in the months after Königgrätz, despite Catholic chagrin over the Prussian-Italian military alliance. It has been suggested even that the bishops were mainly responsible for the dissolution of the *Zentrumsfraktion*,[16] because they hoped Prussia might thereby be induced to assume Austria's former role as the defender of Rome against Italy. From the evidence it seems unlikely that the bishops had anything directly to do with the collapse of the Prussian Center. It appears certain, however, that they did have considerable hope of gaining Prussian support for the Papacy.

In the fall of 1866 Berlin began to show anxiety over the possibility that the Roman question might become explosive, since Italy, having acquired Venetia, could henceforth devote full attention to it. Indeed, the Prussian ambassador at Florence, Count Usedom, reported on October 14, 1866, that Rome was becoming the focus of Italian policy, since French troops were scheduled to leave the city in December, according to the terms of a treaty signed two years earlier.[17] A few days later Goltz, the Prussian Ambassador to France, urged his government to take steps, in cooperation with Napoleon III, to solve the problem of Rome. He feared that Prussia would incur the hatred of all European, as well as German, Catholics if Italy occupied Rome.[18] Berlin was sufficiently worried that King Wilhelm felt it wise personally to convey his interest in the Pope's situation through a communication given to the Pontiff in mid-October by Count Harry Arnim, Prussia's representative at the Holy See. The overly independent ambas-

"Men must be elected who will be able to find a just compromise between the necessary unity of the federal government and the special interests of the states; men who will demand unconditionally the establishment for the north German parliament of the most important constitutional rights, especially parliamentary control of the budget, immunity of members of the Reichstag from prosecution for statements made on the floor, and freedom of the press; men who will work for true parity [of religious faiths] and for the independence of the Church; men who will work to advance the economic interests and the welfare of the people in every way." Hansen, 1:786–87.

[15] Hansen, 1:786.

[16] *Ibid.*, 790.

[17] Usedom to Bismarck, Florence, Oct. 14, 1866, Erich Brandenburg *et al., Die auswärtige Politik Preussens, 1858–1871*, 8: no. 55. This collection will hereafter be cited as *APP*; references are to the document number.

[18] Goltz to Thile, Paris, Oct. 26, 1866 (most secret), *ibid.*, no. 64.

sador, however, apparently exceeded his instructions and suggested to Pius IX the possibility of asylum in Prussia if worse came to worst. The Pope, in a holograph letter on November 1, conveyed his appreciation to King Wilhelm for the latter's "expressions of interest," and voiced the hope that Prussia would assist in guaranteeing the permanent independence of Rome.[19] Arnim delivered the King's noncommittal reply to this letter on December 23, at which time the Pontiff informed him that he sought only "moral support" and not an "effective guarantee." [20]

Nevertheless, Prussia found herself in an embarrassing position, as Undersecretary Thile informed Goltz on November 9. She would be strongly opposed to any move of the Pope to seek asylum in Hohenzollern territories, but she could not refuse him if he did so, for fear he might turn to Vienna again. That, said Thile, could not be permitted, for it would create additional difficulties for Prussia in dealing with her own Catholic citizens. He agreed that cooperation with France was highly desirable.[21]

Although this projected Franco-Prussian *rapprochement* came to nought — in part because of the growing tension between the two governments, in the early months of 1867, over the Luxemburg question — the decision of the Cologne Archbishop to remain neutral in the campaign, approved at least tacitly by other Prussian bishops, was only prudent at the time. Melchers' pronouncement provoked the *Kölnische Blätter* later to complain that the clergy had done little to inform the people either of the importance or of the issues of the election. In the same edict, nevertheless, the Archbishop had suggested that Catholic voters at least consider the religious affiliations of all candidates, and had advised them to cast their ballots whenever possible for Catholics, or at least for "Christians," in order to prevent the triumph of those who wanted to "ban religion from the state, the school, and the family." [22]

The *Kölnische Blätter,* while continuing to support the Progressives, also began to urge voters to examine the religious beliefs of

[19] Bismarck, *Aufzeichnung,* Putbus, Nov. 19, 1866, *ibid.,* no. 90; Pius IX to King Wilhelm, the Vatican, Nov. 1, 1866, *ibid.,* no. 71; Thile to Goltz, Berlin, Nov. 1, 1866, *ibid.,* no. 69.

[20] King Wilhelm to Pius IX, Berlin, Dec. 13, 1866, *ibid.,* no. 130 and note 6.

[21] Thile to Goltz, Berlin, Nov. 9, 1866, *ibid.,* no. 893.

[22] Hansen, 1:786–87.

those seeking election, despite the obvious inconsistency. The result was that in the Rhineland confessionalism indirectly became an issue in the election. Of the thirty-five seats in the Constituent Reichstag allotted to that area, twenty-five were won by Catholics. Whether this result can to any appreciable degree be attributed to the clergy and the Catholic press is not ascertainable. In one Cologne district, endorsement by the *Kölnische Blätter* seems to have been decisive in the election of a clergyman, but, on the other hand, the *Blätter's* support of *Fortschritt* candidates produced meager results. Ten of the Catholics who were elected joined the Free Conservatives, and one attached himself to the National Liberals. Not a single Catholic won election as a Progressive, although four of them did join the *Freie Vereinigung,* the Reichstag equivalent of the old Prussian Left Center. Six remained without party affiliation, and it is reasonably safe to assume that these were the ones elected primarily because they were Catholics.[23]

Of the annexed areas, Hanover was the only one in which Catholics were sufficiently numerous to play even a minor political role. Here also the first impulse of those who opposed the new order was to boycott the election. Catholics, however, formed only a minority of the total opposition. Among the rural population of both faiths there was a strong loyalty to the deposed monarch, which was strengthened by the knowledge that taxes and military service would inevitably be more onerous with the incorporation of Hanover into Prussia. Likewise in the cities, the working class, among whom the Social Democrats had made converts, was generally anti-Prussian, while the Protestant clergy was as solidly particularistic as the Catholic, albeit for different reasons. Few, if any, of these dissidents had hope of effective resistance, but nonparticipation seemed logical, for they feared that the mere act of voting would imply approval of the new order.[24]

However, before the election actually took place, Hanoverian particularists had changed their minds and decided to enter the field. For Catholics especially, a public announcement by the bishops of Hildesheim and Osnabrück of their acceptance of the new situation had some effect. But for all particularists the stand taken by the former minister, Ludwig Windthorst, a Catholic, had the greatest effect in producing the change. Since Windthorst had been for several years the

[23] *Ibid.*
[24] Sybel, 6:15–16; *AAZ*, Jan. 11, 1867, 167; Oncken, *Bennigsen*, 2:20–21.

chief opponent of Bennigsen, Miquel, and the other liberals, his views commanded respect among most conservatives. He now argued that particularists had to enter the campaign for Reichstag seats, because only in that way could the voice of the whole country be heard. Otherwise the field would be abandoned entirely to the supporters of Bismarck. From Berlin, Peter Reichensperger also sought, by similar arguments, to exert influence on the annexed territories. To him, public acceptance of the *fait accompli* was vital, for only through Prussian leadership could the German people "bring themselves under one roof," now that the old *Bund* was gone. At least two important Hanoverian newspapers eventually came to the same viewpoint, and finally the particularists named candidates for every one of the Hanoverian constituencies, nineteen in all.[25]

The hope of the anti-Prussians that the election would take on the character of a plebiscite, which would clearly demonstrate popular hostility to the annexation, was deceived. Of the nineteen seats, ten were won by nationalists. In total number of votes the national party polled 144,188 against 129,885. This result was as gratifying to the pro-Bismarck groups both in Hanover and in the old Prussian districts as it was saddening to the Guelphs and their allies. The only particularist who was elected specifically as a Catholic was Windthorst himself from Meppen. His victory was, however, of considerable significance, for it marked the beginning of a distinguished career on the national stage, inasmuch as Windthorst was later to be recognized as Germany's outstanding parliamentarian.[26]

In the eastern provinces, whose population included about one million Catholics of Polish nationality, the establishment of the North German Confederation, and especially the adoption of universal manhood suffrage, created a unique problem. Since 1848 there had been in every *Landtag,* despite the three-class electoral system which drastically limited the representation of the common people, a group of about twenty members from Polish areas who constantly made difficulties for the government. These Polish delegates had never joined the Catholic Fraction, although they often voted with it. They had,

[25] *AAZ,* Jan. 11, 1867, 167; Bismarck to Arnim, Berlin, Dec. 8, 1866, Prince Otto von Bismarck, *Die gesammelten Werke,* 6: no. 628 (hereafter cited as *GW;* references are to the document number); Hansen, 1:785.

[26] Sybel, 6:36; Oncken, *Bennigsen,* 2:21–22; Hans Herzfeld, *Johannes von Miquel,* 1:46–55.

for example, cooperated with it consistently in combating the liberal program for secularization of the schools. The Poles, in addition to their obvious religious motives, had national objectives as well, and they feared the use of the schools as an instrument of the hated Germanization.[27] The singularity of the situation in early 1867 lay in the fact that a new political union was being created on the basis of German nationality, which would, however, include a large number of Polish citizens who, on national grounds, vehemently denied that they rightfully belonged in the new Germany. Because of universal, equal suffrage, they were now in a position to put forth their objections vociferously and at length.[28] It is not surprising, therefore, that in Polish districts the elections for the Constituent Reichstag produced heated campaigns in which both the religious and the national issue played vital parts.

Evidence of the character of the campaign can be found by examining the claims of fraudulent practices which were submitted to the Reichstag. Most of them concerned events in Posen and other Polish districts of Prussia, and many involved charges of interference by clergymen in favor of Polish-Catholic candidates against German-Protestant office seekers. On several occasions, however, officials were accused of having used various kinds of pressure to force voters to cast ballots against Polish-Catholic candidates. For example, in one district a local official was alleged to have begged his hearers at two campaign rallies not to "vote for the candidate of a party which since Charlemagne had pursued only Roman interests." [29]

The issue of election frauds was thoroughly debated in the Reichstag on March 4, when one of the Polish members, Dr. Motty, a district judge representing a Posen constituency, proposed that the victorious candidate in another Posen district be rejected because of alleged campaign irregularities. Motty argued that election issues in Posen were quite different from those anywhere else in Germany, for in addition to the usual divisions — *grossdeutsch-kleindeutsch,* nationalist-particularist, liberal-conservative — there was one overriding issue:

[27] Bergsträsser, *Politische Parteien,* 63; *AAZ, Beilage,* Nov. 30, 1866, 5494.

[28] *AAZ, Beilage,* Nov. 30, 1866, 5494.

[29] *Stenographische Berichte über die Verhandlungen des Reichstages des norddeutschen Bundes: konstituierender Reichstag,* March 15, 1867, 1:195–96 (hereafter cited as *Stenographische Berichte*). The candidate concerned was General Vogel von Falckenstein, best known for his harsh administration of Frankfurt-am-Main during the Prussian military occupation after the War of 1866!

German or Polish. The landowners, he pointed out, were largely German, while those who worked the land were overwhelmingly Polish. The former, he charged, behaved as if they believed any means legitimate in order to prevent the election of Poles. He accused election officials of refusing to accept ballots marked for Polish candidates, and of securing dismissal from employment of those who insisted on exercising their right. He maintained further that gullible peasants had been told that a vote against the German candidate was a vote in favor of handing the region over to the Tsar of Russia, and that some had been informed that they might vote legally only for Germans. Finally, he insisted that in some cases threats of violence had been used to compel voters to cast ballots as officials directed.[30]

These charges brought Bismarck to his feet with the counteraccusation that, according to information he had received some weeks earlier, a campaign had been carried on in Posen to convince the voters that a ballot cast for a candidate of German nationality was equivalent to a vote against Catholicism. He charged also that propaganda had been spread to make less sophisticated voters believe that the very existence of the Catholic faith was being placed in jeopardy by the formation of the North German Confederation. According to him this campaign had been sufficiently successful that some German Catholics "of the uneducated classes" had felt obliged to vote for Polish candidates for the sake of their religion.[31]

Although Bismarck had not specifically accused Catholic clergymen of perpetrating these frauds, Dr. von Niegolewski, a lawyer representing the eighth Posen district, rose to their defense. He stated that the clergy had remained aloof from the campaign to a degree which was surprising to the inhabitants. He cited as evidence the fact that in the official press at Posen there had been no charges of campaign irregularities by Poles. Niegolewski attributed clerical inactivity to the inexperience of the newly appointed Archbishop of Posen and Gnesen, Count von Ledochowski, who, he said, was not yet aware of "the significance of religion for a nationality which has lost its independence." [32] In support of Niegolewski's argument, the deputy Kantak, from a Bromberg constituency, also denied that the clergy had influ-

[30] *Ibid.*, March 4, 1867, 1:54–56.
[31] *Ibid.*, 1:56.
[32] *Ibid.*, 1:57.

enced the voting. He, however, attributed clerical abstention not to Ledochowski's inactivity, but to his direct order, claiming that if any clergyman took part in a campaign rally, the fact was reported through government channels to the Archbishop, who then reprimanded the offending priest.[33]

Motty's motion was defeated, and a few moments later Niegolewski's election was itself questioned on the grounds of protests alleging that election officials had refused to accept twenty-two ballots marked for his opponent. Since Niegolewski's majority was more than four thousand, the committee's recommendation to ignore the protest was accepted.[34]

Two weeks later the question of election frauds again cropped up, when Bismarck cited six instances in which the Catholic clergy in the province of Posen had allegedly intervened to insure the victory of Polish Catholics. In most cases, he said, priests had taken the position either that Catholics had to be elected to protect the Church, or that Poles had to be sent to Berlin to defend Polish national interests against the Germans. Often, Bismarck claimed, a threat was included: If Germans were elected, the ultimate result would be similar to what had happened in Russian Poland — destruction of Polish Catholic culture.[35]

Since the Reichstag declined to deal with the substance of any of these complaints, it is difficult to judge their validity. Many of the charges are in accord with what one would expect under the circumstances, particularly in the absence of the secret ballot. Furthermore, many of them were substantiated by citations of specific names, places, and dates. It seems likely, therefore, that these, at least, contained more than a kernel of truth. It is probable that the hierarchy, here as in the Rhineland, was striving to preserve cordial relations with the government, but that Catholic laymen and clergymen of the lower ranks did use with considerable effect their influence over their charges. At all events a bloc of a dozen Catholic Polish deputies came to Berlin. National tensions, however, were to make cooperation between them and other Catholics always difficult and sometimes impossible.

By the time the Constituent Reichstag assembled in Berlin on Feb-

[33] *Ibid.*
[34] *Ibid.*, 1:58, 61.
[35] *Ibid.*, March 18, 1867, 1:210–13.

ruary 24 it was clear that Bismarck's hope for a brief session with a minimum of bitterness was doomed. He knew that the national cause would benefit substantially in south Germany if the Reichstag gave an impression of overwhelming enthusiasm for the new union, and, needless to say, he was not unconscious of the effect that such a demonstration would have on foreign governments. Unfortunately, however, the Reichstag was divided among at least seven recognizable parties and two or three splinter groups. No firm majority existed either for or against Bismarck's government, although those who were irreconcilably hostile to the new order were distinctly in the minority. The National Liberal party, which had seventy-nine seats, formed the largest single bloc, and, standing midway between the extremes, held the balance of power.[36]

Most of the important members of the old Prussian *Zentrumsfraktion* had won seats, but here, as in the recently concluded session of the Prussian *Landtag,* all outward signs of unity among them had disappeared. Karl von Savigny, who had once been associated with the Center, had long since entered the government, first as Prussian delegate to Frankfurt between 1864 and 1866, and then as Bismarck's adviser on parliamentary affairs. Although he did not seek election to the Constituent Reichstag, he was instrumental in the founding of the Free Conservative party, and induced several Catholic members to join it. Among them were a Frankfurt priest, Father Thissen, elected from Cologne; Scherer (Aachen); Count Hompesch (Aachen-Geilenkirchen); and Seul (Düsseldorf-Neuss). As indicated above, four Catholic members from the Rhineland, including another priest, Father Dauzenberg (Cologne-Sieg-Waldbröl), joined the *Freie Vereinigung,* as did Rohden (Münster-Tecklenburg-Steinfurt). Peter Reichensperger, representing an Arnsberg constituency, declined to join any party, and became one of the twenty-seven members listed as *wild.* His brother, August, still deeply disillusioned, had refused to stand for election.[37]

Although no clerical fraction appeared, the Constituent Reichstag did witness the birth of a group which was to have considerable significance in the later development of political Catholicism, the *Bundes-*

[36] H. K. Zuchhardt, *Die Finanzpolitik Bismarcks und die Parteien im norddeutschen Bunde,* 35; Sybel, 6:35–36.
[37] Bachem, 3:12–13.

staatlich-konstitutioneller Verein, an alliance of but eighteen deputies, of whom, so far as can be ascertained, only two were Catholics. This party, if the term can properly be applied to an organization so small and composed of so many diverse, even hostile, interests, was largely the creation of Ludwig Windthorst. When Windthorst arrived at the Prussian capital, he discovered that none of the existing parties was inclined to invite his participation in its counsels. Unlike his fellow Hanoverians, Bennigsen and Miquel, he had been outspokenly *grossdeutsch* in sympathy, and had, even after the war, expressed his abhorrence of a Germany dominated by Prussia. These views made him unacceptable to either the Free Conservatives or the National Liberals. Moreover, unlike many other proponents of *Grossdeutschland,* he had not reacted to the destruction of his ideal by retreating to a narrow particularism. The task of the Constituent Reichstag, he had argued during the campaign, was to establish a constitutional structure for north Germany which would be federal, not unitary, which would guarantee external security and internal civil liberty, and which would leave the door open for union with south Germany.[38] Thus, to the Conservatives he appeared too liberal, while to the *Fortschrittspartei* his federalism was unacceptable. Support for his views was, in fact, likely to be found only among individuals who, like himself, came from the annexed provinces or from the smaller states of the Confederation, and were desperate to avoid the complete ascendancy of Prussia. It was, accordingly, from delegates of Hanover, Schleswig-Holstein, Oldenburg, and the Hanseatic cities that the *Verein* recruited its members. Associated with Windthorst in its establishment was the former representative of the Hanseatic cities in the United States, Rudolph Schleiden, elected to the Reichstag from a Schleswig constituency. He was named president of the group. Others included Windthorst's former colleagues in the Hanoverian ministry, Exleben and Münchausen.[39]

The only "old" Prussian, and, other than Windthorst, the only Catholic who chose to join the new group, was Hermann von Mallinckrodt, after Peter Reichensperger the most important figure in the former *Zentrum.* It is primarily because of the association here of these

---

[38] See his letter to a constituent, Celle, Jan. 28, 1867, published in *Germania,* Oct. 2, 1910, quoted by Bachem, 3:16–17.

[39] Felix Rachfall, "Windthorst und der Kulturkampf," *Preussische Jahrbücher,* 135 (1909):225; Hüsgen, 62; Brandenburg, *Reichsgründung,* 2:269–70.

two subsequent leaders of the *Zentrumspartei* that most Catholic historians have seen in the *Bundesstaatlich-konstitutioneller Verein* a bridge between the old Prussian and the later German Catholic parties.[40] Because of the small membership it was possible for the entire group to hold weekly strategy meetings during the Reichstag sessions, and in these meetings Windthorst and Mallinckrodt, hitherto unacquainted, became close friends and collaborators. Whatever effect this collaboration may have had on the establishment of the Center in 1870–71, the *Verein* in 1867 possessed no basis for a clerical party. It was united only by its advocacy of a loosely federal rather than a centralized state. On other questions division was so sharp that no attempt was made in the weekly caucuses to commit members in advance to any specific policy. Necessarily the program, which largely reflected Windthorst's ideas, published in February 1867, had to be couched in very general terms. It favored a federal state with a central government sufficiently strong to guarantee "the independence, honor, and welfare of Germany." It supported parliamentary control of the budget, and ministerial responsibility to the Reichstag. It proposed the establishment of a federal court to decide constitutional disputes, and it demanded guarantees of freedom of the press, assembly, and association. Finally it wanted, somewhat ambiguously, the greatest degree of freedom for individual states consistent with a strong central government. This freedom was to be secured by constitutional guarantees which would, it was believed, make possible the rapid adherence of the southern states to the new *Bund*.[41]

Notwithstanding the dispersion of the Catholic members among several parties with vastly different aspirations and plans, the Reichstag debates give evidence of considerable areas of agreement among many of them on certain basic issues. Moreover, considering their numbers, they occupied the floor for a disproportionately large share of the time. In general, as might be expected, their remarks, with certain notable exceptions, betrayed a lack of enthusiasm for any union solely of north Germany. Most of them were actively hostile toward various aspects of Bismarck's draft constitution on the grounds that it sought to create too strong a central authority and made too little provision for the autonomy of component states. The feeling of most

[40] See especially Bachem, 3:16–17; Hüsgen, 64.
[41] Hüsgen, 62–64; Salomon, *Parteiprogramme*, 128; Zuchhardt, 36, 46.

Catholics was probably represented by Mallinckrodt's extraordinarily able address of March 12. The Berlin lawyer condemned the proposed confederation as unjust. *"Justitia fundamenta regnorum,"* he announced. But justice had not been present at the birth of the North German Confederation, for it was founded solely on expediency. Princes had been deposed, states annexed, the historic bonds that linked the Dutch and Austrian people with Germany had been sundered — all through Prussian aggression. Although the government called this new institution a confederation, it was, Mallinckrodt said, nothing less than a centralized, unitary state, a greater Prussia. In fact, he went on, what Bismarck sought was really "the old Prussia with somewhat broader shoulders, a somewhat stronger back, and a light German overcoat." Moreover, under the proposed constitution, there was no ray of hope for the future. Either north and south Germany would remain permanently connected only by treaties of alliance, or, more probably, the South would be compelled against its will to submit to Prussian centralism. Either outcome would, he was convinced, be disastrous for the nation.[42]

In a similar manner Rohden, while denying hostility to the Confederation as such, had already on March 9 denounced the draft constitution because it treated south Germany and Austria as foreign territories, and because it deprived Prussian citizens of freedoms long cherished. He charged that it superseded provisions of state constitutions without itself containing corresponding guarantees. In this connection he made specific reference to the article which granted the *Bundespräsidium, i.e.,* the Prussian government, the right to declare martial law in any area threatened by internal disturbance.[43]

Along the same lines, Michelis (Düsseldorf-Kempen) had argued, also on March 9, that acceptance of the truncated Germany contemplated by the draft constitution would be an unprincipled surrender to expediency. He stressed too, as he had earlier in the Prussian *Landtag,* the contradictions between the federal and the Prussian constitutions, particularly in reference to parliamentary control of the budget. Appealing for the support of members from Hanover and other annexed territories, he denied that failure to approve the draft would,

[42] *Stenographische Berichte,* March 12, 1867, 1:156–58; Rachfall, "Windthorst," *Preussische Jahrbücher,* 135:226.
[43] *Stenographische Berichte,* March 9, 1867, 1:121–22.

as Bismarck claimed, produce chaos in Germany. Rather, he suggested, astonishingly enough, rejection would mean only that the evil act would be consummated "by Bismarck's own hand without the approval of the representative body," which would thus avoid sharing the responsibility. In closing he returned to the anomalies of the constitutional situation in a paraphrase: "What does it profit us to win the whole world, if, however, we lose our [Prussian] constitution?" [44]

While these Catholics denounced the entire draft on principle, most of their fellows saved their energy for attacks on specific provisions.[45] Scherer, for example, during the final debate on the preamble, sought to win support for an amendment clarifying the ambiguities regarding the locus of sovereignty in the Confederation. He wanted the preamble to state unmistakably that the constitution was a joint creation of the allied governments *and* the Reichstag, so that in the future the governments could not choose to regard it as an *octroi,* and therefore not permanently binding upon them. The motion was lost without a record vote.[46]

As was to be expected, the most heated debates occurred over questions involving the powers of the Reichstag, and its relation to the *Präsidium,* the *Bundesrath,* and the state governments. There was considerable discussion on the controversial question of universal manhood suffrage. Windthorst, on two occasions, gave democratic suffrage his blessing. Furthermore, he supported actively an amendment to establish the secret ballot as a logically necessary complement to universal suffrage. Bismarck, who had accepted a democratically elected Reichstag as unavoidable, raised vehement objections to the amendment, but he could not carry the majority of the house with him, and in the final version of the constitution the ballot was declared to be universal, direct, and secret.[47]

Windthorst failed, however, to arouse any enthusiasm for his favorite project of establishing an upper house, distinct from the *Bundesrath* which represented the governments, as a balance between the democratically elected Reichstag and the Prussian monarchy. He ar-

[44] *Ibid.,* 115–16.
[45] For a general account of the debates and major decisions of the Constituent Reichstag, see Sybel, 6: Chapters 2, 3, and 4. Here only the role of Catholics will be considered.
[46] *Stenographische Berichte,* April 10, 1867, 1: 690–92.
[47] *Ibid.,* March 6, 1867, 1: 76, March 28, 1867, 1: 424–25; Sybel, 6: 91–95. Ward erroneously states that Windthorst opposed the secret ballot and that it was rejected by the Reichstag. See Ward, 2: 362.

gued that political stability made necessary an influential aristocracy, for he was convinced that France could trace most of her troubles to the destruction of the aristocracy in the great revolution.[48] The only evidence of any other Catholic opinion on this scheme is contained in a long speech by Father Thissen against it on March 28. He declared that the concept of medieval *Stände* could no longer meet the needs of the German people, because the vast economic and intellectual changes of the nineteenth century had invalidated old social divisions.[49]

Likewise Windthorst's hope to see established a federal court with jurisdiction over disputes between states, and other constitutional conflicts, which he regarded (quoting Humboldt at the Congress of Vienna) as "the necessary capstone of any federal constitution," was doomed to disappointment. Reichensperger, who supported the idea as strongly as did Windthorst, introduced an amendment authorizing a future Reichstag to establish such a court. He advanced the view that, in the absence of a supreme court, the legislative and judicial functions remained constitutionally confused, a situation which contravened the public interest. His chief worry arose from the fact that, as matters stood, only the *Bundesrath,* in practice controlled by Prussia, could decide legal disputes between the states and the federal government. Windthorst supported Reichensperger's motion, although he would have preferred a more immediate and direct attack on the problem, but it was defeated on a standing vote.[50]

In the light of later German history the most fateful decision of the Constituent Reichstag came on March 26, 1867, when it failed to approve an amendment proposing the establishment of a federal ministry responsible to the Reichstag. To Bismarck the issue was the most crucial of all. He regarded ministerial responsibility as incompatible with the federal structure of the *Bund,* and as an unacceptable limitation on the authority of the *Bundesrath* as constitutional executive. It was the democratic left wing of the *Fortschrittspartei,* led by Schulze-Delitzsch, which introduced the motion to create a responsible ministry; but after the distinguished Hanoverian jurist, Planck, had explored the problem at length, and had concluded that there was in fact no incompatibility between the principle and the authority

[48] *Stenographische Berichte,* March 28, 1867, 1: 425–26; Hüsgen, 68.
[49] *Stenographische Berichte,* March 28, 1867, 1: 419–20.
[50] *Ibid.,* April 9, 1867, 1: 658–60, 663–64; Hüsgen, 70.

of the *Bundesrath,* a sizable number of National Liberals joined in the campaign. Windthorst, the only Catholic who took part in the debate, declared himself solidly in favor of the plan, arguing that otherwise the executive would be responsible only to Prussian interests and completely irresponsible toward the *Bund.*[51]

Despite a spirited defense, the motion fell by a vote of 86 to 177; the vote of those known to be Catholic was divided, with twelve for the motion, eight against it, and six abstaining. Among the major Catholic figures, Windthorst, Mallinckrodt, and Rohden voted for the amendment. Of the three clergymen, Dauzenberg voted for it, Thissen against, while Wegner (Bromberg-Gnesen) abstained. Most of the Polish members likewise abstained.[52]

Although hopes for a responsible ministry were at least temporarily destroyed by this vote, Bennigsen made later on the same day a further effort to whittle down Bismarck's independent power with a proposal to authorize the *Bundesrath* to name not only the Chancellor, but also the heads of administrative departments. Bennigsen's amendment was approved without a record vote, but the article which it amended was then barely defeated, 127 to 126, with the Catholic deputies dividing much as they had before. Thissen, however, on this occasion voted for the proposed change.[53] This vote resulted, of course, in the complete elimination of the office of Chancellor from the constitution, and when on the following day Bennigsen tried to attach his amendment to a proposal resurrecting the office, the entire measure was defeated 140 to 124. Again the Catholics divided as before.[54] At last a compromise offered by Bennigsen, which required all acts of the *Präsidium* to be countersigned by the Chancellor, "who thereby assumes responsibility" for them, was adopted without a roll call.[55]

Another issue involving the relation between Reichstag and Chancellor reached a definitive settlement when, on March 29, an amend-

[51] Sybel, 6:89; *Stenographische Berichte,* March 26, 1867, 1:377.

[52] *Stenographische Berichte,* March 26, 1867, 1:373–74. It has proved impossible to isolate every Catholic member of this and the later Reichstag, since in the case of obscure and otherwise unknown delegates the only clues are found in remarks made on the floor and in other indirect evidence. Enough Catholic *Abgeordneten* have, however, been definitely identified to make possible a picture of the Catholic voting record substantially accurate in all but minor details.

[53] *Ibid.,* 1:380; Sybel, 6:89–90.

[54] *Stenographische Berichte,* March 27, 1867, 1:401.

[55] Sybel, 6:90. The responsibility assumed was moral rather than legal, for the Chancellor could be deposed only by the King.

ment offered by the National Liberal, Braun (Wiesbaden), giving the
Reichstag power to compel attendance of the Chancellor, either in
person or through a representative, failed to pass, 120 to 136. In this
case Windthorst and Mallinckrodt took opposite sides, the Hanoverian
voting with the Conservatives against the proposed amendment, as
did seven other Catholics, while Mallinckrodt and seven more voted
to approve it. Eleven Catholics, for the most part Poles, abstained.[56]

The question of whether Reichstag members were to receive a sti-
pend produced an extremely bitter debate. Bismarck was known to
be unalterably opposed; in fact, the draft constitution included an
article forbidding the payment of any monetary allowance to members. This article provoked the wrath of the democratic wing of the
Progressives, and it was unpopular with many members of other parties. On March 30 Windthorst offered a compromise proposal which
would have left the question to be settled by a future Reichstag, but
withdrew it a few moments later, after the debate had indicated that
his suggestion was unacceptable to the house. Immediately thereafter
the Reichstag went on to adopt an amendment authorizing payment
of a daily allowance and travel costs to members by a vote of 136 to
130. Only five Catholics voted with the Conservative minority, although several of the Poles and a few others abstained.[57]

Defiance of Bismarck and the governments was destined in this
case to fail, however. The *Bundesrath* refused to accept the change, and
on April 15 Bismarck, speaking for the governments, demanded that the
Reichstag reverse its decision. Primarily because the National Liberal
party failed to stand firm, an amendment introduced by the Conservative, Arnim-Heinrichsdorff, that "members of the Reichstag as such
may receive no pay or allowances," received the assent of the house,
178 to 90. The Catholics were found overwhelmingly in the opposition;
even most of the Polish group cast their votes against the measure.[58]

According to the draft constitution Reichstag elections were to take
place triennially. This provision was unsatisfactory to the Conservatives, who introduced an amendment to increase the legislative period
to five years. The amendment was defeated on March 29, 138 to 127;
eight Catholics, including Windthorst, Mallinckrodt, and Rohden,

[56] *Stenographische Berichte*, March 29, 1867, 1: 450–51.
[57] *Ibid.*, March 30, 1867, 1: 477, 481–82.
[58] *Ibid.*, April 15, 1867, 1: 711–12.

voted with the majority, while seven were counted with the Conservatives.[59]

Memories of the Prussian constitutional conflict of the earlier 1860's were certain to stimulate acrimonious controversy on the question of parliamentary authority over the budget. As in Prussia earlier, the axis around which the dispute turned was the specific question of control over military expenditures. The constitutional draft provided that the existing Prussian military laws were to be extended to the entire Confederation, and that for the ensuing ten years the peacetime strength of the army was to be fixed at one per cent of the population. During the same period the commander-in-chief, *i.e.*, the Prussian King, was to be granted 225 thalers per man *per annum*, for which revenues from tariffs, some ordinary taxes, posts, and telegraphs were to be earmarked. In the event that these sums did not suffice, additional amounts were to be raised by special contributions, known as *Matrikularbeiträge*, levied on the states on the basis of population. In effect. this arrangement would have substantially removed the military budget for ten years from control of the Reichstag. Nevertheless, because of the critical international situation there was a large body of opinion, even outside the extreme conservative group, which was unwilling to trust the military security of the Confederation to the whims of parliamentary majorities. As on so many other questions, the National Liberals held the balance of power.[60]

The initial attack on the draft came from the Progressive, Waldeck, who demanded both an annual military budget and a term of active military service shorter than the three years contemplated by the article in question.[61] Waldeck's impassioned plea brought forth strong objections from the professional soldiers in the assembly. The Catholic general, Vogel von Falckenstein, maintained in one of his few utter-

---

[59] *Ibid.*, March 29, 1867, 1: 461–62.

[60] Sybel, 6:137–38. For a full account of the debates on the budget question, see Sybel, 6:133–52. The crisis over Luxemburg reached its peak while the Constituent Reichstag was in session. Because of its larger implications, in particular its significance for south Germany, discussion of the Luxemburg question has been postponed until Chapter Four.

[61] *Ibid.*, 144–45. The *Kölnische Blätter* defended the stand of the *Fortschritt* editorially. For some time it had been advocating cooperation between that party and the Catholics in order "to protect the rights of the people granted by the Prussian constitution against all attacks, open or disguised." On February 22, two days before the opening session of the Reichstag, it had insisted that "not the slightest part of the Prussian parliamentary control of the budget must be abandoned in favor of the military administration." See Hansen, 1: 787–88.

ances that the three-year term was absolutely necessary for the well-
being of the army. In this view he was upheld by Moltke, who argued
also that if the strength of the military establishment were to be left
to the annual decision of shifting Reichstag majorities, the *Bund*
might well perish in case of war.[62]

The debate eventually reached an angry deadlock, which for a time
threatened to produce a crisis similar to that of 1862 in Prussia. On
April 5, in order to prevent the breakdown of deliberations, several
members proposed compromises. The Rhineland Catholic, Kratz (Düs-
seldorf-Gladbach), who was associated with the Progressives, and
Windthorst's friend Exleben of the *Bundesstaatlich-konstitutioneller
Verein* cooperated in introducing a motion to approve the government's plan for three years, *i.e.*, until December 31, 1870, after which
the Reichstag would be required to make permanent arrangements.
Windthorst spoke in favor of this motion, pointing out that in his mind
there was no doubt of the necessity for securing an adequate federal
military force. The vital question, however, was this: How long would
it be necessary to maintain one per cent of the population in military
service during peacetime? Three years would give the government
adequate time to investigate the matter, and it could then recommend a permanent law. Windthorst took considerable pains in this
address to combat the view of Waldeck and the other democrats that
anything except annual budgets would constitute a threat to the
authority of the Reichstag. However, in spite of the Hanoverian's
able argument, the motion was defeated on a standing vote. Another
motion by Kratz, Dauzenberg, and Kleinsorgen — all Rhineland Catholics — to make the military budget after January 1, 1870, dependent
on an annual federal law, suffered the same fate.[63]

The compromise proposal which was ultimately accepted came from
the National Liberal, Forckenbeck. He moved that the government's
proposition be accepted for four years — that is, until December 31,
1871. At that time future arrangements for the army would be established by a permanent law. His motion was approved, 137 to 127, with
all the more important Catholic deputies, except Scherer, voting on

[62] *Stenographische Berichte*, April 3, 1867, 1:545–46. Von Falckenstein is in no way
connected with political Catholicism. His remarks and his votes invariably place him in
the extreme conservative Prussian military tradition, indistinguishable from Moltke,
Roon, and others.

[63] *Ibid.*, April 5, 1867, 1:560–61, 578; April 6, 1867, 1:611.

the side of the majority. Only five voted against the compromise, with many of the Poles, as usual, abstaining.[64] The passage of the Forcken-beck amendment gave rise immediately to a rash of attempts by Conservatives to insure that the arrangements just approved would remain in force after the end of 1871, unless and until the Reichstag adopted a new law. Two slightly different proposals along these lines, offered by Moltke, were defeated on April 5 and 6, respectively. The five Catholic Conservatives who had opposed the Forckenbeck amendment supported these efforts to limit its effect, plus, in each case, one who had voted for the National Liberal compromise. The count on the first of the two was 123 to 136, and on the second, 130 to 138.[65] Essentially the same motion was put forth again on April 16 by Count Stolberg, and it succumbed 110 to 167. On this occasion only four Catholics voted for the motion, and even the Polish group joined with the majority against it.[66]

Finally the National Liberals, Ujest and Bennigsen, who had foreseen that under the arrangement which had been adopted, states could withhold their contributions after December 31, 1871, unless the Reichstag had by that time enacted a new military law, offered an amendment requiring continued payment of the *Matrikularbeiträge* after that date, as required by the interim military law, until it was changed. This amendment was adopted, 202 to 80. The division of Catholics on this question is significant. Those who made a fetish of defending state autonomy naturally opposed it. Sixteen of them, including Mallinckrodt and Windthorst,[67] voted with the minority, while Reichensperger, Thissen, and the Catholic Conservatives, in all ten, supported the motion.[68]

One of the most glaring weaknesses in the draft constitution was the absence of any bill of rights, and, for Catholics, particularly unsatisfactory was the omission of a guarantee of freedom for the Catholic Church from secular political interference. Such a guarantee did exist in the Prussian constitution, and the obvious policy for them, therefore, was to secure its transfer to the *Bundesverfassung*. On the

[64] *Ibid.*, April 5, 1867, 1:578-79.
[65] *Ibid.*, April 5, 1867, 1:579-80; April 6, 1867, 1:611-12.
[66] *Ibid.*, April 16, 1867, 1:720-21.
[67] Windthorst's proposal to subject the *Matrikularbeiträge* to the approval of the Reichstag had met with no success. See Zuchhardt, 4-5.
[68] *Stenographische Berichte*, April 16, 1867, 1:724-25.

general question of civil rights most of the Catholics supported a move of the democrat Schulze-Delitzsch to require appointment of a Reichstag commission charged with drafting a bill of rights along lines of the 1848 *Grundrechte*. However, for most deputies, unpleasant memories of the *Paulskirche* debacle were still too vivid, and Schulze's motion received insufficient backing.[69] Moreover, when the Lutheran pastor, Schrader, of Kiel, proposed an amendment to establish common citizenship for all legal residents of federal territory, with a guarantee of equal civil rights, equal right to public office, and equal right to enter any occupation, this likewise failed, 65 to 189. Thirteen Catholics voted affirmatively; six supported the majority, and five abstained. Windthorst was absent because of illness.[70] The leading Catholics felt too strongly the necessity of constitutional guarantees for the Church to abandon the struggle at that point. Nearly all of them were Prussians, and several took pains to emphasize their loyalty to their government, perhaps in order to counteract the suspicions aroused by certain events of the preceding year. Mallinckrodt, for example, on March 12, speaking "as one whose political opinions generally tend to be based on a calculation of religious interests," expressed his gratitude that Prussia had permitted a freer religious climate than existed in south Germany. He said that he had no objections to the North German Confederation on religious grounds; rather, he expected that religious discrimination would soon disappear within its borders.[71] A week later Rohden echoed Mallinckrodt's sentiments, and took the opportunity to suggest extension of the Prussian guarantees of religious freedom to the entire *Bund*. On the same day Scherer formally introduced an amendment which would simply have inserted Article Twelve of the Prussian constitution into the new federal document. In his remarks, Scherer, usually a strong supporter of Bismarckian policy, took occasion to defend the loyalty of most Catholics to the new order, although he made some pointed references to "good" and "bad" Catholics. Among the latter, he said, were some members of the Reichstag, who regarded the *Bund* itself, the constitution, and the events which had brought them both into being with an obvious lack of enthusiasm. This attack prompted the priest, Father Michelis, to

[69] Sybel, 6:83.
[70] *Stenographische Berichte,* March 19, 1867, 1:265–67.
[71] *Ibid.,* March 12, 1867, 1:156–58.

accuse Scherer of slander, while Rohden, Mallinckrodt, and Klein-sorgen all rose to deny the implication that some Catholics were dis-loyal.[72]

Savigny, speaking for the allied governments, gave a reasoned an-swer to Scherer, in which he stressed the difficulties that had been encountered in securing agreement of governments to the draft con-stitution. He stated that the Prussian administration had not proposed removing religious affairs from the jurisdiction of the states, since it had hoped to bring the Confederation into being with as little contro-versy as possible. It had, therefore, preferred to draw up a document that would deal only with matters most essential for the operation of a federal government. He concluded by stating that the example of Prussian religious toleration, which was so effective in practice, would, he believed, soon induce other states to adopt it for themselves. If not, the possibility still remained of bringing up the proposal later in the regular Reichstag. On the strength of Savigny's argument Scherer withdrew his motion. Mallinckrodt, however, was less impressed by the minister's comments, and immediately reintroduced it. But suffi-cient support was lacking, and the proposal suffered defeat without a roll call, as did a similar motion of Rohden's a few moments later.[73]

Meanwhile from the National Liberal side an attempt was under way to salvage at least the principle of the *Grundrechte*. This time the move took the form of an amendment merely authorizing a federal law, to be enacted later, which would enumerate basic rights that no government might legitimately withhold from its subjects. Specific mention was made of freedom of the press, assembly, and organization. To this proposal Kratz suggested adding the phrase "freedom of re-ligious belief and practice." While the Kratz subamendment was ac-cepted without a roll call, the original proposal, as amended, suffered defeat narrowly, 130 to 128. Seven Catholics voted for, and ten against, the amendment. Twelve, including Windthorst, abstained.[74] Kratz, on April 15, made a final attempt to obtain reconsideration of the ques-tion, when he proposed an amendment giving the federal government power to establish by decree freedom of religion throughout the terri-

[72] *Ibid.*, March 19, 1867, 1:235, 249–51, 261–63.
[73] *Ibid.*, March 19, 1867, 1:250–51, 255–56, 267.
[74] *Ibid.*, March 21, 1867, 1:301, 305–6; Sybel, 6:83–84. Because of the several issues combined in the proposal, the division of Catholics does not indicate clearly their views on the necessity of a federal guarantee of religious liberty.

tory of the *Bund*. He argued that the former motion had failed because it had been joined to others which were unacceptable to the house. However, his success was no greater this time; the Reichstag rejected his amendment decisively.[75]

Foreseeing ultimate failure of these maneuvers, some Catholics had also been attempting to approach the problem from another viewpoint. Kratz had introduced on March 26 an amendment which would have required a two-thirds majority of both *Bundesrath* and Reichstag to amend the constitution, instead of a simple majority in the Reichstag and a two-thirds majority in the federal council, as the draft provided. He argued with considerable logic that, since the federal constitution took precedence over those of the states, the governments could, acting through the *Bundesrath* supported by a simple majority of the Reichstag, deprive citizens of rights which were guaranteed by their own state constitutions. Thus, the Prussian guarantee of religious liberty was, he felt, endangered. Windthorst seconded the Kratz motion in the name of constitutional stability. In his opinion the concept of a centralized state was implicit in the so-called federal constitution. An amendment such as the one under consideration was vital, he believed, for the defense of local interests. Scherer, on the other hand, suggested that the Kratz amendment would place an almost intolerable limitation on future constitutional development, and the proposal failed by a large majority.[76]

It was during this recurring series of debates on the question of constitutional guarantees that the Catholic deputy, Michelis, on March 21, after a caustic interchange with the acting president, Bennigsen, resigned his seat in protest against what he called a *"Scheinparlament."* The Reichstag, he shouted, was engaged in the evil process of destroying constitutional rights of Prussian subjects without establishing even the most rudimentary guarantees in their place.[77]

Rohden all the while was carrying on his private campaign against the article in the draft which authorized the *Präsidium* to declare martial law in areas where public security was threatened, arguing that too much irresponsible power over individuals was thereby placed in the hands of the King of Prussia. He proposed that the Reichstag adopt immediately a rigidly limited definition of what constituted a

[75] *Stenographische Berichte*, April 15, 1867, 1:702–3.
[76] *Ibid.*, March 26, 1867, 1:351–53.
[77] *Ibid.*, March 21, 1867, 1:307–8, 312.

breach of security, and suggested an eventual federal law to specify the conditions under which martial law might legitimately be invoked. Like the other proposals intended to limit further the authority of the central government, this won only a handful of supporters.[78]

From the foregoing it is evident that while Catholic members of the Constitutent Reichstag possessed a considerable degree of common purpose, best defined as a desire to prevent coercion of the states by the federal administration, they demonstrated, except on a very few occasions, no tactical cohesion. Each Catholic deputy customarily voted according to his own convictions, or according to the convictions of the party with which he was at the time associated. Even on questions involving the status of the Church they were divided, at least on the method of reaching the goal.

The Polish Catholics showed the greatest consistency, since a high percentage of them abstained on most roll calls. Their motives were, however, as suggested before, as much national as religious. In fact, whenever the opportunity was offered, they used the debates to draw attention to real or fancied problems of their suppressed nation. Kantak, for example, on March 18, delivered a long address protesting vehemently the absorption of Polish Prussia into the North German Confederation, on the grounds that people of Polish nationality could never legitimately form part of a *German* federal union. He laid much stress on the fact that the Polish provinces had never been included in the earlier *Bund,* while charging once more that the Catholic Church was severely persecuted because it formed a rallying point in the struggle against German domination. Bismarck at that point rose to insist vigorously that the Prussian government had as great an interest in protecting the Catholic Church as had any of its Polish subjects. The Conservative, Hennig, then pointed out for the record that the province of Posen had returned to the Reichstag thirteen Poles and fifteen Germans, striving to cast doubt on the actual strength of the separatist movement in this and other Polish areas.[79]

Kantak took the opportunity afforded by Scherer's remarks of April 10 on the loyalty of Prussian Catholics to deliver another propaganda address, again denying that the North German Reichstag had any right to legislate for the Polish nation.[80] All these expressions of

[78] *Ibid.,* April 8, 1867, 1:618–20.
[79] *Ibid.,* March 18, 1867, 1:206–13, 225.
[80] *Ibid.,* April 10, 1867, 1:691.

Polish nationalism accomplished little except, perhaps, to heighten the dislike of Bismarck and other German nationalists for the Poles. Although German Catholics in the Reichstag showed no noticeable support for Polish nationalism, Bismarck seems always to have believed that some sort of tacit cooperation did exist between them. This belief may well have strengthened his distrust of Catholics in general.[81]

On April 15 acceptance of the amended draft constitution without further changes was moved. Of the nine members who expressed a desire to speak on this motion, five were Catholics: Reichensperger, Windthorst, Rohden, Dauzenberg, and Kleinsorgen. Of the five, only Reichensperger, who had been often absent because of illness, actually got the opportunity to address the house. Presumably his views were fairly representative of those of the other four. He began by denying categorically opposition to the Confederation as such.

After 1866, Reichensperger said, Prussian leadership in Germany was unavoidable. Nevertheless, the constitution, as originally drafted, did not adequately meet the needs or wishes of the German people. Specifically, its "complete silence" on the subject of executive responsibility displeased him. The revised version, however, he found acceptable on that score. Still, he believed that the document left much room for improvement; in particular the budgetary arrangements gave entirely too much power to the Prussian crown, while the refusal to grant any form of pay or allowances to deputies betrayed an unwarranted mistrust of the people. In closing his long address, he appealed to the Reichstag to use its power in such a way that the rights of the people would be made secure. "The will of the parliament," he remarked in an obvious reference to Bismarck, "will triumph over the opposition of any minister."

The Chancellor rose angrily to answer this taunt. He agreed that no minister was indispensable. If, he said, Reichensperger had sufficient parliamentary backing, he would be happy to resign and give his opponent the opportunity "to find out at the head of the majority with which he overthrows me whether he knows as well how to govern as how to talk." [82]

The following day the amended constitution received the Reichstag's approval by the overwhelming majority of 230 to 53. The oppo-

[81] See Bismarck, *Gedanken und Erinnerungen,* 2:154–57.
[82] *Stenographische Berichte,* April 15, 1867, 1:696–99.

sition was composed mostly of the *Fortschrittspartei,* Windthorst's *Bundesstaatlich-konstitutioneller Verein,* and the Polish Catholics. Mallinckrodt had long before announced that he would vote against the constitution, and both Reichensperger and Rohden joined the minority as well. In all, sixteen Catholics voted to reject it, while eleven cast ballots for its adoption.[83]

Immediately after the results were announced, Kantak arose and reminded the chamber of his objections of March 18. He proclaimed that the Poles, having used all "existing means to combat this act of force," had performed their duty, and that they were now, therefore, resigning their seats. They thereupon proceeded to depart in a body — only a few moments, however, in advance of the other members, for adjournment followed almost immediately.[84]

All that was required now to put the constitution into effect was approval by the state diets, in most cases a mere formality. It became the fundamental law of the Confederation on July 1, 1867. In the Prussian *Landtag* the vote was 226 to 91. Here Peter Reichensperger voted for its adoption despite his negative vote in the Reichstag, although several other Catholics and most of the Progressives maintained their adamant opposition. Reichensperger justified the shift on the ground that in the *Landtag* there was no further opportunity to improve the draft; hence rejection would serve no useful purpose, but would, in fact, endanger any political unification of Germany. That alternative his conscience would not let him face. Notwithstanding his belated acquiescence, Reichensperger suffered defeat in his old constituency at the hands of a "government" Catholic in the *Landtag* election of November 1867.[85]

The old order in Germany had at last given way to a new constitutional union of at least part of the German nation. To north German Catholics that union was in many ways unsatisfactory, although, as parliamentary speeches and votes had revealed, there was little agreement among their representatives as to what specifically made it so. There were no signs that Catholicism in north Germany had recovered its former political cohesiveness, and only a few signs that there was

---

[83] *Ibid.,* March 12, 1867, 1:158; April 16, 1867, 1:729; Hansen, 1:788; Zuchhardt, 8.

[84] *Stenographische Berichte,* April 16, 1867, 1:729.

[85] Bachem, 3:22; Hansen, 1:789; *Stenographische Berichte über die Verhandlungen . . . der beiden Häuser des Landtages: Haus der Abgeordneten,* May 1, 1867, 1:19–20; May 8, 1867, 1:108–10.

hope of its doing so. Perhaps the closest approximation to a general Catholic judgment on the *Bundesverfassung* at the time of its adoption is found in the verdict of the *Kölnische Blätter*:

The federal constitution does not satisfy north Germans. It repulses the south German people; it imposes heavy burdens and duties, and grants to the representatives of the people too limited rights. The National Liberals have played a deplorable role through the abandonment of their efforts to achieve civil liberty, for which they once professed to fight. Blinded by the brilliant [military] achievement, doing homage to power, they have sacrificed the most important constitutional rights of the Prussian people.[86]

[86] Hansen, 1:789.

Chapter 4

South Germany and the North German Confederation, 1866-1867

For the four south German governments, defeat in the War of 1866 made necessary a fundamental reorientation of policy. No longer could they use the hostility between Austria and Prussia to insure their own independence. No longer could they depend on Vienna for support against *kleindeutsch* nationalism. No longer could Austro-Prussian co-operation be counted on to thwart Napoleon's dream of the Rhine frontier, although, ironically enough, it was France's aspiration for the Rhine which was largely responsible for the nominal independence of south Germany. For Napoleon, foreseeing the likelihood that a separate union of the southern states would ultimately be forced into the French orbit, had insisted that they be permitted to form a *Südbund*.[1]

The states concerned, however, had no desire to become the tool of French policy in Germany, even if thereby they achieved security against absorption by Prussia. Moreover, assuming that the danger from France could somehow have been obviated, the projected southern confederation would almost inevitably have been dominated by Bavaria, the largest of the four states. Neither Stuttgart nor Karlsruhe was any more inclined to surrender its independence to Munich than to Paris, while for Hesse-Darmstadt the geographical division at the Main made membership in a southern confederation impossible.

Because of their justified fear of French intervention, the southern governments decided at the end of the war that they must swallow their pride and seek military security through ties with Prussia. It proved, therefore, relatively easy for Bismarck to conclude, as part of the peace treaties with Württemberg, Baden, and Bavaria, the secret

[1] Sybel, 5:385; Hermann Oncken, *Napoleon III and the Rhine: The Origin of the War of 1870-71*, 55-56, 66-67.

offensive and defensive military alliances mentioned earlier. In the case of Hesse-Darmstadt no such treaty was deemed necessary, since with the inclusion of Upper Hesse in the North German Confederation, a sizable portion of her single division automatically came under Prussian command.[2]

These treaties without a doubt violated the spirit, if not the letter, of the Nikolsburg Preliminaries, and as Beust, the former Saxon minister who entered the Habsburg service at the end of the war, maintained, they signified a violation *anticipando* of the definitive Peace of Prague, which repeated the Nikolsburg terms regarding south Germany.[3] Nevertheless, they did, for the time being, furnish the only practicable means of checking French demands for compensations out of German territory. And although they produced a storm of protest in south Germany when they were made public later, they did forge a powerful link between North and South, possibly the strongest link which existed between 1866 and 1870.

The peace treaties contained in each case a clause providing for restoration of the *Zollverein,* which the war was considered to have broken. Despite its limitations, the *Zollverein* had served in the past as perhaps the most effective bond between Prussia and the smaller German states. For many years nationalists had hoped to use it as a steppingstone to economic, and later to political, union. Bismarck himself had been working since 1862 to develop it into a central administrative agency for all German commercial affairs. Although nothing in the peace treaties indicated that any change in the form or function of the *Zollverein* was contemplated, in each case it was understood by both sides that a fundamental reorganization would soon be undertaken. By substituting a customs parliament which would make its decisions by a simple majority, the *liberum veto* of each member, which had so frequently hamstrung the organization, would be eliminated.[4] Here again may be seen a violation, in advance, of the intent of the Prague Treaty.

With the possible exception of the Baden government, which had long been favorable to Prussian leadership in some form, the south

[2] For the peace negotiations between Prussia and the southern states, see Sybel, 5:383–98.

[3] Friedrich Ferdinand Graf von Beust, *Aus drei-viertel Jahrhunderten, 1809–1885,* 2:117.

[4] Sybel, 5:384–88.

German states accepted these arrangements only because there seemed to be no other solution to their problems. Economically they could hardly survive outside a larger union such as the *Zollverein*. None of them singly, nor all of them collectively, had any chance of military security without a strong ally. The choice lay between France and Prussia. Both national feeling and state interest in the narrow sense indicated Prussia as the lesser evil. That was true even of Hesse-Darmstadt, although Dalwigk attempted during the peace negotiations to invoke French intervention in her behalf, not knowing that Bismarck had only shortly before rejected a French demand for the annexation of Rheinhessen.[5]

Among the people of south Germany, unaware of the details of international diplomacy, political reactions to events which followed Prussia's victory were mixed. In all four states Prussian sympathizers were actively striving to prepare the way for a union of South and North.[6] In each of them, anti-Prussian parties were for the first time on the defensive and at a real disadvantage. Heretofore they had been able to advocate positive action. They had favored strengthening the old Confederation; they had supported Austria against Prussia. But now they could only oppose further change, and they suffered, therefore, from the difficulties which always beset those who must try to defend something for which they feel no real enthusiasm.

In Hesse-Darmstadt, following the dissolution of the *Landtag* in the fall of 1866, a heated political campaign took place. Catholics, conservatives, particularists, and democrats joined together against the *Fortschrittspartei*, which was already clamoring for annexation of the entire Grand Duchy to the North German Confederation. Using the slogan "First-class Germans or second-class Prussians," the anomalous alliance took advantage of widespread resentment at this "Prussian spearhead" in Hesse. It also profited from the general anger over what citizens regarded as a civil war for which Prussia bore the chief responsibility. Hostility toward Prussia resulted less from the fact that Austria had been excluded from Germany than from the mistaken belief that her exclusion had weakened the entire nation in face of an aggressive France. Catholic supporters of the alliance had, needless to say, additional reasons. Nearly all Hessians were concerned, moreover,

[5] *Ibid.*, 5:388–92.
[6] Rapp, *Öffentliche Meinung*, 71.

with the problems which arose out of the division of the Duchy at the Main. In their unfortunate position they felt even more than others that south Germany was "too weak to live and too strong to die." [7]

In the December election the general dissatisfaction produced a resounding defeat for the Progressives, who had enjoyed a majority in the former chamber. Nearly half the members of the new lower house had not held seats in the preceding *Landtag*. About two thirds of the seats were won by conservatives or particularists, of whom a fair percentage were Catholics. Of the remaining third, only thirteen belonged to the *Fortschrittspartei*.[8]

The division of opinion among the Hessian populace was duplicated by a split within the royal family. Prince Ludwig, nephew of the Grand Duke, had for some years, against the wishes of his uncle, been a partisan of the *Nationalverein*, and was now warmly advocating annexation of the entire Duchy by north Germany. Prince Ludwig was, in addition, bitterly hostile to the Catholic Church. On September 30, when Dalwigk paid him a visit, he took the opportunity to demand forcefully abrogation of the convention which the minister had negotiated with Ketteler in 1854. He maintained that all clergymen, Protestant and Catholic alike, should be considered civil servants, subject to appointment and dismissal by the political authorities. He also made no secret of his belief that Dalwigk was under the sinister influence of the Bishop of Mainz, and objected strenuously to what he felt was undue clerical influence on state policy.[9]

Ketteler was well aware of the difficulties which the convention was causing for the ministry. Ten days earlier, in a letter to the Grand Duke, he had offered to abandon it "in the interest of the state," since he saw that the Progressives were using it as "a means to create disorder of all kinds." [10] Their defeat in the election, however, relieved the government of any necessity to consider the step for the time being, and the convention remained in effect until 1871.

In the neighboring kingdom of Württemberg, the war likewise resulted in an immediate and basic realignment of parties. Again varying attitudes toward incorporation of the kingdom into north Germany served as the axis. Two main positions were apparent from the begin-

[7] Vogt, 137; *AAZ*, Dec. 12, 1866, 5702; Vigener, *Ketteler*, 931.
[8] *AAZ*, Dec. 21, 1866, 5839.
[9] *Dalwigk Tagebücher*, Sept. 30, 1866, 270.
[10] Ketteler to Grand Duke Ludwig III, Mainz, Sept. 20, 1866, *Ketteler Briefe*, 343–44.

ning. On the one side stood the newly organized *Deutsche Partei*,[11] which favored union with the North, and on the other were all those who wished to minimize the significance of Württemberg's defeat in order to justify continued opposition to any closer ties with Prussia. Within each of these general areas of opinion there were important subdivisions. A few individuals, for example, advocated immediate and unconditional north German annexation of Württemberg. The majority of the annexationists, however, favored joining the projected northern confederation only after Württemberg had obtained from Prussia guarantees of continued existence for her "free institutions." The latter point of view represented the official doctrine of the *Deutsche Partei*, whose leaders were, on the whole, convinced that Prussia could and would offer the desired assurances. The particularist side included a large number of individuals who felt that ultimate inclusion of the kingdom in the northern *Bund* was inevitable, but who, having little faith in Prussian benevolence, wanted to resist as long as possible in order to salvage what they could of local autonomy. The difference between this point of view and that of the *Deutsche Partei* is primarily one of emphasis. Finally, there was a sizable group which opposed joining north Germany under any circumstances. A few of these hoped in vain for a restoration of pre-Königgrätz Germany; more were simply unable to overcome their traditional emotional antipathy toward Prussia.[12]

Württemberg Catholics were customarily found in one of the last two groups. Some of the former *grossdeutsch* politicians, seeing the handwriting on the wall, hastened to make their peace with the future. The majority of Catholics among them, however, refused to be swayed from their traditional loyalties. Although, as in Hesse-Darmstadt, they formed a *religious* minority, in both states they were part of the *political* majority, for by far the largest part of the population was hostile to union, except under conditions which were unlikely to be realized.[13]

In a debate which took place in the lower chamber from October 10 through October 13, 1866, on a proposed address to the throne, the Catholic-*grossdeutsch* deputy, von Wiest (Ehingen), expressed what

[11] See Chapter One.
[12] *AAZ*, Oct. 17, 1866, 4750; Pfuel to Bismarck, Stuttgart, Feb. 18, 1867, March 1, 1867, *APP*, 8: nos. 252, 267.
[13] Rapp, *Öffentliche Meinung*, 23, 83; Pfuel to Bismarck, Stuttgart, Feb. 18, 1867, March 1, 1867, *APP*, 8: nos. 252, 267.

seemed to be the typical view of Württemberg Catholics. Wiest was deeply pessimistic, partly because he still believed then that Napoleon III controlled the future of Germany. The North German Confederation, if it ever came into actual existence, said Wiest, would be nothing more than a "frail reed." It was entirely possible that, instead of establishing a confederation at all, Prussia would ultimately annex all north Germany. Therefore, the only safe course for Württemberg was to remain free of the grasp of the northern great power, for "he who carelessly approaches the Prussian flame will be devoured by it." The only really adequate solution for the German problem, thought Wiest, would be found in restoring harmony between Austria and Prussia. Since this appeared improbable, Württemberg could, for the time being, best serve her own and the nation's interest by participating in a league of southern states "without obligation to Prussia." [14] That this possibility no longer existed because of the alliance treaty, he was, of course, unaware.

During the same debate Württemberg's most important Catholic politician, Rudolph Probst, echoed these sentiments with appropriate variations. He strove to make clear that his opposition to Prussia did not derive in any way from religious considerations. He admitted frankly that Prussian Catholics had achieved a status "which leaves little to be desired," and that, in comparison with Austria, the Church possessed great freedom there. Nevertheless, he maintained that while, paradoxically, the interests of the Church might logically draw south German Catholics toward Berlin, they were, as "good south Germans," forced to resist the temptation. The people of south Germany wanted no *Kleindeutschland* because, under Prussian hegemony, there could be no assurance of freedom for Württemberg, or for any of the other small states.[15] The chamber finally adopted an address in accord with the views of Wiest, Probst, and others by a vote of 61 to 25. It called specifically for the establishment of a southern confederation with common parliamentary representation for all member states, and asked further that the Württemberg constitution be reformed to provide greater liberty for the individual citizen and to introduce universal military service.[16]

[14] Rapp, *Öffentliche Meinung,* 79.
[15] *Ibid.,* 77–78.
[16] Sybel, 5:456–57.

The Catholics and German Unity, 1866–1871

In Baden, which stood under the most obvious threat of French aggression, the Liberals commanded a majority in the *Landtag*. The two chambers were convened on October 9, and the peace treaty, without the military alliance and the *Zollverein* agreement, was submitted to them for ratification. A committee named by the lower house to examine the treaty exceeded its instructions and on October 23 reported a proposal for the immediate entry of the four southern states into the North German Confederation. It asked only that the guarantees of autonomy for internal affairs contained in the treaty should remain valid. The head of the ministry, Freydorf, opposed the motion, arguing that the time was not yet ripe. He indicated, however, that he regarded ultimate unification of the nation under Prussia as inevitable. The lower chamber, nevertheless, adopted the committee's recommendation with only eleven negative votes, while the first chamber approved a similar motion unanimously. The upper house also gave its assent, with only three dissenting voices, to a proposal stating that if entry into the North German Confederation was not at the moment feasible, the government should at least negotiate a treaty of alliance with Prussia, and take the initiative in seeking to convert the *Zollverein* into an indissoluble economic union.[17]

Although most of Baden's population was Catholic, the Catholic viewpoint was poorly represented in the *Landtag*, because of a complicated system of indirect election and the absence of a political organization. Consequently there is little evidence concerning the opinion of Catholics toward the government's policy in the fall of 1866. However, considering their almost fanatical dislike for Prussia later, it is reasonable to conclude that even then a majority was at least unsympathetic, and, in many cases, utterly dismayed by the friendliness toward Prussia shown by the ministry and the *Landtag*. Moreover, in some Catholic areas, particularly the Breisgau and the Black Forest, which had once been Habsburg possessions, a sentimental attachment to Austria certainly still persisted.[18]

In the years immediately preceding the debacle of 1866, the conflict between the government and the Church over ecclesiastical appointments and control of the schools had precipitated the first unsuccessful attempts of Catholics to form a political party.[19] That conflict was

[17] *Ibid.*, 458–59.
[18] Bachem, 2:313.
[19] See Chapter One.

90

still in progress, and in the fall of 1866 the liberals added a new demand — compulsory civil marriage. Direct secular interference with one of the sacraments was certain to arouse the faithful, and although this issue did not reach a critical stage until 1869, it furnished one of the most important motives for the later growth of political Catholicism in Baden.[20]

On the other hand there were, even before the end of 1866, signs that some Catholic opinion in Baden had receded from the extreme position on Church-state relations. Generally the concordat between Austria and the Papacy had been viewed as the optimum arrangement. In December 1866, however, the *Badischer Beobachter* published an article which denied that the concordat was of benefit to the Church, since it forced the Church to assume responsibility for mistakes committed by secular authorities. Conversely, it did not benefit the state, which was forced to share the blame for ecclesiastical blunders. The *Beobachter* pointed out numerous examples of both types of error within the year just past. The article censured the Austrian higher clergy, which, it said, had become too wealthy and secular, and asked the Pope to take the initiative in abrogating the concordat, expressing the hope that the Church in Austria would henceforth seek no privileges other than those which both confessions enjoyed under the law.[21] This and other similar observations which appeared in lay Catholic organs during the months that followed the war indicate disillusionment of Catholics with Austria. They also represented attempts to appease south German liberals similar to Ketteler's offer to abandon the convention with Hesse-Darmstadt. It appears certain that to Catholics of Baden, faced with harassment, if not persecution, at home, the Prussian tradition of religious toleration had some appeal. Nevertheless, these tentative signs of a less hostile attitude toward Prussia had no apparent political consequences, and they gradually disappeared under the stress of events during the next two years.

In the first few months after the war, opinion in Bavaria was marked by surprisingly little rancor toward Prussia. Members of the Progressive party, who, in cooperation with the *Nationalverein*, had pushed for Prussian hegemony in Germany, were jubilant, although their joy was tempered by concern over the cost of the war in lives

[20] Dor, 89–91.
[21] *AAZ*, Dec. 24, 1866, 5891; Dec. 29, 1866, 5970.

and treasure. But even among those who had supported Austria most strongly there was, for a time, little bitterness toward Berlin, far less than had been apparent before the outbreak of hostilities. When the Nuremberg-born north German publicist, Lorenz Nagel, toured Bavaria as an agent of the *Nationalverein* shortly after the end of the hostilities, he was highly gratified to find that even in overwhelmingly Catholic Old Bavaria there was "no trace of passionate hatred for Prussia." [22] The astute Hohenlohe, himself nominally Catholic, saw in all classes evidence of growing sentiment in favor of union with Prussia. Neither the Court nor the Pfordten ministry, he added, shared the feeling; to them entry into the northern confederation was tantamount to mediatization. The "ultramontanes," added Hohenlohe, using his favorite term for anti-Prussian Catholics, were also not pleased with the situation. They were, however, accepting it with reasonably good grace, because neither they nor other *Grossdeutsche* were able to come forth with any convincing counterproposals. Not even the Catholic extremists at that time dared propose a tie with Austria or with France.[23]

Although Hohenlohe's prejudice made it difficult for him fully to comprehend the Catholics' viewpoint, his observations do furnish a significant clue to an understanding of it. Its keynote, he implied, was despair. Particularism had failed to save Bavaria; in fact, discerning Catholics could also see therein "the cause of the disaster." They were, then, faced with a *fait accompli* which could only be admitted and tolerated. The Catholic press was bewildered and despondent, seeing little hope for the future. Yet it was not inclined to place the blame solely on the shoulders of Prussia.[24]

The extreme example was that of the *Historisch-politische Blätter,* which during the last half of 1866 took a position so favorable toward Prussia that it could, without overstating the case, be called one of her best friends in the South. As has been pointed out above, the articles of its editor, J. E. Jörg, while deprecating Prussian militarism,

[22] Nagel to Bennigsen, Frankfurt a/M., Sept. 22, 1866, Oncken, *Bennigsen,* 2:69–70. Old Bavaria consisted of the original Wittelsbach domains, and was roughly equivalent to southern, or upper, Bavaria.

[23] Journal, Sept. 1, 1866, Hohenlohe, *Memoirs,* 1:163. See also Müller, *Bayern im Jahre 1866,* 154–55.

[24] Rovère, 46; Hans Spielhofer, "Bayrische Parteien und Parteipublizistik in ihrer Stellung zur deutschen Frage, 1866–70," *Oberbayrisches Archiv für vaterländische Geschichte,* 63:161.

always had comprehended the realities of the Austro-Prussian conflict better than did Catholics in general. The war caused no immediate shift in Jörg's attitude.

The first of his *Zeitläufe* written after the end of hostilities was still far more critical of Austria than of any other power. He fairly raged against "the leaders and the Viennese marionettes of the *Grossdeutsch*-Liberal party." They had forced the country into the war against the will of the Emperor, who had always, claimed Jörg, sought a peaceful settlement. Had Austria striven for peace, had she been willing to solve the Schleswig-Holstein question to Prussia's satisfaction, as Jörg had long advocated, "Venice would now be saved, and the edifice of the Italian revolution would lie in ruins." Austria might be enjoying a position of power and influence; instead she was draining the cup of humiliation. The Austrian liberals, Jörg maintained, had committed the fatal error of wishful thinking, and therefore deserved no mercy.[25]

He went on in the same article to explore postwar issues. The war, he insisted, had settled nothing, and the peace would be merely an armistice while all parties prepared for the next round. The nation had been placed in an even more unstable and dangerous condition than before, for Germany could only survive permanently either as *kleindeutsch* or as *grossdeutsch*; now it was neither. Divided, it would be torn to pieces by the great powers. He had no doubt that the new order would be temporary, for he could not conceive that Prussia would remain satisfied with half a loaf. If for no other reason, she would be driven to complete her alleged "mission" by the pressure of nationalists in north Germany, with the aid of related groups in the South. The middle states were, he noted, suspended between heaven and earth. With a slight mixing of metaphors, he concluded that since they were neither fish nor fowl, the existing situation could not last.

Jörg went on to point out that Catholics now had to abandon all their cherished political ideas. The *grossdeutsch* dream was dead, and those who had represented it on the highest political levels had merited nothing better than a "dishonorable interment." A "new political way of life" had come into being, and Catholics had perforce to judge the world differently than they had in the past.[26] Specifically he gave

[25] "Zeitläufe: Waffenstillstand und Friedenspräliminärien," July 26, 1866, *HPB*, 58: 215–16.
[26] *Ibid.*, 224–26, 231.

the same advice to his readers as he had three years earlier, when, he said, it had appeared presumptuous and even wicked to them. Now, he felt certain, they would see it in its true light, as the product of a justified foreboding: "If no other choice remains, then, without reservation, rather a Prussian Emperor than ever again to be subjects of France and members of a Confederation of the Rhine."[27]

This article is of supreme importance as evidence of "what might have been." By itself it is sufficient to cast considerable doubt on Bismarck's often expressed opinion that south German Catholics had always been irreconcilably hostile to Prussian leadership in Germany.[28] Far more important, however, is the fact that Jörg was for the first time calling upon Catholics to abandon their prejudices and to ally themselves with Prussia in building a new Germany, for to him only the Prussian army stood between south Germany and domination by Napoleon III. Had it proved possible to establish a Catholic party in Bavaria along the lines proposed here, many of the difficulties of the next five years might well have been avoided, and perhaps some of the darker pages in the early history of the Empire — in particular, the *Kulturkampf* — might not have been written. Such a party could have exercised profound influence on Catholics in the other southern states, and might have been instrumental within a year or two in creating a united sentiment south of the Main in favor of a federal union with Prussia. But it was not to be. In the final analysis, it was Bismarck and the National Liberals who stood in the way.

In his next issue Jörg presented what to him were the necessary conditions for entry of the southern states into the projected *Nordbund*. The overriding one was that there should be no annexation by Prussia of former members of the German Confederation north of the Main. Unless states such as Hanover, Electoral Hesse, and others were permitted to enter the new federal union as entities, the term "confederation" would be meaningless. Whatever it was called, it would be nothing more than an enlarged Prussia. With a Prussia unjustly swollen by the extinction of her smaller neighbors' independence, the South, he insisted, could never unite. If, however, the new union were to be truly federal, with a parliament that was capable of giving real protection to all the people, then the south German governments would

[27] *Ibid.*, 231–32.
[28] See, for example, his letter to Arnim, Berlin, April 12, 1868, *APP*, 9: no. 722.

be morally bound immediately to sign treaties of alliance with Prussia which would prevent any foreign intervention.[29]

In these statements can be seen the germ of what later turned Jörg into the most bitter enemy of Prussia in all south Germany. By her annexations in the North, Prussia betrayed the federal principle, as the Munich editor understood it. Any connection between Bavaria and the enlarged Prussia was thus unacceptable to him, because he feared that eventually Bavaria would lose the power to control her own internal affairs. Nevertheless, throughout the remainder of 1866 he continued to hope for the best. In this same article he propounded the thesis that war between Prussia and France was inevitable. Therefore, the southern states had to choose one or the other. If they attempted to remain neutral, the danger would be very great that the two powers would, at the end of such a war, come to an agreement at south Germany's expense. An alliance with France was out of the question, for she could not be trusted to defend the interests of south Germany when the Bavarian Palatinate stood high on her list of territorial objectives. Hence Prussia was the only possible choice, and he suggested that the best that could happen would be immediate war, while Germany was still armed and while south Germany could still force Prussia, as the price of alliance, to make acceptable terms for entry into the new Confederation.[30]

In a succeeding issue Jörg attempted to convince his readers that Prussia had not, as many believed, been guilty of plotting war against Austria. She had, he wrote, been forced by the necessity of maintaining her status as a great power to acquire both Schleswig and Holstein for herself. Otherwise she could hardly have justified the battles of Düppel and Alsen to her own people, and the dynasty itself might have been endangered. At the very least, failure to acquire both duchies would have reduced her to the level of a second-rate power.[31] At the end of the year he returned to his attack on past Austrian policy, claiming that Catholics, as such, had lost little by her defeat. Austria, by preferring to fight for Schleswig-Holstein rather than for the rights of the Church in Italy, had forfeited any claim that she had pursued a "Catholic" policy. Moreover, the mere fact that a Protes-

---

[29] "Zeitläufe: Das deutsche Volk zwischen heute und morgen," Aug. 13, 1866, *HPB*, 58:327.

[30] *Ibid.*, 316–26.

[31] "Zeitläufe: Was Preussen eigentlich gewonnen hat," *HPB*, 58:389–90.

tant of the character of Beust, the former Saxon minister, could now become chief minister of the Empire gave the lie to any such assertion. The past was dead; in the future Berlin, not Vienna, would be the scene of the great spiritual battle.[32]

The attempt of the *Historisch-politische Blätter* to convert south German Catholics to active support for the Hohenzollerns ended in failure. By the end of the year Catholics in Bavaria had again become extremely bitter toward Prussia. In part the change can be explained simply as a product of the passage of time; despair is usually a temporary phenomenon. As the war receded into history, Bavarian Catholics who loved their little country intensely found themselves unable to forgive the power that had humbled her pride.[33] Partially it can be explained by the fact that others besides Jörg had expected something from Prussia which did not materialize. A state which had not hesitated to extinguish dynasties in the North had little appeal by 1867 for those who regarded their own dynasty with an affection equal to that which they felt for their Church. Anti-Prussian feeling among Bavarian Catholics was further strengthened by the fact that in the fall of 1866 the *Fortschrittspartei,* anticlerical as well as *kleindeutsch,* added to its propaganda for union with north Germany a demand for the secularization of the schools. The lower chamber, elected by a restricted franchise which overrepresented urban areas to the detriment of heavily Catholic rural Bavaria, showed after the war increasing sympathy for both of these demands. The result was that, in the mind of the average Catholic, friendship for Prussia became, even more than before, confused with hostility to the Church.

On August 28, 1866, a group of forty-two members of the chamber, calling themselves the "Union of the Left," moved that the division at the Main and the proposed south German Confederation both be rejected in favor of a union of all German states, excluding Austria. The sovereign would be an all-German parliament, although a degree of autonomy would be left to the component states. The group further proposed that, should the union prove impossible at that time, Bavaria should press for a reestablishment of the *Zollverein,* and for the negotiation of an agreement providing military collaboration with Prussia in time of war. The motion was adopted by the chamber on

[32] "Zeitläufe: Die confessionellen Leidenschaften im Ruine Deutschlands," *HPB,* 58: 796.
[33] Spielhofer, *Oberbayrisches Archiv,* 63:161; Ziekursch, 1:246–47.

August 30, but the senate on the following day overwhelmingly rejected it, with only Hohenlohe, who had spoken in its behalf, and three others voting for it. Nevertheless, the minimum objectives of the motion had, unknown to most of the deputies, been achieved with the signature of the peace treaty a few days earlier. On August 31, the senate, however, approved a bill adopted previously by the house, requesting the King to have drafted immediately legislation to reorganize the educational system "on the basis of the absence of tests, and the assurance of full freedom of conscience." On this measure only six nays were recorded, including those of the two archbishops, von Scherr and von Deinlein, and that of Bishop von Dunkel.[34] No matter how little the two bills were inherently related, the fact that they came to a vote at the same time, and were sponsored by substantially the same group, could hardly be overlooked by Catholics. Moreover, the parliamentary strength of the Progressives was increasing perceptibly during the same period. In one by-election in late September a "decided Progressive" won a seat in a district which had returned a conservative *Grossdeutscher* by 160 votes three years earlier.[35]

Perhaps even more disconcerting for Bavarian and other south German Catholics was the increasing tendency of individuals in both parts of Germany to equate the Prussian victory with the final triumph of Protestantism.[36] The *Historisch-politische Blätter* published a long article, alternately belligerent and querulous in tone, cataloguing at least a hundred instances of alleged persecution of Catholics in Prussia during the war. It charged that officials had used anti-Catholic propaganda, specifically the claim that all Catholics were pro-Austrian, to whip up the war spirit.[37] Jörg devoted one of his *Zeitläufe* to a discussion of anti-Catholicism, taking considerable pains to distinguish between two varieties of Protestants. One, he said, was motivated by the spirit of freemasonry. It had been this group which was responsible

---

[34] Rapp, *Öffentliche Meinung*, 71; Rovère, 46; Journal, Sept. 1, 1866, Hohenlohe, *Memoirs*, 1:163.

[35] *AAZ*, Oct. 4, 1866, 4538.

[36] Cf. the letter of the historian, J. G. Droysen, to a friend, August von Haeften, Berlin, Aug. 2, 1866. "[Prussia's victory] means at last the triumph of the true German spirit over the false, the spirit of 1517 and 1813 over Roman and Austrian scorn and oppression." Rudolph Hübner (ed.), *Johann Gustav Droysen Briefwechsel*, 2:872. See also Bachem, 2:231.

[37] "Die Katholikenhetze in Preussen während des deutschen Krieges," *HPB*, 58: 654–80.

for nearly all the attacks on Catholics in the press. The more orthodox Protestants had been, for the most part, more restrained, although, he said, since the end of the war they had been slowly moving in the direction of their more radical fellows.[38] He went on to warn that in the long run the "masonic" Protestants were likely to be as hostile toward orthodox Protestantism as they were toward the Catholic Church, for their views were closely related to those of the liberal politicians whose goal, with reference to religion, was creation of a "German national church." He predicted, therefore, that they would not for long tolerate the state churches of Hanover, Schleswig-Holstein, and Electoral Hesse, all of which, though Protestant, were dissimilar.[39]

Inevitably, as the prestige of the liberal unionists swelled, the position of Pfordten as head of the Bavarian ministry became increasingly untenable, since he was the author of the anti-Prussian policy of the prewar period. By late December he had lost all his following except for a few zealous Catholics, and on the last day of the year he resigned in favor of the liberal nobleman, Hohenlohe, who had already demonstrated marked sympathy for union with north Germany.[40]

The advent of Hohenlohe served to crystallize Bavarian public opinion. The liberals, of course, lined up solidly behind him, while almost immediately a violent campaign began in the Catholic press against the man and his program. From the presses of the *Münchener Volksbote,* under sponsorship of its hotheaded editor, von Zander, emerged a whole series of *Flugblätter* which were notable for their vehemence. The opposition, mostly confined to the press, was, for the time being at least, ineffective in exerting pressure on the new ministry. The prewar Catholic-Conservative party still held eleven seats in the lower chamber, but had power only to protest noisily. Nevertheless, a new opposition was taking root in the country under the nominal leadership of Jörg and Dr. Ruland, a Würzburg librarian and member of the

[38] Jörg quoted Dr. Krause, editor of the *Protestantische Kirchenzeitung* of Berlin as follows: "In the battle of Königgrätz the Thirty Years War finally came to an end . . . for not only has Austria's power and influence been excluded from Germany, but also the Papacy has lost its last secular support in Europe. . . . Under Prussia's leadership, once again the independent German nation can and will reconstitute itself on thoroughly Protestant principles." Quoted from the *Süddeutsches Evangelisch-protestantisches Wochenblatt,* Aug. 20, 1866, *HPB,* 58:784.

[39] *Ibid.,* 790–95.

[40] *AAZ,* Dec. 28, 1866, 5954.

chamber, assisted by Freiherr von Thüngen of the senate. The new opposition, largely spontaneous in origin, was conservative in character, but bore little relation to prewar conservatism. The older brand had been essentially feudal and dynastic in inspiration. The new movement, not yet well enough organized to merit the title of party, sought to win adherents by stressing much more heavily the loyalty of Catholics to their Church. From the beginning it was associated with the Casinos, which had just been imported from Baden by the twenty-three-year-old Count Conrad von Preysing. The Munich Casino especially became a center for the political education of young Catholics. Preysing, as well as most of the older leaders, was hostile to democracy, but very early the new conservative movement developed within itself a faction whose members were known as "clerical democrats." Its chief spokesmen were Bucher, editor of the *Donauzeitung* of Passau, and a chaplain in the Bavarian army, a Father Lukas. Jörg, though he could not at this period be classified as a democrat, had, because of his interest in the social question, already developed some leanings in that direction.[41]

Early in 1867 a sudden change in the tone of Jörg's contributions to the *Blätter* became apparent, indicating his growing absorption in the task of creating a Catholic opposition in Bavaria. His former attempts to win sympathy for Prussia were abandoned. Instead, Prussia became almost the sole object of his attacks. In his New Year greeting to his readers, significantly entitled "The Beginning of the End," he predicted a year full of political crises. Prussia, he wrote, had betrayed the German people by abandoning federalism in order selfishly to advance the interests of the House of Hohenzollern. If, after the war, Prussia had invited the other states to cooperate in founding a *kleindeutsch* federal union, in accordance with her own proposal of June 10, 1866, she would not by the beginning of the new year have had an enemy worthy of consideration anywhere in Germany. However, her selfish policy was certain, if continued, to destroy the very idea of a German nation. It was perfectly true, he admitted, that Germany might be united outwardly by means of Prussia's current policy, but the union would not possess the moral character which alone could

[41] Spielhofer, "Bayrische Zentrumspartei," *HPB*, 165:354–56; Spielhofer, "Bayrische Parteien," *Oberbayrisches Archiv*, 63:154–55; Bachem, 2:232–33; A. Doeberl, "Preysing," *Gelbe Hefte*, 2:844–45: Theodor Schieder, *Die kleindeutsche Partei in Bayern in den Kämpfen um die nationale Einheit, 1863–71*, 161.

make of it a real state.[42] And even superficial unity was not inevitable, for:

On the road which it has entered through its policy of annexations for the House of Hohenzollern, Prussia will inevitably collide with the total armed might of France. This collision will be the signal for the last and greatest catastrophe of a purely political nature in Europe, and in the hour of crisis the call will go out to all the rest of the German states to come to Prussia's aid with all their strength — to come to her aid in support of a policy which, at best, must lead to the mediatization of her allies and, at worst, to their abandonment to foreign powers.[43]

Until at least the middle of the year 1867 the embryonic Catholic opposition played a negligible role in Bavarian affairs. However, the ministry, dependent on the *Fortschrittspartei* for its existence, continued to press for secularization of the schools as well as for union with the North. Moreover, its economic policies favored the growing industrial cities against the interests of the Catholic farmers. For these and other reasons, Catholic-conservative leaders were gradually able to increase their popular following. By the fall of 1867 the new conservative movement was powerful enough to worry Hohenlohe considerably.[44]

Meanwhile another event of highest importance for the future of political Catholicism in Germany had taken place. In January of 1867 Bishop von Ketteler published his most important political tract, the book *Deutschland nach dem Kriege von 1866*. Any pronouncement on a political subject by Germany's best known and most dynamic Catholic clergyman was certain to be of interest to almost all individuals, whatever their faith, who were concerned with national problems. Before the war Ketteler, as indicated above, had been outspokenly *grossdeutsch* in sympathy. The Catholic newspapers of Mainz, which could hardly escape his influence, had helped align the Hessian populace behind Austria in 1865 and early 1866. On the day before the battle of Königgrätz, Ketteler had issued a statement to the clergy of Rheinhessen, charging that "reckless envy [on the part of Prussia] has led to this war between brothers." [45] After the battle of Aschaffenburg he had personally given spiritual consolation to Austrian wounded in the

[42] *HPB*, 59:1, 15–16, 18.
[43] *Ibid.*, 19–20.
[44] Spielhofer, *HPB*, 165:354; Wöhler, 22–23.
[45] Vigener, *Ketteler*, 489–92.

military hospital at Mainz, for which he received a personal letter of thanks from Franz Joseph.[46] He had written in his answer to this letter, "Only a united Germany, with the heirs of the old imperial crown at its head, is in accord with the real requirements of Germany and with the place that God has given her in the history of the world."[47]

Germans were surprised and, in many cases, shocked, therefore, to learn from the Bishop's book that he had now become an advocate of German unity under the scepter of the Hohenzollerns. Ketteler, like Jörg, sought to refute the claim that Prussia was solely responsible for the war. He argued that there had been three causes for the catastrophe: first, the Schleswig-Holstein question, in which Austria as well as Prussia had pursued immoral and selfish ends; second, and most important, the pressures which had developed in Prussia from the constitutional crisis; and, third, the *idée fixe* that Prussia had a divine mission to bring unity to the nation, which, in the last analysis, left no place in Germany for Austria.[48] Although most of the guilt, then, devolved on Prussia, both powers, said Ketteler, had pursued narrow state interests; both had sought to use religion as the handmaiden of their policy, in defiance of the eternal law of God. Consequently the German Confederation had perished, and with it the conviction that war between Germans was impossible. A host of new dangers, therefore, faced the nation and the people.[49]

Nevertheless, he went on, no human act was wholly bad, and with God's mercy, what was basically evil might result in good. Austria's defeat, for instance, could mean the beginning of her internal regeneration, while, for the rest of Germany, real unity was now, for the first time, possible. As Ketteler reviewed the situation, there were three prerequisites for the future welfare of the German people. First, there had to be a solution of the German problem satisfactory both to Austria and to German national sentiment. The only practicable answer to this question, he believed, was a federal union of non-Habsburg Germany under the leadership of Prussia, united with Austria by an indissoluble alliance. The second requirement was the abandonment in Germany of French *étatisme* and a return to what he called the

[46] Franz Joseph to Ketteler, Schönbrunn, Aug. 14, 1866, *Ketteler Briefe*, 341–42.
[47] Vigener, *Ketteler*, 492–93.
[48] Wilhelm Emanuel Freiherr von Ketteler, *Deutschland nach dem Kriege von 1866*, 13–19, 20–22, 29, 30–31, 35.
[49] *Ibid.*, 48–65.

true German ideal of human freedom, founded on religion and morality, not on abstract principles and economic relationships. The final necessity was the establishment of suitable arrangements for the Church and the school within the state, so that "true peace" between them would become possible.[50]

Ketteler regarded the provisions of the Prussian constitution as completely satisfactory in regard to the relation between Church and state, and indicated that they could serve as a "true Magna Charta" for the nation. He warned, however, against those who sought to destroy all guarantees of religious freedom and to subvert the schools to anti-Christian purposes. Those people he called enemies of Germany.[51]

After a chapter defending the proposition that in a religiously divided country the principle of equality for all faiths did not conflict with the doctrines contained in the Syllabus of Errors,[52] the Bishop concluded his book with the observation, considerably elaborated, that all current problems could be resolved into a single question: "whether we stand with or against Christ." The future, he added, depended on the answer.[53]

The immediate reaction of Catholics was distinctly unfavorable. Most of Ketteler's own circle at Mainz was bitterly opposed to the *kleindeutsch* tone of the work. Even the *Mainzer Journal* condemned it. Furthermore, many south German Catholics were shocked by the Bishop's views on religious parity. Cardinal Reisach predicted shortly after the book was published that if Bismarck "crossed the Main," the Catholic Church would soon find itself the victim of persecution.[54] At Würzburg, the historian, Franz Brentano, spoke bitterly of the "Prussian Bishop" who, he felt, was propagating a dangerous error. Jörg wrote that he agreed with Ketteler's basic idea, but on details he found much to criticize in the book. Particularly, he thought that the Bishop had underestimated the significance of Austria's exclusion from Germany.[55] In Prussia, on the other hand, the Catholic scholar, Peter Volkmuth, charged Ketteler with "unprincipled" criticism of the Ho-

---

[50] *Ibid.*, 68–69, 72, 75–76, 81–83, 88, 101, 105–8, 113.

[51] *Ibid.*, 118–19, 121, 123, 131.

[52] *Ibid.*, Chapter XII.

[53] *Ibid.*, 211.

[54] Vigener, *Ketteler*, 515–21.

[55] Hertling, 1:66–67; "Zeitläufe: Der Bischof von Mainz über unsere gegenwärtige Lage," *HPB*, 59:454–63.

henzollern kingdom, denouncing especially his remarks on the Prussian mission.[56]

Despite the immediate unfavorable reaction, it is difficult to overestimate the ultimate importance of *Deutschland nach dem Kriege* in molding opinions of Catholics in Germany. As Bachem points out, the program of the Center party after 1871 was largely based on it, but even before that date, it was of tremendous importance in clarifying issues for Catholics and in making it possible for them finally to think in terms of the present and future, rather than in those of the past.[57]

Whatever chance there had been that Ketteler's book might immediately produce a decrease in the hostility of south German Catholics toward Prussia was destroyed by the effects of the Luxemburg crisis in the spring of 1867. Many historians have dealt with its complexities,[58] and they need not concern us here. Suffice it to say that the little Grand Duchy had been a member of the German Confederation, although it was joined in a personal union with the Netherlands. During the peace negotiations in 1866, Bismarck had suggested to Napoleon's ambassador that he had no objection to France's acquiring Luxemburg in compensation for the Prussian gains in Germany. Early in 1867 Napoleon offered to purchase the Duchy from the King of Holland, who was not averse to the sale. He would, however, not act without Bismarck's express approval. The Prussian statesman then discovered that it would be politically disastrous for him to give that approval, for, to his surprise, German public opinion appeared to regard Luxemburg as part of the nation's sacred soil, not to be bartered away. Bismarck's refusal to honor his promise infuriated Napoleon, and the resulting imbroglio roused public opinion in both countries to a pitch that for a time made war seem unavoidable. Finally, the problem was solved by Napoleon's favorite tactic, an international conference, which neutralized Luxemburg under a general European guarantee.

Of most significance for the present study is the fact that on March 19, 1867, at the height of the crisis, Bismarck, in order to calm the fears of the north German public and to answer critics in the Reichstag, authorized publication of the treaties of alliance with the southern

[56] Vigener, *Ketteler*, 513–14.
[57] Bachem, 3:7.
[58] See e.g., Sybel, 6:98–130; Oncken, *Napoleon III and the Rhine*, 69–95; Ward, 2:385–400; Eyck, *Bismarck*, 2:342–68.

states.[59] In north Germany the stroke had the desired effect. In the South, however, it contributed a great deal to the growing internal tension in each of the four states, and everywhere heightened the distrust which all anti-Prussians felt toward Bismarck and the North German Confederation.

In part their reaction resulted from a sense of betrayal by their own governments. Pfordten, for example, had denied to the Bavarian parliament the very existence of a treaty which he had helped negotiate. Hohenlohe, in his first address to the Bavarian Reichstag after he became head of the ministry, announced that his policy would be *to seek* a military alliance which would place Bavarian troops under Prussian command in time of war. At the same time he made public his intention to strive for a reorganization of the Bavarian army along Prussian lines in order to make unified command possible. He promised to work out, if possible, an agreement with the other southern states by which they would similarly reorganize their forces. Accordingly, he did arrange a military conference at Stuttgart early in February 1867, at which the four agreed to adopt the basic outlines of the Prussian military system.[60]

Aware that Bavaria could not safely remain isolated, Bavarian Catholics had not actively opposed the Hohenlohe proposals when they were made. The sudden knowledge, however, that a binding alliance, instead of being projected, had already existed secretly for months was a crushing blow. It demonstrated with startling clarity how thoroughly Bismarck dominated post-Königgrätz Germany, as well as the unwillingness, or inability, of the Bavarian government to resist north German pressure. Some Catholic extremists were so angry and frightened that they supported a suggestion of a radical democrat that Bavaria break all ties with the rest of Germany and join the Swiss Confederation. In the capital a few hotheads openly advocated a Bavarian alliance with France, and, hopefully, with Austria, against Prussia. The justified public impression that Bismarck was perfectly willing to dispose of Luxemburg to France contributed a great deal to the violence of the outburst.[61]

On the other hand, early in April when the tension was at its worst,

[59] Sybel, 6:80–82.
[60] *Ibid.*, 207–9.
[61] *Ibid.*, 209; Werthern to Bismarck, Munich, March 22, 1867, April 30, 1867, *APP*, 8: nos. 326, 560; Legation Secretary Krause to Bismarck (private letter), *ibid.*, no. 356, note 1.

Jörg argued more defensibly in the *Blätter* that an immediate German war against France over Luxemburg would be the most satisfactory outcome of the crisis, since internal circumstances in Germany were more favorable then than they were apt to be later. The military reforms, for example, were not yet in effect. Hence in an immediate war south Germany would fight under her old military arrangements. In case of a German defeat, "the future military law of Prussia will be made in Paris," but if German arms were victorious, "no one can require us [*i.e.*, Bavaria] to take upon ourselves the oppressive weight of Prussian military organization." [62] During those critical days, almost all Bavarian organs of public opinion demanded that Prussia defend the rights of Germany at any cost, although not always for precisely the same reasons. Most Catholics seem to have hoped with Jörg that a Prussia at war with France would be forced to compromise with south Germany to secure aid. A few extremists wanted to see Prussia defeated and humiliated by France so that she would lose prestige in Germany. Therefore, when war appeared probable, they spread propaganda to the effect that Prussia was unable to defend south Germany, in order to thwart any plans for the mobilization of the Bavarian army.[63]

A little later, after the crisis had become less acute, Jörg took time to discuss the role of the Pfordten government in the establishment of the alliance. He admitted that the particularists had, as liberals charged, been responsible for bringing the country to disaster. Pfordten and his colleagues had always acted on the assumption that Austria was more dangerous to Bavarian interests than Prussia. The alliance treaty had been the ultimate result of that policy. The treaty itself, however, he found to be not without merit, for it did ally Bavaria with the rest of Germany, and to him no other alternative could be considered. What he condemned was the manner in which Pfordten, by accepting the treaty without requiring any concessions from Bismarck, had abandoned the possibility that Bavaria could in the future exercise influence in Germany. Bavarian diplomacy, he feared, would be forever controlled by Berlin, for Prussia could now with justification claim, "I am Germany." He argued that it would have been far better

[62] "Zeitläufe: Der Luxemburgische Handel und die Bismarckische Politik auf dem Prüfstein," April 10, 1867, *HPB*, 59:631.

[63] Werthern to Bismarck, Munich, April 2, 1867, *APP*, 8: no. 394; Fleming to Bismarck, Karlsruhe, April 25, 1867, *ibid.*, no. 529; Wilhelm Schüssler, *Bismarcks Kampf um Süddeutschland, 1867*, 152.

for Pfordten to have accepted the loss of the Palatinate, which Prussia had at one point proposed to annex, rather than sign such a treaty. For then Bavaria could at least have preserved a free hand, and been able to serve as a bridge between Berlin and Vienna. Aside from these factors, he felt that both Pfordten and Hohenlohe had acted immorally in concealing the existence of the alliance from the Bavarian people.[64]

Some weeks later, at the time of the London conference, Jörg renewed his criticism of Prussian policy. By that time he had concluded that peace might be maintained, although not by means of an international conference. The real hope, he again insisted, lay in an understanding between the two German great powers, which would again create a solid German front against France.[65] While the event belied his pessimism, and peace was preserved despite the absence of any *rapprochement* between Berlin and Vienna, Prussia's handling of the Luxemburg crisis had done her cause irreparable harm in Bavaria. Most Catholics were thereafter even less able than before to believe that she was to be trusted. Although passions did cool to a degree after Bismarck divested himself of his role of one who was willing to alienate German territory to foreign nations, the fact that he had been willing was enough for Bavarians. The Prussian ambassador at Munich claimed considerable credit for quelling the enthusiasm of ultramontane extremists in Bavaria for an alliance with France. He reported telling the Archbishop of Munich that, according to his information, Napoleon had offered Rome to Victor Emanuel in return for an alliance against Prussia. There does not seem to have been any basis in fact for his allegation, or for his claim that it influenced Catholic opinion.[66]

In Württemberg, too, the publication of the Prussian alliance treaty came as a stunning blow to Catholics, although it produced, naturally, a wave of jubilation in the *Deutsche Partei*. The latter immediately demanded that the treaty be given force by passage of a law which would practically have incorporated the Württemberg military establishment in the Prussian army. Catholics attacked the proposal bit-

[64] "Zeitläufe: Behandlungen über die äussere und innere Lage Bayerns," *HPB*, 59:697–700, 702–6, 709–11.

[65] "Zeitläufe: Preussen und Deutschland zur Zeit der Londoner Conferenz," *HPB*, 59:775, 779.

[66] Werthern to Bismarck, Munich, April 30, 1867, *APP*, 8: no. 560.

terly, and partly for that reason some conservative Protestants decided to support it. The scheme came to naught in the end.[67] The whole Luxemburg crisis, however, produced far less internal conflict in Württemberg than it did in Bavaria, possibly because hostility toward Prussia had been in general somewhat less acute than in the Wittelsbach Kingdom.

The reaction of Baden Catholics was not unlike its counterpart in Württemberg, except that in the absence of effective parliamentary representation their opposition had necessarily to be confined almost entirely to the press. Some articles in the Catholic press condemning Prussian duplicity were reprinted in official French papers, which sought to bolster the impression that public opinion in Germany was badly divided. Roggenbach was so concerned over the international implications of these attacks that he warned Bismarck on March 30 against yielding to Napoleon on any point. He feared that any sign of weakness by the north German government would give the signal for particularists in Baden openly to take the part of France.[68]

Hesse-Darmstadt, as pointed out above, had no treaty of alliance with Prussia. Bismarck considered such a treaty unnecessary, and he loathed Dalwigk personally because of the Hessian minister's success during the peace negotiations in securing French and Russian intervention to prevent Prussian annexation of Upper Hesse. The Chancellor also believed, probably correctly, that it would be impossible to keep an alliance with Hesse secret from France, and equally impossible to keep the others secret if Dalwigk knew of their existence. Consequently, the publication of the treaties came as a shock not only to the public, but also to the government. Dalwigk was both surprised and angry at the Grand Duchy's omission from the list of allies. It was a personal affront, and it was certain to increase his difficulties with the nationalist party, which was now recovering from its defeat of the preceding December.

The clerical press of Hesse, particularly the *Katholisches Volksblatt*, attacked the alliances violently in terms not unlike those of Jörg in Bavaria. The treaties, it said, represented still another attempt of

---

[67] Rosenberg to Bismarck, Stuttgart, March 27, 1867, *APP*, 8: no. 344.

[68] Neumann to Bismarck, Karlsruhe, March 24, 1867, *APP*, 8: no. 334; Fleming to Bismarck, Karlsruhe, April 25, 1867, *ibid.*, no. 529; Roggenbach to Bismarck, March 30, 1867, *ibid.*, no. 356, note 1.

Prussia to set up a unitary, centralized state in Germany. The southern states, by consenting to sign them, had abandoned their sovereign
independence and had become military vassals of the Hohenzollerns.
Many members of Ketteler's circle at Mainz were in complete agreement with these views. They had, along with Dalwigk, been thinking
in terms of another war in which south Germany, allied with Austria
and France, would fight for "the reuniting of Germany." Ketteler himself, of course, did not share those opinions.[69]

In spite of his own personal inclinations, Dalwigk was constrained
to conclude, on April 7, a military convention with Prussia which
ended the illogical separation of the Hessian division into two brigades
under different command. Four days later he affixed his name at last
to a treaty of alliance with Prussia similar to the others, largely to
satisfy the national party. In the midst of the negotiations, three Upper Hessian deputies in the North German Reichstag interpellated
Bismarck, apparently by prearrangement, on his attitude toward entry of the entire Grand Duchy into the *Bund*. Bismarck replied that
if Austria had no objections on the grounds of the Peace of Prague, it
was then up to the Hessians. The national party at Darmstadt was
overjoyed at the tone of Bismarck's answer, while most Catholics were,
as usual, incensed. Vienna failed to heed Dalwigk's frantic appeal for
an objection which would counteract the pressure. As a result, in June
a motion proposing immediate entry of Hesse-Darmstadt into the
North German Confederation won approval in the lower house of the
Ständekammern. The only notable speech against it was by the Catholic deputy, Seitz. The former loose anti-Prussian alliance had collapsed
in face of growing awareness that the Grand Duchy's position was untenable, leaving Catholics as the only wholehearted advocates of complete isolation. The upper chamber, however, rejected the motion by a
great majority. Here Canon Moufang, Bishop Ketteler's representative, was one of the leaders in the fight against it.[70]

While the attitudes of politicians and editors are indicative of the
state of mind of Catholics, they do not present the entire picture.
What Catholic citizens who were not in public life thought and felt

[69] Vogt, 112–14, 120, 139–40; Wentzel to Bismarck, Darmstadt, March 28, 1867, *APP*,
8: no. 349; Vigener, *Ketteler*, 495–96.
[70] Vogt, 139–42, 153, 155; Dalwigk to Beust, Darmstadt, April 9, 1867, *ibid.*, 213–15;
H. von Gagern to Dalwigk, Vienna, April 16, 1867, *ibid.*, 215–16; Wentzel to Bismarck,
Darmstadt, April 15, 1867, *APP*, 8: no. 489.

is much more difficult to ascertain. Count Hertling, in 1867 still pursuing his studies, found that after the publication of the alliance treaties, despair among his friends and acquaintances was even greater than it had been following the appearance of *Deutschland nach dem Kriege*. His own feelings, perhaps typical of those of others in his station, appeared in a letter to his mother:

If I still had any political illusions, the most recent events would have destroyed them for me. I never expected anything from the north German parliament; but that it would be to such a degree the show place of abject servility and complete barbarity with reference to morality and justice, I would never have believed. . . . All that is ideal has disappeared from the world.[71]

The impression of most south German Catholics that the Prussian noose was tightening around their necks grew even stronger during the remainder of 1867. In both Baden and Bavaria the problem of relations between Church and state remained acute. The Baden minister of commerce, for example, issued an administrative order on May 31 depriving Church officials, as of the following January 1, of their franking privilege, and in September a law was introduced in the *Landtag* proposing the legal separation of Church and state. Although the measure did not come to a vote, Catholics saw in it a warning that there would be further attempts to abridge rights guaranteed the Church by law.[72]

In Bavaria the Progressives continued to agitate for reform of the educational system. As a countermeasure, a group of Catholics established a special committee at Regensburg to circulate propaganda against the scheme. The editor of the *Historisch-politische Blätter*, in an article dealing with the conflict in Baden, but with references to the same problem elsewhere, again called for Catholics to organize politically to vindicate their rights. Legal guarantees, he wrote, were no longer sufficient to protect the Church. Since 1866 only strength could assure that rights would be respected, for the modern liberal state, no longer inspired by a Christian conscience, recognized no law but itself. The Church, and Catholics, had no choice but to use liberal principles such as freedom of the press and assembly in their own behalf, in order

[71] Hertling, 1:167.
[72] "Zeitläufe: Der neue badische Kirchenstreit," *HPB*, 60:777–79; *ibid.*, 805–7; A. Doeberl, "Preysing," *Gelbe Hefte*, 2:845.

to save themselves from oppression by liberal governments. While they could not expect any special privileges, they could insist that in the education of their own children the state had no right to interfere.[73]

Relations between south Germany and the North German Confederation reached their next critical phase with the negotiation of the new *Zollverein* treaties in June 1867. It has been pointed out above that the peace treaties provided for tentative restoration of the Customs Union in its prewar form. Bismarck, however, and his chief economic adviser, Rudolph Delbrück, had no intention of permitting the former *liberum veto* to endure indefinitely, now that they had power to eliminate it. Accordingly, in December 1866, Prussia gave the required six months' notice of her desire to terminate the Union, preparatory to beginning negotiations for the establishment of a reformed *Zollverein*. Any other action was postponed until the final approval of the north German constitution by the Reichstag in late April 1867, and until the Luxemburg crisis had run its course, Bismarck, at last, on May 28 invited the four southern states to send representatives to Berlin. Conversations began on June 3, and five days later a series of treaties drafted by the Prussian government were signed. The new *Zollverein* was to function through a *Zollbundesrath* and a *Zollparlament*. These were to be the *Bundesrath* and Reichstag of the North German Confederation, enlarged for the purpose by members representing the south German states. The *Zollparlament* delegates from the South were to be elected on the same terms as members of the North German Reichstag — *i.e.*, by direct, universal manhood suffrage. Thus for the first time since 1848 truly democratic elections would take place in south Germany. Tariff legislation would require a simple majority of both bodies, and no subsequent ratification by state diets would be necessary. The Prussian Crown was to exercise executive functions, with the right to enforce tariff laws and negotiate trade treaties.[74]

Almost immediately nationalists in south Germany saw in the *Zollparlament*, the first body since the Frankfurt parliament in which all Germany would be represented, an instrument through which political unification of Germany might be secured. It was only necessary

[73] *HPB*, 60:805–7; A. Doeberl, "Preysing," *Gelbe Hefte*, 2:845.
[74] Sybel, 6:223–27; Bismarck to Prussian missions in Munich, Stuttgart, Karlsruhe, and Darmstadt, Berlin, Feb. 15, 1867, *GW*, 6: no. 685.

that south Germany send to the first session a delegation favorable to union. A motion to extend the competence of the *Zollparlament* to include *all* legislation could then be introduced, with every hope that it would prove irresistible. As they put it, the *Zollparlament* would become a *Vollparlament*. Even Bismarck, who was known to favor proceeding with caution, would hardly be able to stem the tide. At a meeting on August 3, 1867, at Stuttgart, the leading south German nationalists agreed to work toward this goal.[75]

Unfortunately for their purpose, the possibilities were equally apparent to their opponents, and, therefore, anti-Prussians in all four states soon began a campaign to prevent ratification of the *Zollverein* treaties. Since the alliance treaties, and the agreements for military reform, were also up for ratification, they too became objects of a similar attack. Always Catholics were in the thick of the fight; often they furnished the leadership.

In Baden, when, late in May, several members of the lower chamber again circulated a declaration advocating a closer union with Prussia, it was the Catholics alone who, as a group, refused to sign. At the beginning of the *Landtag* session early in September, Lindau, elected in July, made his maiden speech opposing an address to the throne which asked the government to work for Baden's entry into the North German Confederation. Lindau made no effort to minimize the shattering effect of events during the preceding year. He did, however, deny that because of those events his country had to "submit blindly" to the state which had "painted its motto, 'Blood and Iron,' on the battlefield with the blood of its German brothers." Joining the North would give no security to Baden, he said, for the burdens assumed thereby would destroy her economic existence. He felt qualified as a merchant to express an authoritative opinion on the new *Zollverein*, which would merely sacrifice former privileges of the southern states to north Ger-

---

[75] Brater to Oetker, Munich, July 25, 1867, Oncken, *Bennigsen*, 1:76–77; *ibid.*, 76, note 2, 155–56, 156, note 1; Bismarck to Fleming, Berlin, Nov. 13, 1867, *GW*, 6a: no. 934; Bismarck to Fleming, Berlin, Dec. 3, 1867, *ibid.*, no. 974; Bismarck to Werthern, Berlin, Jan. 25, 1868, *ibid.*, no. 1030. Schüssler, in *Bismarcks Kampf um Süddeutschland*, 279–81, maintains that Bismarck himself was behind this move as the one best calculated to bring the southern states within the fold most rapidly. At best this theory represents a possibility only, and it is difficult to harmonize with the Chancellor's well-known hesitancy at involving the fledgling North German Confederation in a war with France prematurely. He was certainly under no illusion that Napoleon III would stand peacefully aside while the four states were absorbed by north Germany.

man interests. What was needed, instead, was the restoration of the *Zollverein* along the lines which had existed before the war, so that member states could not be compelled to act against their own interests. Furthermore, adoption of the Prussian military system would be of no benefit to Baden, for the only real solution to her military problem lay in ending the breach between Habsburg and Hohenzollern. Armament *à la Prusse* would only impose unbearable economic burdens. He demanded, in closing, that the government ask for no new taxes for military purposes until it had sought first to meet its financial needs by cutting other expenditures.[76]

On October 8 Lindau cast the only vote against ratification of the alliance treaty, and two weeks later he voiced the lone dissent to adoption of universal conscription. Even he, however, relented on the *Zollverein*, which passed the lower chamber, as it did the upper, unanimously. By the same token, the law governing the election of *Zollparlament* deputies received the unanimous assent of both houses. Lindau, although his arguments obviously made little impression on his colleagues, did not abandon his efforts. On November 8 he renewed his demand that there be no tax increases. During this debate the liberal, Lamey, accused him of being the leader of the "Ultramontane party." The merchant denied the existence of any such party, maintaining that he spoke only for the people. The first half of his answer was certainly true, while the second half, in terms of the situation in 1867, was, to say the least, exaggerated.[77]

The *Ständekammern* of Hesse-Darmstadt also approved both the *Zollverein* and the belated military alliance, against inconsequential opposition from Catholic and other particularists. Württemberg, on the other hand, underwent a period of serious internal tension before its *Landtag* ratified both agreements. The anti-Prussian coalition used every possible means to defeat them. In small towns and in cities meetings were held at which speakers sought to convince the people that ratification meant loss of political independence and economic ruin for Württemberg. Wherever Catholics were numerous they participated wholeheartedly in the campaign. Nevertheless, the *Deutsche Partei* carried the day, notwithstanding an earlier decision of the *Land-*

[76] Dor, 67, 71–75; Fleming to Bismarck, Baden, May 25, 1867, *APP*, 9: no. 38.
[77] Dor, 78–79; Walter Schübelin, *Das Zollparlament und die Politik von Baden, Bayern, und Württemberg, 1866–1870*, 59.

tag that, since the two treaties meant a fundamental alteration of the
constitution, a two-thirds majority was necessary for adoption. In the
lower house the vote was 73 to 16. The minority included the leading
Catholic deputies, Probst and Österlen.[78]

As might be expected, the most bitter struggle took place in Bavaria.
Even before the *Zollverein* negotiations of June, Jörg, Edel, Ruland,
and other Catholic politicians had begun to agitate against the military alliance. Jörg carried on a campaign of increasing malevolence
against Prussia in the pages of his journal. On the *Bundesverfassung*
he wrote: "On our side we can see nothing in this constitution except
an institution adapted to the inevitable absorption of individual states
by way of financial and military arrangements." Later he repeated his
charges that Bismarck had exploited the victory in Bohemia for the
selfish ends of the Hohenzollern Monarchy, not for the interests of
Germany. Again he insisted, as Lindau would later in the Baden chamber, that the only remedy for the evil times which had befallen the
nation was elimination of Austro-Prussian hostility. Otherwise Germany was doomed to be crushed by France or Prussia, perhaps by
both.[79]

By the summer of 1867, the Bavarian clergy was for the first time
beginning to take part in a political campaign on what would be called
in America the grass-roots level. As early as May 19, a popular meeting was held at Beuersberg, a village in Old Bavaria, to protest both
the liberals' proposed educational reforms and the alliance with Prussia. Werthern, the Prussian ambassador, in reporting this incident, indicated that the rural population in Old Bavaria was being strongly
influenced against Prussia by the clergy, and also by the popular ultra-
montane-democratic newspaper, the *Münchener Volksbote,* allegedly
the voice of the episcopate. Werthern judged that in Old Bavaria the
ratio of friends of Prussia to those who hated her was roughly one to
five hundred. In September, at Passau, a self-appointed committee of
clerics adopted a petition asking dissolution of the chamber before the
Zollverein treaty came to a vote, because, the petition stated, the
lower house did not represent the true feelings of the country. The
Passau *Königsadresse,* as it became known, was circulated among par-

[78] Vogt, 153; Rosenberg to Bismarck, Stuttgart, Oct. 22, 1867, *APP,* 9: no. 242; Schübelin, 63–65.
[79] *HPB,* 59:454–68; 60:80, 84.

ishes in Old Bavaria, Lower Bavaria, and the Upper Palatinate. In all, it received nearly two thousand signatures. It is not clear what degree of clerical pressure was represented in the decisions of individuals and groups to sign the petition.[80]

Agitation for new elections was unavailing. Jörg and his friends were forced to continue their fight against the same hostile chamber. From the tribune the editor denounced the military reforms on the ground that "not more, but fewer, soldiers" were needed to solve Bavaria's and Germany's problem. Adoption of the Prussian military system, like the new *Zollverein,* promised only an "irresistible descent from one level to another into the arms of Prussian hegemony."[81] Against the Customs Union he charged "centralism, saber rule, Caesarism," stating that it would mean "unconditional subjection of Bavaria to the economic dictation of Prussia and its parties." The treaties were "for Prussia only a means of fiscal exploitation of the southern states, for the purpose of furthering her [Prussia's] armaments, and her unproductive militarism." It is significant that these arguments were based primarily on political, not economic, premises. The opposition made no effort to claim at this time, as Lindau did in Baden, that the economy of rural Bavaria was being sacrificed to the demands of north German industry, or to those of Bavarian cities.[82]

When the treaties came to a vote, however, on October 22, only seventeen deputies were willing to reject the *Zollverein,* and on the next day the electoral law was approved with only fourteen negative votes. The military reforms, likewise, were adopted against inconsequential opposition. According to the Bavarian constitution the alliance treaty itself did not require legislative ratification. The *Reichsräthe,* on the other hand, gave its consent to the *Zollverein* treaty only after strong pressure had been exerted from Berlin, and from economic interests at home which would have suffered great hardship had they lost the advantage of inclusion within an all-German customs frontier.[83]

As the year came to an end, it was obvious that north and south

[80] *APP,* 9: no. 39, note 2; Schübelin, 67–68; A. Doeberl, "Preysing," *Gelbe Hefte,* 2:845; Spielhofer, "Bayrische Zentrumspartei," *HPB,* 165:418; Julius Fröbel, *Ein Lebenslauf,* 2:508–9.

[81] Wöhler, 22; Schieder, 169.

[82] Wöhler, 22; Schieder, 161–62; Schübelin, 69.

[83] Schübelin, 69; Sybel, 6:271–72. For the role of the North German Reichstag in the Bavarian ratification of the *Zollverein* treaty, see Chapter Five.

Germany had been bound together constitutionally in ways that few had foreseen a year earlier. To nationalists in both sections the way seemed open for rapid completion of a *Kleindeutschland*. Their most important opponents, the Catholics, were again, as after Königgrätz, filled with despair. Jörg wrote during the last weeks of the year: "European international law has come to pure nothing, and actually, thereby, the idea of justice has disappeared from our world. Everywhere might comes before right in international, as well as in internal, affairs." [84] The principle of nationalism, bequeathed to the world by France, he went on, was the evil force which had brought about this catastrophe, and only "a great general spiritual outpouring that will overcome the destructive individualism of the bourgeoisie" could help. Otherwise revolution and social democracy were inevitable.[85] The following months were to find Jörg more and more involved with other Catholics, both north and south of the Main, in trying to bring about in Germany that hoped-for defeat of bourgeois liberalism and its brand of nationalism.

[84] "Zeitläufe: Rom und die Conferenz-Werbung Frankreichs," *HPB*, 60:982.
[85] *Ibid.*, 982–83.

Chapter 5

Reichstag and Customs
Parliament, 1867–1868

In north Germany, by the summer of 1867, public support for the feudal Conservatives, the Progressives, and the particularistic Catholics had declined to such a degree that effective opposition to Bismarck's policy was for the time being impossible. In the elections for the first regular North German Reichstag, which took place on August 21, the *Fortschrittspartei* won fewer than thirty seats. The number of Catholic deputies elected was not strikingly different from that of the Constituent Reichstag, although a number of the more important Catholics did not return. Among them were Michelis, Scherer, Seul, Rohden, and Father Thissen. Mallinckrodt, Windthorst, Peter Reichensperger, and Kratz were reelected, as were most of the Polish Catholics who had sat in the Constituent.[1] The majority of new Catholic members came from the Rhineland, although Archbishop Melchers of Cologne, on July 17, had forbidden the clergy to take any part in the campaign. Thus, potentially the most effective means of influencing Catholic voters was allowed to go by default. It is not surprising, therefore, that Catholics elected from Rhineland constituencies were, for the most part, supporters of Bismarck who, either before or after they arrived at Berlin, joined the Free Conservatives.[2] The *Kölnische Blätter* attempted, without success, to stem the tide. When Savigny was entered as a candidate from Koblenz, it warned voters "who do not seem to have had [sufficient] experience that 'government Catholics' are the most dangerous for the cause that lies closest to their [the

---

[1] Sybel, 6:237–39; *Stenographische Berichte über die Verhandlungen des Reichstages des norddeutschen Bundes, I. Legislatur-Periode, Session 1867* (hereafter abbreviated as *Stenographische Berichte, 1867*), Namenverzeichnis der Mitglieder des Reichstages, 1:x–xxvi.

[2] Hansen, 1:789–90.

voters'] hearts, freedom of the Church." [3] It complained that Melchers had caused "a stony indifference" among Catholics by tying the hands of the clergy." [4]

Similarly, in the Prussian *Landtag* elected in November, most of the Catholics were members of the Free Conservative party. A few, however, who preferred to consider themselves *wild*, often acted more or less together. Windthorst, for the first time eligible to sit in the *Landtag*, was elected to represent Meppen (Hanover). He found none of the existing parties or groups congenial, and declined to join any of them. He was, nevertheless, able, because of his exceptional parliamentary talents, to exercise considerable influence on affairs, winning the respect, if not the affection, of his colleagues, and earning the distinctive sobriquet, *Fraktion Meppen*.[5]

With the establishment of the North German Confederation, the Prussian *Landtag* began to decline in importance, and the significant decisions and debates were generally thereafter to occur in the Reichstag. The first regular session of the Reichstag, however, was productive of fewer noteworthy debates than the Constituent. Catholic members likewise played a far less important role, even as obstructionists. During the interminable process of validating elections, which occupied the first days of the session, charges of election frauds in the province of Posen again were raised. This time only Kantak spoke at length for the Poles, and his arguments, unlike those at the beginning of the Constituent, did not play upon the religious issue, but dealt wholly with considerations of nationality. The house declined, as before, to go into the substance of the charges.[6] Several were dismissed on the ground that they were motivated by "party spirit," which prompted Reichensperger at one point to observe that public affairs were of necessity judged in terms of party objectives, and that such claims, therefore, should be dealt with on their merits, rather than be rejected on irrelevant grounds. His speech appears to have impressed few members.[7]

[3] *Ibid.*, 796.

[4] *Ibid.*, 789–90.

[5] *Ibid.*, 790; Hüsgen, 73–74.

[6] *Stenographische Berichte, 1867*, Sept. 25, 1867, 1:99–103. The Reichstag did, however, refuse to seat General Vogel von Falckenstein because of obvious violations of the election regulations in his district. The religious question was in no way involved, and the majority of Catholic deputies declined to vote. See *ibid.*, 1:61. The general reappeared in the 1868 session, having won a by-election.

[7] *Ibid.*, 34–36.

The first debate of more than routine importance took place on a National Liberal motion to adopt an address to the throne expressing the "thanks and satisfaction of the nation over the results achieved up to this time [by Bismarck and Prussia] through a truly German policy," and the hope that the work would soon be completed by the entry of the south German states into the *Bund* under provisions of Article 79 of the constitution. The motion gave Kantak another opportunity to strike an ineffective blow for Polish independence. He pointed out that Poles could not assent to a vote of thanks for a "truly German policy," since that policy had meant forcible subjection of the Polish nation. He claimed further that the reelection of so many of the Polish deputies who had resigned their seats at the final session of the Constituent Reichstag was proof that an overwhelming majority of Prussian Poles shared this viewpoint. Kantak's remarks had no discernible effect on the house.[8]

Reichensperger objected to the first portion of the address because its phraseology implied that the Reichstag approved the events of 1866. The parliament was thus gloating over the misfortunes of south Germany. In order to avoid that implication, which the proponents of the address denied was intended, he proposed to substitute a paragraph which would simply express gratitude for the adoption of the north German constitution. His amendment found little support, and the house adopted the address in its original form by a vote of 157 to 58. Catholics were by no means solidly opposed; eight voted for the address and nine against it, while eight did not vote. The majority included most of the "government Catholics."[9]

The second major item of business was the budget for the fiscal year 1868, which aroused *per se* surprisingly little controversy. For the present study the importance of the budgetary debate derives almost entirely from the attempt of Peter Reichensperger and others to attach to the budget an amendment which would have made the Chancellor responsible at civil law for unauthorized expenditures. This represented an effort to introduce a very mild version of ministerial responsibility, which, in a more orthodox form, had been rejected by the Constituent Reichstag. The Reichensperger amendment provided for the creation of a five-man Reichstag committee empowered to

[8] *Ibid.*, Sept. 24, 1867, 83–84.
[9] *Ibid.*, 82–83, 90–91.

bring suit for damages against the Chancellor in the *Oberappelations-gericht* at Lübeck. Reichensperger argued that unless the Reichstag had some means of compelling observance of its wishes, its right to control the budget was meaningless. The nominal responsibility of the Chancellor provided in the constitution, he regarded as completely insufficient. The National Liberal, Twesten, countered with the observation that the Reichstag always had the recourse of rejecting a subsequent budget, unless it received satisfaction from the Chancellor, but Reichensperger insisted that no representative body had an ethical right arbitrarily to refuse assent to a budget. It might decline to approve portions, it might change others; but outright rejection would mean that a parliament regarded itself as above and outside the state. The Reichstag, acting on such a principle, could easily, he maintained, destroy the Confederation. Only some sort of effective legal responsibility could suffice. The Reichensperger amendment, opposed by the National Liberals, was defeated on a standing vote.[10]

During the discussion of the naval budget, the Catholic deputy, Kratz, introduced an amendment which, because of the excitement it aroused, illustrates the serious consequences of religious division in Germany. The apparently innocuous Kratz amendment simply proposed naming a Catholic chaplain for the north German fleet. According to its author, Catholic sailors were unfairly deprived of normal spiritual guidance. They had no resort, he said, except to civilian clergymen, which was possible only in port and during off-duty hours. Bismarck spoke against the proposal, denying that the government had any intention of discriminating against Catholics in the naval service. The budget, he said, had not made provision for a Catholic chaplain simply because only eleven per cent of naval personnel were of the Roman faith. Roon, the war minister, rose to point out that most of that eleven per cent did not belong to the seagoing forces, but consisted either of marines or of noncommissioned officers assigned to technical services in naval yards. The vast majority of them, he said, were stationed at Kiel, where the services of civil priests were easily available. The omission implied no discrimination, Roon went on, for it simply reflected the fact that men who enlisted for sea duty nor-

[10] *Ibid.*, Oct. 8, 1867, 297–99, 307–9; Aktenstücke, no. 68; *ibid.*, 2 : 131; Zuchhardt, 53, 60–61. The *Oberappelationsgericht* had been recognized during the period of the German Confederation as the court of highest jurisdiction in Germany. Its status after the war of 1866 was somewhat anomalous.

mally came from coastal areas which were, by historical accident, overwhelmingly Protestant.

Kratz was, however, not satisfied. He insisted that the government's policy discriminated, on purely religious grounds, against the enlistment of Catholics. Moreover, it was almost certain to increase resentment against the North in south Germany. He denied any intention of introducing a religious issue into the debate, although it was impossible to make his proposal without mentioning religion. Because of the possible effects that refusal to adopt the motion might have on south Germany and on foreign countries, some Protestants were willing to support it. The Lutheran university professor, Aegidi, for example, asked that it be approved. Its rejection, he argued, was certain to be misinterpreted, while its passage would demonstrate to the whole world that there was no religious discrimination in the North German Confederation. Dr. Künzer, a Catholic, echoed Aegidi's request in similar terms. At the last moment, Bismarck attempted conciliation, stating that the Navy Department had no fundamental objection to the appointment of a Catholic chaplain. He assured the house that in case the Kratz amendment was not adopted, the government would consider the question when it prepared its next budget. The amendment was defeated on a standing vote.[11]

Catholics took no important part in the debate on the new military service law made necessary by the annexations of 1866, the establishment of the Confederation, and the alliance treaties with the southern states. Criticism of the government's bill, and counterproposals, of which there were many, dealt only with details, and relatively little basic discord was revealed. Only one question came to a roll call. The government bill provided for compulsory service for seven years, including two years on active duty and five in the first line reserve, unless annual maneuvers, "necessary strengthening of the army," or mobilization for war required calling up the reserves. It was perhaps the bitter memory of the Prussian crisis of 1861 which led the Progressive deputy, Freiherr von Hoverbeck, to propose an amendment striking out the clause quoted above, for it seemed to give the government power to increase the number of men under arms without sanction of the Reichstag. When the amendment came to a vote, Catholics were divided, ten for it and nine against. Of the major fig-

[11] *Stenographische Berichte, 1867,* Oct. 1, 1867, 1: 194–95, 199–201.

ures, Kratz, Mallinckrodt, and Windthorst voted for the change, while
Reichensperger abstained, as did most of the Poles. It failed by a vote
of 81 to 165.[12]

During this first regular session, the North German Reichstag passed
a series of laws designed to wipe out many of the more archaic aspects
of the legal systems in north Germany. Among them was an act ending all restrictions on the right of citizens to travel, settle, own property, or conduct business anywhere within the *Bund*, and one granting
workers the right to form unions for the purpose of securing higher
wages or better working conditions. In neither case did Catholics figure prominently in the debates. The law on freedom of settlement was
passed without a roll call, and the labor legislation received the assent
of the house, 206 to 70. Only two Catholics voted against it, although
eleven did not vote at all. Among the abstainers were Mallinckrodt,
Reichensperger, and Windthorst, none of whom explained his reasons.
Thirteen Catholics voted with the majority. The government had not
opposed the bill in principle, although Delbrück had announced that
it would prefer to deal with the matter later as part of a general industrial code. Because of this attitude, and because of its more conservative character, the *Bundesrath* rejected the measure, although it made
no difficulty in regard to the law on freedom of settlement.[13]

Among the large number of petitions received by the Reichstag during the session were several from individuals and groups in the two
Mecklenburgs, asking the federal government to take steps toward
elimination of disabilities arising out of the reactionary, feudal state
constitutions still in effect in the duchies. It was no secret to the
Reichstag that, as nearly all the petitions charged, constitutional practice in the Mecklenburgs was completely contradictory to principles
accepted by all modern states, and that it was glaringly at variance
with the north German constitution. The committee on petitions, dominated by the National Liberals, recommended, therefore, the adoption
of a resolution asking the Chancellor to take steps to secure reform of
the offending constitutions.

For the advocates of states' rights, including many of the Catholics,
this motion presented a dilemma. If they supported it, they were up-

[12] *Ibid.*, Oct. 18, 1867, 488.
[13] *Ibid.*, Oct. 14, 1867, 416. Freedom of labor to organize was enacted into law in 1869
as part of the north German industrial code.

holding the principle that the federal government could legitimately interfere in the internal affairs of member states. Opposition, however, was tantamount to defending two of the most reactionary régimes in Europe. For Catholics the problem was complicated by the fact that the Catholic minority suffered severe legal disabilities in the overwhelmingly Lutheran Mecklenburg region. Windthorst was the only one of them to speak against the motion. His remarks reveal the difficulty which many Catholic members must have felt. As a citizen, he said, he admitted the desirability of sweeping reforms in the constitutions of the Mecklenburgs, but as a member of the Reichstag, a body which had been created by treaties between sovereign states to carry out certain functions enumerated in the constitution, he could not vote for the motion. For it was clearly outside the competence of the Reichstag to intervene in the internal affairs of either Mecklenburg or those of any other member state. The three-class system by which the Prussian *Landtag* was elected was also incompatible with the north German constitution. Did the Reichstag have a right or duty to intervene here also? He thought not.[14]

When the motion came to a vote, eleven Catholics, as might be expected, abstained. Six, including Mallinckrodt and Windthorst, voted no, while eight voted for the proposal. Since it failed by a very narrow margin, 106 to 102, the division of the Catholic vote had more significance than usual, although the most important reason for the failure was the refusal of the Free Conservatives to follow the National Liberals on this question. Catholics who voted for the bill were, for the most part, those to whom religious considerations were of transcendent importance, and it may be conjectured that the plight of the Church in the duchies was the paramount factor in their decision.[15]

The final important item on the Reichstag agenda was the *Zollverein* treaties of June. It must be kept in mind that the Reichstag and the south German parliaments were dealing with the treaties at the same time. Therefore, what happened in Munich or Stuttgart, for example, had an important effect on events in Berlin, and vice versa. It was, in fact, the initial refusal of the Bavarian upper chamber to ratify the *Zollverein* treaty unless the *liberum veto* for Bavaria was restored which provoked the more dramatic aspects of the Reichstag

[14] *Ibid.*, Oct. 23, 1867, 599–600, 608.
[15] *Ibid.*, 608–9.

debate. On the evening of October 26, shortly after the *Reichsräthe's* decision, Hohenlohe and Freiherr von Thüngen, leader of the opposition in the senate, left Munich for Berlin, intending to open further negotiations with Bismarck on the question. When they arrived the next morning, they discovered that the Reichstag, upon learning by telegraph of the delay in Munich, and already aware of the reluctance of the Württemberg chambers to ratify the military agreement, had adopted a proposal offered by the National Liberal, Braun of Wiesbaden, which made ratification of the military alliance in effect prerequisite for entry into the *Zollverein* at all. Although this move was ostensibly directed at Württemberg alone, since no parliamentary ratification of the alliance was constitutionally necessary in Bavaria, it gave unmistakable evidence to the two Bavarians that no further limitation on either agreement would be tolerated by north Germany.[16]

It was Mallinckrodt who had led the fight against the Braun amendment. He argued that there was no logical connection between the alliances and the *Zollverein,* and that it was unjust to require the southern states to abandon economic union in order to avoid the burdens of the alliances. Those states, however, might well do just that, in which case north Germany might suffer more than the South. He found it difficult to understand, in any case, why so much emphasis was placed on the alliances. Only in case of an attack by France could they conceivably have value, but if that happened, no treaties would be necessary. The best method of binding the two sections together was not through treaties imposed upon the South in defeat, but rather through convincing it that north Germany had no wish to endanger its independence. By adopting the Braun amendment, "You will at best," he concluded, "create a Germany in which it will be open to question whether within its boundaries are more people who are there by choice or by compulsion." [17]

The answer of the National Liberals was that it was unfair for the South to reap the benefits of the *Zollverein* without sharing the burdens of defending Germany. Miquel went so far as to impugn the patriotism of Mallinckrodt and his co-religionists on both sides of the Main, professing to see in their attitude a strong inclination toward France. Mallinckrodt hotly denied the charges, both for himself and

[16] Sybel, 6: 271–73.
[17] *Stenographische Berichte, 1867*, Oct. 26, 1867, 1: 671–72.

for his fellow Catholics in north and south Germany. He insisted, particularly, that he had as good a claim to being regarded a German patriot as anyone in the house.[18]

Mallinckrodt's efforts went, of course, for nought. The final vote was 177 to 26. Only four Catholics — Windthorst, Mallinckrodt, Fühling, and Kantak — voted against the motion, although only eight voted for it.[19] The large number of abstentions grew out of an inability to choose between conflicting desires. On the one hand, most Catholics did not want south Germany to be coerced, but on the other, they did hope to see the country united, and the *Zollverein* appeared to be a necessary step in the process. A few moments after the vote was taken, the Reichstag adjourned, and, as indicated in the preceding chapter, the Bavarian *Reichsräthe,* faced with a practical ultimatum, and under heavy pressure at home, abandoned its opposition shortly thereafter. The Württemberg *Landtag* followed suit a few days later.

With the ratification of the *Zollverein* treaties, the focus of attention must again be shifted to south Germany, where preparations immediately began for election of delegates to the first *Zollparlament.* Both the nationalists and their opponents knew that the character of the representatives sent by south Germany to Berlin would have crucial significance for the future course of national development. The nationalists' campaign had actually begun with the Stuttgart meeting of August 1867, at which representatives from the national parties of the four southern states had agreed to contest the election on the issue of extending the competence of the *Zollparlament.*[20] They proposed giving it power to enact legislation for all Germany on such matters as migration between, and domicile within, states, and entry into professions or trades. By going beyond the letter of the treaties, they hoped to set a precedent for further steps which sooner or later would convert the *Zollparlament* into a fully competent legislative body.[21] Moreover, if they could create an impression of overwhelming popular enthusiasm for their project, it would be difficult for France, Austria, or hostile groups in Germany itself successfully to appeal to restrictions of the Treaty of Prague.

Until a few weeks before the election, scheduled for early February

[18] *Ibid.,* 680; Sybel, 6:273–74.
[19] *Stenographische Berichte, 1867,* Oct. 26, 1867, 1:681–82.
[20] See Chapter Four.
[21] Schübelin, 71–72.

1868, the *Fortschrittspartei* in Bavaria had few doubts that the result would be as it desired, for not until then did the opposition show signs of more than passive resistance. Nevertheless, cooperation between Catholic conservatives and radical democrats was quietly developing. The only common grounds between them were distrust of Prussia and hatred for the Bavarian liberals. These ultimately proved, however, to be sufficient. The liberals' open advocacy of Bavarian entry into the North German Confederation, combined with their drive to reform the educational system, finally angered Catholic conservatives to such a degree that, shortly after the new year, they began actively to campaign for the election of anti-Prussian deputies. The democrats had entered the field earlier, and the two campaigns soon merged. The *Zollverein* itself rapidly became a secondary issue, replaced by a more vital question: Was there to be a national union under Prussian leadership, or not? The Clericals and democrats raged against "Prussian militarism," demanding that there be no further surrender of Bavarian sovereignty. Their battle cry became "*Hie Bayern — Hie Preussen.*" [22]

The emotional fervor which sustained Catholics once they had entered the fight is typified by the feelings of young Count Preysing, who, early in 1868, was sojourning in Rome. He wrote to a friend two weeks before the election:

The party which carries treason and godlessness as its banner has enjoyed its triumph long enough, trusting our complacency and weakness. Those men have dared to speak to us of love of country, while they throw at us the phrase "ultramontanism." Must it be that this should happen at the very time when they are busy working to destroy our fatherland by evil laws, by open treason? It is necessary to make clear the meaning of the words with which they wantonly play, and, by God, it shall and will be done! [23]

As feelings grew more bitter, it was almost inevitable that religious issues would become directly involved in the campaign. In the Palatinate, for example, it began in an orthodox fashion, with a conventional division between conservatives and liberals, between particularists and nationalists, with Catholics generally favorable to the conservative particularists. Some of these, of course, were Catholics, but they were

[22] A. Doeberl, "Preysing," *Gelbe Hefte*, 2:845; Schübelin, 98–100; "Report to the King on the South German Question," April 10, 1868, Hohenlohe, *Memoirs*, 1:277–79.
[23] Preysing to Count Ludwig von Arco-Zinneberg, Rome, Jan. 28, 1868, A. Doeberl, "Preysing," *Gelbe Hefte*, 2:850.

not campaigning as such. However, soon liberal newspapers began to use the term "ultramontanism" to refer to the viewpoint of the opposition. In the Landau-Neustadt district, for example, the *Neustädter Zeitung* insisted upon the defeat of the conservative candidate because his election allegedly would play into the hands of the "ultramontanes." The *Pfalzer Kurier,* on the day before the election, reported that prominent Catholics in the Zweibrücken-Pirmasens area had received letters, presumably from clergymen, asking them to vote conservative. It also charged that priests were campaigning so actively in the district that the landscape appeared "completely black." Clergymen held, according to the *Kurier,* frequent meetings whose purpose was "without question solely connected with the burning election situation." [24] Whether or not these charges were exaggerated (and it appears from other evidence that they were not), they helped to bring religious tension to a pitch which had been unknown for a long time, with the result that the confessional division played an inordinately large role in the late stages of the campaign. As the *Pfalzer Kurier* itself put it on election eve, "*Hie Katholik — Hie Protestant* has, to our horror, become the slogan of the day." [25]

That the Catholic clergy, not only in the Palatinate, but over the entire country, intervened at the last moment seems indisputable. Practically all sources, Catholic and Protestant, make the point. It is not, however, clear whether their decision to take part was the result of instructions from the bishops. Werthern, the Prussian ambassador at Munich, concluded from his observations in the fall of 1867 that the lower and middle clergy constituted the most dangerous Bavarian enemies of Prussia. They feared, he said, that unification of Germany under Prussia would subject the Church to the domination of a Protestant government, and would make more difficult the accomplishment of their mission. The higher ranks, on the other hand, were pleasantly impressed, Werthern thought, with the favorable situation enjoyed by the Church in Prussia. He concluded at that time that if the attacks of Austrian liberals on the Church were to continue, the Bavarian episcopate would eventually come over *en masse* to the Prussian side.[26] Ten days after the election, however, Werthern informed Berlin that

[24] Ludwig Allmann, *Die Wahlbewegung zum ersten deutschen Zollparlament in der Rheinpfalz,* 56–57, 63, 65, and *passim.*

[25] *Ibid.,* 60.

[26] Werthern to Bismarck, Munich, Oct. 5, 1867, *APP,* 9: no. 198.

the rural areas had been completely dominated by the clergy, acting under direct orders of the bishops. He cited cases of peasants who had promised to vote for their landlord, but who, at the last moment, had shifted their support to the " 'ultramontane candidate,' *since they did not dare to act against the commands of their priest*" [italics in the original].[27]

Werthern's judgment must be regarded with caution, but in any event, the clergy, with or without instructions from above, threw its weight into the scale with tremendous effect. Apparently, the significance of universal direct suffrage, in use for the first time in Bavaria, did not become clear to either side until very late in the campaign. The parish priests, however, once they had become aware of the political power inherent in their ability to gain the confidence of the average voter, were the decisive factor in the election.[28] When the ballots were counted, the clerical particularists had won twenty-six of the forty-eight seats, while the democratic particularists gained only one. The *Fortschrittspartei* elected twelve candidates, while the remainder of the seats went to minor groups. Not only the number of seats won by Catholics, but also the majorities by which some of them were elected, astonished political observers. Jörg, for example, polled 10,599 votes out of 11,708 in his district. Werthern, in his report to Berlin, called these results "astounding" and "surprising," attributing them to the "infamous means" used by the Clericals. To him the election proved "that the great mass [of Bavarians] are still irresponsible and are completely in the hands of a powerful, secret party [the Papacy, the Jesuits, or both?], which has its roots outside the country." [29]

The outcome of the election came as an equally great surprise to the victors. Catholic political leaders had never advocated universal manhood suffrage, yet in the first truly democratic election they had been far more successful than ever before. The obvious conclusion was that the hated domination of the liberals might be broken through mobilizing the masses. Very shortly thereafter the Catholic-conservative minority in the *Landtag* began to command much more respect than

[27] Werthern to Bismarck, Munich, Feb. 20, 1868, *ibid.*, no. 608.

[28] Schübelin, 100; Hajo Holborn (ed.), *Aufzeichnungen und Erinnerungen aus dem Leben des Botschafters Joseph Maria von Radowitz*, 1:158.

[29] Schübelin, 100–1; Bachem, 2:233; *Stenographische Berichte über die Verhandlungen des durch die allerhöchste Verordnung vom 13. April 1866 einberufenen deutschen Zollparlaments* (hereafter abbreviated as *Stenographische Berichte Zollparlament, 1868*), 1:28; Werthern to Bismarck, Munich, Feb. 15, 1868, *APP*, 9: no. 596.

formerly, as the majority showed itself "shaken and reeling." The Catholic members became what Hohenlohe described as "arrogant," and what Catholics themselves, then and later, termed "confident." They lost no time in pressing their view that the people had spoken, that no closer ties with Prussia could, therefore, be justified.[30] Almost by accident a new and formidable political force had come into existence.

The *Zollparlament* election in Baden produced, relatively, an even more spectacular victory for the enemies of Prussian hegemony than in Bavaria. Here also Catholics played the most prominent role. Although they comprised roughly two thirds of the 1,400,000 people of Baden, in the fall of 1867 Jakob Lindau was the only member of the lower chamber who consciously represented Catholic interests. As explained above, the rural population's lack of political maturity, together with the system of indirect elections, public (*i.e.*, nonsecret) voting, and gerrymandering of districts, had kept opposition to the prevailing liberal government disorganized. Baden liberals hoped to see demonstrated by the *Zollparlament* election solid backing for the existing régime as well as overwhelming support for union with the North. The liberal-nationalist slate, therefore, was hand picked by the government, and the minister-president, Freydorf, personally signed the election manifesto of the party. Neither the government nor the majority of the chamber made any effort to conceal their intention to seek extension of the Customs Parliament's competence. Hence the word went out that it was more important for delegates to have "correct political principles" than to be experts on tariffs and taxes. Little effective opposition was expected.[31]

As in Bavaria, organized opposition of Catholics was late in making its appearance. Perhaps it might not have arisen at all had the liberals been less cocksure, and less blatantly favorable toward immediate entry of the Grand Duchy into the *Nordbund*. Opposition candidates, were, of course, named, but for a long time nothing more than a desultory campaign was undertaken in their behalf.[32] Many prominent

---

[30] Schübelin, 101; Bachem, 2:233; Journal, Feb. 19, 1868, Hohenlohe, *Memoirs*, 1:273; Gagern to Dalwigk, Munich, April 23–24, 1868, *Dalwigk Tagebücher*, Anlagen, 394.

[31] "Die badischen Wahlen zum Zollparlament," *HPB*, 61:760–62, 768. This long article should be nominated for honors as one of the most brilliant pieces of political reporting of the nineteenth century.

[32] The liberals conceded the probable election of one opposition candidate, Lindau. See *ibid.*, 761.

Catholics wanted to express disapproval of the government's policy by a complete boycott of the election, coupled with a public statement of the reasons for it. But as the date for the election drew near, it became more and more evident that there was widespread dismay in the countryside at the liberal platform. The Catholic majority of the population, still *grossdeutsch* in outlook, resented bitterly the outspoken demand for *Anschluss,* which meant to them that Baden would be swallowed up in an enlarged Prussia. Likewise, an attempt to join the Confederation, it was felt, would bring about war with France, a war which was likely to be fought largely in the fields and villages of Baden. Moreover, most people, while accepting in principle the recently enacted military reforms, were not, for obvious reasons, enthusiastic over three years of military service. In addition, taxes were already high, and the free-trade doctrines of the liberals would, if adopted by the *Zollparlament,* probably force them even higher. There still remained also the bitterness engendered by attacks on the status of the Church and the campaign to secularize education.[33]

Although conclusive proof is lacking, it may have been the results of the Bavarian election which caused Catholic leaders, only a few days before election day, to decide to make a real contest. Here too clergymen took an active part in the last stages of the campaign, and, as in Bavaria, they proved able campaigners because of the respect in which they were held by the average citizen.[34]

The final days were marked by fanatical outbursts on both sides. Liberals charged "ultramontanes" with wanting to destroy all freedom, and with planning a political reaction to be engineered with the aid of Napoleon III. Protestants heard that their faith would be endangered by the victory of "ultramontanes." Catholics, on the other hand, played on the fears of peasants and workers that the economy of the country would be ruined unless men linked with the régime were defeated. "Give your vote to Christian-thinking men who will

[33] *Ibid.,* 761, 778–88; Bachem, 2:316.

[34] The explanation offered by the correspondent of the *Historisch-politische Blätter* for the intervention of the Baden clergy, which may reveal more about the correspondent than about the situation in Baden, was this: "Persecuted, derided, reviled, and mishandled by the Liberal party and its minions, the Catholic clergy recognized its civic duty, and realized that it could not continue in inert indifference when circumstances cried for it to defend the rights and liberties of the person, the family, the community; the security of religion and the Church. The Liberals themselves have driven and forced priests into the ranks of their enemies." "Badische Wahlen," *HPB,* 61:766. See also Schübelin, 80.

know how to defend the position and the rights of the Church and the school" was one of their final admonitions.[35] The liberals made much of an alleged tie between the "ultramontanes" and the radical democrats. This, Catholics, within and outside Baden, denied vehemently, pointing out that the theory of democracy was an extension of secular liberalism, with the domination of the masses substituted for control by the bourgeoisie. Catholics, said their spokesmen, could not ally themselves with such a philosophy. Allies or not, there is no doubt that in February 1868, as in Bavaria, Catholics and democrats fought on the same side against the liberals.[36]

Once the decision for an active campaign had been taken, the Opposition, as it called itself, chose its remaining candidates quickly but carefully. It avoided naming Catholics in all the fourteen constituencies in order to minimize the clerical issue as much as possible. Likewise no candidates were named to run against the few governmental choices who were regarded as experts on economic affairs, provided they appeared willing to defend the economic interests of the Duchy. Because it was decided so late to contest the election seriously, there was no possibility of presenting a full slate of candidates in any case. The liberals on election eve were little concerned over the outcome.[37]

Under these circumstances, the result was even more remarkable. When Baden went to the polls on February 18, not one, but six Opposition candidates won seats, and two others had pluralities only slightly short of the necessary absolute majority. These two, however, were defeated in the subsequent runoff. The delegation which went to Berlin, therefore, consisted of six liberal nationalists, six of the Opposition, and two "experts" who had been unopposed. The latter two were, however, of nationalist sympathies. Lindau was victorious in two of the three districts in which he had been entered, and was replaced in one of them by Dr. Bissing in the subsequent by-election.[38] Moreover, five of the six Opposition deputies were elected as Catholics.[39] Still

[35] "Badische Wahlen," *HPB*, 61:766; Schübelin, 76–78.
[36] "Badische Wahlen," *HPB*, 61:775–77.
[37] *Ibid.*, 761–64.
[38] *Ibid.*, 768–71; Dor, 114.
[39] Bissing, Rosshirt, Lindau, Dahmen, and Freiherr von Stotzingen. In the eighth district, Lindau won by 9,140 to 7,187. Rosshirt in the sixth had 9,357 to 7,454. In the by-election Bissing polled 10,588, or 1,844 over an absolute majority. The Catholic Count Andlaw lost to Roggenbach in the fourth district, 5,324 to 8,737. See *Stenographische Berichte Zollparlament, 1868*, 1:14–15.

more noteworthy was the fact that in the original balloting the Opposition polled 90,078 votes to the liberals' 86,890, and in the runoff, the liberals, even though now forewarned, managed to garner fewer than 500 votes more than their opponents. The result might have been more striking still had not conservative Protestants, although actually hostile to the régime, been induced in some districts to vote for liberal candidates by the fanaticism of the final stages of the campaign.[40]

As might be imagined, the Catholic press broke forth in a loud chorus of rejoicing over the "victory." The attempts of the liberal press to point out that a majority of seats had in fact been won by nationalist candidates made no impression. For, although the triumph of the Catholic-*grossdeutsch* partisans was only moral, they felt fully justified in claiming that the people, for the first time given an adequate opportunity to make their opinions known at the polls, had rejected the liberals. The result was interpreted specifically as a protest against Prussianization, and as a vote for *"das ganze Deutschland,"* i.e., the reincorporation of Austria into Germany. Almost immediately Catholic leaders began to demand the introduction of universal, direct, and equal suffrage for *Landtag* elections. As the weeks went by, and the government took no such action, cries for dissolution of the *Landtag* swelled to a roar.[41]

The significance of the Baden *Zollparlament* election for the future of political Catholicism was not lost on Catholic leaders, either there or elsewhere in south Germany. The correspondent of the *Historisch-politische Blätter* pointed out, with his attention fixed as much on Munich as on Karlsruhe, that it had demonstrated the power of Catholic farmers when they became aroused against the liberal bourgeoisie. "The people," he wrote, "have now seen what can be done by decisive action." Although the liberals would, he judged, still remain the dominant party, and although popular (read "Catholic") enthusiasm for political action would probably wane, it was comforting to know that in time of crisis the masses could be aroused.[42]

The election in Württemberg resulted in an equally rude setback for

[40] "Badische Wahlen," *HPB*, 61:772, 774. Ketteler predicted that the runoff would give a great majority to the Catholic-*grossdeutsch* group. See *Dalwigk Tagebücher*, Feb. 24, 1868, 397.

[41] Schübelin, 83–84; "Badische Wahlen," *HPB*, 61:773–74, 789; Fleming to Bismarck Karlsruhe, Feb. 26, 1868, APP, 9: no. 620.

[42] "Badische Wahlen," *HPB*, 61:77–78, 793.

the national party. Clericalism, however, never became a direct issue in the campaign, although indirectly it did play a role. The government of Freiherr von Varnbüler, which had attempted to steer a course that would avoid the Charybdis of isolation, while escaping the Scylla of annexation to north Germany, had accepted the alliance treaty and the restoration of the *Zollverein* with good grace. It was, on the other hand, determined that the Customs Union should not become the agency through which the country's independence would vanish. The government, therefore, chose an official slate of candidates, committed to the moderate views of the chief minister. Nevertheless, the unbridled campaign of the *Deutsche Partei* to secure election of annexationist deputies soon stirred up the then more or less dormant anti-Prussian sentiment, with the result that Varnbüler lost control not only of the situation in general, but also of his own candidates. The *grossdeutsch*-conservatives and the *grossdeutsch*-democrats, between them including most of the Catholics, combined forces as the *Volkspartei* to combat the unionists. Soon the government candidates felt obliged to align themselves with the outright enemies of Prussia in order to avoid defeat, while the minister strove desperately to maintain a middle position.[43] Some government officials used the prestige of their offices to impress their views on the voters, inquiring of them individually, or in political meetings, whether they wanted to remain Württembergers or become Prussians. The north German constitution, according to a grim political joke that made the rounds, had only three articles: (1) Pay! (2) Be a soldier! (3) Shut up!

Catholics seem often to have been involved in this sort of vituperation. The most important Catholic newspaper, the *Deutsche Volksblatt,* commented editorially that the *Deutsche Partei* was the only enemy. It demanded that Catholics be represented in the *Zollparlament* by some of their fellows, but, since Probst and Oesterlen were men of considerable importance in the *Volkspartei,* the question seems academic.[44]

Since the Württemberg election took place more than a month later than those in Baden and Bavaria, north German politicians had plenty of time to worry about its outcome. Weeks before election day, north

[43] Schübelin, 93; Sybel, 6:312–13; Rosenberg to Bismarck, Stuttgart, March 9, 1868, *APP,* 9: no. 657; Freiherr Hermann von Mittnacht, *Rückblicke,* 74, note 1.

[44] Rosenberg to Bismarck, Stuttgart, March 9, 1868, *APP,* 9: no. 657; Schübelin, 94; *Stenographische Berichte Zollparlament, 1868,* 1:35.

Germany knew that, whatever the result there, the once expected nationalist majority in the *Zollparlament* could not possibly be realized. Rosenberg reported to Berlin on March 13 that the *Deutsche Partei* would not elect a single candidate, and the voters subsequently proved his judgment correct. Of the entire delegation, Varnbüler was probably the most sympathetic toward Prussia. At least three Catholic *Grossdeutsche* were included — Probst, Oesterlen, and Schäffle. Probst received more than five thousand votes above an absolute majority.[45] The *Deutsches Volksblatt* puckishly referred to the outcome of the election as "a most striking practical joke,"[46] which they will respect out there in the world, whether they rejoice or wail over it." [47]

In Berlin the reaction was understandably gloomy. The Württemberg minister there reported, at the end of March, that there had been a great opening of eyes in the Prussian capital. After the Bavarian and Baden elections, a favorable outcome had not been expected, but no one had foreseen the magnitude of the defeat which the Swabian national party suffered.[48] Only in Hesse-Darmstadt did the vote go as expected. The unpopularity of Dalwigk and his policies made possible in nearly all districts the victory of men favorable to union with the North. In the final tabulation, the four south German states sent to Berlin forty-nine particularists against only thirty-six nationalists.[49]

Bismarck and his colleagues had not been overly enthusiastic about the plans of the more sanguine south German nationalists. They feared that if the southern delegation was strongly in favor of immediate German unity through the *Zollparlament,* an insoluble dilemma would arise. Either north Germany would have to honor the request, in which case war with France at an inopportune moment could hardly be avoided, or she would have to rebuff the southerners and chance the probable cooling of annexationist sentiment.[50] Moreover, Bismarck

[45] Könneritz to Freiherr von Friesen (foreign minister of Saxony), Berlin, Feb. 26, 1868, *APP,* 9: no. 622; Rosenberg, Report, Stuttgart, March 13, 1868, *ibid.,* no. 689, note 3; Rosenberg to ———?, Stuttgart, March 25, 1868, *ibid.,* no. 689, note 1; *Stenographische Berichte Zollparlament, 1868,* 1:59; A. E. F. Schäffle, *Aus meinem Leben,* 1:140. The *Deutsche Partei* did not count on winning more than four or five seats. See August L. Reyscher to Friedrich Oetker, Cannstadt (Württemberg), Feb. 24, 1868, Heyderhoff, *Liberalismus,* 1:410–12.

[46] "Urkräftigen Schwabenstreich." The pun is lost in translation.

[47] Schübelin, 96–97.

[48] Spitzemberg to Varnbüler, Berlin, March 30, 1868, *APP,* 9: no. 692.

[49] Sybel, 6:314; Vogt, 168; Ziekursch, 1:247.

[50] Spitzemberg to Varnbüler, Berlin, March 30, 1868, *APP,* 9: no. 692. See also Chapter Four, note 75.

had no desire to see a parliament get the credit for completing the union. What he did hope was that the *Zollparlament* would demonstrate a widespread desire for unity, without, however, forcing the issue. In view of the election returns the fear was unnecessary, and the hope was vain.

In order to give psychological emphasis to the *Zollparlament* as the embodiment of a Germany united in spirit, it had been decided to sandwich its sessions between two halves of the 1868 North German Reichstag meeting. Accordingly, the Reichstag was convened on March 23, with the understanding that after four weeks it would recess for the duration of the *Zollparlament,* in which, of course, its members would sit as the north German representatives. Upon adjournment of the Customs Parliament, the Reichstag would resume its session.[51]

Under the circumstances, it was with trepidation rather than anticipation that the National Liberals awaited the opening of the *Zollparlament.* When the deputies assembled on the afternoon of April 27, they listened to an address of welcome by the King of Prussia in his capacity as *Zollverein* president. The speech was filled with the customary platitudes. Conspicuously absent, however, was reference to any possible significance of the new body for the political unification of Germany.[52] In view of the bitter disappointment of nationalists over the results of the south German elections, it is not surprising that those elections themselves produced hot debates during the early days of the session. The formalities of seating the south German deputies gave the National Liberals an opportunity to accuse the Württemberg government of grossly illegal political activity during the campaign. The substance of the charges made by the Prussian, Braun of Wiesbaden, and the fiery Metz from Hesse-Darmstadt was that government pressure had been widely used to secure the election of deputies hostile to Prussia. It was further charged that the government in Stuttgart had closed its eyes to a campaign of terrorism against nationalist candidates. To prove their claims, Braun and Metz cited specific instances and read election propaganda which had been circulated in Württemberg by officials, presumably under the control of the ministry. Both men maintained that the defeat of the *Deutsche Partei* had

[51] Sybel, 7:3. Both halves of the Reichstag session will be dealt with in the following chapter.

[52] *Ibid.; Stenographische Berichte Zollparlament, 1868,* April 27, 1868, 1:2–3.

resulted from an open alliance between the government and the *Volkspartei*, the latter composed largely of "ultramontanes." [53] According to Metz, the only link between the members of this "unholy alliance" was "dislike for the present trend of German development, and hatred for the state which is the leader of the new Germany to be created." [54]

Varnbüler answered, denying that there had been any agreement between the government and the *Volkspartei*. The *Deutsche Partei*, he pointed out, had campaigned on the issue of extending the competence of the *Zollparlament*. The election had simply registered the will of the people against that proposal. Aroused Swabian patriotism had overwhelmed the supporters of Prussia. If the *Deutsche Partei* had been willing to abide by the purposes of the *Zollverein* treaty, it would undoubtedly have elected some candidates. But, he concluded, "one can love his country, though it be small." [55] Mittnacht, Varnbüler's ministerial colleague, gave fundamentally the same argument. The Württemberg government, he said, certainly had had no reason to love the *Deutsche Partei*, which had openly promised that it would propose at Berlin to ignore "this worthless and foolish *Zollverein* treaty." The government had opposed the *Deutsche Partei*, but not in alliance with any other group, for "to defeat this party, no alliance was necessary." [56]

The debate had arisen technically over a motion to request the *Präsidium* of the *Zollbundesrath* — i.e., the Prussian government — to begin negotiations with Württemberg with a view toward securing revision of her election laws to prevent repetition of these and other alleged abuses. The motion passed by a vote of 162 to 105. In the minority, however, were found practically all the particularists from the southern states, a high percentage of whom were Catholic, plus the antigovernment Catholics from the North German Reichstag.[57] This was the first striking instance of political cooperation between north and south German Catholics. Here for the first time was seen in action what soon became known as the south German fraction.

This parliamentary group, which in a sense was to dominate the entire session, consisted primarily of the forty-nine particularist deputies from Bavaria, Baden, and Württemberg. For many of these men,

---

[53] *Stenographische Berichte Zollparlament, 1868,* May 1, 1868, 1: 35–37, 39–40.
[54] *Ibid.,* 39.
[55] *Ibid.,* 45–46.
[56] *Ibid.,* 42–43.
[57] *Ibid.,* 50–52.

the journey to Berlin represented their first contact with the world outside the narrow frontiers of their own state, or, in some cases, district. The north German capital was strange to them, and, because of their prejudices, it was likely to remain so. Moreover, the procedure of the Reichstag, which the *Zollparlament* followed, was unfamiliar to them.[58]

Under the circumstances, it was only to be expected that these lonely men, who felt themselves in hostile territory, would form some sort of association. In a fashion which strikingly resembles the formation of the clubs that were the nuclei of later political parties during the early days of the great French Revolution, or in the Frankfurt of 1848, these south German particularists began to congregate in the evenings at the Hotel de Petersbourg, 31 Unter den Linden, where Thüngen, Hafenbrädl, and some of the other Bavarian Catholics were residing. The hotel was only a stone's throw from the meeting place of the parliament, which added an element of convenience.

The original impetus for organizing a political fraction out of this nebulous group, which shared little but a dislike of union with north Germany and a determination to prevent widening the competence of the Customs Parliament, seems to have come from Probst of Württemberg.[59] However, had it not been for the cooperation of Prussian Catholics — Reichensperger, Mallinckrodt, and especially Windthorst — the group, because of the political inexperience of its members, could hardly have achieved its objective of bringing to nought the plans of the ardent nationalists. Windthorst, who, like the others, was invited to the *Petersburger Hof* as a guest of the south German Catholics, offered his services as adviser on Reichstag parliamentary procedure, thus lessening the danger that the newborn fraction would come to grief on technicalities.[60]

[58] Speakers for either side in every debate, for example, were chosen by lot from lists of those who indicated a desire to be heard. Lindau never got to speak during the entire session, and left before it ended. See Dor, 114–16.

[59] Zuchhardt, 36; Ziekursch, 1:247; Schübelin, 105; Spielhofer, "Bayrische Zentrumspartei," *HPB*, 165:419. Jörg wrote later that the elements of the *Süddeutsche Fraktion* were approximately as compatible as fire and water. "Aus dem Berliner Zollparlament" (Part I), May 10, 1868, *HPB*, 61:811.

[60] Schübelin, 105–6; Spielhofer, "Bayrische Zentrumspartei," *HPB*, 165:419; Zuchhardt, 36; Rachfall, "Windthorst," *Preussische Jahrbücher*, 135:228. Jörg gave Windthorst credit for the organization of the fraction. See "Berliner Zollparlament" (Part I), *HPB*, 61:810. See also Schäffle, 1:142; Roggenbach to Queen Augusta, Berlin, May 26, 1868, Julius Heyderhoff (ed.), *Im Ring der Gegner Bismarcks*, 86–87. The Prussian gov-

The intimate relationship of Windthorst, Reichensperger, and Mallinckrodt to the south German fraction emphasizes one of the most important points about it: that it was basically, although by no means entirely, an organization of Catholics. Five of the six members from Baden, the vast majority of the Bavarians, and several of the most important Württembergers were Catholic. Dr. Bissing, Lindau's friend, was elected chairman.[61] That the majority was Catholic was, however, important, fortuitous; for such unity as the fraction possessed came not from that fact but from the aversion, shared by all its members, to a Prussianized Germany. It included a number of Protestants — Varnbüler, Mittnacht, and Moritz Mohl of Württemberg, for example. It embraced, besides, aristocrats and democrats, protectionists and free traders, *Grossdeutsche* and narrow particularists. Among its "guests" were the atheistic Saxon Social Democrats, Bebel and Liebknecht.[62]

To its enemies the south German fraction represented three distinct trends: particularism, "ultramontanism," and democracy. Except for the opprobrious reference to Catholicism, this characterization is not far from the mark. Because of the fantastically diverse interests represented, it could put forth no positive program, yet for a group whose outlook on almost all questions was totally negative, it had phenomenal success.[63] It had also, as will appear later, an important bearing on the subsequent development of political Catholicism in Germany.

The question of extending the *Zollverein*'s competence, which had occupied the minds of German politicians for months, finally reached the floor in a somewhat watered-down form on May 7, as a motion for an address to the throne authored by the two fiery Hessian unionists, Metz and Bamberger. It was signed by nine other south Germans and by most of the north German National Liberals. The proposed

ernment brought home Joseph Maria von Radowitz, a Catholic member of the embassy at Munich, in an attempt to establish liaison with the Bavarian Catholic delegates, hoping that their intense particularism might be broken. Needless to say, the move failed. See Holborn, *Radowitz*, 1:165–66.

[61] Bachem, 3:24–25; Schübelin, 105–6; "Berliner Zollparlament" (Part I), *HPB*, 61:808–10; Zuchhardt, 36; Spielhofer, "Bayrische Zentrumspartei," *HPB*, 165:419; Rachfall, "Windthorst," *Preussische Jahrbücher*, 135:228.

[62] Jörg called Bismarck the "real patron" of the fraction, for he alone, through his policy, held it together. "Berliner Zollparlament" (Part I), *HPB*, 61:806.

[63] Schübelin, 105–6; "Berliner Zollparlament" (Part I), *HPB*, 61:808; Ludwig Bamberger, Letter to His Constituents, Aachen, June 3, 1868, *Vertrauliche Briefe aus dem Zollparlament*, 46–47.

address referred to the *Zollparlament* as "the representative of the German people," and spoke of the necessity of "complete unification of the entire German fatherland," adding that the "unavoidable necessity of a national representation for all branches of public life cannot be denied our people permanently." Finally, it referred to Austria in a manner that left no doubt of the permanence of her exclusion from Germany.[64]

Reichensperger began the attack on the address by seeking to have it ruled out of order on the ground that it went beyond the competence of the house. As he doubtless expected, the attempt failed.[65] Then Bennigsen, speaking as *Referent* for the committee which had conducted the preliminary discussion, made a speech which was both logical and moderate, seeking to calm the fears of the south Germans. The motion, he insisted, was in no way an attempt to "majoritize" them. Any attempt to convert the *Zollparlament* into a *Vollparlament* would require the approval of all the governments which had signed the original treaties, for the treaties themselves did not confer any such power upon the esteemed gentlemen before him. All that the address proposed was to set forth the spirit of German unity for all the world to see. That, to him at least, was nothing less than a national duty.[66]

Freiherr von Thüngen, one of the most important members of the Bavarian senate, answered Bennigsen for the south German fraction. He began by dashing whatever hopes there had been that Bennigsen had impressed the recalcitrant southerners. Thüngen admitted that he suffered from a severe disadvantage. Bennigsen could talk about national duty, while he himself had to adhere to the treaties and to their intended purpose. The majority of the south German people opposed any ties to Prussia more binding than those provided in the treaties because they feared loss of their independence. That fear was not, he added, based purely on emotion, but on calculation of interest as well. The South, which loved Germany as much as any other section, would, therefore, honor the treaties of alliance, and would fight willingly if any foreign power were to attack Germany. The *Zollverein* treaties, he was glad to agree with Bennigsen, could not be altered without the approval of the south German governments and parliaments. How-

[64] *Stenographische Berichte Zollparlament, 1868*, 2: Drucksache no. 7, pp. 1, 3–4. One Prussian Catholic Conservative, Hosius, from the Rhineland, signed the motion.

[65] *Ibid.*, May 7, 1868, 1:85–87.

[66] *Ibid.*, 91–95.

ever, the proposed address, although it dealt only with aspirations and not with actualities, expressed hopes that south Germany could not share. Moreover, the *Zollparlament* had to have regard for far more than its own wishes, since whatever opinions it expressed were bound to be heard throughout Europe. The south German deputies, he again reminded the house, represented their constituents for one purpose alone, the purpose defined in the *Zollverein* treaties. Any attempt of the assembly to arrogate to itself rights which it did not lawfully possess could only increase southern distrust of north Germany's motives. Since, in any case, the *Zollparlament* was incompetent to do so, whatever action it took along those lines would have no legal significance.[67]

The Heidelberg professor, J. C. Bluntschli, entered the fray for the southern nationalists with an impassioned speech against a motion to table the address. "I recognize," shouted Dr. Bluntschli, "no south German people! I recognize four south German governments; there is no south German people! I recognize only one German people." Though his address received a thunderous ovation from the National Liberals, the south German fraction was not visibly impressed.[68] An impasse appeared to have been reached.

Actually two motions had been offered to reject the Metz-Bamberger proposal. One, providing that it be simply passed over without comment, bore the signatures of Reichensperger, Mallinckrodt, Windthorst, Kleinsorgen, and others. The second, offered by Waldeck (*Fortschrittspartei*), proposed to table the address "in consideration that" the efforts of the *Zollparlament* in the economic sphere would contribute to the ultimate establishment of an all-German parliament. This, of course, was also propaganda for German unification, but in a much milder form than the Metz-Bamberger draft address. Bismarck, who, because of his worry over possible foreign reaction, was hostile to the address, hoped to see the Waldeck resolution adopted. He realized that the debate which would inevitably arise on its wording would produce manifestations of German national sentiment which he could later use as he saw fit. He was, however, doomed to disappointment, for the Reichensperger version was adopted by the house, 186 to 150. The south German fraction voted for it *en bloc*, while only a small handful of northern Catholics failed to support their fellows. Bismarck, fore-

[67] *Ibid.*, 95–96.
[68] *Ibid.*, 101.

seeing the probable unanimity of the southern particularists, at the last moment signaled the Prussian Conservatives to go along with the majority, in order to avoid subsequent difficulties which might have resulted from a very close vote. The *Fortschrittspartei* voted for the motion on similar grounds.[69]

Much of Bismarck's desire not to press the issue came from his knowledge that the south German fraction had already commissioned five of its members — Jörg and Freiherr von Zu Rhein of Bavaria, Probst and von Neurath of Württemberg, and Rosshirt of Baden —[70] to draft a "declaration of right." This was to be read to the assembly in case the address was adopted, after which the fraction intended to walk out *en masse*.[71]

There could be no doubt that the absolute unwillingness of the south German fraction to compromise stopped the national party in its tracks, and the Catholic press of south Germany did not hesitate to gloat over the discomfiture of the *Kleindeutsche*.[72] The *Badischer Beobachter* rejoiced that "what we predicted has been fulfilled, only more impressively [than we hoped], namely that the halo with which party spirit surrounded the . . . heads of a limited circle among us has been unmercifully torn off in Berlin." [73] "A Badener," writing in the *Kölnische Blätter,* called the parliamentary victory *"summa summarum."* [74]

Deprived of its hoped-for political significance by the defeat of the address, the *Zollparlament* turned now to the more prosaic tasks for which it had been elected. The details of most of its debates and decisions need not concern us here. The most important item of business was the ratification of a new treaty between the *Zollverein* and the Habsburg Empire. Although it leaned definitely in the direction of free trade, the majority of the protectionists from Baden and Bavaria, members of the south German fraction, hesitated, because of their sentimental attachment to Austria, to vote against an arrangement which Vienna so obviously desired. It was consequently approved with only seventeen negative votes, nine of them cast by south German

[69] *Ibid.*, 106–8; Wimpfen to Beust, Berlin, May 9, 1868, *APP,* 10: no. 18; Oncken, *Bennigsen,* 2:162; "Berliner Zollparlament" (Part I), *HPB,* 61:811–12.
[70] Neurath was the only Protestant.
[71] Schübelin, 114–15.
[72] *Ibid.*, 115; Spielhofer, "Bayrische Zentrumspartei," *HPB,* 165:420.
[73] Schübelin, 115.
[74] *Ibid.*

Catholics. There were also fifteen Catholic abstentions, including several of the Poles and a few of the southerners.[75]

The adoption of the treaty meant a serious loss of revenue for several members of the *Zollverein,* with the Prussian government suffering the greatest injury. Anticipating this, Delbrück had proposed to recover the losses through tax increases and higher import duties on tobacco and petroleum. The south German fraction opposed both tariff measures since either would cause economic hardship to south Germany. When the final vote was taken, Catholic members of the Reichstag supported the fraction practically unanimously, and thus the occasion furnishes another example of parliamentary cooperation between north and south German Catholics. Only two Catholic members, both north Germans, voted for Waldeck's amended version of the tobacco tariff, which was adopted 167 to 131 on its second reading, May 16. The Poles, as usual, abstained.[76] Moreover, only three north German Catholic votes were cast in favor of the duty on petroleum at its second reading two days later, at which time it failed, 149 to 86. On this ballot, however, a number of south Germans, as well as the Poles, abstained.[77] The third and final reading of either measure became unnecessary when Bismarck announced the unwillingness of the *Bundesrath* to accept the tariff on tobacco unless the petroleum duty were also enacted, and, therefore, withdrew the entire measure. Again Catholics had made a contribution to the defeat of Bismarck's plans, although the petroleum tariff failed largely because of National Liberal opposition.

During the debates on the Austrian treaty, and on the tariff measures related to it, the question of German unity periodically injected itself into the discussions, usually through the attempts of rabid unionists to reap from the *Zollparlament* whatever propaganda harvest was still possible. The south German fraction was usually able to defeat these efforts by chorusing "Keep to the subject," until the speaker subsided.[78]

[75] Sybel, 7:25–29; *Stenographische Berichte Zollparlament, 1868,* May 11, 1868, 1:153–54, 176–77, 186–89.

[76] Sybel, 7:26–27; *Stenographische Berichte Zollparlament, 1868,* May 16, 1868, 1:229–31, 237–39.

[77] Sybel, 7:45–46; *Stenographische Berichte Zollparlament, 1868,* May 18, 1868, 1:376–78.

[78] *Stenographische Berichte Zollparlament, 1868,* 1:109–385, *passim*; Schübelin, 117.

The most important political debate following the rejection of the address came on May 18 when Bamberger, speaking ostensibly on economic problems which the *Zollverein* treaty with Austria would cause for Hesse-Darmstadt, wandered off into a discussion of the political misfortunes of that divided Grand Duchy. Repeated shouts of the south Germans *"zur Sache"* this time failed to halt the contentious Hessian, and several of his fellow nationalists also managed to add their voices to what soon turned into another appeal for national unity through extension of the *Zollparlament*'s competence. After the debate had gone on for some time, Probst issued a warning in behalf of the south German fraction. The accusation that hatred of Prussia was the reason for south Germany's reluctance to consider expanding the functions of the body was false, he said. The true reason was that south Germany believed the *Zollparlament,* as originally conceived, to be capable of rendering a real service to the nation. If, however, it was to be of any value, some degree of harmony between the various groups was vital. That harmony was possible only if political controversies were excluded from the discussions, for, in the face of existing disagreements, the constant recurrence of political arguments could only increase, not lessen, tension between the sections.[79]

Seeking to calm the atmosphere, Bismarck rose quickly to deny any desire, either of himself or of the northern confederation, to exert pressure on south Germany. "You consider us," he added with grim humor, "more oppressive than we are." [80] The National Liberal, Lasker, nevertheless returned to the attack, denying the right of Probst to speak for south Germany. He reminded the house that at least a third of the Bavarian delegates did not "have the honor to be represented either politically or religiously" by Probst. Furthermore, he thought that perhaps the representatives of Baden and of Hesse might prefer to speak for themselves. Probst, he suggested, represented only Würt-

[79] *Stenographische Berichte Zollparlament, 1868,* May 18, 1868, 1:259–65; Bamberger, Letter to His Constituents, Berlin, May 22, 1868, *Vertrauliche Briefe,* 25.

[80] *Stenographische Berichte Zollparlament, 1868,* May 18, 1868, 1:265. Bismarck's expressed wish to let the South choose its own time was apparently sincere. See his interview with the British journalist, W. Beatty-Kingston, Berlin, Sept. 22, 1867: "But we have since [the War of 1866] been very careful about south Germany, and have remained quite passive. We can stop as we are for ten years or more, only insisting on the terms of the treaty of Prague, but the southerners will not let us, and if they come to offer us an accession of power, we shall certainly not kick them downstairs." Heinrich von Poschinger (ed.), *Conversations with Prince Bismarck,* 93.

temberg. Rosshirt of Baden, however, came to the defense of Probst. Although, he said, the discussion had turned into a second address debate, he could not, despite his resolution to avoid political questions, remain silent. Lasker, he insisted, assuming his goal was actually the unity of Germany, should not have brought up the religious issue, which was in no way relevant to the question. Yet he felt impelled to stress again the point which had been made often before, that in case of foreign attack Germany would be united, even without an address to the King, even without treaties of alliance.[81]

Up to this point the south Germans had been carrying on the debate unaided by members of the Reichstag. But now Windthorst took occasion to second the remarks of Probst and Rosshirt, and, if possible, to restore harmony to the discussion. Like the others, he denied any desire to enter upon a political debate. Yet some of Bismarck's words deserved comment. He agreed completely with the Chancellor that no pressure ought to be exerted to force the southern states into the *Nordbund*. Many words had been spoken for and against *extension* of the *Zollparlament*'s competence. The argument, however, avoided a much more important question: What *was* the actual competence of the *Zollparlament*? This question could not be answered merely by perusing the treaties, for they were cold and lifeless, acquiring vitality only through the interpretations of those who implemented them. If there were agreement among members of the *Zollparlament* that the treaties should furnish a basis for political unification, then unity through extension of its competence would be easily accomplished. It was precisely because such agreement did not exist that the almost daily recurrence of rash and provocative speeches was causing irreparable harm to the national cause.

For the unification of Germany there is necessary first of all a meeting of minds. I question whether this debate today has contributed to a meeting of minds. I am inclined to deny it. One must look not only into his own mind but also into the minds of others. If we continue in this manner, we shall not succeed in extending the competence of the parliament, but, rather, we shall destroy it.[82]

Windthorst's address, plus, perhaps, the weariness of the delegates, brought the discussion back to its ostensible purpose. At its close

---

[81] *Stenographische Berichte Zollparlament, 1868*, May 18, 1868, 1:265–66, 271.
[82] *Ibid.*, 273–74.

sometime later, however, Probst felt impelled to inject a "personal remark," denouncing Lasker's attack on his patriotism, and on that of south Germans generally. The Luxemburg affair, he reminded the house, had proved the willingness of south Germany to make any necessary sacrifice for the nation.[83]

The first session of the *Zollparlament* came to an end on May 23 with a farewell address by the King of Prussia. The irreconcilable division within the body made it necessary that King Wilhelm's remarks again be confined to generalities. After reviewing the accomplishments of the session with warm approval, he said a few words about the political future of Germany, but made, naturally, no specific recommendations. His fondest hope, he said, was that the session had increased the confidence of North and South in one another, and that it had destroyed some of the preconceived notions which had so long hindered expression of that "love for the common fatherland which is the equal inheritance of all the German peoples." [84]

The King at first had been so disappointed with the meager accomplishments of the *Zollparlament* that he had declined, with Bismarck's approval, to deliver the closing address in person. The Chancellor, however, after consultation with Hohenlohe and other southern nationalists, became convinced that a bad situation ought not to be made worse, as would certainly be the case if the King gave the parliament an impression of *mauvais humeur*. He accordingly prevailed upon his sovereign to reconsider.[85]

A considerable number of the south German deputies did not hear the King's address, for the exodus from Berlin had already begun several days before. Nevertheless, on the day following the close of the session, some of the southern delegates, before dispersing, issued to the press a "Declaration of the South German Fraction to Its Constituents." This manifesto contained a stinging rebuke to those who were working for entry of the southern states into the North German *Bund*. Its key paragraph stated:

We have again recognized that the entry of the southern states into the North German Confederation would further neither the unity of the whole nation, nor the constitutional freedom and special interests

---

[83] *Ibid.*, 283.
[84] *Ibid.*, May 23, 1868, 387–88.
[85] King William to Queen Augusta, Babelsberg, May 21, 1868, *APP*, 10: no. 37, note 1.

of south Germany. Rather, . . . the constitution of north Germany makes much more desirable maintenance of the independence of the south German states. Especially the overwhelming preference given to military preparations in the North German Confederation interferes with the pursuit of material and spiritual interests, and leads, without lessening the burdens on the Prussian people, to increasing them for her confederates. As a necessary result of the traditional policy of Prussia, this burden will be a lasting one.[86]

The authors of the declaration favored, instead, the establishment of a loose federal union — more cultural than political in character — of the southern states, which would remain connected to Prussia only by the existing military alliances. They expressed confidence that these goals could be achieved "through a decidedly liberal policy." [87]

None of the deputies who had departed before the conclusion of the session were party to the declaration. Others refused to sign it "for diplomatic reasons," and, in fact, a few seem to have hastened their departure to avoid committing themselves. Still others, of whom Jörg is the most striking example, objected to it because they felt it did not go far enough, and because of its mild endorsement of liberalism.[88] Jörg remarked in the next issue of the *Blätter* that in some respects he shared the hope of its authors, but not their faith that the desired result was possible. He condemned the declaration, moreover, as self-contradictory, since he felt that the independence of south Germany was incompatible with the Prussian alliances. Finally, the line of action proposed by the declaration could only fail in the end, for its authors were themselves obviously liberals at heart, and would, therefore, inevitably fall prey to their professed enemies, the liberal nationalists.[89] Jörg's retreat from his 1866 position was now complete. The Prussian annexations in north Germany had severely shaken his faith in Bismarck's conservatism, and the Chancellor's continued cooperation with the National Liberals was beyond forgiving.

Most of the south German deputies, however, less extreme and less politically sophisticated than Jörg, left Berlin in high spirits, with the

[86] H. Schulthess, *Europäischer Geschichtskalender*, 4 (1868): 73–74; Hoffmann to Dalwigk, May 23, 1868, *APP*, 10: no. 37, note 1.
[87] Spielhofer, "Bayrische Zentrumspartei," *HPB*, 165: 420; "Aus dem Berliner Zollparlament" (Part III), June 13, 1868, *HPB*, 61: 980, 982.
[88] Schulthess, *Europäischer Geschichtskalender*, 4 (1868): 74; "Berliner Zollparlament" (Part III), *HPB*, 61: 979, 982.
[89] "Berliner Zollparlament" (Part III), *HPB*, 61: 979–80.

conviction that they had laid the foundation for the resurrection of a *grossdeutsch* party which could successfully withstand the pressure of liberals for national union on their own terms. As the Catholic, Schäffle of Württemberg, expressed it, obviously parodying Miquel's famous *mot* of 1867, the south German fraction had brought the Prussian locomotive to a *permanent* halt at the Main. In order to give some continuity to the parliamentary alliance before leaving Berlin, the group which had issued the declaration named a committee, consisting of Thüngen (Bavaria), Probst (Württemberg), and von Stotzingen (Baden), to consult periodically on future policy. That the latter two were Catholics is not without significance.[90]

The extent of the disaster for those who had hoped to use the *Zollparlament* as an instrument to achieve national unity is apparent from the almost universal gloom which reigned in Berlin among government and National Liberal circles after the end of the session. Bismarck's often expressed belief that eventually the South would voluntarily seek to join the northern Confederation had apparently been proved an illusion. According to an Austrian diplomat in Berlin, the chief topic of conversation after the adjournment of the *Zollparlament* was how to strengthen the North German Confederation, rather than how to convert it into a German Empire. He predicted that ultimately this line of thought would result in the complete disappearance of the smaller states of the *Bund*.[91] No one in Berlin, wrote the Hessian minister to Bavaria, showed any satisfaction with the *Zollparlament*. "It has become clear to all that the political fruits of this institution will ripen more slowly than most had believed."[92]

Nothing which happened in succeeding months did anything to dispel this gloomy atmosphere. In retrospect, therefore, the first *Zollparlament* session does appear to mark the end of a period and a policy. The enthusiastic and naïve belief of the National Liberals that the North German Confederation would be a brief transitional stage gave way to a realization that the existing state of affairs might endure for perhaps a decade. Bismarck, who had long believed that war with France would be a prerequisite for completion of the Hohenzollern Empire, found his viewpoint confirmed, except that obviously the war

[90] Spielhofer, "Bayrische Zentrumspartei," *HPB*, 165:420; Schulthess, *Europäischer Geschichtskalender*, 4 (1868): 74.

[91] Münch to Beust, Berlin, June 24, 1868, *APP*, 10: no. 78.

[92] Hoffmann to Dalwigk, Berlin, May 23, 1868, *ibid.*, no. 37, note 1.

would not arise out of French resistance to an attempt of the southern states to join the *Nordbund,* as he had apparently once felt. Since Catholics of both sections were among the chief architects of the rebuff, Bismarck's anger and that of National Liberals toward "ultramontanes" increased. Hence the first session of the *Zollparlament* is also a significant milestone on the road to the *Kulturkampf.*[93]

The defeat of the nationalists at Berlin in no way produced a relaxation of south German fear of Prussia. The entire Württemberg delegation, with the possible exception of Varnbüler, returned home convinced that Prussia was determined to absorb her north German confederates into a greater Prussia, and that if the South was to escape a similar fate, means of defense had to be devised quickly. Despite the unwillingness of some Württemberg members of the south German fraction to sign the Berlin Declaration, there was to be no rebirth of sentiment favorable to the *Deutsche Partei,* which continued to see its already narrow base of popular support further undermined.[94]

In Bavaria the adjournment of the *Zollparlament* was followed by a period of increasingly violent agitation against Hohenlohe by the Catholic opposition. The Clericals, still a minority in the lower chamber, demanded ever more vociferously the dismissal of the minister, dissolution of the chamber, and new elections. The *Münchener Volksbote* raged at Prussia, calling her, among other things, the cause of Europe's ruin, the destroyer of commerce and trade, and the sole threat to the peace of the continent.[95] Jörg, disillusioned with the liberal tendencies of the Berlin Declaration, continued to castigate the south German fraction. No southern confederation was possible, he expostulated in the *Blätter,* when "two ministers and a member of the diplomatic staff of Bavaria have regularly assisted" in the *Zollparlament* those who wanted to force Bavaria under the Prussian yoke.[96] He recognized also that the tactics which had been followed in Berlin by the south German fraction could not be continued indefinitely. The fraction had stood firm as if "on a rock in the heaving sea," but the

[93] Oncken, *Bennigsen,* 2:162–63; Bismarck, *Gedanken und Erinnerungen,* 2:71–73; Bismarck's conversation with Carl Schurz, Berlin, Jan. 29, 1867, *GW,* 7:235–36. On the *Zollparlament* elections and Bismarck's attitude toward Catholicism, see Bismarck to Arnim, Berlin, April 12, 1868, *APP,* 9: no. 722.

[94] Von Gasser (Bavarian minister to Württemberg) to King Ludwig, no date, *APP,* 10: no. 37, note 1.

[95] Spielhofer, "Bayrische Zentrumspartei," *HPB,* 165:420; *APP,* 10: no. 47, note 4.

[96] "Berliner Zollparlament" (Part II), *HPB,* 61:904.

southern states had to choose between "escaping from their lonely rock to the firm shore, or being swept away by the pounding surf." [97]

In what direction did that "firm shore" lie? There had to be established, Jörg wrote, a new conservative party on a new basis, "a party which must find its support in the people." [98] That party had to take a stand against the liberal bourgeoisie on the great social questions of the age, not on purely political or confessional issues, which were rapidly declining in importance.[99] The editor was calling here for the creation of a new Catholic popular party. His minimizing of confessionalism, though sincere, meant merely that, in his view, Catholics had to devote their energies to a more vital cause than combating Protestantism as such. They had to close ranks against the godless doctrine of liberalism, which was, he was convinced, destroying the moral character of man and society. They had to fight against the men who propagated that doctrine in Bavaria; they had to prevent the bloodless conquest of south Germany by those who, under the guise of unifying the nation, would fix permanently the domination of an omnipotent, devouring state over all the German people.

The call of Jörg and others for a party which would organize the Catholic masses was heard in Bavaria almost immediately, and in Baden a little later. In Württemberg, Catholics were already deeply involved in the fortunes of the *Volkspartei*. Even in Hesse-Darmstadt there were signs that the Catholic minority would attempt again to build a party dedicated to overthrowing the friends of Prussia who controlled the *Landtag*.

Ironically enough, it was Bismarck who, more than anyone or anything else, was responsible for the alliance of Catholicism and democracy in south Germany. Universal, direct suffrage, which had come to south Germany at his behest, had given Catholics their first great political victory. The weapon chosen by the Prussian statesman to win the German masses in 1866 had been used two years later with devastating effect against him in three of the south German states.[100] And during 1869 and 1870 it was to give south German Catholics the means to place the completion of the German Empire itself in jeopardy.

[97] *Ibid.*, 900.
[98] *Ibid.* (Part III), 981.
[99] *Ibid.*; "Das Verhältnis von und zu Oesterreich," *ibid.*, 62:79–80.
[100] See Schäffle, 1:142–43.

Chapter 6

North and South during the Pause, 1868–1869

I₦ ᴛʜᴇ period immediately after the close of the first *Zollparlament* session, eager *kleindeutsch* nationalists and their bitter enemies alike found ample cause for wondering whether the War of 1866 had actually settled the German question decisively in favor of Prussia.[1] However, neither the dejection of the one group nor the elation of the other was completely justified. Both arose more from the failure properly to anticipate the results of the elections than from the results themselves, or from the subsequent effectiveness of the south German fraction. The improbable, even the impossible, had happened, and the ultimate outcome of the struggle no longer seemed certain to either side.

Bismarck, however, never having shared the sanguine expectations of his more enthusiastic supporters, suffered proportionally less disillusionment. In a dinner conversation, which took place while the *Zollparlament* was meeting, between Bismarck and General von Suckow, the Prussian officer who had been appointed in 1867 to command the Württemberg military establishment, the Chancellor gave the impression of calmness. He observed that, in view of the election results, north Germany could not legitimately seek to move beyond the existing tariff and alliance treaties. For Germany to become united by the end of the century, he remarked, would be a considerable achievement, while if unity were realized within five or ten years it would represent "an unhoped-for manifestation of the grace of God."[2] He

[1] Observers noted, for example, at the third German *Bundesschiessen*, held in Vienna in August 1868, with sportsmen from all over Germany participating, that the *grossdeutsch* idea was still very much alive. It appeared, wrote one witness, as if the battle of Königgrätz had never occurred when one listened to the tenor of the speeches, or to the cheers for the Habsburgs. See Ziekursch, 1:247.
[2] Conversation between Bismarck and General von Suckow, Berlin, May 11, 1868, *GW*, 7: no. 201.

had no doubts, he said, that the ultimate effects of the *Zollparlament*, in which men from both sections sat together in one body, would be salutary, for the South would gradually lose its fear that Prussia intended to use force to complete the national union. "Force we will not and may not use." [3]

Bismarck reverted to this theme several months later in a conversation with the ubiquitous south German journalist, Julius Fröbel. The unification of Germany, he stated, ought not to carry with it the seeds of an unhealthy hostility between sections. Rather, the South could successfully be assimilated into a new national state only through its own free choice, "even if it takes thirty years to accomplish the task." [4]

Sufficient evidence is lacking for a final judgment on whether Bismarck's protestations of unconcern represented a pose adopted to influence public opinion in south Germany, or whether they approximated his actual views at the time. Any accurate appraisal must take into account his concern over the rising threat of political Catholicism in Bavaria, Baden, and Württemberg. His official correspondence at the time of the *Zollparlament* elections [5] indicates a high degree of anxiety on that score. He may well, however, have still believed that the situation ultimately could be retrieved via diplomatic pressure on Rome itself. Whatever his personal conviction, it is clear that the months following the close of the 1868 *Zollparlament* saw a subtle but decided shift in his tactics. During the final half of 1868 and throughout 1869 few, if any, steps were undertaken in Berlin designed to create new bonds between north and south Germany. Instead, the focus of activity came to be more and more institutional stabilization within the existing confederation, with particular emphasis on the necessarily tedious process of integrating the military potential of all north Germany under the Prussian system.

Bismarck, as he later admitted, seems to have overestimated the military threat of France during those years.[6] The danger from that quarter, and the knowledge that south Germany had come as far toward Prussia as could be expected for the time being, indicated a pause during which the situation could be reassessed and, perhaps, allowed to mature. Most of the ardent nationalists in the South accepted Bis-

[3] *Ibid.*
[4] Fröbel, 2:545ff.
[5] See Chapter Five, note 93.
[6] Bismarck, *Gedanken und Erinnerungen*, 2:72.

marck's appraisal and held their peace, although the impetuous Hessian, Bamberger, found it ironical in 1869 that the *Zollparlament* should debate the virtues of a trade treaty with Japan, as if the road from Berlin to Stuttgart and Munich ran through Yokohama and Nagasaki. "Wonderfully complex are the ways of Providence," he wrote in a letter to the voters at home.[7]

Because of Bismarck's decision to tread softly, debates during the second half of the 1868 Reichstag session and those of the entire 1869 session have less interest for the present study than the earlier ones. Likewise debates during the 1869 meetings of both the *Zollparlament* and the Prussian *Landtag* are relatively devoid of interest. Even in the first half of the 1868 Reichstag, which met before the tariff parliament convened, there was little reference to the German question as such, perhaps because of the desire of the government and the National Liberals not to prejudice the deliberations of that body. Catholic members took relatively little part in the debates, although Windthorst did appear as a leader of the opposition to Lasker's bill which sought to establish a federal guarantee of parliamentary immunity for members of provincial and state diets. The Hanoverian's chief argument, as in the past, was that the measure, although in itself good was not within the competence of the Reichstag, since it meant an unconstitutional intervention in the internal affairs of individual states. Windthorst was unable to convince even the majority of his co-religionists, for only four other Catholics voted with him, and the bill was adopted by the unusual majority of 119 to 65. Ten Catholics voted with the majority, while the rest failed to vote.[9]

Windthorst and Reichensperger were the only Catholics who participated in a lengthy debate on a proposed law dealing with the administration of the federal debt. This technical piece of legislation acquired political importance when Miquel and forty-four others introduced an amendment which would have empowered the Reichstag to prosecute treasury officials who were deemed delinquent in their duties. Since constitutionally the entire administration was an ap-

[7] Hermann Oncken, *Grossherzog Friedrich I von Baden und die deutsche Politik von 1854 bis 1871: Briefwechsel, Denkschriften, Tagebücher*, 2:109, note 3; Letter to His Constituents, Berlin, June 7, 1869, Bamberger, *Vertrauliche Briefe*, 78.

[8] *Stenographische Berichte über die Verhandlungen des Reichstages des norddeutschen Bundes, I. Legislatur-Periode*, Session 1868 (hereafter cited as *Stenographische Berichte, 1868*), April 3, 1868, 1:81–82.

[9] *Ibid.*, 89. The *Bundesrath* rejected the bill. See Sybel, 7:10.

panage of the Chancellor, this amendment was another indirect attempt to establish ministerial responsibility. Reichensperger made a long speech in its behalf, defending, as before, the principle of responsible government. Windthorst, on the other hand, while stressing once more his belief in the desirability of a responsible chancellor — or, better yet, a responsible ministry — opposed the Miquel amendment. In his judgment, it approached the problem in the wrong way, since in effect it transferred executive powers directly to the Reichstag in violation of the constitution.[10] By a margin of one vote, 114 to 113, the house adopted the amendment, with Reichensperger voting for it, Windthorst against, and Mallinckrodt abstaining. Catholics as a whole were divided sixteen to nine in favor of the proposal, with five abstentions. The Chancellor answered by withdrawing the entire law.[11]

The post-*Zollparlament* portion of the 1868 Reichstag, in addition to dealing with various financial problems, enacted several highly important pieces of social legislation, among them an extension of Prussian laws on labor unions to the entire territory of the *Bund,* elimination of some legal restrictions on the right of individuals to enter various trades and professions, and practical abolition of imprisonment for debt.[12] The first of these represented an initial step toward establishment of freedom for trade unions. Catholic participation in these debates was limited almost entirely to an unsuccessful attempt of Reichensperger to amend the bill eliminating imprisonment for debt with a provision abolishing personal arrest as a means of execution in civil suits. The house adopted instead a substitute motion, bearing the signatures of Lasker and Windthorst, which specifically permitted arrest as a means of compelling payment of damages awarded by a court in cases involving intent to defraud.[13]

In many respects the 1869 session was a duplicate of the previous year's meeting. The question of German unity received little attention, while the process of converting the Confederation into a modern state was further advanced. An industrial code was adopted which gave legal status to trade unions; a law was passed prohibiting loans to workingmen on the security of their current and future wages. The principle of comity between the courts of the various states was estab-

---

[10] *Stenographische Berichte, 1868,* April 22, 1868, 1: 146–50.

[11] *Ibid.,* 163–64.

[12] Sybel, 7: 60–63.

[13] *Stenographische Berichte, 1868,* May 27, 1868, 1: 196–200; May 28, 1868, 1: 211–12.

lished by federal law, and the Prussian commercial code was extended to all members of the Confederation. Finally, a uniform election law was enacted.[14] As in 1868, Catholic deputies played, in these instances, only minor roles. Moreover, they did not participate to any marked degree in the lengthy proceedings over the budget for 1870.

For the most part it was only on the perennial constitutional questions — parliamentary immunity for members of state diets, pay for members of the Reichstag, and ministerial responsibility, all of which came up again — that even the major Catholics contributed anything noteworthy to the debates. Both Mallinckrodt and Windthorst again argued against the resurrected Lasker motion to establish a federal guarantee of parliamentary immunity at the state and local level. As before, they claimed that the Reichstag was not competent to pass such a law.[15] It is, however, a significant indication of the lack of solidarity among Catholic deputies that eight of them appeared as co-signers of the Lasker-Waldeck motion.[16] Künzer, one of the eight, explained that he wanted to aid German unity by removing a major cause for the widely held opinion that north Germany was in the iron grip of the military. Mallinckrodt was the only Catholic who voted against the motion on its first reading, on which occasion it passed 100 to 51, although the other important Catholics abstained. The bill was subsequently adopted on the final reading by a standing vote, although there was no hope of securing the *Bundesrath*'s agreement.[17]

Seven of the eight Catholics who had joined in sponsoring the Lasker motion also acted as co-signers of a bill offered by Twesten and Graf Münster to set up responsible federal ministries for foreign affairs, finances, war, navy, and trade and commerce.[18] The opposition of Windthorst was implacable, despite his well-known advocacy of responsible government. Although, he said, no constitutional state could endure permanently with a single executive officer, he could not support the bill under debate because it violated the constitution by extending the competence of the central government. The bill was approved,

---

[14] Sybel, 7:154–56. During the debate on the election law, Windthorst expressed dislike of the secret ballot. See *Stenographische Berichte . . . I. Legislatur-Periode*, Session 1869 (hereafter abbreviated as *Stenographische Berichte, 1869*), March 20, 1869, 1:195.

[15] *Stenographische Berichte, 1869*, March 16, 1869, 1:89–90; March 18, 1869, 1:132.

[16] *Ibid.*, Anlagen, no. 24, 3:149. The seven were Blum, Fühling, Göddertz, Hompesch, Hosius, Kratz, Künzer, and Tobias.

[17] *Ibid.*, March 16, 1869, 1:98–100; March 18, 1869, 1:134.

[18] The exception was Künzer. *Ibid.*, Anlagen, no. 37, 3:169.

111 to 100. Windthorst voted, along with five other Catholics (including, incidentally, Hompesch, who had signed the petition), with the minority. The majority included six Catholics, only four of whom had originally supported the proposal.[19]

The only Catholic who felt impelled to take part in the renewed debate on the question of pay and allowances for Reichstag members was Künzer, who opposed such payments on the familiar, if in this case somewhat incomprehensible, ground that such a law would unconstitutionally extend the competence of the Reichstag. On two roll calls, the Catholics divided much as they had on earlier occasions when this measure had been defeated. As before, it failed by a narrow margin.[20]

The now stereotyped charge of incompetence recurred when Windthorst, during the debate on extension of the Prussian commercial code, fought the establishment of a supreme court to hear cases involving the code. While maintaining stoutly that the constitution did not authorize any federal courts, he admitted that he objected to this court primarily because it was to be located in Berlin. *Unter den Linden,* he warned the house, was far too close to the *Wilhelmstrasse* for comfort. Presumably, except for his *pro forma* objections on constitutional grounds, he was reasonably well satisfied with the ultimate decision to situate the court at Leipzig.[21] Reichensperger, however, arguing from entirely different premises, offered much more vigorous opposition to the bill. He protested that the erection of any courts with specialized jurisdiction was an unjustifiable expenditure of public funds, since it would tend to create a privileged judicial class. A federal supreme court might well be desirable, but not unless it was given appellate jurisdiction over all types of cases. During this debate the long standing personal hostility between Reichensperger and Lasker erupted once more when the Jewish National Liberal again took occasion to impugn the loyalty of Reichensperger and of all who agreed with him. This attack brought about another defense of Catholic patriotism by Reichensperger.[22]

On two other occasions Windthorst raised the monotonous charge of Reichstag incompetence. His opposition to a constitutional amend-

---

[19] *Ibid.,* April 16, 1869, 1:407–8, 412–13.

[20] *Ibid.,* May 5, 1869, 2:818, 821–22; May 12, 1869, 2:938–39.

[21] *Ibid.,* May 4, 1869, 2:791–92; Sybel, 7:156–57.

[22] *Stenographische Berichte, 1869,* May 4, 1869, 2:785; June 19, 1869, 2:1308, 1310, 1312.

ment, introduced by Lasker and Miquel, placing all civil law, legal procedure, and the organization of courts within the province of the federal government is easily understood. He did, however, present the novel argument that the normal constitutional provision for amending the *Bundesverfassung* was inapplicable whenever the amendment would result in an extension of the federal government's competence. In such cases, he insisted, approval by all the state governments and by all the state diets was necessary. He undoubtedly was not unaware that were his principle to prevail, any increase in the authority of the central government would be rendered permanently impossible.

Künzer, the only other Catholic who spoke on this question, took the opposite viewpoint. The amendment, he stated, would not in any way increase the competence of the federal government, for it was certainly within the rights of the north German people to decide through the Reichstag that they wanted all to be judged by the same laws. Although the amendment was approved by "a great majority" on a standing vote, the *Bundesrath*, as was expected, declined to grant its necessary assent.[23]

Far more surprising was Windthorst's opposition to a bill sponsored by the Jewish lawyer, Moritz Wiggers, to eliminate in all states any remaining religious qualifications for the exercise of civil and political rights. The motion, signed by three Catholic deputies, Kratz, Kleinsorgen, and Fühling, was attacked by Windthorst with his customary argument: The Reichstag was not constitutionally empowered to enact such legislation, no matter how beneficial its purpose might be. Despite his formal objections, and the more substantial opposition of some Protestant conservatives from the small states, the bill received the overwhelming approval of the Reichstag and became law on July 3, following its adoption by the Federal Council.[24]

From the foregoing examples, it is clear that Catholics showed even less tendency to act as a bloc in the Reichstag during 1868 and 1869 than they had in either of the 1867 sessions. Windthorst, Mallinckrodt, and Reichensperger were often poles apart, and the lesser individuals, although they remained for the most part silent, revealed by their votes that there was a very small area of agreement among them. Only

---

[23] *Ibid.*, April 10, 1869, 1:292; April 19, 1869, 1:457–60; April 28, 1869, 1:651–52; May 5, 1869, 2:835; Sybel, 7:158–59.

[24] *Stenographische Berichte, 1869,* June 2, 1869, 2:1246; Anlagen, no. 221, 3:690; Hansen, 1:802–3.

Windthorst seems consistently to have been interested in fighting a rear-guard action on the issue of federalism. The others appear to have lost enthusiasm for the struggle. Both Kratz and Reichensperger became deeply involved in several debates on highly technical questions with little immediate political significance, and the latter, particularly, had demonstrated his extraordinary legal talents.[25] But Bismarck's change of emphasis had left the north German Catholics, as well as the National Liberals, suspended between the past and the future. The sluggish pace was frequently the subject of remarks during the 1869 session. On April 16, for example, Windthorst answered one of the complaints on that score by denying that there had been any slowdown in matters which legitimately belonged to the competence of the federal government. If by lack of progress was meant that the individual states had ceased rapidly to be deprived of their independence, then the halt was welcome. "We cannot destroy public welfare in Germany and in Europe any more effectively than by progress in limiting [the independence of] individual states. . . ."[26]

In view of the trend in the Reichstag, it is not surprising that the second meeting of the *Zollparlament,* again sandwiched between halves of the Reichstag session, was also a very tame affair compared with its predecessor. Neither the Prussian government nor the moderate National Liberals wanted to chance another rebuff like that of 1868 from the south German particularists. Consequently, political questions were carefully excluded from the agenda. The opening address of the King on June 3 was devoid of direct political references, mentioning only economic legislation which was to be laid before the body for enactment.[27] Hohenlohe, although his party had suffered a major defeat in the recently concluded Bavarian elections, was reelected vice-president by a large majority, while Thüngen, the candidate of the south German fraction, garnered only thirty-two votes. Most of the important southern Catholics were back, the only prominent exception being Schäffle, who had resigned to accept another post.[28]

[25] See, *e.g.,* his several speeches during the debate on the bill to establish comity between the state courts. *Stenographische Berichte, 1869,* 2: *passim,* especially 865–67.

[26] *Ibid.,* April 16, 1869, 1: 408.

[27] *Stenographische Berichte über die Verhandlungen des durch die Allerhöchste Verordnung vom 23. Mai 1869 einberufenen deutschen Zollparlaments* (hereafter abbreviated as *Stenographische Berichte Zollparlament, 1869*), June 3, 1869, 1–2.

[28] *Ibid.,* June 4, 1869, 8; June 7, 1869, 13. For the Bavarian election of May 1869, see below, pp. 183–185.

North and South during the Pause, 1868–1869

The chief concern of the 1869 *Zollparlament* was consideration of a new schedule of tariffs. Although most of the bill aroused little controversy, heated debates took place on two clauses. The first was a proposal to levy a tax on beet sugar; the second, a revival of the measure defeated a year before, to tax imported petroleum products. Most Catholics were opposed to both, although Reichensperger, again the lone wolf, spoke for the former. The house eventually approved the beet sugar tax, 148 to 110, but, as before, rejected the oil tariff, this time by a vote of 155 to 93. The south German fraction and most of the northern Catholics cooperated in the defeat of the petroleum clause, although the Polish group abstained. The alliance, however, did not hold firm on the sugar tax. In neither case did the Catholic vote appear to be the decisive factor.[29]

The new tariff law, as amended, was approved finally on June 21. The key roll call on the second reading indicated 139 for and 129 against. The Catholic vote was divided in such a way as to indicate that economic considerations, rather than any ascertainable political or religious interests, furnished the primary motivation. Fourteen Catholics, most of them north German, voted with the majority, while 21, mostly from the South, cast negative votes. Twenty-one others, including Windthorst, Reichensperger, the Polish group, and some of the more moderate southerners, such as Lindau and Thüngen, either were absent or did not vote.[30] An innocuous address by the King closed the session on the following day.[31]

Contemporary appraisals of the session ranged from bitter denunciation to qualified approval of its achievements. Bamberger, as mentioned before, was contemptuous because of its political inactivity. The *Zollparlament* behaved, he wrote, "as if it were nothing more than a poor, simple tariff parliament."[32] Roggenbach, on the other hand, indicated in a letter to the Queen of Prussia that he considered passage of a new tariff schedule against the opposition of the south German fraction a minor triumph. In any event, he concluded, the real benefit came from the simple fact that South and North were meeting together annually. He saw evidence that the gulf between the sections

[29] *Ibid.*, June 16, 1869, 137–39; June 17, 1869, 167–69.
[30] *Ibid.*, June 21, 1869, 231–32, 242.
[31] *Ibid.*, June 22, 1869, 251–52.
[32] Letter to His Constituents, Berlin, June 7, 1869, Bamberger, *Vertrauliche Briefe*, 77.

was narrower in 1869 than it had been in 1868, and predicted that it would become still narrower a year hence.[33]

Jörg, however, perhaps allowing the wish to convince him of the fact, interpreted the obvious relaxation in the tempo of events as evidence of Prussian fears. Bismarck, he wrote at the close of the session, was a "plunger." He had been supremely competent at destroying the old Germany, but he was now powerless to organize a new order to replace it. "Briefly stated, in Prussia they have, in spite of everything, begun to be afraid." [34] The victors of 1866, having made expansion of Prussia their sole goal, were now faced with the realization that territorial expansion had meant internal weakening. The dilemma would inevitably become worse unless Prussia could end the provisional state of affairs in Germany. That could be done in only one way — by precipitating a war with France. And Bismarck, Jörg gloated, was afraid of the consequences.[35] As usual his analysis was not far wrong. As usual also, his penchant for exaggeration led him to underestimate the resources of his enemy.

The growing attention paid by the Reichstag to strengthening the central government of the Confederation in 1868 and 1869 produced serious repercussions in the Prussian *Landtag*, which, in turn, did not go unnoticed in south Germany. The readers of the *Historisch-politische Blätter* were treated in the spring of 1869 to a detailed report on attacks made by Windthorst and Mallinckrodt in the Prussian lower chamber on a law sequestering funds of the former King of Hanover. This law had revoked the settlement made in 1867 with George V in retaliation for his support of the Guelphic Legion. Windthorst charged that it confiscated property without due legal process, and accused the *Landtag* of seeking to be "accuser, witness, evidence, judge, and legislator at the same time."

Mallinckrodt, on the other hand, stressed the more ominous fact that the law had placed at Bismarck's disposal a sizable fund which was completely removed from public control. For whatever purpose the fund might be used, said Mallinckrodt, its mere existence could only undermine constitutional government.[36] By calling special atten-

[33] Roggenbach to Queen Augusta, Berlin, June 22, 1869, Heyderhoff, *Im Ring der Gegner Bismarcks*, 103–4.

[34] "Zeitläufe: Paris, Bayern, und Berlin," *HPB*, 64:78–79.

[35] *Ibid.*, 83.

[36] "Zeitläufe: Die Verfahren im preussischen Abgeordnetenhause vom 29. und 30. Jan. 1869," *HPB*, 63:343–47.

tion to this debate, Jörg doubtless succeeded in heightening his readers' apprehension over Bismarck's intentions.[37]

Near the close of the year the *Blätter* again called attention to the debates of the Prussian *Landtag*. During November 1869, the federal law establishing a supreme tribunal to hear cases arising under the north German commercial code provoked a series of bitter debates in both Prussian houses. Because the Conservatives were incensed at what appeared to them an unconstitutional intervention in Prussia's internal affairs, these debates inevitably turned into general discussions of the federal government's powers. Jörg quoted large sections of the debates in the *Blätter* to prove that in north Germany a trend had clearly developed toward interpretation of the *Bundesverfassung* in a sense not only different from its original intent, but in some cases diametrically opposed to it. He argued that this was attributable primarily to the National Liberals, but went on to charge that the government had made no real objection. Lasker, he pointed out, had read to the *Abgeordnetenhaus* a letter allegedly in Bismarck's own hand, which declared that Prussia's German policy was so firmly grounded that no change would result even if Bismarck himself were replaced. To the Bavarian editor the letter, and in fact the whole course of the debates, demonstrated that the North German Confederation was inevitably developing into an *Einheitsstaat*. No one in Berlin, he wrote, regarded the existing order as anything but temporary, and no one in the Prussian lower chamber, except Windthorst and a few other Catholics, had had the courage to resist the trend. In the *Herrenhaus*, Graf zur Lippe had proposed adoption of a declaration that no modifications of the federal constitution which effected changes in the fundamental law of Prussia be recognized in the future without prior consent of the *Landtag*. His proposal, however, had fallen upon deaf ears.[38] The lesson of these debates, as Jörg put it for his readers, was that "no one can any longer doubt that there is no permanent place in this Confederation for the idea of independence for individual states."[39] *Caveat Bavaria!*

In a similar vein, although less exaggerated, was the judgment given

[37] The suspicions of Mallinckrodt and Jörg were well founded, for Bismarck used the fund primarily to pay for "planting" inspired articles in various "independent" newspapers.
[38] "Zeitläufe: Der norddeutsche Bund," *HPB,* 64:990–1003.
[39] *Ibid.,* 1001.

by the Württemberg minister and *Zollparlament* deputy, von Neurath, when he stopped at Darmstadt after the 1869 *Zollparlament*. He told Dalwigk that Prussia was in a serious financial plight, citing Windthorst, that "little, ugly, but exceptionally gifted man," as the source for his statement. The seriousness of Prussia's economic condition, he quoted Windthorst as saying, ought not to be ignored by the south Germans, for if they persisted in refusing money grants to the *Zollverein*, Prussian officialdom might feel compelled by sheer economic necessity to "cross the Main" in order to retrieve the rapidly worsening finances of the *Bund*. To Neurath this argument carried considerable weight, since he regarded the Hanoverian as perhaps the most talented opponent of Prussia. Moreover, his own observations had led him to the same conclusion.[40]

Although the relaxation of pressure on south Germany in no way lessened the fear of Berlin felt by south German Catholics, that fear was no longer of the paralyzing variety which had been so apparent in the first year after Königgrätz. The particularist "victory" in the *Zollparlament* elections had given them a weapon with which to fight back. The victory had been engineered largely by Catholics, and in the flush of success there was a momentary revival of *grossdeutsch* hope, which found expression in the declaration of the south German fraction mentioned earlier.[41] However, political, religious, and economic tensions within and among the southern states soon put that hope beyond the possibility of attainment. Consequently, the Catholic political movements which arose in parts of south Germany during 1868 and 1869 had only a nominal orientation toward Vienna. Ultimate reunion of Habsburg Austria with the rest of Germany was universally adopted as a slogan, but, for the most part, south German Catholics now recognized that the clock could not be turned back. Their political efforts, therefore, were to be confined to preventing it from moving inexorably ahead.

In the two states where Catholics formed a minority of the population, they did not succeed in establishing by themselves a political party. They do not even seem to have tried very hard. The already existing alliance between Catholics and democrats continued to function in Württemberg, with the former endeavoring "[to stress] the

[40] *Dalwigk Tagebücher,* June 25, 1869, 405.
[41] See Chapter Five.

160

Christian content of democracy, and to exclude the evil modern elements, as well as their hypocritical representatives," in the words of Rudolph Probst's brother.[42] The momentum generated in the *Zollparlament* campaign carried the clerical-democratic forces through to a victory in a *Landtag* election early in July 1868. The government party had expected to gain a majority of five or six in the lower house, but it found itself instead in the minority by about that number of seats, since clericals or democrats carried twelve districts upon which Varnbüler had counted heavily. According to the Prussian minister at Stuttgart, a decisive factor was the fear in the minds of many voters that Varnbüler, with a parliamentary majority behind him, might prefer to deal with Prussia rather than to continue wrangling with the democrats in the *Landtag*.[43]

Anti-Prussian sentiment in Württemberg continued to grow throughout the last half of 1868 and all of 1869 as the burdens resulting from the military reforms came to be felt by all classes of the population. Especially resented were the Prussian general, von Suckow, who commanded the Army, and the Prussian sympathies of the minister of war, Count von Wagner. In 1869 hostility toward the latter culminated in a successful move to oust him. It seems likely that had not the Franco-Prussian war come providentially in the summer of 1870, the opposition would have been able to muster sufficient strength to strike at Varnbüler himself.[44]

The failure of a clearly defined Catholic political party to develop in Württemberg may in part be explained by the relative calm which prevailed in relations between Church and state throughout the sixties. Militant Catholics objected periodically to the government's refusal to allow the establishment of masculine religious orders, although these were permitted by the law of 1862 regulating the status of the Church. No effort was made by secular authorities, however, to interfere with existing feminine orders, which were quite active. The issue never passed beyond the stage of chronic grumbling. At no time were there serious struggles over school administration or investiture, like those which kept the atmosphere in Baden and Bavaria troubled.[45]

[42] Pastor, *Reichensperger*, 1:599. See also Letter to His Constituents, Berlin, May 22, 1870, Bamberger, *Vertrauliche Briefe*, 141.
[43] Ziekursch, 1:247; Rosenberg to Bismarck, Stuttgart, July 13, 1868, *APP*, 10: no. 93.
[44] Ziekursch, 1:247.
[45] Bachem, 2:258–59.

The absence of a significant Catholic political party in Hesse-Darmstadt is more difficult to explain, since the episcopal palace at Mainz was in many ways the pivot of German Catholicism. From Bishop Ketteler emanated a long series of essays, pastoral letters, and sermons which were read and commented upon by intellectuals of all faiths and by ordinary Catholic citizens the length and breadth of the land. Mainz also was the nerve center of the growing Social Catholicism.[46] Yet after the abortive attempt of Canon Moufang to found a Catholic party in 1862, further efforts in that direction were abandoned. Part of the answer is undoubtedly to be found in the fact that Ketteler himself violently disagreed with his fellow Catholics on the question of Germany's political future. The reception accorded his book, *Deutschland nach dem Kriege*, gave him certain proof, if proof were needed, that he stood almost alone among south German Catholics. Even his associates at Mainz, who cooperated so magnificently in pushing his socio-economic views within the Church, and in his struggle to defend it against anticlericalism in Hesse and Baden, would not help him here.[47] It seems logical, therefore, to conclude that the necessary common ground upon which a cohesive party could be erected did not exist.

It must not, on the other hand, be assumed that the politico-religious area remained outside the realm of conflict in Hesse during the years between the Austrian and the French wars. A bitter campaign was carried on against Ketteler in the liberal and Protestant press, not only there, but throughout Germany. In December 1867 the Bishop felt obliged to reply to charges made against him by the *Kölnische Zeitung* that he had used his office to stiffen Dalwigk's opposition to the North German Confederation, and, further, that he had acted as spiritual adviser for the Protestant Archduchess of Hesse-Darmstadt. The paper asserted that Ketteler, allegedly the leader of an insidious party, had wrung from the Hessian régime "unheard-of concessions."[48] Ketteler published his denials in the *Mainzer Journal*, in a series of articles entitled "Political Lies." Here he met the attacks upon him by means of violent countercharges, whose general import was that the "persecution" heaped upon the Church by liberals formed

---

[46] See Hertling, 1:205.

[47] Vigener, *Ketteler*, 536, 540.

[48] "Open Declaration of Bishop von Ketteler," Dec. 17–22, 1867, reprinted from the *Mainzer Journal*, nos. 293–98 (1867), *Ketteler Briefe*, 355–56, 359.

part of a plan to destroy its independence. If, he warned, these tactics of arousing religious passions to a level where real issues were forgotten were to succeed in south Germany, they would soon be applied in Austria, and eventually Prussia herself would feel the lash. He warned that the liberals might eventually "reduce the Prussian government to dust." [49] His conclusion was that

all those men who are responsible for this religious agitation, through all their political lies, are the true enemies of the German people and of the German fatherland. Our fatherland needs nothing more than it needs religious peace. He who ceaselessly raises these questions, he who stirs up the truly Christian people, and destroys the rights of the Catholic Church has no love for his German fatherland, but instead pursues lower party interests. [50]

At the same time Ketteler wrote a letter to the Lutheran Bishop, Zimmermann, who had earlier in the year claimed before the assembled Hessian clergy that Ketteler had for a long time been responsible for "calumnies and detractions" against the Lutheran faith. Zimmermann had cited as examples various articles in the Catholic press and Ketteler's pastoral letters. Ketteler denied any connection with the Catholic press, and, therefore, any responsibility for what it printed. As far as the other charges were concerned, he demanded either proof or a public retraction. Again he stressed his belief in the necessity of peace between the branches of Christian believers. [51]

Shortly afterward, the official organ of the Lutheran Church in Hesse published an answer to Ketteler's articles. It repeated Zimmermann's accusations, with elaboration, for the Bishop was now portrayed as the evil genius of the Dalwigk régime, exercising such a powerful influence that he could be actually regarded as "co-regent of the country." Furthermore, it argued, Ketteler was endeavoring to use his political influence to destroy the hitherto excellent relations between the royal family and the Dalwigk ministry, in order to aid north German annexation of the Grand Duchy. The Bishop was able, in his subsequent refutation, to point out gleefully the impossibility of his being both the agent of Austria, as charged by the *Darmstädter Zeitung* (liberal), and the tool of Bismarck, as the *Kirchenblatt* maintained. Both charges, he wrote, were further examples of political lies,

[49] *Ibid.*, 355–63.
[50] *Ibid.*, 363.
[51] Ketteler to Bishop Zimmermann of Darmstadt, Mainz, Dec. 21, 1867, *ibid.*, 363–65.

serving only the interests of parties, not the interests either of Hesse or of the German nation.[52]

The lengths to which some Lutheran clergymen went in their attacks on Catholicism is revealed by the fact that Dalwigk himself, during the summer of 1868, was accused by the *Evangelisches Kirchenblatt* of being secretly a Catholic because he had failed to put in an appearance at Worms for the dedication of a monument to Luther. "There is nothing," he wrote in his diary, "more absurd and intolerant than a Protestant minister!" [53]

Despite these tensions, relations between Ketteler and Dalwigk remained cordial throughout the period under consideration. In 1868, for example, the Hessian minister acted as the Bishop's unofficial emissary in a vain effort to induce Beust to take a firmer hand against Austrian liberals, who were then pressing for complete secularization of elementary education. Although the mission failed, Ketteler later informed Dalwigk, presumably for transmission to Vienna, of his continued regard for the Beust ministry, which, he said, ought not to have difficulties placed in its way by clerical interests. He thus expressed his gratitude for the Austrian minister's past service in defense of the south German cause, and promised him his future support.[54]

Nevertheless, Ketteler never wavered from his conclusion that the ultimate solution of the German problem would exclude Austria. On the eve of his departure for the Vatican Council in the fall of 1869 he paid a courtesy call on Dalwigk, during which the two discussed contemporary political issues. Again the Bishop stressed that despite his dislike for Prussia because of her behavior in 1866, he saw no way out of the German dilemma except through the inclusion of all non-Habsburg Germany within the Prussian orbit. The internal tensions within the Habsburg Empire, particularly the problem of the subject nationalities, would, he thought, forever prevent consummation of any scheme to reunite Austria with the rest of Germany. Dalwigk, however, was not convinced and still hoped that changed circumstances would one day alter the situation.[55]

Despite the failure of Catholic laymen in Hesse-Darmstadt to organize politically before the Franco-Prussian War, a few signs had

[52] "Political Lies," reprinted from the *Mainzer Journal*, Jan. 15–16, 1868, *ibid.*, 372–79.
[53] Darmstadt, Aug. 7, 1868, *Dalwigk Tagebücher*, 380–81.
[54] Feb. 24, 1868, *ibid.*, 367; April 6, 1868, *ibid.*, 370.
[55] Nov. 10, 1869, *ibid.*, 417–18.

appeared by 1869 that political Catholicism would ultimately take root here also. In that year a Catholic *Leseverein* appeared in Mainz under the sponsorship of a well-to-do meat packer, Johann Falk III. This association served in Hesse, as similar groups were serving in other states, to direct the political education of Catholic laymen. Once the dichotomy within the ranks of the clergy was ended by the war, Hessian Catholics were adequately prepared for the founding of the Center.[56]

In marked contrast to the slow progress of Catholic political organization in Hesse and Württemberg, events had, by the summer of 1868, set the stage in the other two south German states for the rapid development of strong Catholic parties. In Baden, as indicated above, the hostility of Catholics toward the régime had been increasing for a number of years, in part because of the conflict over German unity, but also because of the chronic strife between the state and the Church locally. After the end of the War of 1866, a group led by the Heidelberg professor, J. C. Bluntschli, began to agitate for the introduction of compulsory civil marriage. The contest over control of the lower schools remained unsettled. The long-standing clash between the aged Archbishop Vicari and the government was still much in evidence. The Catholic press periodically grumbled at the discrimination suffered by Catholics. One representative article, which appeared on May 8, 1867, in the *Freiburger katholisches Kirchenblatt,* the official organ of the episcopate, charged that Catholics were unjustly excluded from public office, that universities were entirely under the control of secular or Protestant officials, and especially that the government's efforts to extend its control over the entire educational system constituted an intolerable interference with legitimate functions of the Church. The *Kirchenblatt* maintained that the south German governments were under a moral obligation to grant their subjects at least the rights enjoyed by Prussian Catholics, since after the signature of the *Schutz- und Trutzbündnisse* the South was obliged to fight beside Prussia in any future war.[57]

The death of Archbishop Vicari on April 14, 1868, at the age of eighty-four, ushered in another crucial stage in the Church-state controversy, and this, in turn, led ultimately to the founding of a Catholic political

[56] Bachem, 2:354.
[57] "Zwei Postscripta zu den badischen Briefen," I, *HPB,* 62:59–60, 73–75.

party. The chief minister, the liberal nationalist Julius Jolly, was determined that the Archbishop's successor not be another Vicari, who had for nearly a quarter century been a thorn in the flesh of successive governments. By law, no archbishop could be named without prior approval of the government. The cathedral chapter, however, immediately appointed *Domdekan* Lothar Kübel as vicar, giving him the legal right to exercise the authority of the archbishop's office until a permanent appointment was made. The fact that Kübel was known to be under the direct influence of the Jesuit coterie which had surrounded Vicari boded ill for Jolly's hopes. On May 6, 1868, the chapter, in accordance with the law, submitted to the government a list of eight names from which the archbishop would be chosen. The secular authorities were to designate those on the list who were unacceptable. At its head stood the name of Bishop von Ketteler; all eight were men of known Jesuit associations. Cardinal Hohenlohe, brother of the Bavarian minister-president, whom Jolly had confidentially indicated to the chapter as his choice, was conspicuously absent. Jolly first sought to by-pass the chapter and to deal directly with Rome, but he failed to find a suitable person to act as intermediary. Consequently, the government returned the list, designating seven of the eight as *personae non gratae*. Since the law gave ecclesiastical authorities the right to make the final choice from at least two candidates acceptable to the government, no appointment was possible. The cathedral chapter promised to submit another list, but failed to do so, and after considerable useless diplomatic activity at Rome and at Berlin—the Hohenzollern principality belonged to the Freiburg archdiocese—a complete deadlock developed. No archbishop could be named, but Kübel could not be removed as vicar. Neither side would yield, and the stalemate endured no less than fourteen years![58]

The government had several weapons at its disposal, all of which it shortly began to use. The law of 1860 regulating appointments to Church offices required candidates to receive a liberal education in addition to their theological training. Heretofore the law had not been strictly enforced, but now Jolly issued regulations requiring all Catholic theological students to present for their degrees evidence of having taken two courses in philology, one in general philosophy, and one in secular history. Upon graduation, they were henceforth required to

[58] Bachem, 2:314; Baumgarten and Jolly, 126–31.

pass a state examination demonstrating their proficiency in Latin, Greek, philosophy, world history, literary history, and ecclesiastical law. Kübel, of course, forbade clerical students to take the examination. The entire clergy adopted passive resistance; all attempts at negotiation failed.[59]

For those who believed that the conflict between the Church and the liberal state was irreconcilable, no better proof could be imagined. The *Historisch-politische Blätter* followed the Baden struggle with close attention. It accused the Liberal party of seeking "quietly to undermine the Church by police regulation, and to introduce a Catholic-Protestant 'national church' under a liberal German tsar."[60] Its advice: "The complete freedom of the Church [from the authority of states such as Baden] must be the goal for which Catholics, firmly united, strive."[61]

Cries of anguish from Catholics were soon more than matched by angry outbursts from a section of the Baden National Liberal party, which claimed, among other things, that Jolly was betraying an intolerable softness toward the Catholic Church. This attack came to a head when, on November 8, 1868, fourteen members of the party met in the town of Offenburg and adopted a resolution of no confidence in the ministry. The resolution cited two major objections to Jolly. First, he was condemned for his failure to secure admission of Baden into the North German Confederation. Second, he and his government were castigated for what the rebels termed favoritism toward the orthodox churches, both Catholic and Protestant. Particularly, the insurgents demanded that the government cease what they called emulation of the Prussian minister of public worship, von Mühler, "whose support of a limited orthodoxy and a moribund pietism is contrary to the spirit of our century, and does injury to the spiritual interests of the German nation."[62]

The Offenburg insurgents planned no open attack on Jolly until they were sure of sufficient parliamentary support to oust him. Consequently, the declaration was circulated secretly among radical liberal members of the *Landtag*. Nevertheless, it was soon divulged to the *Karlsruher Zeitung,* which immediately published it. Jolly, thus faced

[59] Bachem, 2:315–16.
[60] "Die Erzbischofswahl zu Freiburg," *HPB*, 62:657.
[61] *Ibid.*
[62] Baumgarten and Jolly, 131–32; Ziekursch, 248.

with an open break in his own party, felt obliged to use whatever means were at hand to restore unity. By giving unmistakable proof of his anticlericalism, he could eliminate one of the main objections of the rebels. His first step, therefore, was to order the immediate closing of a small convent in one of the minor towns. The action was based on a local official's report that Church authorities had failed to secure the necessary governmental authorization before installing the cloister. The nuns, however, acting either on impulse or on the instruction of Kübel, refused to vacate, and the government was forced to evict them. The natural resentment of Catholics at this exercise of secular power was not lessened when, after some of the dispossessed sisters reoccupied their former quarters, the government removed them forcibly a second time.[63]

Scarcely had excitement over this incident abated when a second round in Jolly's campaign began. In 1867 the government had taken from control of the Church a heavily endowed hospital in Constance, claiming that before the year 1820 the hospital had been under secular jurisdiction, and that, therefore, its possession by ecclesiastical authorities was illegal. The government acted on information furnished by the mayor of Constance, Stromeyer, a liberal Catholic. The mayor had also been closely associated with a campaign to end the rigid confessionalization of the schools in that city. Having been warned on three occasions, Stromeyer, on January 14, 1869, suffered excommunication on the grounds that his conduct had violated his duty as a Catholic. Kübel's emissary who delivered the notice of excommunication, moreover, informed Stromeyer that he was thereby relieved of his seat on the municipal commission for charitable foundations, which belonged by law to any Catholic mayor. It was this latter action which gave Jolly the opportunity to strike another blow at Kübel, and thereby further to impress the rebellious members of his party. He ordered the mayor reinstated on the commission and instituted legal proceedings against the acting archbishop and his emissary, charging that the two had illegally attempted to remove a public official from a secular office. Although the supreme court of Baden, as expected, dismissed the case, ruling that the excommunication affected Stromeyer only as a Catholic and not in his capacity as mayor, the case aided in the accomplishment of Jolly's political objective, to heal

[63] Baumgarten and Jolly, 131–33, 141.

the Offenburg breach. The revolt came to an end at a second meeting in Offenburg, in May 1869 — this time of the entire party — at which it withdrew its objections to Jolly, and agreed to support the ministry and its policies.[64]

Nevertheless, as some cooler heads had warned, Jolly had created martyrs.[65] More than any other single factor, indignation aroused by the minister's provocations made possible the success of Lindau and others in their efforts to establish a Catholic political party. Early in 1869, while Jolly's attacks on the Church were at their height, Lindau, Bissing, and Dr. Leopold Fischer set themselves up in Heidelberg as a provisional committee to undertake arrangements for contesting the forthcoming election, scheduled for August, in which one third of the membership in the lower chamber would be renewed. On May 1 the committee issued the first manifesto of what it called the *Katholische Volkspartei*. It demanded, first of all, dissolution of the chamber and the calling of an extraordinary *Landtag* to write a new suffrage law based on universal, direct, secret manhood suffrage. In this demand the new party acted in cooperation with the then newly organized Electoral Reform League, a democratic and *grossdeutsch* organization without religious orientation.[66] Other proposals contained in the *Volkspartei*'s manifesto were (1) complete separation of Church and state, to end "repression by liberal officialdom"; (2) complete freedom of the Church to manage its own affairs and to control its property; (3) freedom of instruction "without prejudice to the right of the government to supervise the schools"; (4) unification of Germany, including Austria, on a federal basis; and (5) a whole series of clauses asking what amounted to a reversal of practically the entire past legislative policy of the government.[67]

It became apparent that the new party could not be ignored when, on May 9, its first scheduled rally at Bruchsal attracted around six thousand persons. Lindau, Bissing, Andlaw, and others addressed the meeting. All of them attacked the Jolly ministry, citing the Offenburg

[64] *Ibid.*, 141–43, 145–56; Roggenbach to Queen Augusta of Prussia, Freiburg, Dec. 23, 1868, March 14, 1869, Heyderhoff, *Im Ring der Gegner Bismarcks*, 96, 100–1.

[65] Roggenbach to Queen Augusta of Prussia, Freiburg, March 14, 1869, Heyderhoff, *Im Ring der Gegner Bismarcks*, 100–1.

[66] Bachem, 2 : 318–19; Baumgarten and Jolly, 143. The biographers of the Baden minister speak of an agent of Beust as the midwife for both organizations. They neither mention the name of the alleged agent nor cite evidence.

[67] Bachem, 2 : 318–19; Dor, 76.

crisis as evidence that the government had lost the confidence of everyone. A second rally took place at Freiburg on May 17, attended by perhaps three thousand, and a third at Engen on May 23. At the Freiburg meeting, Lindau was elected president of the party by acclamation, and in his acceptance speech he sought to justify the establishment of a confessional party. "The *Katholische Volkspartei*," he told his audience, "has to exist because our established rights have been taken away from us by legislative enactment." The party had been created for one purpose: "to bring about by legal means freedom in ecclesiastical affairs." At each of these meetings leaders of the new party continued to clamor for the dismissal of Jolly and dissolution of the *Landtag*.[68]

As a means of realizing their goal the leaders asked their supporters, both orally and through the five Catholic daily newspapers of Baden,[69] to circulate petitions addressed to the Grand Duke asking for the immediate election of a new *Landtag* by universal, direct suffrage. Members of the clergy were enlisted to campaign for signatures. The receipt of petitions from 123 separate parishes furnished the government in Karlsruhe with a demonstration that the new party was not without strength. So impressed, in fact, were the liberals that they soon began to circulate counterpetitions to discount the *Volkspartei*'s campaign, while the *Badische Landeszeitung*, a paper with official connections, came out with a series of personal attacks on Lindau, allegedly originating with the clergy, intended to discredit him.[70]

On July 1, the *Katholische Volkspartei*, having failed to induce the Grand Duke to dissolve the *Landtag*, published its election manifesto. All Catholics were urged to vote, in order to give evidence that their wishes were no longer to be ignored. Because of the indirect ballot, the party had no hope of winning more than a few seats. Considering its handicaps, however, it did surprisingly well at the polls on August 24. Three of its candidates, Baumstark, Bissing, and Lender, were elected. Baumstark, in fact, was victorious in two districts, although in the runoff the party lost the seat which he relinquished. The three

[68] Bachem, 2:319–20; Dor, 80–81. The figures given for the attendance at these rallies, derived from partisan Catholic sources, may be suspect.

[69] The five papers were, in approximate order of importance: (1) *Badischer Beobachter*, (2) *Pfalzer Bote*, (3) *Freiburger Bote*, (4) *Der Trompeter von Säckingen*, (5) *Die Freie Stimme vom See*. See "Zwei Postscripta zu den badischen Briefen," I, *HPB*, 62:60–61.

[70] Bachem, 2:320; Baumgarten and Jolly, 143–44; Dor, 83.

newly elected Catholics joined Lindau to form a parliamentary bloc, symbolically referring to themselves as "the Quadrilateral," after the great fortresses in northern Italy which Austria had successfully defended against the French and Piedmontese in 1859. Later the four were joined by Rosshirt, who, although he had belonged to the lower chamber since 1863, had not heretofore been regarded as a specifically "Catholic" deputy.[71]

The moderate success of the *Katholische Volkspartei* forced the government and the National Liberals into an even closer alliance than before, since, with a Catholic majority of two to one in the country as a whole, and with various non-Catholic democratic groups in opposition as well, liberals could easily foresee the ultimate upset of their plans unless they maintained an unbroken front. The *Volkspartei*, despite its diminutive parliamentary representation, passed to the attack immediately after the opening of the *Landtag* on September 24. During the address debate, the Catholic group criticized the government's policy on nearly all points. It proposed abandonment of the alliance with Prussia, and resurrected the defunct idea of a *Südbund* allied with Austria. However, the main objective of the Quadrilateral was the ecclesiastical policy of Jolly. Baumstark accused the ministry of having an irrational hatred for the Church, and again made the point that the *Katholische Volkspartei* saw as its main task the fight to free the Catholic Church from control by the bureaucratic state.[72]

Early in the session, Lindau introduced a bill to reform the suffrage law in line with the party's program. Jolly was sufficiently alarmed that he was willing to give ground. Consequently, the government introduced a counterproposal which, although it met some major objections of the opposition, avoided the dreaded issue of universal, direct, manhood suffrage. Jolly's bill conceded the secret ballot and simplified requirements for voting. It redistricted the country in a somewhat more equitable manner, and it provided that all seats in the lower chamber would be renewed quadrennially, instead of, as before, every eight years. In addition, the lower chamber was to gain the right to elect its own president and was to be granted a greater measure of control over its agenda. Most of these reforms had been included in the Offenburg program, and Jolly was obviously trying to appease

[71] Bachem, 2:320–21; Dor, 85–86; Baumgarten and Jolly, 53
[72] Baumgarten and Jolly, 147, 153–54; Bachem, 321–22.

the former rebels in his own party as well as making a gesture toward popular sovereignty in line with Catholic demands. Although it was practically foreordained that the government bill would be passed, the Quadrilateral won a considerable moral victory by even getting its own proposal to the floor for debate.[73] Jolly and others attacked the Lindau bill as unwise because of the alleged tendency of the masses to favor radical programs without adequate consideration. However, as Jolly's biographers admit candidly, "The ground most important for Baden, the strengthening of the ultramontane party to be expected from a general direct suffrage law, remained unmentioned." [74]

Lindau's bill was introduced into the upper chamber by Freiherr von Bodmann, a Catholic aristocrat. Kübel spoke for it, although he was chided by government supporters for having taken a position in conflict with the Syllabus of Errors. In the *Herrenkammer* Jolly revived the old bogey that Catholics sought to subject German culture to a foreign authority. The Lindau motion, of course, had even less chance here than in the lower chamber.[75]

On two other major questions the Catholic People's party also went down to defeat. The first was a bill to introduce compulsory civil marriage. Already in the statute books was a law, passed over heated but ineffectual Catholic protests, which permitted civil marriage whenever the Church refused to perform the ceremony, provided no legal impediments existed. However, according to this law, recourse to religious authorities had to be made first, which forced the couple to accept the onus of defying clerical prohibition. Moreover, the Church had refused to recognize the validity of any marriage performed by secular officials. It was this latter situation which made possible Jolly's claim that it was the Church which had forced the government to act. The bill, quite understandably, came as a profound shock to the majority of Catholics. Consequently, an exceptionally large audience was present at a protest meeting held October 24, 1869, at Hardheim bei Walldürn, in Lindau's electoral district. This gathering adopted by acclamation a resolution condemning unconditionally obligatory civil marriage. It went on to denounce also a proposed law on charitable

[73] Bachem, 2:322; Baumgarten and Jolly, 149; Dor, 86–88.
[74] Baumgarten and Jolly, 149–50.
[75] *Ibid.*, 154–55; Bachem, 2:322–23.

foundations,[76] and to reaffirm the party's opposition to incorporation of Baden in the North German Confederation. Finally, it protested again the government's adoption of the Prussian military system.[77] Nevertheless, despite widespread public agitation, the law on civil marriage was passed by the lower chamber on November 17 with only six negative votes, and later received the assent of the *Herrenkammer,* again with only six voices raised against it.[78]

As the Hardheim protest reveals, Catholics opposed the government's bill to transfer control of charitable foundations to the state almost as violently as they did the civil marriage legislation. Since the law dealt with property valued at about twenty million marks, their resentment had an economic, as well as a purely religious, motivation. The Quadrilateral fought the measure with all weapons at its command: denunciation, argument, parliamentary maneuver — all to no avail, despite the fact that at least some sections of the law were as offensive to Lutherans as to Catholics. During the final debate in the lower chamber early in May 1870, Catholics seem to have packed the galleries in an effort to impress the legislators. At its conclusion the five Catholic members dramatically stalked out, refusing to participate in the final ballot. The majority for the bill was therefore 49 to 3, instead of the expected 49 to 8. The three negative votes were cast by conservative Protestants.[79]

The only chance to defeat the law was in the more conservative upper chamber. Jolly was sufficiently worried that he felt obliged to answer there the fanatical attacks which had been made upon him by the clergy and by the Catholic press. Throughout the period during which the bill was under consideration, there had been repeated cries from both: "spoliation of the Church," "violation of the constitution," and "interference with religious liberty." Before the *Herrenkammer,* Jolly defended the bill not on its merits, but chiefly on the grounds that its defeat would play into the hands of the ultramontane party. "Our only support," he declared, "lies in the anticlerical party. In our country there is no basis at this time for a national government other than intense anticlericalism."[80] Although the bill would

[76] See below.
[77] Bachem, 2:323–24; Baumgarten and Jolly, 160–61; Dor, 89–90.
[78] Bachem, 2:323; Dor, 92.
[79] Bachem, 2:323; Dor, 97–98.
[80] Baumgarten and Jolly, 156–59.

doubtless have passed in some form without this appeal to prejudice, Jolly's impassioned speech may account for the fact that nearly all the moderating amendments were voted down.[81]

The Catholic party achieved only one significant victory during the session. That came when the government instituted criminal proceedings against the *Rastatter Anzeiger* for "slander and misrepresentation," because it published the text of the Hardheim resolution mentioned above. In order to raise in the courts the issue of freedom of *speech*, as well as freedom of the *press,* and to protect the editor of the *Anzeiger* as far as possible, Baumstark and Lindau, the authors of the resolution, issued a statement publicly accepting responsibility for it, thereby practically forcing the government to bring charges against them also. The court of original jurisdiction acquitted the editor, but remanded the others to the *Obergerichtshof* at Mannheim, Baden's supreme court for criminal cases. This court, however, refused the case on the ground that a criminal court had no jurisdiction. In effect, it thus acquitted the defendants, and established a legal precedent for the future.[82]

Although the *Katholische Volkspartei* secured enactment of no part of its legislative program during the 1869–70 session of the *Landtag,* its activities were not without political importance. The constant vocal opposition of Lindau and Baumstark served to emphasize for the public the conflict between Catholic and liberal viewpoints and to make the issues understandable to the unsophisticated Catholics who made up the majority of the population. It could, for example, hardly have been without some effect on opinion when Lindau announced during the budget debate in November 1869 that his conscience forbade him to approve the grant of a "single kreutzer to this unholy ministry" because of its antireligious policy.[83] In fact, so dejected did some of the liberals become over the party's strength among the masses that they openly predicted the next election would increase its representation to fifteen or twenty seats. Their concern seemed justified when, shortly after the close of the *Landtag,* elections were held for local officials in the Grand Duchy, and the Catholic party made significant gains.[84]

[81] *Ibid.,* 160.
[82] Dor, 94–95.
[83] Bachem, 2:324.
[84] "Der ausserordentliche Landtag des Grossherzogthums Baden vom 12. bis 21. Dezember, 1870," *HPB,* 67:81.

Nevertheless, its strength in the countryside grew at a comparatively slow pace. It found considerable difficulty in creating an effective organization on the lower levels, perhaps because of the political inexperience of the average Badener. Leadership remained almost entirely in the hands of the party's five parliamentary representatives. Furthermore, despite several attempts, the *Volkspartei* was not able to establish liaison with its potential friends in Bavaria and Württemberg until after the Franco-Prussian War.[85]

Lindau, however, was one of the first Catholic laymen in south Germany to realize fully that the battle against secular liberalism could not be won entirely within state boundaries. In September 1869 he made use of the opportunity afforded by an invitation to speak on political developments in his native state before the *Generalversammlung der katholischen Vereine Deutschlands* at Düsseldorf, to argue against particularism. After announcing the formation of the *Volkspartei,* he strongly urged all German Catholics to found "a great political party" dedicated to resisting the drive of liberalism toward the destruction of the Church's independence.[86] This appears to be the first concrete proposal for an all-German Catholic party. It implies, despite Lindau's advocacy of *grossdeutsch* federalism at home, a willingness to accept Bismarck's *Kleindeutschland,* or at least a realization that it could no longer be avoided.

Although the question of what might have happened had south German Catholics been able to surmount their particularistic tradition between 1868 and 1870 is academic, the astounding success of political Catholicism in Bavaria during those years suggests the possibility that, with adequate cooperation between Catholics of the four states, the denouement of Bismarck's policy might have been quite different. For here Catholics, organized under the banners of the Bavarian Patriot party, succeeded by the fall of 1869 in ending *kleindeutsch*-liberal domination of the *Landtag,* and in February of 1870 they forced the resignation of Hohenlohe himself. Moreover, as will appear later, the Patriots came very close, in the summer of 1870, to preventing Bavaria's entry into the Franco-Prussian War, while at the beginning of 1871 their attempt to prevent a peaceful consummation of the new *Reich* failed only by a hair's breadth.

[85] Bachem, 2:324.
[86] *Ibid.,* 321.

The impetus for the Patriot party is ultimately derived from the events of 1866. Bavaria's defeat, followed by the appointment of Hohenlohe, who was committed to the union of Germany under the Prussian aegis, brought to a focus all the submerged fears of the mass of Bavarians who still preserved their sentimental attachment to the old Germany. Moreover, Hohenlohe, liberal and anticlerical, sharpened those fears by sponsoring internal reforms which ran counter to the tradition and the faith of most Bavarians.[87]

The major points of conflict between Catholics and the Hohenlohe ministry up to the middle of 1868 have been outlined above.[88] The alliance treaty, the *Zollverein* treaty, Hohenlohe's support of Bismarck — all combined to create an active political consciousness among the Catholic masses, and helped to produce leaders for them. Internally, events conspired to the same end. The most hotly debated issue was the proposal to reform the educational system, introduced into the lower chamber of the *Landtag* on October 31, 1867. The intent of the bill was to give the state primary responsibility for the conduct and supervision of schools, with the exception of those existing for purely religious instruction. Local clergymen were no longer to be the sole school inspectors; that task would be taken over by a board on which the clerical representative could be swamped by members speaking for other interests. District officials appointed by the state were to be given actual administrative control over instruction. Although the government did not press for its immediate enactment, the measure provoked a tremendous amount of agitation among members of the hierarchy and among Catholic laymen, who felt that their children would thereby be turned over to the mercies of the godless state. On October 13, 1868, the bishops submitted a petition to the King, asking for "careful and unbiased consideration" of the bill, before any irrevocable steps were taken.[89]

In order to counteract the attack on confessional schools, a Catholic educator, Ludwig Auer, founded the *Katholischer Erziehungsverein* in 1867. The organization established offices throughout the country which sought to keep the average Bavarian acquainted with the Church's viewpoint on education. The society began publishing the *Ka-*

---

[87] Schieder, 193; Bachem, 2:237–38.
[88] See Chapters Four and Five.
[89] Hohenlohe, *Memoirs*, 1:328; Bachem, 2:233–37.

tholische Schulzeitung in 1868 to secure publicity for its labors. As might be expected, the *Erziehungsverein* was the victim of considerable enmity on the part of the government, which found it a constant annoyance. Only halfhearted attempts, however, were made to curb its activities.[90]

It was during the months following the close of the 1868 *Zollparlament* that the amorphous Catholic opposition to Hohenlohe's liberal and *kleindeutsch* program coalesced into a party. In part, the foundations of the *Bayrische Patriotenpartei*, or the *Bayrische Volkspartei*, were laid in Berlin during the *Zollparlament* meeting, for it was there, as indicated in the preceding chapter, that Bavarian Catholic politicians got their first real lesson in cooperation against Prussia. Yet since the party never acquired a closely knit formal structure or centralized control, it can just as accurately be considered to have taken form during the winter of 1868–69, when popular resentment against the government burst forth into more or less spontaneous political action. Following the disaster of the *Zollparlament* election, the government became considerably more aggressive toward Catholics. The minister of the interior, late in the summer of 1868, forced into retirement two well-known Catholic district officials, one of whom had been a *Zollparlament* delegate, and effected the transfer of a third from Augsburg to a heavily Protestant area, where, it was felt, he could do less harm.

In the fall it became apparent that the government was going to press for early enactment of the school reform law in order to put it into effect before the constitutional end of the *Landtag* in 1869. The most important leader of the Patriots, Joseph Edmund Jörg, and nearly all later Catholic commentators, have maintained that the Patriot movement was a spontaneous protest of the unorganized masses against such actions, which indicated the government's espousal of the twin evils — liberalism and Protestant Prussia. Such writers have stressed that the Patriot party functioned through a series of independent uncoordinated groups, each having its roots in the problems and interests of local areas. So considered, it can hardly be regarded as a party at all in the conventional sense.[91] The same writers [92] have also

---

[90] Bongartz, 41–43.

[91] Wöhler, 23; Schieder, 195, 199–200, 206–7; "Staat und Kirche," *HPB*, 65 : 909–10; "Zeitläufe: Bayern und seine Zukunft," *ibid.*, 66 : 718.

[92] See, *e.g.*, Bachem, 2 : 238, 241.

consistently maintained that the *Patriotenpartei* was not confessional in character; the fact that from the very beginning it bore the imprint of Catholicism they attribute merely to the refusal of Protestants to join it. This argument, while technically correct, fails to take into account that, so close was the connection in the popular mind between the Patriots and the Church that no sincere Protestant or freethinker could have aided the party in good conscience without severe damage to his intellectual or religious convictions.

The first obvious signs that a Catholic party was in the making are found in the increasing violence of the attacks on Hohenlohe in the Catholic press immediately after the end of the 1868 *Zollparlament*. At approximately the same time there was organized in Munich the *Verein patriotischer Männer,* parent cell of the party and source of its name. The founders were three ex-ministers of the pre-Hohenlohe era, plus several representatives of business interests, who were worried over dangers for Bavarian economic life arising from the *Zollverein's* low tariff policies.[93] Meanwhile, the Casinos in Munich and other cities were becoming more active. In July the Munich Casino established a press committee, headed by a clergyman, which disposed of considerable funds from an unidentifiable source. It projected the founding of a new newspaper to compete with the popular *Münchener neueste Nachrichten,* one of the government's major supporters, but decided that the funds could be more advantageously used to influence the editorial policy of existing Catholic papers. By midsummer Catholics in official positions who were bold enough to associate openly with the Casinos began to find themselves in difficulties with their superiors. In July, for example, a professor at the Royal Lyceum in Passau was warned by the Ministry of Education that his critical remarks on the proposed school reforms, made in an address at the Munich Casino, constituted a violation of his duty as a state official. Several other cases of a similar character are recorded.[94]

One of the chief difficulties faced by the Patriot movement was the seemingly irreconcilable division in the ranks of politically conscious

[93] Spielhofer, "Bayrische Zentrumspartei," *HPB*, 165:420. Investigation has failed to yield the names of the founders.

[94] *Ibid.*; Radowitz to Bismarck, Munich, Sept. 1, 1868, *APP*, 10: no. 126; Count Ludwig von Arco-Zinneberg to Preysing, Kaltenhausen bei Salzburg, July 29, 1868, A. Doeberl, "Preysing," *Gelbe Hefte,* 2:855; Preysing to Arco-Zinneberg, Moos, July 21, 1868, *ibid.,* 851.

Catholics between those who wanted to maintain the traditional dynastic-conservative character of the state, and those who saw the
only hope of combating liberalism in an espousal of democracy. Both
groups had cooperated in the *Zollparlament* election, for both were
equally hostile to Prussia. But if the Hohenlohe régime was to be
ousted, some means of allaying the conflict had to be found. Among
laymen, the division tended to reflect social stratification. Commoners
like Jörg and Bucher, as pointed out before, had become convinced of
the usefulness of the democratic approach because of its startling success in the *Zollparlament* election. A number of other conservatives
were beginning to see the problem in a similar light. However, young
Catholic aristocrats like Count Konrad Preysing, a leading figure in
the Munich Casino, felt that democracy would lead as rapidly to the
destruction of Bavarian independence as would an attack by the Prussian army.[95] His friend, Count Ludwig von Arco-Zinneberg, expressed
the typical antidemocratic view in a letter to Preysing, written on July
29, 1868:

A good Catholic can never be a democrat in Bavaria, if he speaks
honestly to the people. It is an absolute impossibility. One can hold the
democratic form of government as better in principle, but a Catholic
cannot, in a country where a venerable dynasty rules, declare himself
openly a democrat, because thereby he only undermines the authority
established by God.[96]

The problem was complicated by the fact that this conflict over
tactics extended to the clergy, potentially the most effective source of
leadership for the movement. The parish priests, recruited from the
lower social and economic strata, and therefore sharing somewhat the
feelings which were arousing the peasants, were often sympathetic to
the democratic appeals of Jörg and the others. A number of priests
were associated with the Casinos of Munich and Passau, in some cases
as "guests" and in others more actively. The hierarchy, on the other
hand, although in no way friendly toward Hohenlohe, was reluctant to
approve any program which set the masses politically into motion.
The Archbishop of Passau delivered a festival sermon in July 1868,
calling on the peasants to obey constituted authorities, and advising

[95] Preysing to Arco-Zinneberg, Moos, July 21, 1868, A. Doeberl, "Preysing," *Gelbe
Hefte,* 2:852.
[96] Arco-Zinneberg to Preysing, Kaltenhausen bei Salzburg, July 29, 1868, *ibid.,* 855.

them to be suspicious of malcontents who sought to lead them into disobedience and disorder. At approximately the same time the Archbishop forced the Passau Casino to abandon the use of the word *Catholic* in its title, and ordered clergymen under his jurisdiction to cease participation in its activities. Nevertheless, despite pressure from the bishops and the government, many parish priests continued to use their close connection with the common people in behalf of the new party. Not all the bishops were actively hostile. Some merely hesitated because they felt that the time was not yet ripe. Indecision, however, robbed them of the opportunity to influence either side.[97]

The Catholic press was likewise divided into democratic and dynastic-conservative wings. Zander's *Volksbote* and Jörg's *Historisch-politische Blätter* were outstanding examples of the former, while the *Augsburger Postzeitung* and the *Bayrischer Kurier* were the most important representatives of the latter. Catholic aristocrats and most bishops resented the tactics of such organs as the *Volksbote*, but as the tide of popular feeling rose, conservative Catholics found themselves ever less able to control the situation. The democrats gradually pushed them out of positions of authority in the Casinos, and the parish priests proved themselves willing to ignore restraints which the episcopate attempted to place upon their political activities.[98]

Much of the distrust felt by the bishops toward the Patriot movement arose from the extreme and untenable position which some of the Catholic radicals took on the German question. The *Volksbote*, for example, was almost openly pro-French, and it promoted a continuous campaign of vilification against Prussia. Several times during the summer of 1868 and later, it gave the impression of hoping for a French victory in the war which it, along with nearly everyone else, foresaw between Prussia and France. Since many parish clergymen regularly read this inflammatory journal, the bishops had considerable reason to fear its ultimate effect on the Bavarian masses. The fear was in no way reduced when Jörg, regarded as the leader of the extremists, emerged as chief spokesman for the Patriots. As should have been apparent from his former pronouncements, Jörg was no French sympathizer.

[97] Preysing to Arco-Zinneberg, Moos, July 21, 1868, *ibid.*, 851–53; Spielhofer, "Bayrische Zentrumspartei," *HPB*, 165:420–21.

[98] A. Doeberl, "Preysing," *Gelbe Hefte*, 2:846; Spielhofer, "Bayrische Zentrumspartei," *HPB*, 165:420; Martin, *Zeitschrift für bayrische Landesgeschichte*, 6:61; Spielhofer, "Bayrische Parteien," *Oberbayrisches Archiv*, 63:155.

It was, however, in no way illogical to fear that the extremists, by opposing any binding ties with north Germany, would force Bavaria willy-nilly into the arms of Napoleon.[99]

As the Patriot movement crystallized during the winter of 1868–69, a more or less consistent doctrine finally developed. All the Patriots could agree that there should be no closer union with north Germany and Prussia. All of them likewise agreed in their opposition to the proposed educational reforms. Most of them were willing to support suffrage reform to abolish the electoral colleges and to introduce direct voting for the lower house of the *Landtag*. The last was adopted more for the sake of expediency than of principle, for a democratic suffrage seemed the most adequate way to bring an end to what Jörg called "party government," *i.e.*, the liberal régime.[100]

The Patriots professed, as did their counterparts in Baden, to aim at creation of a *Grossdeutschland* as the ultimate goal. Practically every one of their local groups specifically rejected any thought of an alliance between Bavaria and a non-German power. It appears, however, that their adoption of *grossdeutsch* federalism was, as in Baden, a gesture to the past, since nearly all Bavarians recognized that the *grossdeutsch* ideal was in fact dead. The real goal of the Patriots was preservation of Bavarian sovereignty completely unfettered. This they managed to rationalize with their professed federalism by arguing that it was necessary to preserve a foundation in south Germany upon which a federal structure could later be erected. Like the *Volkspartei* in Baden, the Patriots spoke hopefully of a southern confederation. It is easily seen that all the practical and achievable parts of their program were negative and particularistic, while the few positive suggestions were survivals from the past.[101] Jörg revealed the true nature of the movement when he wrote, "Bavarian particularism is only the result of the customary piety of the people and their loyalty to their sovereign." Although the King had failed in his duty to defend his own

[99] Döllinger was of the opinion that there was no real sympathy for France in Bavaria in 1868. The priest who headed the press committee of the Munich Casino was quoted, however, as saying, "We have to work in two directions and for two goals: In the religious sphere we proceed decisively with Rome; in the political sphere, with France." See Radowitz to Bismarck, Munich, Sept. 1, 1868, *APP*, 10: no. 126. See also Martin, *Zeitschrift für bayrische Landesgeschichte*, 6:61; Schieder, 201.

[100] Bachem, 2:237–38; "Zeitläufe: Bayern," *HPB*, 64:651–52, 656.

[101] Martin, *Zeitschrift für bayrische Landesgeschichte*, 6:61; Schieder, 202.

rights and those of his people, they would defend his.[102] On another occasion, the Munich editor explained the connection between the Patriots and the Church in a similar vein by writing, "What is called 'ultramontanism' in Bavaria today is nothing more than the loyal and honorable expression of the general popular feeling.[103]

Closely connected with the Patriots in outlook and objectives were the *Bayrisch-patriotische Bauernvereine,* the first of which was founded by Count Hafenbrädl in 1868. These societies, originally designed to protect the economic interests of agricultural producers, soon developed general political significance. They enrolled many large and small landowners, some members of the clergy, and even a few individuals from the middle class in the smaller towns. In many ways the *Bauernvereine* served as the chief contact between Catholic politicians and their most important single bloc of voters, the rural landowners.[104]

The first showdown between the government and a revitalized political Catholicism came in February 1869, when the ministry, faced with the approaching constitutional end of the *Landtag,* sought to take advantage of the still bitter divisions within Catholic ranks to force passage of the school reform law. In the chamber the debate occupied the week of February 15–23. It was marked by a successful drive of left-wing liberals to add to the bill amendments providing a degree of separation of Church and state far beyond what Hohenlohe had contemplated. In the *Reichsräthe,* however, the bill ran into heavy opposition from the Catholic aristocracy. Hohenlohe himself addressed the upper chamber on April 19, arguing that it was vital to settle the matter favorably before the beginning of the forthcoming Vatican Council. In his view, expressed in a circular dispatch to the German governments a few days earlier,[105] the Council meant nothing less than a declaration of war by the Church against all things modern. It was necessary that Bavaria put herself on record before it was too late. Despite the minister-president's direct intervention, the bill failed to receive a majority. Therefore, the last important action of the expiring *Landtag* represented a major defeat for the government, a defeat which ominously foreshadowed events of the next nine months.[106]

[102] "Zeitläufe: Bayern und seine Zukunft," *HPB,* 66:719.
[103] "Zeitläufe: Bayern," *ibid.,* 63:766.
[104] "Zeitläufe: Bayern," *ibid.,* 64:654–56; Schieder, 199–200. See Chapter Two.
[105] See Chapter Seven.
[106] Schieder, 194–96; Hohenlohe, *Memoirs,* 1:328–29, 332.

North and South during the Pause, 1868–1869

The campaign which preceded elections to the new *Landtag* was one of the most savage in nineteenth-century German history. All issues tended to become simplified into one: support for, or opposition to, the Hohenlohe program. Consequently, the various liberal groups, despite their disagreements, closed ranks against the Patriots. The latter, professing to view the contest as a class struggle between the bourgeoisie and the traditional *Stände,* made effective use of the Catholic press and of organizations, such as the Casinos and the *Bauernvereine,* to mobilize public opinion. To a much greater degree than ever before, popular distrust of Prussia became a weapon against Hohenlohe and all he stood for. Among typical slogans of the Patriots were "Down with the eternal tax squeeze of military despotism!" and "The bloodsucking military state must be curbed." The country was flooded with pamphlets predicting that Bavarian independence was doomed unless evil men who were working for a Prussianized Germany were thrown out of office.[107]

Nor was the appeal to violent passions limited to the Patriots. All restraint was cast off by government supporters as well. They hurled the epithet "ultramontane" at all their opponents with reckless abandon. Some of the more extreme among them publicly admitted that they would rather see a Prussian army in Munich than permit ultramontane control of the Bavarian government. Jörg commented that one did not need to be even a Catholic in Bavaria to be dubbed ultramontane. One had only to oppose Hohenlohe. Both sides made constant reference to a coming European war. Government supporters stressed the naked position of a Bavaria without ties to Prussia, while Patriots harped on danger of the existing alliance to Bavarian independence.[108]

Perhaps the feature of the campaign which aroused the greatest liberal indignation was the direct intervention of the Catholic clergy in behalf of the Patriots. Clergymen often refused to grant absolution to Catholics who persisted in reading liberal newspapers, and many of them campaigned actively for Patriot candidates. In such a situation, religion itself could hardly escape becoming an issue. As the campaign progressed, anticlericalism, and even anti-Catholicism, became more

[107] Schieder, 195–201, 203.
[108] *Ibid.,* 199–200, 204; "Zeitläufe: Bayern," *HPB,* 63:766; "Zeitläufe: Der Krieg," *HPB,* 65:474.

and more the focus of the liberal attack. Ever more frequently was heard the demand that the people of Bavaria and of Europe be freed from the domination of an obscurantist clergy. Catholic supporters of Hohenlohe, such as Döllinger, had foreseen such an outburst. Döllinger himself proposed confidentially to the minister during the campaign that much might be gained if Hohenlohe would take conciliatory steps toward the clergy. He suggested particularly that the proposed educational reforms be referred to responsible clerics for consideration, so that the bill might find a more hospitable reception in the coming *Landtag*. Many clergymen, Döllinger indicated, feared that the law was directed against the Church itself, and the government, through its own diffidence, had allowed the religious issue to be injected into the campaign. The result could only be evil. There is no evidence that Hohenlohe took any action on Döllinger's suggestion.[109]

Jörg defended clerical participation in the campaign by arguing that the government had deprived the people of all their natural leaders by patronage, and the priests were thus the only ones whom the average Bavarian could in confidence follow. Moreover, if universal direct suffrage, as advocated by the Patriots, were adopted, clerical intervention would become unnecessary, for the people would then develop their own leaders.

If these guarantees [direct, secret ballot] were once achieved, then the clergy could sooner save its breath in political affairs. So long as the cleverly contrived apparatus of the electoral colleges exists, however, just so long will the clergy be the destined aid for the people in their opposition; it must give the people all the help it can, according to law and conscience, wherever it finds itself capable of doing so and sees the ground prepared.[110]

The moral implications of active participation in a political movement caused considerable anxiety within the ranks of the clergy itself. The *Historisch-politische Blätter* discussed the problem on at least two occasions. One issue carried the substance of a letter from a Bavarian priest who admitted that he had undergone a terrible inner conflict before deciding what he should do. He had concluded that since the Church was not of this world, the form of the state was of no matter to him as a clergyman. His sole concern with the election was its effect on the Church. Since he felt unqualified to judge, he decided

---

[109] Schieder, 206–7; Döllinger to Hohenlohe, April 15, 1869, Hohenlohe, *Memoirs*, 1:329.
[110] "Zeitläufe: Bayern," *HPB*, 63:765–66, 771–72.

that he could only remain aloof.[111] Jörg expressed considerable sympathy for the state of mind which motivated this viewpoint. Nevertheless, he felt it was wrong. The clergy, he insisted, had a duty to defend its own rightful domain, which was under violent attack by the liberals.

> The Bavarian clergy in the present generation can, whatever it wishes, support and advance, either directly or indirectly, no other policies than the instinctive one of the real people or the well-thought-out one of their uncompromising enemy.[112]

There was no middle ground. Compromise was of no avail, for the liberals regarded willingness to compromise merely as a sign of weakness, which served only to increase their contempt and hatred for the Church. Jörg advised that the clergy had no course to follow but "the generally valid rule, *Est modus in rebus.*" [113]

Before the campaign ended, a large number of rural clerics did abandon their traditional conservatism and disregarded the strictures of the bishops. At the last moment, even many of the latter came out for the Patriots, and counseled voters that it was a religious duty to elect Catholic deputies. The people went to the polls on May 12, 1869, and the Patriots reaped the harvest of the fears and the passions they had helped sow. When the ballots were counted in the electoral colleges, which met on May 20, it appeared that the Patriots had won an absolute majority in the lower chamber. The results demonstrated to what degree the Patriot movement represented a revolt of agricultural districts against domination by urban interests, for the liberals won all the cities except three — Freising, Regensburg, and Bamberg — while the Patriots were almost everywhere else victorious. Their success was attributable largely to the rural clergy and to the *Bauernvereine,* with some help from the Casinos in the cities.[114]

---

[111] "Gedanken über das persönliche Verhalten des katholischen Klerus zu den politischen Zeitfragen," *HPB*, 63:581–96, *passim*.

[112] "Zeitläufe: Bayern," *HPB*, 63:770–72.

[113] *Ibid.*, 772.

[114] Spielhofer, "Bayrische Zentrumspartei," *HPB*, 165:421–22; Schieder, 209–10; Rovère, 98–99. It is now generally agreed that the Patriots were entitled to a small majority. Bachem, for example, gives the Patriots seventy-nine seats; the Liberals, fifty-five; and the Center, *i.e.*, the ministerial party, twenty. See Bachem, 2:240. Hohenlohe, however, seeking to minimize the disaster, chose apparently to regard two disputed elections as already decided against the Patriots. According to his calculation, the Patriots would have seventy-seven seats; the Liberals, fifty-six; the Center, twenty; and the Popular party (Independent Democratic), one. Since the last three were equally anticlerical, Hohenlohe

In the months which intervened between the election and the assembling of the *Landtag*, enmity between the Patriots and their opponents increased. The former loudly demanded the immediate resignation of the entire Hohenlohe ministry, claiming that the election had demonstrated how little confidence the country had in the government. The press of each side heaped abuse on the other. Hohenlohe remained officially deaf to all cries for his departure. In a communication to Bavarian legations abroad, he indicated his own and his colleagues' satisfaction that the clericals had been able to gain no more than they had. The Patriots, he pointed out, apparently did not feel strong enough to demand abrogation of the treaties between Bavaria and Prussia. While the division in the lower chamber would, he admitted, make enactment of further reforms impossible, the government's reverse was not sufficiently great to destroy what had already been done. There could, he felt, be no justification for his resignation at that time.[115]

By late September, when the Landtag convened, the situation had deteriorated so far that to some people civil war did not appear to be beyond the realm of possibility. The virulent conflict which had been raging all summer immediately broke forth in the chamber. Control of this body depended on its decision in several disputed elections. Each of the blocs proceeded, from partisan motives, to disqualify as many of its opponents as possible. In all, nine seats were declared vacant. They were so distributed that seventy-two Patriots and seventy-two Hohenlohe supporters remained. In the resulting impasse, it proved impossible even to elect a president of the chamber. The government faction withdrew its favorite candidate, Marquard Barth, and put forth the moderate liberal, Edel, in the hope of dislodging a few votes from the solid Patriot phalanx. The Patriots backed Weiss, who was considered an extremist. On the one ballot which was taken, the division stood seventy-one to seventy-one. Hohenlohe then began negotiations with Patriot leaders, and, having failed to find the slightest crack in the support for Weiss, asked the King to dissolve the chamber. Dissolution followed on October 6. The Patriots believed, or

judged that the chamber would divide evenly. See Circular to the Royal Legations, May 29, 1869, Hohenlohe, *Memoirs*, 1:340.

[115] "Zeitläufe: Bayern," *HPB*, 64:650–51; Circular to the Royal Legations, May 29, 1869, Hohenlohe, *Memoirs*, 1:340–41.

professed to believe, that Hohenlohe had refused any compromise in the hope that a second election would produce different results. This judgment appears to have been erroneous, for the minister noted in his journal the day the chamber was dissolved that he feared nothing was to be gained by the step. It seems more likely that he was taking the only possible way, other than capitulation, out of a situation which would have made a constitutional crisis inevitable.[116]

Bavaria thus faced a second election in less than a year. To liberals it seemed that the prospect was somewhat better than in the spring. First of all, the government in the interim took the opportunity to rearrange a few electoral districts, defending the action as necessary to correct certain inequalities, while the Patriots called it illegal gerrymandering. In the second place, during the intervening months a tendency appeared among some German bishops who were attending the Vatican Council to resist efforts of the Roman Curia to dogmatize papal infallibility.[117] It was hoped that a split in the ranks of the Patriots would result. The government again used every possible means to insure a liberal-nationalist victory, turning, as Jörg charged, every branch of the administration down to the forest rangers into a "compact, hostile army against the Patriots." On the other side the clergy was again active. The campaign surpassed in ferocity even the earlier one of the same year. The result this time, however, was a decisive victory for the Patriots. Even Munich returned a Patriot majority. In the Allgäu, which in May had sent 134 liberals to the electoral college, against 49 Patriots, the Patriots elected 104 and the liberals 79. The chamber, as first constituted, included 80 Patriots and 74 pro-Hohenlohe deputies. After all disputes had been decided, the figures were 83 and 71. The Center party, *i.e.*, the group most closely identified with Hohenlohe, suffered near annihilation. Many of the most prominent individuals on the liberal side in former chambers failed of reelection.[118]

The minister-president, on the day after the final results became known, discussed with his colleagues whether the resignation of the

---

[116] Schieder, 213; Wöhler, 23; Bachem, 2:240; "Zeitläufe: Bayern," *HPB*, 64:650–51, 657–59; Journal, Sept. 28 and 29 and Oct. 6, 1869, Hohenlohe, *Memoirs*, 368, 370.

[117] See Chapter Seven.

[118] The people voted on November 16; the electoral colleges on November 25. Schieder, 215, 218; Bachem, 2:240; "Zeitläufe: Paris, Bayern, und Berlin," *HPB*, 64:75–76; "Zeitläufe: Bayern," *ibid.*, 649–50; Journal, Nov. 26, 1869, Hohenlohe, *Memoirs*, 1:375.

entire ministry, or of himself alone, was required. No decision was reached at that time, but later the same day Hohenlohe decided to tender his personal resignation. King Ludwig, however, refused to accept it, indicating his complete confidence in the minister. The latter, in a touching letter, expressed his thanks to the King and agreed to retain his post, at least temporarily. He advised his sovereign, however, that, although he believed the existing lines of foreign policy could be continued, drastic changes in the conduct of domestic affairs would be inevitable. It would be obligatory for the ministry to accept universal, direct suffrage, against which the King had always taken a firm stand. It would be equally vital for it to agree to reform of the upper house. Patriot demands that legislative initiative be given to the chamber could no longer be resisted, and some ministerial changes would have to be made. Only if the King agreed to these conditions could Hohenlohe remain. Furthermore, he advised Ludwig to consult with Patriot leaders to discover what were the minimum concessions they would consider.[119]

The *Landtag* met on New Year's Day, 1870. Weiss, this time, was elected president without difficulty. Jörg, as the leader of the majority party, became *Referent*, or first secretary. The speech from the throne, written by Hohenlohe and delivered on January 17, stressed the necessity of ending the bitter party strife which had rent the country for a year and a half. It assured the *Landtag* that the treaties with Prussia in no way threatened the independence of Bavaria. On the following day, the lower chamber elected a committee to draw up an address to the throne. Jörg became chairman of the committee, and, under his direction, it drafted an address which contained a declaration of no confidence in the entire ministry.

Sincere loyalty to Your Majesty and unshaken fidelity to the country and its independent development have produced among the majority of the people a feeling of mistrust to which the result of the elections has given expression, a feeling accentuated by the party spirit of the ministry.

The noble words of Your Majesty are calculated to calm excited feelings; but thorough confidence will not be restored until Your Majesty succeeds in finding, as advisers of your crown, men who combine

[119] Journal, Nov. 26, 1869, Letter to the King, Dec. 1, 1869, Hohenlohe, *Memoirs*, 375, 378–80.

good intentions with firm action, and possess alike the confidence of Your Majesty and of the country.[120]

While Jörg's committee was laboring on the address, the upper chamber, which had always been hostile to Hohenlohe, adopted a resolution of no confidence in the minister personally. Only twelve votes were cast in his favor. Hohenlohe had appeared in person before the *Reichsräthe,* concluding his address with the defiant charge that the only reason for the chamber's lack of confidence was that he had loyally carried out Bavaria's treaty obligations to north Germany. Early in February, the draft address came up for debate in the lower chamber. Jörg led the attack, denouncing Hohenlohe's alleged refusal to carry out the will of the country, which, according to the *Referent,* required that the alliance treaty with Prussia be revoked. Here, too, the minister defended his record in person, directing his remarks specifically to Jörg, but with no ascertainable effect. At the last moment the Patriots decided, as a tactical move, to concentrate their efforts on Hohenlohe alone. Jörg dramatically withdrew the original motion of censure and substituted another which eliminated all references to the other members of the government. The house adopted this version of the address by a vote of seventy-seven to sixty-two on February 10, 1870. Again Hohenlohe offered his resignation, and again Ludwig refused to accept it on the grounds that to give way to such pressure was a sign of weakness which might be dangerous for the monarchy itself. At length, however, the King was persuaded that there was no alternative. In a letter accepting the resignation, he stated for the record that he was acting solely because Hohenlohe had adduced strong personal reasons for wishing to be relieved, not because of the *Landtag*'s lack of confidence. The minister-president stepped down on February 18.[121]

The Patriots had thus won a victory potentially of vast significance for the future of Bavaria and of Germany. They had forced out of office the man who was without a doubt Prussia's most influential friend south of the Main. In so doing they had well-nigh destroyed one of the keystones upon which Bismarckian policy toward south Germany had been built: the assumption that south German nationalists would be able to bring about union of the two sections without the di-

[120] Spielhofer, "Bayrische Zentrumspartei," *HPB,* 165:424; Wöhler, 23; Hohenlohe, *Memoirs,* 1:385.
[121] Schieder, 234; Bachem, 2:240, 242; Hohenlohe, *Memoirs,* 1:389–90, 400, 403–4.

rect intervention of Prussia. As Bavaria went, so, very likely, would go Baden and Württemberg, particularly since nationalists were already under heavy attack in those states as well. The victory was, however, not complete. The remainder of Hohenlohe's cabinet still held office, and the King, by his appointment of the Bavarian ambassador to Vienna, Count Bray-Steinberg, as Hohenlohe's successor, insured that the demands of the extremists for abrogation of the alliance treaty would not be carried out. Bray, a close friend of Beust, and certainly no champion of Prussia, could be counted upon to keep the treaty in force — if for no other reason than that he could see, as Jörg and the Patriots could not, that the defense of Bavaria against France depended on it.[122]

The Patriots themselves were only slightly discouraged by this turn of events. Their victory had been too sweeping for them to be disheartened by a minor check. As early as midsummer of 1869 Jörg had attributed the "tame" session of the *Zollparlament* to the outcome of the first Bavarian election, and had gloated over the reaction to that election in Paris as well as Berlin.[123] The second, and decisive, victory of the Patriots could not but furnish an even greater impediment to the achievement of the North German Chancellor's designs. Even if it had not been possible to effect a complete sweep of the Hohenlohe influence, the man himself was gone. The initiative had passed out of the hands of the *kleindeutsch* nationalists, and the challenge of liberalism had been met and hurled back. Barring some untoward happening, the Patriots could block any further concessions to the North, and might hope eventually to revoke those which had already been made.

The above represents the judgment of the vanquished as well as that of the victors. Both Hohenlohe and Werthern, the Prussian ambassador at Munich, were convinced that the disaster was directly attributable to the stagnation in Berlin which had allowed the initiative in the South to be wrested from the hands of the national party.[124] Prussian sympathizers in Bavaria were saying early in December 1869, "If the

---

[122] Schieder, 234; Wöhler, 23; Bachem, 2:242; Spielhofer, "Bayrische Zentrumspartei," *HPB,* 165:424; E. Salzer, "Fürst Chlodwig zu Hohenlohe-Schillingsfürst und die deutsche Frage," *Historische Vierteljahrschrift,* 11 (1908):63, 73–74. Bismarck, in a report to the King, Nov. 20, 1869, referred to the possibility of Hohenlohe's fall and replacement by a "Catholic-Austrian minister" as a "calamity." See *GW,* 6b: no. 1449.

[123] "Zeitläufe: Die letzten Ereignisse in Paris, Bayern, und Berlin," *HPB,* 64:74.

[124] Bismarck, *GW,* 6b: Introduction to no. 1459.

German question is not brought to life again quickly and decisively, then the process of crumbling will inevitably go on, and in three years more Bavaria will be completely in the hands of the priests." [125] Moreover, as the winter of 1869–70 merged into spring, not only was the clerical party in the saddle in Bavaria, but a clerical party was showing signs of considerable vitality in Baden, and the democratic-*grossdeutsch*-clerical opposition in Württemberg was becoming dangerous to Varnbüler's government. The Vatican Council was clearly pressing onward toward promulgation of the Dogma of Papal Infallibility, which would strengthen ultramontane elements everywhere. Clearly the next move, if move there was to be, was up to Bismarck.

[125] *Ibid.*, no. 1459.

Chapter 7

Bismarck and the Church, 1866–1870

SINCE this study seeks primarily to explore the growth of political Catholicism in Germany during the years of transition between the old Confederation and the new Empire, it has dealt only infrequently with the Papacy, the hierarchy, and their relations with the various German governments. Nevertheless, the mounting antagonism of the Roman Curia toward liberal and scientific intellectual trends of the nineteenth century, culminating in the decrees of the Vatican Council of 1869–70, had a profound effect upon the relationship of German Catholics, individually and collectively, and of the Church itself, with those governments. Moreover, diplomatic relations between the Papacy and the German governments, especially between the Papacy and Bismarck, had an influence by no means negligible upon the development of political Catholicism. Finally, the whole politico-religious conflict had considerable bearing upon the origins of the War of 1870. It is necessary, therefore, to interrupt the main narrative at this point in order to bring these developments in the realm of *haute politique* into proper focus.

Evidence of Bismarck's hostility to Catholic politicians has already been presented on several occasions. Nothing in his career, however, suggests that he had any religious prejudice against Catholics as such. His own religious beliefs, although deep and sincere, were highly unorthodox,[1] and not of the sort that led to religious bigotry. In general, he had little patience with organized churches of any variety, for he viewed them all essentially as political blocs which frequently stood

---

[1] Georges Goyau, *Bismarck et l'église: le culturkampf, 1870–1878*, 1:1, 9. Bismarck as an elderly man described his youthful religious views as "pantheistic." See *Gedanken und Erinnerungen*, 1:19.

in the path of what he sought to accomplish. Moreover, while he had come to distrust the Papacy during his sojourn as Prussian envoy to the Federal Diet at Frankfurt, largely because of the close alliance which then existed between the Curia and the Habsburgs, it appears that his aversion to political Catholicism dates primarily from the events of 1866. Certainly, except for the constant difficulties he faced as Prussian minister-president in dealing with the Polish Catholics, there is little evidence of friction before that date.

In 1851 the young Bismarck had referred to Prussian Catholics as the most loyal subjects of the King, and during the fifties and early sixties he apparently viewed the Catholic clergy of the Rhineland, along with the landed aristocracy in the east, as main bulwarks against bourgeois liberalism. Something akin to this attitude was still visible even in 1866, for the Catholic masses of the Rhineland seem to have formed one of the chief groups to whom his proposal for reform of the Federal Diet was designed to appeal. He hoped, through espousal of universal, equal suffrage, to enlist them, along with others in the lower economic strata, in defense of the monarchical principle — again to counteract the influence of the liberal bourgeoisie. There is no evidence that he ever intended to establish a single national German Church through amalgamation of the Protestant and Catholic faiths, as some Catholics charged during the *Kulturkampf*.[2]

For the first eighteen months after the end of the war with Austria, Bismarck, as indicated above, was faced with the determined antagonism of a few Catholic politicians as he strove to establish the North German Confederation, and to forge bonds between it and the southern states. Their opposition was generally ineffectual, but always irritating. Polish delegates to the Reichstag repeatedly protested inclusion of any part of their national territory in the new German state. The Hanoverian Catholic, Windthorst, persistently refused to abandon his fight in behalf of the deposed Guelph dynasty. Prussian Catholics like Mallinckrodt more than once denounced Bismarck's *Bund* in the name of abstract justice. In south Germany sullen acceptance of the military decision gradually disappeared, and was replaced, especially on the part of Catholics, by a vehement animosity toward Prussia, notably after the publication of the secret treaties early in 1867. The constant accumulation of these minor grievances caused Bismarck, a few months

[2] Hansen, 1:782; Ziekursch, 1:108; Pastor, *Reichensperger*, 2:60.

after the war, to become thoroughly angry. He wrote to Arnim at Rome in December 1866, that the "Catholic fraction" was the most hostile group in the Prussian *Abgeordnetenhaus*, accusing it of an antagonism toward the government which surpassed even that of "red democracy." [3]

Bismarck's conception of how to deal with this problem reveals one of his few political blind spots. For then, as later, he tended to blame the intransigeance of German Catholics directly on the Papacy, failing completely to realize that their hostility toward him arose very largely out of resentment of his ruthless destruction of the old order in Germany. It was, then, by pressure on the Vatican that Bismarck first sought to end Catholic opposition. The defeat of Austria had enormously increased the danger that the Italian government might forcibly occupy Rome, particularly since the scheduled departure of French troops in December 1866 would leave it practically undefended. Throughout the fall of that year the Roman question occupied the attention of Prussian diplomacy, while, as has been pointed out,[4] Pius IX attempted to arrange a possible sanctuary in the Hohenzollern domain. The letter to Arnim cited above was the beginning of a not too subtle attempt to blackmail the Pontiff, on the assumption that it was within his power to end obstructionism of Catholic deputies in the Prussian *Landtag*. Bismarck wrote, "If Rome either has not the will or the power to exercise a calming and moderating influence upon its adherents, and to make the cause of governments its own, what interest can governments have in making the cause of the Pope *their* own?" [5]

It is extremely unlikely that this blackmail could ultimately have succeeded in any case. Bismarck, however, was prevented from carrying it through to a conclusion because of the complex situation which arose as a result of the withdrawal of French troops. In the summer of 1867 the old republican, Garibaldi, led a filibuster into papal territory, and, after twice being captured and twice escaping, on October 27 he defeated a papal force sent to apprehend him for the third time. The following day a French detachment debarked at Cività Vecchia and marched again into Rome. A few days later Garibaldi's troops suffered a crushing defeat at the hands of a combined French and papal army.

[3] Bismarck to Arnim, Berlin, Dec. 8, 1866, *GW*, 6: no. 628.
[4] See Chapter Three.
[5] Bismarck to Arnim, Berlin, Dec. 8, 1866, *GW*, 6: no. 628.

Although the Italian government disclaimed any responsibility for Garibaldi's expedition, relations between Florence and Paris naturally became strained. Bismarck, who desired to retain the friendship of Italy, could not, therefore, act in the Pope's behalf himself. Because he also feared to precipitate war with France at that time, or over that issue, he could not afford to intervene in favor of Italy. He was forced, then, officially to maintain a neutral attitude. His official correspondence makes it perfectly clear that the decisive factor in his decision was the possible effect of any action on the thirteen and a half million German Catholics.[6] On October 21 he informed Usedom in Florence that he opposed any Prussian intervention to assist Italy in acquiring Rome. Germany's destiny, he explained, was achievable only through a united citizenry. The preservation of religious peace was a prerequisite for that unity, and was, therefore, far more important than the possible loss of Italy as an ally. The "ultramontane party," he argued, had been hitherto unimportant in Prussia, and had not yet succeeded in exercising undue influence south of the Main.

This situation would alter to our disadvantage as soon as the mass of devout Catholics should become convinced, rightly or wrongly, that Prussia was in open conflict with the supreme head of the Church, and had undertaken a bloody and difficult war with France to deprive her [France] of her status as defender of the Pope.[7]

He went on to predict that in such an event the eight million Catholics of north Germany would no longer elect ten or twelve (*sic*) obstructionists to the Reichstag from areas where they possessed an absolute majority. They would then be fully capable of sending to Berlin as many as a hundred deputies, every one of whom would be implacably hostile to the government. Moreover, the blow at the religious sensitivities of Catholics in south Germany would be even more serious, and the new basis of unity only recently achieved through the *Schutz- und Trutzbündnisse* would be jeopardized. On the other hand, he concluded, *if France were to attack Germany over some issue which did not involve the religious question* (italics by the author), German national feeling would be immeasurably strengthened.[8] The significance of this analysis can scarcely be overestimated in view of subsequent

[6] Bismarck to Usedom, Berlin, Oct. 13, 1867, *GW*, 6a: no. 885; Goyau, *Bismarck*, 1:28.
[7] Bismarck to Usedom, Berlin, Oct. 21, 1867, *GW*, 6a: no. 899.
[8] *Ibid.*

events, for it throws new light on the complex question of Bismarck's later tactics in dealing with France. In particular, it suggests why, in 1869–70, with such a wealth of legitimate disputes to draw upon, he chose to make use of the fantastic issue of the Hohenzollern candidacy to force France into declaring war.

While Bismarck was not inclined in 1867 to go to war with Napoleon in defense of Italy's hypothetical right to Rome, he was no more disposed to assist the Emperor in getting out of his own difficulties with the Italian government. Thus, Napoleon's proposal for an international conference to settle the Roman question fell upon deaf ears in Berlin. In Darmstadt, however, Dalwigk, seeing another opportunity to embarrass the north German Chancellor, as well as to demonstrate his own independence, openly supported the Emperor's project. Bismarck's anger became apparent when a series of violent denunciations of Dalwigk began to appear in the *Norddeutsche Allgemeine Zeitung,* the Chancellor's favorite organ. This train of events reached its culmination on November 24, 1867, when Bismarck sent a message to Darmstadt threatening to have Hesse declared in violation of the *Bundesverfassung,* unless the position of its government was reversed. But Dalwigk refused to bow to pressure from Berlin, stating that duty required him to defend the interests of Catholics who lived in the section of the Grand Duchy which was not part of the North German Confederation. He denied that anyone had reason to doubt Hesse's loyalty to the obligations it had assumed toward north Germany. Significantly, Dalwigk received congratulations from Beust for his "independent attitude and policy." The possibility that this conflict between Bismarck and Dalwigk would develop into a major crisis in German affairs disappeared when Napoleon abandoned the conference scheme because of his failure to induce any major power to support it.[9]

Meanwhile, Rome was attempting to keep open its lines of communication with Berlin. One faction within the Curia had recommended since the end of the war that Prussia's new status in Germany be recognized by sending a prelate of high rank to Berlin as Papal Nuncio. Bismarck was not unfavorable to the idea, believing that he could deal with German Catholic opposition more effectively through an official representative of the Vatican than through the Catholic section of the Prussian *Kultusministerium.* The latter, he was convinced, took its orders from

[9] Vogt, 165–67.

Rome, but the Papacy could in no way be held responsible for its actions. King Wilhelm, however, could not be persuaded that it was appropriate for a Protestant sovereign to receive a Papal Nuncio. Moreover, Pius IX himself did not believe that such a step was wise, since he felt, in common with the majority of the Curia, that the unfortunate effects which it might have upon the sensibilities of France and Austria would more than counterbalance any advantages. On the other hand, the Pope was willing to take cognizance of Prussia's new position by offering a satisfactory compromise on the long-discussed problem of religious arrangements for Catholic soldiers in the Prussian army. According to the terms of an agreement reached in 1868, all such soldiers were placed under the exclusive religious jurisdiction of a military bishop appointed by the Pope with royal consent. Several German prelates cautioned against acceptance of this arrangement, fearing that it would create a special clergy under direct control of the military authorities, but the Pontiff considered that the gesture of friendship could hardly be withheld.[10]

Against this backdrop of cool, but not unfriendly, relations between the Papacy and the Prussian government, the *Zollparlament* elections of February 1868 must once again be considered. As already indicated, the disaster suffered by the national parties in these elections was responsible for a decided shift in Bismarck's German policy. In addition, it marked the beginning of his active antagonism to the Catholic Church as such, and thus represents an important milestone on the road to the *Kulturkampf*. When the north German Chancellor had sufficiently mastered his disappointment and recovered his calm, he prepared a careful analysis of the whole problem of the Church in Germany as he saw it in the light of recent history. This he dispatched to Arnim on April 12, 1868, with instructions to make use of its contents "in the proper manner to enlighten the Roman Curia on the state of things."[11]

Bismarck began by observing that the Church, during the preceding twelve months, had taken a position toward events in Germany so striking that it compelled attention. For a quarter of a century, he went on, churchmen had regarded the status of Catholics in Prussia

[10] Goyau, *L'Allemagne religieuse*, 3:317–18; Bismarck, *Gedanken und Erinnerungen*, 2:156–57.

[11] Bismarck to Arnim, Berlin, April 12, 1868, *APP*, 9: no. 722.

as in some ways ideal. He cited several well-known statements of important ecclesiastics as evidence. Nevertheless, it was a "notorious fact" that in the conflict which led to the War of 1866 Catholic circles in Germany had taken Austria's part, although the Curia itself, he took pains to make clear, was in no way responsible. The behavior of some Prussian Catholics had been little less than treasonable. The good sense of the people and of most clergymen had prevented this subterranean campaign from becoming dangerous. But, had the course of military events taken a slightly different direction, the government would have found it of real concern.

The Chancellor found no difficulty in explaining the attitude of clerical sympathizers under the circumstances of early 1866. But since the end of the war, too, this "overt and covert war of Catholic-ecclesiastical circles against Prussia" had been continued, most obviously in the political campaigns which preceded the *Zollparlament* elections. "Everywhere, and almost without exception, the Catholic clergy has appeared as the opponent, really, as the enemy, of Prussia and the North German Confederation." He reviewed examples of clerical hostility in every one of the southern states except Hesse-Darmstadt, pointing out that Catholics had been willing to ally with any group, provided only that such an alliance would contribute to the defeat of candidates friendly toward Prussia. Clericals had thus associated with democrats, and worse. These "unnatural alliances" Bismarck regarded as the chief explanation for the victory of the particularists. This claim, he insisted, was based not so much on the laments of the defeated as it was upon the boasts of the victors. The *Augsburger Postzeitung*, for example, had openly congratulated the clergy for its aid in defeating nationalist candidates.

Bismarck went on to point out that the Catholic press had not hesitated to use slander, libel, and outright provocation to violence in order to arouse the populace against Prussia. In this it had been ably seconded by Catholic organs in foreign lands, particularly those in France and Belgium. From his reading of the evidence, he could only deduce that there was actually a "Catholic policy" purposing the humiliation and ultimate destruction of Prussia. He warned that such a policy could lead only to a sharpening of Protestant hostility toward the favored constitutional position of the Catholic Church in the Hohenzollern domain. Many north German Catholics were themselves concerned over what was happening. In this way he explained the widespread opposition to the appointment of a Papal Nuncio, for, he said, north German Catholics were afraid that he would become a tool of the ultramontane forces "now dominating the German clergy."

The Chancellor reiterated his desire for good relations between Prussia and the Church. But for such relations to continue, he warned, it was vital that Rome meet the government halfway. Otherwise Prussia might well come to regard the interests of the Church in south Germany as inimical to her own interests and to those of the Confederation.

The voices which maintain that a lasting peace between Prussia and the Catholic Church is not possible . . . find in the manifestations [I have] cited only too strong a support. Should further experience prove them right, should we have to recognize that the party which is the open enemy of Prussia really exercises control in the Church, and that the Church itself on its highest level has either not the will or the power to impress another character upon the attitude of the German clergy, we would be forced thereby to a position toward the Catholic Church which I, in the interest of both the state and the Church, and in the interest of the civil order as a whole, would most deeply regret.[12]

Although mindful that opposing interests were contending within the Church for papal support, Bismarck was convinced that "high-ranking and influential prelates in Rome" approved what was happening in south Germany. He hoped, however, that the Curia would be able to judge its own interests from a point of view superior to that of its own members who were responding merely to the passions of the day. He concluded the long dispatch with a final expression of hope for a "moderating influence," possible only through a "serious intervention of the Pope," and a final threat that "it would pain Prussia to have to find that Rome favors what is happening, or that it is not strong enough to put a stop to it; to find in Rome not an ally against the revolution, but a more or less conscious enemy."[13]

The significance of this note has been overlooked by most writers on Bismarck[14] and on the Church. It is, however, of enormous importance in any effort to analyze the development of his views on the

[12] *Ibid.*

[13] *Ibid.* The final version of the note deleted a paragraph of an earlier draft which spoke of the behavior of German Catholics as a "crusade against Prussia." See *ibid.*, note 12.

[14] Eyck, for example, although familiar with it, ascribes to it no special significance. See Eyck, *Bismarck*, 3:82. A. O. Meyer, *Bismarck*, does not mention it at all.

relationship between Church and state, especially since it makes possible a reasonably accurate determination of the date of a major shift in his attitude. Heretofore he had been merely impatient with the obstructionism of German Catholic politicians. Henceforth he was actively hostile toward the Church itself, which could not, or would not, compel its members to abandon opposition to Prussian hegemony in Germany. Although Bismarck's remarks were couched in belligerent terms, they constituted, nevertheless, as Eyck correctly points out,[15] an appeal for papal intervention in German politics. The effort failed. Rome, then, could no longer be regarded as a friend.

Arnim, in a preliminary answer, attempted to defend the Pontiff, although he offered no hope that anything useful could be accomplished at Rome. Pius, he argued, was well enough disposed toward Prussia, and might, were he a free agent, be induced to support Bismarck's policy. A free agent, however, he was not, for he was surrounded by a coterie of prelates who hated and feared the Hohenzollern monarchy. Thus he was effectively insulated from the influence of any bishops who wished to promote cooperation with Berlin. Arnim suggested that some benefit might result if the Crown Prince, who was on the point of departing on a state visit to Italy, were to call upon the Pope and take up the matter personally.[16] To this Bismarck, however, was unalterably opposed, partially because of his dislike for the Prince, but also, probably, for fear of angering the Italian government. The King had considerable sympathy for Arnim's suggestion, and Bismarck, to close the matter, asked his envoy not to mention it again officially.[17]

After Arnim had had an opportunity to study his superior's long communication, he submitted his own analysis of the issues as they appeared from his vantage point. This, too, gave Bismarck no grounds for hope that a solution could be found in Rome. In fact, Arnim suggested that cooperation between Prussia and the Vatican was, in the final analysis, impossible. The objectives of Prussian policy, he thought, might best be achieved by completely ignoring the Vatican. It was faintly possible that German unity might be accomplished without a complete break with the Papacy, but he emphasized "faintly." Nevertheless, he still maintained that the Pope was not the organizer of

[15] Eyck, *Bismarck*, 3:82.
[16] Arnim to Bismarck, Rome, April 21, 1868, *APP*, 9: no. 750.
[17] Bismarck to Arnim, April 26, 1868, *ibid.*, no. 769.

the "alliance between the Church and the revolution" in Germany. Rather, he was in a sense a prisoner of the ultramontane bishops, who alone could help him achieve his goal of absolute monarchy within the Church. He could not then, be expected to break with his ultramontane supporters in those parts of Germany where they were strong. Within very circumscribed limits a *modus vivendi* might be possible between Prussia and the Vatican, but nothing more than that.[18]

A day or two later, Arnim at last got the opportunity to present Bismarck's impressions to Cardinal Antonelli, the papal secretary of state. He received, as he had expected, little satisfaction. The Cardinal denied that the Holy See was the partisan of any political party in Germany or elsewhere. In answer to Bismarck's complaint about the Catholic press he reminded Arnim that the Church did not advocate freedom of the press, and suggested that the civil governments in Germany certainly had sufficient power to solve the problem of abuses in that sphere without assistance from Rome. Arnim closed his report of the conversation with a reminder to his chief that he had conducted similar talks with Antonelli on at least a dozen occasions before. Always he had asked substantially the same questions; always he had received essentially the same answers.[19]

Bismarck, despite his increasing disillusion with the Catholic hierarchy, apparently still continued to believe, even after the *Zollparlament* elections, that the loyalty of Prussian Catholics at least could be relied upon. As he put it in May 1868, Prussian clerics were "first of all Prussians, and only then Catholic clergymen." [20] Presumably laymen would follow their lead. Nevertheless, more and more evidence accumulated during the succeeding twelve months which indicated that his optimistic view might have to be revised. For example, Bismarck's concern over Polish separatism, which he had always suspected of being supported by some segments of the clergy, became sufficiently great by December 1868 to justify a circular letter on the subject to missions in all major capitals. The dispatch charged that liaison had been established between Poles and other dissatisfied elements in Germany, including dispossessed princes and south German democrats. The Poles were allegedly using these connections to stir

[18] Arnim to Bismarck, Rome, July 2, 1868, *ibid.*, 10: no. 86.
[19] Arnim to Bismarck, Rome, July 4, 1868, *ibid.*, 10: no. 88.
[20] Conversation between Bismarck and *Ministerialrath* Freiherr von Völderndorff, Berlin, middle of May 1868, *GW*, 7: no. 203.

up anti-Prussian feeling throughout Germany, while, conversely, south German particularists were using their Polish friends to spread their own propaganda in Prussia itself.[21] Two months later, the Chancellor informed the heads of missions in St. Petersburg and Warsaw that signs of cooperation between Polish Catholics and the dispossessed Guelphs of Hanover were unmistakable. He cited an article in the *Sächsiche Zeitung* (Leipzig) of February 6, 1869, which put heavy stress on the common interests of both. The immediate goal, according to the article, was the establishment of a federation of nationalities in Austria, and then reconstitution of Germany on an autonomous federative basis. Thus, it maintained, restoration of Polish independence would be achieved at the same moment that the German states again became free of Hohenzollern domination.[22]

Meanwhile, from other sources, Bismarck's worst fears about the objectives of ultramontane circles in south Germany were being strengthened. Early in September 1868, he received a report from Munich which confirmed his view that the Papacy itself was linked with the campaign to destroy Prussian influence. The Prussian special envoy, J. M. von Radowitz, reported that the Papal Nuncio in Munich, Father Meglia, had been striving to convince King Ludwig that German national feeling was inimical to the interests of the Church. Meglia had allegedly told the King that in the event of war between Prussia and France, Bavaria's interests would be best served if she took the French side. The Nuncio was also charged with being indirectly responsible for the pro-French tone of much of the Catholic press.[23] Whether or not Bismarck was convinced of the truth of these specific charges is not recorded, but he certainly was in a mood to take them seriously. Several months later, in March 1869, he protested to the prelate, Monsignor Wolanski, about the hostility of the south German press toward Prussia. He informed Wolanski that the offending papers were backed by "the clergy, the hierarchy, and the Curia."[24]

The progressive deterioration of relations between Berlin and the

[21] Thile to the Prussian missions in St. Petersburg, Brussels, Paris, and London (Berlin, Dec. 20, 1868), *APP*, 10: no. 352.

[22] Bismarck to Prince Reuss (St. Petersburg) and Rechenberg (Warsaw), Berlin, Feb. 13, 1869, *ibid.*, no. 517.

[23] Radowitz cited the historian Döllinger as the source for this information. Radowitz to Bismarck, Munich, Sept. 1, 1868, *ibid.*, no. 126.

[24] It has not been possible to identify Wolanski, except that it appears he had access to the Papal Court. Bismarck to Arnim, March 15, 1869, *GW*, 6b: no. 1343.

Holy See was paralleled, as indicated previously, by growing tension between Rome and several other German governments. The entire situation was complicated by the preparations for the Vatican Council, which were nearing completion in the spring of 1869. The impetus for the Council of 1869–70 can be traced to the long chain of events which had already produced the Syllabus of Errors in 1864, *i.e.*, the increasing estrangement of the Church from major currents of nineteenth-century life and thought. The bull, *Aeterni Patris,* of June 29, 1869, which officially summoned the bishops of the Catholic world to meet in Rome the following December, represented the culmination of three and a half years of planning. Pius had announced secretly to the College of Cardinals his intention to convene an oecumenical council as early as December 6, 1864. Shortly after the new year, thirty-six other bishops were informed of the design, and a formal announcement was made in the Papal allocution of June 26, 1867. During the long period which intervened between the inception of the idea and the proclamation of the Council, the Church's temporal position suffered disastrously. The most important blow was, of course, the defeat of Austria in the War of 1866, for it was the root of the others. Moreover, the spiritual authority of the Church seemed to be crumbling before the onslaught of secular liberalism, scientific materialism, and the pretensions of the state to final jurisdiction in all aspects of life. From the beginning the Pope had viewed the Council as a means of combating modern "errors" more effectively than had been possible in the Syllabus. He sought to obtain assent of the entire hierarchy to a positive formulation as dogma of its negative articles. By 1868, however, it was clear that some of the Pope's most powerful supporters, in particular the Jesuits, were determined to go even further in the war against modernism. As time went on, more and more was heard from Jesuit sources about the desirability of defining as dogma the infallibility of the Pope, a belief long held and taught by many clergymen, although not as a necessary article of faith.[25]

Whether or not the original impulse for this step came from the Pope himself is not clear; that he approved it is indicated by an over-

<hr />

[25] Bachem, 3:84–85; Vigener, *Ketteler,* 569; Holborn, *Radowitz,* 1:184. The background of the Vatican Council is treated by all histories of the Church in the nineteenth century, and by most national histories of the period. Treatments vary according to the preconceptions of the writer. The most objective general treatment is probably in Fernand Mourret, *Histoire générale de l'église,* 8: part 1.

whelming weight of evidence. Two of the publications especially favored by the Pontiff—the Roman daily, *Civiltà Cattolica*, and the journal, *Stimmen aus Maria Laach*, published from a Rhineland monastery—were the most ardent proponents of the infallibility dogma. Both were edited by Jesuit fathers. The *Laacher Stimmen*, founded only in 1865, emitted a constant stream of articles on the Syllabus and on its implications for the modern world, always from the most extreme ultramontane viewpoint. Moreover, the bishops who were summoned to Rome in the fall of 1868 to prepare for the Council were in almost all cases men known to favor promulgation of the dogma. Since the bull of convocation contained no reference to an agenda, these and other similar indications gave the only clues to what was contemplated.[26]

From the historical perspective of more than eight decades it is difficult to comprehend the excitement, the bitterness, the actual hatred which the Council aroused in Europe, beginning long before the prelates had assembled at Rome. To freethinkers the world over, arrogantly confident that their answers to the eternal problems were the true ones, it represented an abominable resurgence of all that was evil in the Middle Ages. To many Protestants it seemed that Rome was endeavoring to undo the work of the sixteenth century. Several governments were concerned over the possible effects of the Council's decisions upon their relations with the Church, and upon the loyalty of their Catholic subjects. All these fears were accentuated in Germany because the country was in the midst of one of the great political crises of the century.

The first reaction of most German Catholics to the announcement that a Council would meet was enthusiastic. In 1867 Jörg regarded it as the salvation of humanity from the "absolutism of the egoistic spirit of man, degraded to the finite." [27] This judgment, however, was made before the issue of papal infallibility became public. As that question gradually grew in importance, more and more German Catholics found themselves troubled. Although loyal to their faith, they had no wish to see the Church converted into an absolute monarchy governed by decrees from Rome. Those of north Germany, most of

---

[26] Friedrich Nippold, *The Papacy in the 19th Century*, 149–50; Holborn, *Radowitz*, 1:185; Löffler, 69.
[27] "Zeitläufe: Das allgemeine Conzil und die allgemeine Verwirrung," *HPB*, 60:246.

whom had lived in a climate of comparative religious freedom, were completely unsympathetic with the ultramontane point of view. Others, including many of the important north German Catholic politicians, as well as men like Jörg in Bavaria, believed that whether or not the dogma was wise in itself, its definition under the circumstances of 1869–70 would be highly unfortunate, because of the inevitable political repercussions. Windthorst, for instance, was desperately anxious to avoid anything that might destroy the bond which had been built up between northern and southern Catholic politicians through the *Zollparlament*. He likewise feared that extreme action by the Council would render impossible the working alliance which had been fairly consistently maintained between Protestant and Catholic particularists. Of further concern was the possibility that Bismarck himself might intervene in the contest on the side of the German anti-infallibilists, so that, by confusing the issue, he might enlist their support for Prussian hegemony in Germany. Windthorst foresaw that in the end the dogmatization of papal infallibility might mean the destruction in Germany both of the budding Catholic political movements and of the independence of the Church itself.[28]

Most German bishops were likewise opposed to definition of the dogma, some on principle, and others, like many laymen, because they believed it inopportune. In the Prussian Rhineland ecclesiastical opposition was open and almost unanimous. Farther south, Bishop Ketteler of Mainz, no more circumspect on this than on other questions, had committed himself against papal infallibility in his book *Deutschland nach dem Kriege* at the end of 1866. Moreover, in a letter to the Papal Nuncio in Munich about the time the book came out, Ketteler conspicuously omitted dogmatization of papal infallibility from his long list of desirable reforms in the Church. In May 1868 the Bishop addressed two communications to the editors of the Berlin *Kreuzzeitung*, which had attacked him as an ultramontane because of his brochure, *The True Bases of Religious Freedom*, published shortly before. In both, Ketteler affirmed the infallibility of the Church, but specifically asserted the liability to error of every individual Christian. He went so far as to deny unequivocally that he believed any statement in the Syllabus on the relationship between Church and state

---

[28] Vigener, *Ketteler*, 538; Rachfall, "Windthorst," *Preussische Jahrbücher*, 135:228–30; Hansen, 1:797.

was infallible. As was so often the case, Ketteler was at odds here with his own colleagues at Mainz, most of whom did not share his enthusiasm for bishops independent from control of the Holy See. Perhaps their experience with Ketteler is sufficient explanation.[29]

Although it thus appears from his entire career up to 1869 that Ketteler was fundamentally opposed to the dogma on principle — it was presumably for this reason that, in spite of his being recognized as the leading German prelate, he was not taken into the Pope's confidence in 1865 — he did not maintain that position during the period of the Council. Rather he joined the group of bishops who chose to combat the dogma not on its merits, but on the ground that it was inopportune. Most of his German colleagues took this position publicly, perhaps because the political tensions were so acute in their country that, even more than the bishops of other countries, they were aware of the dangers of stirring up a hornet's nest. Here even Moufang, Ketteler's assistant, though an ardent ultramontane, supported his superior.[30]

In Germany, public interest in the Council became general in February 1869, following the reprinting in the German press of an article which appeared initially in the *Civiltà Cattolica* on February 6. Ostensibly this dealt with the religious situation in France, but it did so in a fashion which made clear that the anonymous author expressed the attitude of the Pope and the Curia on Catholicism in general. The article spoke of Catholics in France, and by implication elsewhere, as divided into two groups. "One group [may be called] simply Catholics; the other includes those who call themselves liberal Catholics." The "Catholics," the article continued, hoped that the forthcoming Council would be short and noncontroversial, and that it would define as dogmas the principles proclaimed already in the Syllabus of Errors. Moreover, they would greet definition of papal infallibility with enthusiasm, while many of them would be happy also to see defined as dogmas the immaculate conception and the assumption of Mary.[31]

The article produced an enormous furor in Germany. In effect the Papacy had charged that all Catholics who did not accept the Sylla-

[29] Hansen, 1:797; Ketteler to the Papal Nuncio to Bavaria, R. F. Meglia, Mainz, Jan. 5, 1867, *Ketteler Briefe*, 347–51; Ketteler to the editors of the *Kreuzzeitung*, Mainz, May 1, 1868, May 6, 1868, *ibid.*, 379–82, 382–84; Vigener, *Ketteler*, 539.
[30] Vigener, *Ketteler*, 569, 571; Hansen, 1:797.
[31] Mourret, 8:530; Ludwig Hahn, *Geschichte des "Kulturkampfes" in Preussen; in Aktenstücken dargestellt*, 9.

bus *in toto,* all those who were willing to live on amicable terms with the liberal state, all those who opposed definition of the infallibility dogma were heretics. If this viewpoint were to prevail, if all Catholics were to be required to subscribe to it, how would it affect the loyalty of Catholics toward civil authorities to whom they owed allegiance? And how would it affect the position *vis-à-vis* the Church of the various governments which had Catholic subjects?[32]

The *Allgemeine Zeitung* of Augsburg began the counterattack on the *Civiltà* with a series of articles by "Janus," the pseudonym adopted for the purpose by Ignaz von Döllinger. The Munich professor, long a leader of liberal Catholics in Germany, was now ready to fight to the bitter end against what seemed to him a hopeless attempt to return to the Middle Ages. The nineteenth-century Janus, like his mythological counterpart, had looked both backward and forward, and concluded that adaptation to the modern world was not only desirable, but mandatory, if the Church was to play a significant role in the future. The first of the "Janus letters," published in the middle of March 1869, charged that the Jesuits, the Curia, and the Pontiff himself had committed an "outrage against the rights of the Church" in the *Civiltà* article. As the year went on, Döllinger's articles attacking ultramontanes became progressively more bitter, until he seems finally to have abandoned all pretense at objectivity.[33]

In Hohenlohe the Bavarian Janus found a kindred spirit who was more than willing to cooperate. On March 23, 1869, Döllinger submitted to him a draft letter for circulation among Bavarian ambassadors in various European capitals, suggesting that all governments concerned with the issues posed by the Council take concerted action to warn Rome against any decisions which would unilaterally alter

---

[32] "Memoir: Das bevorstehende Konzil," May 1869, Holborn, *Radowitz,* 1:183.

[33] Mourret, 8:531–33; Vigener, *Ketteler,* 517. The letters were collected and published in book form in December 1869 under the title, *Der Papst und das Konzil.* The book was immediately translated into Latin and into all the important modern European languages. The English version, *The Pope and the Council by Janus,* has been used here. Some of the letters were reprinted in Döllinger's book, *Römische Briefe vom Konzil,* published in 1870, also immediately translated into the major languages. This work contains, for the most part, Döllinger's letters to the *Allgemeine Zeitung* from the period when the Council was in session. The English version, *Letters from Rome on the Council,* has been used. This book is often known as the *Quirinus Letters,* since Döllinger chose that pseudonym when he went to Rome, and will be hereafter cited as such. Upon Döllinger's death in 1890, a definitive edition of his writings on the Council appeared under the title, *Briefe und Erklärungen über die vatikanischen Dekrete, 1869–1887.*

existing relationships between Church and state.[34] The draft began with a discussion of the questions which were likely to come before the Council, pointing out that the chief one would be the infallibility dogma:

But this [question] goes far beyond the domain of purely religious questions, and has a highly political character, because the power of the Papacy over all princes and peoples, even those in schism from Rome, would thereby be defined in secular affairs, and elevated into an article of faith.

Now this question, highly important and pregnant with results as it is, is preeminently of a nature to draw the attention of all Governments having Catholic subjects to the Council. But their interest — or rather, perhaps, their anxiety — must needs be still further heightened when they see the preliminaries already in preparation, and the composition of the committees formed at Rome to carry out these [sic]. Among these committees is one in particular whose sole business is to concern itself with politico-ecclesiastical matters. So it is beyond a doubt the deliberate intention of the Roman Curia that the Council shall lay down, at any rate, some decisions on politico-ecclesiastic matters or questions of a mixed nature. . . . Governments are confronted with the serious question whether, and in what form, they would have to advise either the Bishops subject to their authority, or, at a later stage, the Council itself of the perilous consequences to which such a deliberate and fundamental disturbance of the relations of Church and State must inevitably lead.[35]

Döllinger ended the draft by proposing that interested governments "endeavor to arrive at some mutual understanding on this very serious matter." So complete was Hohenlohe's agreement that he merely added a covering paragraph, and, on April 9, transmitted the draft to the Bavarian representatives all over Europe.[36]

The general reaction to the Hohenlohe circular was not particularly satisfactory to either of its proponents. France refused to cooperate on the ground that troubles which might not arise ought not to be anticipated, although she did vaguely hint at the possibility of assistance if Hohenlohe's fears became realities. The Bavarian minister regarded the reply as adequate. In Vienna Beust was even more reserved.

[34] Holborn, *Radowitz*, 1:182; Michael, *Döllinger*, 65–66; circular letter to the Bavarian ambassadors abroad, April 9, 1869, Hohenlohe, *Memoirs*, 1:326–27.

[35] Circular letter to the Bavarian ambassadors abroad, April 9, 1869, Hohenlohe, *Memoirs*, 1:326–27.

[36] *Ibid.*

He informed Hohenlohe that religious freedom was a basic principle of the Austrian constitution. Since any action of the type contemplated would interfere with that freedom, Austria could not go along. Moreover, Austria had no desire to interfere with legitimate rights of the Church, and, considering that the Council's agenda was still in the realm of conjecture, Beust felt it would be best to wait at least until the dangers materialized. If, as he expected, many German bishops were interested in preserving peace between Church and state, their hands would be strengthened if secular authorities remained neutral. Therefore, so long as the Church's action did not "collide with the standpoint of the state," Austria would not intervene.[37]

Hohenlohe was both disappointed and angry at Beust's response, especially since the traditional ties between Vienna and Rome might have made assistance from him particularly valuable. A short time later the Bavarian minister attacked what he called Beust's duplicity in an anonymous article contributed to the *Allgemeine Zeitung*. He charged that Beust, while cynically professing neutrality toward the Council, was secretly working with the Jesuits to create difficulties for the Bavarian government, so that Austria might profit from the hoped-for overthrow of Hohenlohe's ministry.[38] Despite his anger, however, Hohenlohe was not willing to abandon efforts to secure Austrian backing for his scheme. In August 1869, he visited Vienna and held further conversations with Beust. The latter was now willing to agree that the ultramontanes' intentions could no longer be doubted, but he continued to counsel patience. He was still strongly convinced of the likelihood of a split within the Austrian hierarchy on the question of papal infallibility, but only if the government kept discreetly silent. Any attempt to put pressure on the bishops would push them all into the ultramontane camp.[39]

The crucial problem for Hohenlohe was the attitude of Prussia. Before the memorandum was circulated, Bismarck was inclined to look upon the excitement as a tempest in a teapot. On the very day that Döllinger submitted his draft letter, the North German Chancellor showed his complete unconcern over the forthcoming Council in a

[37] Beust to the Austrian ambassador in Munich, Count Ingelheim, Vienna, May 1869, Hahn, 10–11; Hohenlohe, *Memoirs*, 1:335–36; Roggenbach to Queen Augusta, Berlin, June 22, 1869, Heyderhoff, *Im Ring der Gegner Bismarcks*, 106.

[38] Text in Hohenlohe, *Memoirs*, 1:336–38.

[39] Journal, Vienna, Aug. 25, 1869, Hohenlohe, *Memoirs*, 1:363.

communication to the Prussian minister in Bern. He judged that it would affect the interests of Prussia very little, and, therefore, no pressure would be put by the government upon the Prussian bishops. Actual participation of government representatives in the Council was, in his opinion, quite out of the question. He had apparently paid little heed to a request from Usedom as early as September 1868, approved by King Wilhelm, that the government prepare possible lines of action in advance to support the moderate bishops. Moreover, he made no recorded objection to the mission of the Duke of Ratibor, who, early in April 1869, represented the King of Prussia at a celebration marking the fiftieth anniversary of the Pope's entry into holy orders.[40]

Bismarck's initial reaction to the Hohenlohe circular was, therefore, only a milder version of Beust's. He telegraphed to Werthern in Munich on April 20 that the Council was an internal affair of the Church, which, in all likelihood, would not interfere with the rights of secular governments. He was willing, however, to cooperate with any government through a conference or other appropriate means to clarify the whole issue. On the same day he dispatched a second message, classified secret, to Werthern, suggesting that he advise Hohenlohe that Bavaria as a Catholic power might herself issue a warning along the lines proposed in the memorandum. Bismarck made no promise, however, that Prussia would support such a move officially.

Two weeks later Bismarck amplified and somewhat clarified his ambiguous instructions. In another message to Werthern he pointed out that the Hohenlohe proposal assumed the possibility of winning over many ultramontanes to a milder point of view. He was convinced, however, that this hope would prove vain, fearing, rather, that the attempt itself would be exploited as a sign of weakness. A friendly warning by Catholic Bavaria, acting alone, probably would not be so regarded, and could certainly do little harm.[41]

Members of the Prussian diplomatic staff who were in closer touch than Bismarck with the situation at Rome, nevertheless, were convinced that his lack of concern was dangerous. They began, therefore,

[40] Usedom to Bismarck, Florence, Sept. 15, 1868, *APP*, 10: no. 137; *Randbemerkung* of King Wilhelm on same, *ibid.*, note 4; Bismarck to Roeder (Bern), Berlin, March 23, 1869, *GW*, 6b: no. 1353; Hahn, 6.

[41] Bismarck to Werthern, Berlin, April 20, 1869, *GW*, 6b: no. 1372; Bismarck to Werthern (secret), Berlin, April 20, 1869, *ibid.*, no. 1373; Bismarck to Werthern, Berlin, May 5, 1869, *ibid.*, no. 1384.

to subject their chief to considerable pressure. From Munich came the dire predictions of Radowitz on the probable effect of the Council on relations between Church and state. From Rome itself Arnim wrote on May 14 that the situation was so serious that Berlin was duty bound to take action against an obvious plan to alter those relations unilaterally. He suggested again that Prussia send representatives to take part in the Council directly, as secular governments had in the past.[42] Both Bismarck and King Wilhelm decisively rejected this proposal, and Bismarck informed Arnim that the Papacy, in any case, probably would not recognize the representative of a Protestant, *i.e.*, heretical, power. He went on to say that "to make protests is always a thankless task, and can have meaning only when it lies within the power of the one protesting to prevent what he is protesting against."[43] No Protestant government in this matter had that power.

Bismarck, however, was sufficiently impressed by these communications from his subordinates to inform Munich a few days later of the conditions under which he was willing to support secular action at Rome. These were four in number: First, the action had to be secret. Second, it had to be framed, not as a protest, but as a friendly warning that the governments concerned would not countenance unilateral decisions affecting existing concordats or other legal arrangements regulating the status of the Church. Third, he insisted that dogmatic issues be ignored, except in so far as they had political significance. Papal infallibility he regarded as politically important. Finally, he declined to join in any action unless all, or nearly all, German governments, without distinction between Protestant and Catholic, also took part.[44] Obviously Bismarck was burning no bridges behind him.

On the basis of these conditions Bismarck, Hohenlohe, and Varnbüler worked out a more detailed plan in Berlin on June 12, 1869.[45] Bavaria was to make specific proposals, and those, plus comments of the various German governments on them, would be forwarded to Rome by an "unofficial plenipotentiary" whom Bavaria would select. This individual, it was agreed, would have to be someone who could assume the status of a "distinguished traveler," and his activities on

[42] "Das bevorstehende Konzil," May 1869, Holborn, *Radowitz*, 1: 182–85; Arnim to Bismarck, Rome, May 14, 1869, Hahn, 11–12.
[43] Bismarck to Arnim, Berlin, May 26, 1869, Hahn, 12–14.
[44] Bismarck to Werthern, Berlin, May 28, 1869, *GW*, 6b: no. 1396.
[45] The latter two were in Berlin for the 1869 session of the *Zollparlament*.

behalf of the German states would be kept secret. It was further decided that each government would issue warnings to bishops under its jurisdiction at the time they were given leave to attend the Council. Since it proved impossible to agree at this meeting on a suitable "distinguished traveler," the first part of the scheme had to be held in abeyance for the time being.[46] Ultimately it was dropped altogether, for the same reason. The second portion was eventually carried out.

Although Bismarck's unwillingness to see the Church-state issue brought into the open at this time prevented the Hohenlohe circular from having the full effect its authors desired, it cannot be regarded as unimportant. The public impression which it made strengthened Hohenlohe's hand in Bavaria during the period just after the first crucial election of 1869, and may have made it possible for him to retain his precarious hold on the reins of government. Moreover, the memorandum and the reaction to it did bolster slightly the will of German anti-ultramontane bishops to fight against definition of the infallibility dogma. Bismarck, however, had underestimated his opposition, or perhaps he had only failed to appreciate fully the importance of the issues involved.[47] In the absence of his full support, Hohenlohe's project only succeeded in angering south German Catholics, without influencing appreciably the Council itself. Jörg, for example, who had originally been opposed to the dogma, became a good deal less hostile toward it after the flurry produced by the Hohenlohe circular. In late summer, 1869, he wrote:

From such a document one can easily show how the gentlemen understand "freedom" and the "modern state" — the gentlemen who must grow pale at the thought of an infallible highest authority in the Church, . . . because they want to believe so much more firmly in their own infallibility.[48]

The Janus letters had much the same effect upon him, and presumably on other south German Catholics. A little later Jörg wrote in reference to one of Döllinger's outbursts:

[46] Conversation with Bismarck, June 12, 1869, Hohenlohe, *Memoirs*, 1: 346–47; Abeken memorandum, Berlin, June 14, 1869, *ibid.*, 348; conference between Bismarck, Hohenlohe, and Varnbüler, Berlin, June 12, 1869, *GW*, 7: no. 220.

[47] Eyck, *Bismarck*, 3: 80–81; Döllinger's observations on the answers of the powers to Hohenlohe's circular to the Bavarian ambassadors, Hohenlohe, *Memoirs*, 1: 338–39; Bismarck to Hohenlohe, Aug. 11, 1869, Hahn, 14.

[48] "Zeitläufe: Das oekumenische Concil, seine Benergler und seine Gegner," I, *HPB*, 64: 168.

And are we fallible laymen to believe that a man who renounces and relinquishes everything in order to serve the Lord, be he Jesuit or not; that such a man possesses less enlightened conviction and understanding in matters of the kingdom of God than a learned man who, covered with orders and honors, revels comfortably in the treasures of libraries, and on that alone bases his claims? To me such a claim is once and for all incomprehensible.[49]

The controversy in the German press raged unabated throughout the summer and fall which preceded the opening of the Council. It was marked by such episodes as Döllinger's claim on May 20 that dogmatization of papal infallibility would *ipso facto* elevate the bull, *Unam Sanctam* of Boniface VIII, with its doctrine of absolute papal sovereignty, to the status of a belief required of Catholics. The debate in the press, if anything, increased in tempo after the fathers assembled in Rome. Early in 1870 Döllinger's articles were answered by the infallibilist Bishop Hergenröther of Würzburg in a book entitled *Anti-Janus*, which sought to demonstrate how the Munich theologian had willfully misquoted historical texts to advance his own heretical views.[50]

Meanwhile, the summer of 1869 witnessed strenuous efforts by important German Catholics to resist the drive for definition of the controversial dogma without descending to Döllinger's tactics. Many of them, as suggested before, suspected that the latter was not far wrong when he accused the Pontiff of seeking to turn the clock back, however much they deplored the venomous character of his attacks.

In May a member of the faculty of the Catholic Gymnasium in Koblenz drew up a petition addressed to the Bishop of Trier against definition of the dogma. This petition, dated May 17, 1869, usually known as the *Koblenzer Laienadresse*, was signed by about fifty-five important Catholic laymen of the Trier diocese. In one of the classic understatements of the century, it expressed the fear that dogmatization of papal infallibility and of the assumption of Mary "would not make easier reunion with our Christian brothers now separated in belief." [51] It went on to state that "it appears to us, in the interest of the freedom and independence of the Church, most essential that the

[49] *Ibid.*, III, 64:322.
[50] *AAZ*, May 20, 1869, reprinted in *Quirinus Letters*, 1–3; Mourret, 8:533; Hertling, 1:207.
[51] Michael, *Döllinger*, 66–67.

coming Council leave no doubt that the Church has completely broken with the wish to establish the theocratic form of the state of the Middle Ages." [52]

The signers of the petition referred to themselves as liberal Catholics and offered impassioned objections to the imputation of the *Civiltà Cattolica* that such were not "real Catholics." Jörg, in commenting on the address, agreed that the Koblenzers were correct, for he could take no exception to their Catholicism, only to their liberalism. At the time it was assumed that there was a direct connection between the Koblenz petition and the Hohenlohe circular; this seems, however, not to have been the case.[53]

A similar protest came in June from a somewhat more widely known group of Catholics. At the end of the 1869 *Zollparlament* session, twenty-eight of its Catholic members decided to hold a conference on possible action in regard to the approaching Council. Windthorst, Jörg, and Peter Reichensperger were important members of the group, which met in Berlin on June 17. This unofficial gathering became known as the *Berliner Laienkonzil*. It was Windthorst who favored the most drastic action. He proposed that the German bishops who were soon to hold their annual conclave in Fulda be asked to inform the Vatican bluntly that there was serious resentment over the proposed dogma among wide segments of the Catholic population in Germany. Most of the others were unwilling to go so far, and Windthorst's suggestion was fatally modified before an agreement was reached. It was decided first to inquire secretly of the bishops in what form they preferred the resolution to be presented. This destroyed any chance that the *Laienkonzil* could influence public opinion, for it necessarily followed that no petitions could be circulated, and that no news of the meeting should be communicated to the press.[54] As might be expected, secrecy could not be maintained,[55] but the very mildness of the tactics employed meant also that neither Fulda nor Rome was apt to be seriously impressed, although the German bishops certainly took the resolution into account at their conclave.

[52] Hahn, 16.

[53] "Zeitläufe: Das oekumenische Concil, seine Benergler und seine Gegner," II, *HPB*, 64:239; Michael, *Döllinger*, 67.

[54] Rachfall, "Windthorst," *Preussische Jahrbücher*, 135:228–29.

[55] Roggenbach, for example, knew of it by June 22. See Roggenbach to Queen Augusta, Berlin, June 22, 1869, Heyderhoff, *Im Ring der Gegner Bismarcks*, 107.

Bismarck and the Church, 1866–1870

The Fulda meeting of German bishops, September 1–6, 1869, was summoned to consider urgent problems facing the Church. The two most important of these were (1) what attitude should the bishops take toward the proposed dogma, and (2) what action should be recommended to the Council on the "social question," especially with reference to combating the Social Democrats. In both matters Bishop Ketteler dominated the conference. His interest in the working class has been dealt with before, and it was, in fact, almost entirely because of his efforts that this problem was placed on the agenda of the Fulda meeting. He hoped that the bishops would endorse his view that the social and economic welfare of the factory worker was a concern of the Church, and that they would support strongly his desire to see the problem made part of the agenda in Rome. The Protestant philanthropist, Victor Aimé Huber, with whom the Bishop had been in communication for over a year, was partially responsible for his decision to push the matter at this time. Huber had convinced him that the Catholic Church, with its larger resources, had to take the lead in what both men regarded as a Christian duty. Ketteler had prepared a long, formal report for the conference, entitled *Provision of the Church for the Factory Worker*. In the opening paragraph he spoke of this as "the most difficult and important problem of the present." [56] He argued that the Church could not carry out its true function so long as it allowed the working class to be treated solely as a means of production. The worker, crowded into slums, without opportunity for adequate family life, without leisure, was little subject to the saving grace of Christianity. The Church as an institution had to combat the abuses of modern capitalism, and this ultimately involved educating the worker to understand his responsibilities.[57] First, however, the Church had to create "institutions for the humanization of these bewildered masses," for only then would it be possible "to think of their christianization." [58] Throughout the report the basic assumption was that "all economic activities which are separated from religious and moral bases deepen the gulf between capital and labor, *i.e.*, between

[56] Vigener, *Ketteler*, 556; Victor Aimé Huber to Ketteler, Bad Ems, June 16, 1868, *Ketteler Briefe*, 385–86; Goyau, *L'Allemagne religieuse*, 3:161; Bongartz, 7; text of the "Report of the Fulda Bishops' Conference (1869) on the Social Question," Bongartz, 7–28.

[57] "Report," Bongartz, 7–28, *passim*.

[58] *Ibid.*, 10.

rich and poor." [59] The viewpoint is essentially that of the 1891 Encyclical of Leo XIII, *Rerum Novarum*, which indeed was largely derived from this and other writings of Ketteler.

The Bishop failed to carry his colleagues as far as he wished. The conference declined to adopt his proposal that the social question should be stressed by the German bishops at Rome, agreeing only to move that the Council reaffirm the duty of the Church to care for the poor. The bishops did, however, authorize publication of Ketteler's report in the *Christlich-soziale Blätter*, which in turn requested its republication by other Catholic organs. To a modest degree this followed. [60]

Ketteler's report was of great importance in the decision of the *Generalversammlung der Katholikenvereine*, which met at Düsseldorf a few days after the close of the Fulda Conference, to establish a standing committee "to further the creation of Christian-social organizations for the economic . . . [and] moral elevation of the working class." Catholic socialists regard this decision as the beginning of efforts to contest organization of German workers with the Social Democrats. [61]

On the other important question before the Fulda assembly, the infallibility dogma, the majority of the bishops were in outward agreement. Fourteen of the twenty present — bishops or their representatives — approved a resolution drafted by Franz Brentano, then still in holy orders, condemning definition of the dogma as "unpropitious" in view of the situation in Germany. This was also, of course, in line with Ketteler's reasoning. The six who refused to sign the resolution had a long ultramontane record and would not, therefore, associate themselves with a remonstrance to be transmitted to Rome. [62] Following the adoption of this resolution, the conference decided to issue a pastoral letter to German Catholics designed to calm fears raised by the wild charges of Döllinger, Hohenlohe, and others. The Fulda *Hirtenbrief* pointed out that the Council could not establish new dogmas, since it was incompetent to proclaim any doctrine which was not contained in the scriptures or in the tradition of the Church. Thus no

[59] Ketteler, *Deutschland nach dem Kriege*, 221.

[60] Vigener, *Ketteler*, 561; Bongartz, 7.

[61] Bongartz, 29–31, 84; Nitti, 132.

[62] Vigener, *Ketteler*, 579; "The Bishops and the Council," *AAZ*, Nov. 19–20, 1869, reprinted in *Quirinus Letters*, 42.

German needed to fear that the Council would act to compromise the Church with secular authorities, nor was there any reason to fear an attempt to revive the pretensions of the medieval Church. The bishops sought also to scotch rumors that the opposition at Rome would not be permitted freedom of discussion. These statements were all subject to varying interpretations, and the ultramontane minority was able, therefore, conscientiously to give its approval.

The Fulda Remonstrance and the Pastoral Letter together served to put infallibilists in Germany and in Rome on notice that there would be a German opposition to definition of the dogma. The *Hirtenbrief*, however, promised more than could possibly be delivered. Wishful thinking led men like Döllinger to interpret it as a promise to the nation that the bishops would resist to the end.[63] Many others apparently saw it in the same light and were, therefore, only the more disappointed later.

The German prelates departed for Rome at the beginning of December, carrying with them in most cases warnings from their governments as agreed upon earlier in Berlin. Hohenlohe, whose authority was for all practical purposes at an end because of the Patriot victory in the election only a few days before, praised the Fulda Pastoral highly in a conversation with the Archbishop of Munich. The Prussian *Kultusminister*, in a communication to the Archbishop of Cologne, expressed his trust that Prussian bishops "would remain conscious of their duty as citizens of the *Reich* [sic] and as subjects of the King." More specifically, he hoped that they would resist efforts to change existing legal relationships between Church and state. Namzanowski, military bishop of the Prussian army, was advised by the King personally to do as he chose at the Council, "but do not support infallibility, for this can only result in trouble." [64]

The Vatican Council opened on schedule, December 8, 1869. From the very beginning, the overriding topic of interest was the infallibility dogma. Unfortunately for those who wished to defeat it, their ranks were divided in such a way that cooperation was difficult. A few were opposed because they thought, along with Döllinger, that the dogma,

[63] "The Bishops and the Council," *AAZ*, Nov. 19–20, 1869, reprinted in *Quirinus Letters*, 35–36, 42; Vigener, *Ketteler*, 579; Hahn, 17–18; Ketteler to the editors of *Germania*, Oct. 21, 1872, *Ketteler Briefe*, 459.

[64] Mühler to Melchers, Oct. 10, 1869, Hahn, 18–19; Diary, Jan. 10, 1870, Johann Friedrich, *Tagebuch während des vatikanischen Concils*, 79.

difficult but not impossible to defend on theological grounds, was intellectually intolerable in the modern world. Others did not publicly question either its truth or the wisdom of defining it *per se,* but were unwilling to see it promulgated immediately, because of its political implications. These were the "inopportunists," led by the Bishop of Orléans, Dupanloup; the Archbishop of Paris, Darboy; and Ketteler. A relatively large group, including most of the German bishops, still maintained that the doctrine was false. Its leaders were Schwarzenberg of Prague, Héfelé of Rothenburg, Rauscher of Vienna, and Strossmayr, Archbishop of Diakovar. Finally, there was a group which included the bishops who were undecided, and who, therefore, hoped to see the whole issue avoided if possible. Bonnechose of Rouen was the outstanding example. In all, at the beginning of the Council, the opposition appeared to number about two hundred of the seven hundred and fifty bishops.[65]

Because the preparations for the Council had been carried out entirely by the Curia and prelates chosen by it, the proposed rules of procedure placed control over the agenda almost completely in the hands of the Holy See. The only Germans who had served on the preparatory commissions were Cardinal Reisach, a staunch papalist; the Jesuit, Schrader; and Hergenröther, the author of *Anti-Janus.* Thus, despite the fact that the opposition was later able to obtain a slight liberalization of the rules, the whole course of the Council was almost predetermined from the beginning.[66] Such liberalization as did take place was largely the result of interest manifested by secular governments and of such evidences of dissatisfaction as the Fulda Remonstrance and similar protests from the Hungarian and Bohemian bishops. The bishops of Austria proper had been too deeply divided to make a united protest in advance. So complete was the control of the ultramontanes that when the all-important twenty-four member committee *de fide* was elected on December 14, the liberals were unable to place a single member on it.

Although the Curia had long since abandoned any hope that the dogma could be defined by acclamation, early in January 1870 a peti-

[65] Mourret, 8:540–42; 545–46.

[66] *Ibid.,* 534, 542–43; Nippold, 150; Hertling, 1:207; *AAZ,* June 11, 1869, reprinted in *Quirinus Letters,* 7–8; Second Letter from Rome, Dec. 18, 1869, Fifth Letter from Rome, Dec. 23, 1869, Sixth Letter from Rome, Dec. 24, 1869, Seventh Letter from Rome, n. d., *Quirinus Letters,* 83, 104–5, 116, 117–19.

tion was circulated in secret, asking the Pope to place the question on the agenda immediately, so that it might quickly be brought to a vote. The petition received a large number of signatures — Döllinger reported 500, later corrected to 410 — before the opposition bishops became aware of its existence. It contained one significant modification of the earlier Jesuit position, which presumably was the result of the widespread antagonism to the dogma which had developed during the preceding year. Now the Pope's infallibility was to be limited to occasions when he spoke to the entire Church, a relatively infrequent occurrence. Once the bishops who were known to be hostile or doubtful became aware of the petition, they were subjected to a great deal of psychological pressure. It was, for example, at this time that Ketteler was greeted by the Pope with the query *"Amas me?"* [67]

Several of the German and Austrian anti-ultramontane prelates, including Ketteler, Haynald (Kolocza), and Strossmayr, almost immediately drew up a counterpetition in which they sought to uphold the inherent rights of bishops as divinely instituted officers, and demanded that the Council not depart from the traditions of the Tridentine assembly. The tone, however, was too belligerent for many of the Germans and Hungarians. Consequently, a milder protest, drafted by Rauscher, was substituted. This version was initialed by forty-six bishops, including most of the German and Austro-Hungarian representatives. Although its style was less truculent than that of the first draft, in substance it was not greatly different. It, too, pledged its signers to combat all efforts to elevate papal infallibility to a dogma. At the same time similar petitions were circulated among bishops representing other national groups, and in all about 145 signatures were obtained to various protests against the dogma.[68]

The "managers" of the Council, in order to hinder the opposition, finally secured a directive from the Pope himself forbidding unauthorized meetings of more than twenty bishops. The directive was consistently disregarded, particularly by the German and French contingents. Moreover, between January 25 and February 3, on three separate occa-

[67] *AAZ,* Nov. 19–20, 1869, reprinted in *Quirinus Letters,* 40–41, 44; Third Letter from Rome, Dec. 19, 1869, Eighth Letter from Rome, Jan. 8, 1870, Ninth Letter from Rome, Jan. 9, 1870, Thirteenth Letter from Rome, Jan. 30, 1870, *Quirinus Letters,* 92, 129–31, 139, 172. In connection with the Pope's greeting to Ketteler, see the Gospel according to St. John, Ch. xiv, 15.

[68] Ninth Letter from Rome, Jan. 9, 1870, Tenth Letter from Rome, Jan. 15, 1870, Thirteenth Letter from Rome, Jan. 30, 1870, *ibid.,* 137–38, 150, 153–54, 172–73; Hahn, 23–24.

sions, German and Austrian bishops addressed the assembled fathers in a fashion which was highly critical of the past conduct of the Holy See. Each of these speakers proposed a number of reforms to curb the independence of the papal office. As might be expected, their proposals were regarded as little less than sacrilegious by the majority, and had almost no influence on the ultimate decision.[69]

They did, however, have considerable effect outside Rome. For, although most sessions of the Council were secret, Döllinger and others, acting as correspondents for various European newspapers, received detailed reports on almost every session as soon as it was concluded. It was largely on Döllinger's highly colored accounts, published in the *Allgemeine Zeitung,* that Germany depended for its information on the proceedings. Even the anti-infallibilists felt the professor's lash, and some of them may thereby have been influenced to accept the decrees of the Council with better grace than would have been the case otherwise. On several occasions Ketteler, for example, felt obliged to send "open declarations" to the *Mainzer Journal* denying imputations which Döllinger had made about him or other bishops. On February 8 he accused the theologian of denying not only the infallibility of the Pope, but also the infallibility of the Church. Once, he wrote, when he had studied at the feet of the Munich scholar, he had held him in great esteem. But he could now no longer have any connection with a man "who heaps honor on the enemies of the Church." This outburst was in answer to Döllinger's claim, made in one of the *Quirinus Letters,* that the majority of German bishops shared his own views on infallibility. On February 19 Ketteler dispatched another open letter to the same newspaper, which called the entire Döllinger series "a system of errors" that sought intentionally to delude the German people. This time he used the term "lies" several times in reference to the writings of his erstwhile professor. Some months later, on June 4, he again labeled as a lie a report in the *Allgemeine Zeitung* that he had ceased to be an "inopportunist" and had become an outright opponent of the dogma.[70] As an indication of what was happening in the Bishop's mind this denial is of more than ordinary significance. Once he had certainly held the view which Döllinger ascribed to

---

[69] Tenth Letter from Rome, Jan. 15, 1870, Twelfth Letter from Rome, Jan. 26, 1870, Fifteenth Letter from Rome, Feb. 4, 1870, *Quirinus Letters,* 166–68, 195, 197.

[70] Declarations of Bishop von Ketteler, Rome, Feb. 8, Feb. 19, June 5, 1870, *Ketteler Briefe,* 400–2, 403–5, 412–13.

him, but now he grew angry when taxed with it. The tremendous pressure exerted on him from both sides — for his article of February 19 he received a message of praise from Pius IX personally [71] — was apparently causing him intolerable mental anguish.

From the information which filtered out of Rome it soon became apparent to many that the worst fears of Hohenlohe were apt to be realized. Bismarck, however, as late as the beginning of 1870, viewed events at the Vatican serenely, despite the increasing anxiety of his ambassador, who was on the scene. On New Year's Day "one of the most important German diplomats in Rome," probably Arnim, talked rather freely with Döllinger's colleague, Friedrich, on the role of the German bishops.

We Germans must really be very ashamed of the miserable role which the German bishops are playing here. If it were not for the Hungarian bishops, who can be considered in this case half German, they would be running about like lost sheep. The German clergy, especially the episcopate, has absolutely no feeling for the nation.[72]

A few days later Arnim wrote to Döllinger himself, urging continuation of his efforts to stimulate a public outcry in Germany "that will have an effect all the way to Rome." At about the same time he warned Bismarck again that the Papacy was an enemy, and that dogmatization of papal infallibility would be a declaration of war upon all governments, to which they should reply in kind. He insisted that for Bismarck, action was especially necessary, since the Papacy was "piling up a gigantic amount of war material in our own country." Bismarck noted on the margin, "*Phrasenpomp*," and complained that Arnim viewed everything with alarm, but never made any practical suggestions.[73]

The North German Chancellor apparently felt that he could ignore these warnings because, as he informed Arnim on January 5, 1870, he believed that "we have the wisdom to find means to overcome any crisis [which might result from the Council's action] in the field of legislation, supported by the power of public opinion and by enlightened political consciousness." As before, he asked his ambassador to give all possible moral assistance to the German bishops, and especially to

[71] Pius IX to Ketteler, Rome, Feb. 21, 1870, *ibid.*, 405.
[72] Diary, Jan. 2, 1870, Friedrich, *Tagebuch*, 52.
[73] Arnim to Döllinger, Jan. 8, 1870, Michael, *Döllinger*, 101–2; Eyck, *Bismarck*, 3: 79–80.

assure them that their rights would be defended *"in their own country"* (italics Bismarck's). But it was again made clear that he would not take the initiative in any diplomatic remonstrance.[74] Here is one of the most important clues to Bismarck's policy on relations between Church and state throughout the period. He seemed unable to realize that the question of papal infallibility, for example, although of interest to governments only because of its constitutional, legal, and political implications, could not be dealt with successfully on the legislative and administrative levels alone. For it involved, as did so many other issues, all the moral, religious, and historical preconceptions of Catholics, clerics and laymen alike. That Catholicism was a political force he comprehended perfectly; that it was far more he never seems really to have understood. Hence he always found it difficult to appreciate why Catholics behaved as they did. So often they chose to ignore what was clearly to their political advantage! His error was to assume that everyone was a realist like himself, or at least that everyone else defined realism as he did.

On January 21, 1870, the proposed *Schema de Ecclesia* was distributed to the assembled fathers by the committee *de fide*. Its content immediately became known to the public through an unauthorized disclosure to the press. The fifteen chapters dealt with the legal relationship of Church and state, with the rights of civil society in relation to the Church, and with the temporal power of the Holy See. In general, it simply restated as positive dogma the negative clauses of the Syllabus. Specifically it maintained that the temporal power was ultimately subject to the supreme authority of the Church, and that there was "no salvation outside the Church." All who refused assent were to be declared anathema. Conspicuously absent, however, was any mention of papal infallibility. Nevertheless, Döllinger and other liberal critics within and outside the Church judged that the *Schema,* if adopted, would require Catholics to violate the laws of their own countries if those laws conflicted with ecclesiastical pronouncements.[75]

The reaction of most governments was understandably adverse. From the French foreign minister, Daru, came, on February 20, a note protesting the apparent intent of the Church to interfere in the sphere of secular government. The premier in the ministry of January 2,

[74] Bismarck to Arnim, Jan. 5, 1870, *GW*, 6b: no. 1467.
[75] Mourret, 8:563; Fifteenth Letter from Rome, Feb. 4, 1870, *Quirinus Letters*, 203–4.

Émile Olivier, was himself of ultramontane sympathies, and Daru's note, therefore, had to be more circumspect than would have been the case had he had the full support of his chief. Bismarck in mid-February conferred with the Austrian ambassador, Count Wimpffen, and found Vienna now much concerned that the Council was apparently moving across the fine line which separated reform within the Church from intervention in temporal affairs. Bismarck was of the opinion that the Hofburg had been under considerable pressure from the Hungarian bishops to take a stronger stand, but he appeared still to regard the situation calmly. He told Wimpffen that he agreed, of course, in principle that governments had to defend themselves against ecclesiastical usurpation; nevertheless, he was not yet convinced but that confidential warnings would best accomplish the goal. He also maintained his former position that the most Prussia would do was join her own protests with those made by governments of predominantly Catholic countries. He had this information transmitted to the Prussian legations abroad, presumably to inform other governments that Prussia's attitude had not changed significantly.[76]

After considerable discussion in secret sessions, the *Schema* was returned to the committee for revisions, and on March 6 the revised version was distributed to the bishops. The only important change consisted in the addition of the fateful clause: *"Romanum pontificem in rebus fidei et morum definiendis errare non posse."* It was now certain that the infallibilists intended to pay no heed to the opposition within the Council. Again Bismarck was subjected to frantic appeals from Arnim for action which would bolster the German bishops. Still the Chancellor held back. He informed his envoy on March 13 that the government of the North German Confederation could not act against the Curia so long as the latter remained formally within the realm of ecclesiastical matters. In no case, he added, could it go beyond what the bishops themselves were willing to do, and then only after the prelates had acted. He asked that Arnim make it clear to the Germans that Berlin would not abandon them, that Prussia would render them all possible assistance so long as they persisted in defending their own rights. When France, again through the initiative of

[76] Bismarck to the Prussian Legations in Munich, Florence, Brussels, Dresden, and Rome (Berlin, Feb. 21, 1870), *GW*, 6b: no. 1513; Bachem, 3:87; Sybel, 7:210–11; Pierre de la Gorce, *Histoire du second empire*, 6:72–73.

Daru, sent a moderately strong protest to the Pope on April 10, Bismarck, although he regarded the French note as too weak to be effective, finally consented to the dispatch of a similar communication from the North German Confederation.[77] The most important paragraph in this note, dated April 23, 1870, ran:

> Such decrees [as are being considered by the Council], far from being solely a vague menace for the future, seem rather calculated in a manner to cause a rebirth, enveloped with a new dogmatic sanction, of old pontifical claims, sufficiently known and constantly combated by civil society in every epoch and in every nation. To attempt to proclaim these principles today from the height of the pontifical throne, to attempt to sustain them by all the means of persuasion which the Church possesses, would be, we fear, to cause disturbance in the entire range of relations of the Church with the state, and to lead to crises of which the pontifical government, in spite of its traditional wisdom, does not perhaps take into account, because it is less able than we to judge the state of opinion in our country.[78]

Bismarck was still, however, unwilling to take extreme measures to force moderation upon the Council, for he exercised considerable care to make even this blow as soft as possible, stressing more than once that he was motivated solely by a desire to preserve religious peace in Germany. "We have," the note stated in another paragraph, "no interest in weakening the authority of the sovereign Pontiff."[79] Notes of approximately the same content were forwarded to Rome by the governments of Austria, Bavaria, and Portugal. Papal authorities received the protests courteously, but declined in every case to take action upon them. Antonelli told the French ambassador that it was impossible officially to lay his note before the Council.[80]

Meanwhile debate on the portion of the revised *Schema* dealing with papal authority had already begun on March 13. It was not until June 14, however, that the Council completed discussion of the original articles and was ready to deal with the new dogma. During the intervening period the whole weight of papal prestige was thrown

[77] Fifteenth Letter from Rome, Feb. 4, 1870, *Quirinus Letters*, 193; Mourret, 8:563–64; Nippold, 159; Eyck, *Bismarck*, 3:81; Bismarck to Arnim, Berlin, March 13, 1870, *GW*, 6b: no. 1527; Legation of the North German Confederation in Rome to Antonelli, April 23, 1870, Friedrich, *Tagebuch*, Beilage IV, 449–51.
[78] Legation of the North German Confederation in Rome to Antonelli, April 23, 1870, Friedrich, *Tagebuch*, Beilage IV, 450.
[79] *Ibid.*, 451.
[80] Sybel, 7:212; Bachem, 3:87.

against the opposition bishops to break down their resistance. By the middle of June the logical weakness in the inopportunist argument had become all too apparent even to those who had held it most strongly. The Pope wished the dogma defined, and those who opposed him were faced with the choice of acquiescing or of going into open revolt against the head of the Church, thus turning their backs on tradition. In the case of Ketteler, in many ways the leader of the group, the inner struggle was particularly severe. As early as December 1869, Friedrich had pointed out to one of the diplomats at Rome that Ketteler's whole background, especially his long association with the Jesuits, made it most unlikely that he could be counted upon to resist to the end. In March 1870, Cardinal Hohenlohe, brother of the Bavarian minister and one of the most outspoken opponents of the dogma, expressed the fear that Ketteler was leading the German bishops into a trap, with the intent to betray them at the crucial moment. This judgment was much too harsh. All evidence points to the conclusion that Ketteler was entirely sincere in his opposition to the dogma, but that he was at last unable to justify in his own mind a step abhorrent to his personality and training — an open break with the Pope. At the time of his reply to the papal commendation for his attack on Döllinger in February 1870, Ketteler spoke of his inner conflict, and then expressed the hope that he might be relieved of his burden and be permitted to return home, offering, however, to continue if the Pontiff desired it. His last public utterance before the Council took final action came on June 5, when he once more charged the *Allgemeine Zeitung* with lies about his attitude toward the dogma. His words were again a measure of the pressures upon him, for now he flatly denied that he had ever opposed the infallibility of the Pope — certainly a direct contradiction of the evidence from 1866 and 1867. He admitted to having believed that definition was inopportune, but now attacks on him such as those in the *Allgemeine Zeitung* had led him to doubt the wisdom of that belief.

In July, only a few days before the final session on the dogma, Ketteler's utter weariness was evidenced by his curt refusal to debate theological issues any further with Archbishop Deschamps, one of the leading infallibilists. "The wretched dissension which now divides the bishops makes me so weary that I prefer to lay down my pen." To his niece he wrote two days later that he hoped for unity among the bishops, but doubted that it would be possible. He mentioned the difficult time he had had in Rome, but recognized it would have been foolish to expect otherwise. The whole impression is one of fatigue, some bitterness, and considerable nausea over the course that the Council had followed.[81]

On July 13 the revised *Schema* was submitted to a vote in general congregation, equivalent to a committee of the whole. This meeting, which was secret, afforded the last opportunity for the opposition to contest the issue without an open break with the Papacy; for in the succeeding public session every bishop would have to bear responsibility for his vote, not only before the Church, but before the entire world. Of the 601 prelates who attended, 451 voted *placet*; 88, *non placet*; and 62, *placet juxta modum, i.e.,* to approve conditionally. Thirty-six German and Austro-Hungarian bishops formed the core of the dissidents. Among the most prominent were Cardinals Schwarzenberg and Rauscher, Archbishop Scherr, and Bishops Ketteler and Héfelé. Following the congregation, the opposition resolved to make one further effort, and on July 15, six of its members, including Ketteler and Scherr, requested of the committee *de fide* that it adopt an amendment which would require assent of the Church as a whole before any decree could be regarded as infallible. The committee, which had already accepted one limiting modification — "when he speaks *ex cathedra*" — in an effort to secure unanimity, refused to compromise further. In fact, it closed the door to reconciliation by itself inserting a new clause: "Decrees of the Roman Pontiff [are] in and of themselves, and not by consent of the Church, irreformable." [82] Some of the opposition bishops saw no course open to them, in the face of this gratuitous insult, but open resistance. They had, however, little time to consider their action, for the final public session, originally scheduled for Sunday, July 24, had been moved up to Monday, July 18, because of the imminent outbreak of the Franco-Prussian War. More than fifty of the dissidents met on July 17, and tentatively decided to vote *non*

[81] Diary, Dec. 18, 1869, Friedrich, *Tagebuch*, 29–30; Cardinal Hohenlohe to Prince Hohenlohe, Rome, March 18, 1870, Hohenlohe, *Memoirs*, 2:3; Ketteler to Pius IX, Rome, Feb. 26, 1870, Ketteler to Archbishop Deschamps, Rome, July 9, 1870, Ketteler to Countess Droste zu Vischering, Rome, July 11, 1870, *Ketteler Briefe*, 405–6, 417–18, 420–21; Declaration of Bishop von Ketteler, Rome, June 5, 1870, *ibid.*, 412–14; Tenth Letter from Rome, Jan. 15, 1870, *Quirinus Letters*, 151.

[82] "*Romani Pontificis definitiones esse ex sese, non autem ex consensu ecclesiae, irreformabiles.*"

placet. Bishop Dupanloup of Orléans, who arrived late at the meeting, succeeded, however, in convincing them that the best policy would be abstention. Accordingly they decided to avail themselves of permission granted by the Pontiff earlier in the month for those who felt "the pressure of duties" to leave before the public session. A letter was therefore drawn up explaining that rather than vote *non placet* the signers were returning home immediately. All the bishops promised to submit to the decision of the Council. The letter, with fifty-five signatures, was dispatched to the Pope. Ketteler, in addition, wrote a personal letter explaining that his action had been finally determined by the fact that the substitute motion which he had helped to prepare had proved unacceptable. He was, therefore, departing, to avoid finding himself "in a position abhorrent to my soul" of being obliged to oppose publicly the Pope's will.[83]

On the following day, at the last public session of the Council, only two bishops voted *non placet,* while 535 assented to the dogma. The two who refused to compromise were Monsignor Riccio of Cajazzo and Monsignor Fitzgerald of Little Rock. Neither had been party to the minority decision of July 17, but both also agreed to submit to the decrees of the Council.[84]

On the following day came the French declaration of war against Prussia, and two months later, the withdrawal of French troops from Rome. The Council was still technically in session when the Italian army, on September 20, invaded the Eternal City itself, to the accompaniment of an artillery bombardment. A few weeks thereafter papal territories were declared by the Italian government to be incorporated into Italy as the "Roman province." The next day Pius IX suspended the Council. Not a hand had been raised by any European power to aid the Papacy. Several governments found a perverse satisfaction in seeing the Pope drain the cup of misfortune after he had so obstinately ignored their requests for moderation.

In Germany, although the war immediately overshadowed all other questions, conflict over the Council's decrees continued to rage for the remainder of the year. Most of the German governments filed protests over the infallibility dogma and refused to permit publication

---

[83] Mourret, 8: 571–73; Hahn, 32; Bachem, 3:88–89; Bishop Fessler to Ketteler, Rome, July 9, 1870, Ketteler to Piux IX, Rome, July 17, 1870, *Ketteler Briefe,* 419, 421–22.
[84] Mourret, 8:572–73; Bachem, 3:88–89.

of the decrees within their territories. Austria went so far as to denounce her concordat. In August 1870, the German bishops reconvened at Fulda, and from there issued another *Hirtenbrief* which advised all Catholics to submit. Some of the bishops did so with extreme reluctance. In particular, Héfélé of Rothenburg appeared crushed by the collapse of German resistance at Rome. He gave one observer who visited him the impression of being "mortally wounded." Most Catholic laymen bowed without hesitation.

Jörg, late in the summer, issued from Berlin a public declaration addressed to the Archbishop of Munich, which affirmed that all loyal Catholics accepted the decisions of the Council without question. He had thus totally reversed his earlier position on papal infallibility. The shift had been foreshadowed in the first issue of the *Historisch-politische Blätter* for 1870, published just after the beginning of the Council. He had written then that the world stood at a "great turning point of history," and that the Church might have influence on the future of humanity only if it took positive action through the Council. The Syllabus had pointed the way, and the Church could continue on the proper road by acting "to combat anti-Christianism," and by becoming an influence "in every field of social life." The Hohenlohe circular had begun Jörg's conversion from an anti-infallibilist, and the virulence of Döllinger's attacks on the supreme Pontiff had completed it.[85]

Irreconcilables like Hohenlohe viewed the German clergy's submission as a sign of the "moral ruin of the bishops." Misinformed about the terms of the July 17 decision, Hohenlohe accused them of breaking their pledged word to one another. A few Catholic intellectuals refused to yield. Döllinger, several of his Munich colleagues, and some from other south German universities met at Nuremberg on August 27, and issued a denunciation of the dogma so violent that young Hertling commented there was nothing left for them but to become Protestants. A similar meeting, held on August 14 by several professors at Bonn, produced a similar dissent. Most of these individuals were excommunicated, and later became leaders in the Old Catholic movement. Döllinger, whose opposition was by far the most bitter, suffered excommunication on April 23, 1871, after ignoring several warnings

---

[85] Mourret, 8:573, 577–78; Hahn, 36–38; Journal, Nov. 30, 1870, Hohenlohe, *Memoirs*, 2:28; Wöhler, 24; Hertling, 1:214; "Das Conciliums-Jahr," *HPB*, 65:20. See also "Zeitläufe: Das oekumenische Concil, seine Benergler und seine Gegner," I., *ibid.*, 64:159–68; "Zeitläufe: Die liberalen Katholiken und das Concil," *ibid.*, 65:557.

from Archbishop Scherr. Unlike the others, however, he remained aloof from the *Altkatholiken,* and died in 1890 with the ban still in effect, long after the others had been received again into the Church.[86]

Upon Germany the Council had a severely disturbing influence. It tended to divert the attention of Catholics from important political questions at a time when great events were in the making.[87] In north Germany it helped to produce an ugly outbreak of anti-Catholicism which Bismarck was not able completely to keep in bounds.[88] Thus it emphasized the deep religious division within the country at a time when the Chancellor was making every effort to prevent any hindrance to the cause of German unity. By so emphasizing those divisions it helped to create the basis for a new Catholic political party.[89]

How is it possible to explain Bismarck's almost negligent attitude toward the Council and toward the politico-religious issues it posed for Germany? In part the answer may be found in the already mentioned difficulty of the great realist in understanding why others should become so aroused over questions which to him had an air of unreality. But even more it may be traced to the fact that Bismarck at this time felt an almost desperate necessity to avoid any action of his own that would further sharpen divisions in Germany which had been produced by the religious conflict, and by others over which he had as little control. During the months when the Council was meeting, Bismarck walked a tightrope, and a false step might have produced disastrous consequences.[90] Only after the French declared war, on July 19, did he to a degree regain control of the domestic situation in Germany. Even then he felt constrained to instruct Arnim: "Keep away from any . . . demonstration. Infallibility is at the moment without interest for us." [91] With a military victory, this and other domestic issues could be settled realistically and satisfactorily. But here again he failed to comprehend that reality had different meanings for different people.

[86] Journal, Nov. 30, 1870, Hohenlohe, *Memoirs,* 2:28; Hertling, 1:216–17; Scherr to Döllinger, Munich, Jan. 4, 1871, Feb. 14, 1871, March 17, 1871; Dr. Joseph von Prand to Döllinger, April 5, 1871, April 18, 1871, Döllinger, *Briefe und Erklärungen,* 61–65, 69, 72, 98–99, 103; Mourret, 8:577.

[87] Vigener, *Ketteler,* 538.

[88] See Chapter Eight.

[89] See Chapter Nine.

[90] See Chapter Eight.

[91] Bismarck to Arnim, Berlin, July 20, 1870, *GW,* 6b: no. 1684.

Chapter 8

Catholics and the Founding of the Empire, 1870–1871

IN MIDSUMMER of 1870 the deceptively quiet interlude in Bismarck's efforts to bring the German states under the Prussian mantle came to an abrupt end with the sudden outbreak of the Franco-Prussian War. It is not intended here to go deeply into the origin of the war — although a great many aspects of the problem are still obscure — except to explore the role which Catholic Germany played in forcing the Chancellor's hand. For it seems probable that Bismarck's relations with the Church and with Catholics had much more to do with his abandonment of inaction than has been realized. As late as June 22, 1869, when the second annual session of the *Zollparlament* came to an end, Bismarck appeared not at all disquieted by the course of events. Although the session itself had been totally devoid of political importance, he told Hohenlohe that it had served at least one useful purpose: The leaders of the national party on both sides of the Main had at last come to see that it was folly to bring up political questions so long as the majority from south Germany was determined that they should not be discussed.[1]

This satisfaction, moderate and essentially negative though it was, evaporated rapidly during the following months. The growth of the *Katholische Volkspartei* in Baden, even if there was no immediate likelihood of its gaining control of the government, posed a threat to the hopes of nationalists in the Southwest. Moreover, the Patriots' victory in the second Bavarian election of 1869, and the subsequent fall of Hohenlohe, was a real disaster, for the *Landtag* would now be

---

[1] *Stenographische Berichte über die Verhandlungen des durch die Allerhöchste Verordnung vom 23. Mai 1869 einberufenen deutschen Zollparlaments, passim*; Conversation with Hohenlohe, Berlin, June 23, 1869, *GW*, 7: no. 221.

controlled by the most bitter enemies of Prussia to be found in all Germany. Although the Bray ministry was not the worst possible — the mere suggestion of a government headed by Jörg made all nationalists shudder — there was no guarantee that Bray would remain in office for long, or that, if he did, he would be able to withstand the demands of the Patriots to cut all ties with north Germany.[2] At the very least there was great danger that he would have to appease them by scrapping the military reforms of the Hohenlohe era.

In Württemberg, too, opposition to the military reforms adopted in accordance with the *Schutz- und Trutzbündnis* became dangerous by the early months of 1870. In January the *Volkspartei* circulated petitions throughout the country protesting the new military service law. About a hundred and fifty thousand signatures were obtained. When the *Landtag* reconvened on March 8, after an interval of fourteen months, forty-five members of the *Volkspartei* introduced a motion demanding that the government immediately introduce legislation to bring the military establishment into line with the financial capabilities of the kingdom. It asked especially that the number of men under arms be drastically cut. Behind the whole move was the hope of reintroducing the militia system. Varnbüler and Mittnacht wanted to avoid a showdown, for they knew they might well be defeated, and eventually a compromise was reached by which the military budget was pruned considerably, but the two-year compulsory service was retained. Thus, although a drastic curtailment in the number of Württemberg troops was avoided, their training and equipment were bound to suffer. The direction of the wind was obvious in Berlin.[3]

Meanwhile, in north Germany also, as astute men on both sides of the Main had long recognized, there were pressures which made indefinite prolongation of the existing order more and more difficult. Jörg had several times pointed out that the *Nordbund* was unstable

---

[2] The *Kreuzzeitung* in 1870 gave the Patriots a "large share of the responsibility" for the War of 1870 on the somewhat farfetched grounds that Hohenlohe's fall had encouraged France to believe that a party was in power at Munich which would look to the Tuileries rather than to Berlin. See "Zeitläufe: Der Krieg und die Parteien in Süddeutschland," *HPB*, 66:475. The analysis is faulty — the Patriots were capable of seeing little beyond the frontiers of Bavaria, except for passing glances at Vienna and Rome — but it is one of the few contemporary references which suggest that there was a direct relationship between Catholicism in Germany and the origins of the war. Cf. also Bismarck's reference, on Nov. 20, 1869, to Hohenlohe's fall as a "calamity." *GW*, 6b: No 1449, and note 122, Chapter Six, above.

[3] Mittnacht, *Rückblicke*, 30–31; Sybel, 7:366–67.

because of its constitutional anomalies. Early in 1870 he reverted to this theme. It was now apparent, he wrote, that the annexations of 1866 had weakened the fabric of Prussian society, for indigestible elements had been incorporated in the kingdom, adding "considerable ferment to the old mash." State finances had been ruined, he claimed, and serious deficits in 1868 and 1869 for both Prussia and the *Bund* bore him out. He argued further that the proverbial efficiency of Prussian administration had been irreparably wrecked by the too sudden expansion of her frontiers, and by the consequent addition of large numbers of disaffected individuals.[4] In his comments on the opening of the North German Reichstag session in February he scrutinized in detail the contradictions in the north German constitutional structure. There was a Reichstag but no *Reich*. The Reichstag had been opened by a speech from the throne, but there was no throne; there were twenty-odd thrones. The address was delivered by the King of Prussia, but he spoke not as king but as president of the Confederation, and so on.

If one understands only these difficulties and contradictions in formal nomenclature, it appears at first glance that the North German Confederation can have no permanent existence as such, even if it had been established "forever" ten times.[5]

Prophetically he added that this monstrosity would either dissolve into a "real confederation," or it would be converted into an empire, in which the thrones would be replaced by one throne. This had always been Bismarck's objective, he charged, and now none of the nationalists in Berlin, from the Chancellor himself to Lasker, thought of anything but a centralized state which would destroy forever the traditional divisions. Thus pressures were increasing in the North to force a crossing of the Main, however strongly south Germany was opposed.[6]

In the same article Jörg reviewed with high praise a book published only a few weeks before by the Prussian scholar, Constantin Frantz, entitled *The Darker Side of the North German Confederation Considered from the Prussian Viewpoint.*[7] Frantz took the position that

---

[4] "Zeitläufe: Das Conciliums-Jahr," *HPB*, 65:16.

[5] "Zeitläufe: Die Eröffnung des norddeutschen Reichstages und die preussische Thronrede," *ibid.*, 375–76.

[6] *Ibid.*, 375–76, 381.

[7] *Die Schattenseite des norddeutschen Bundes, vom preussischen Standpunkt betrachtet.*

Prussia had turned her back on her entire historical tradition in 1867, not for the sake of something higher and better, but simply in order to become a "modern" state. Inevitably the result could be nothing but the destruction of the German national character, for the Confederation was itself, as Frantz put it, "a laboratory for political experimentation," which ignored all history and tradition, good and bad.[8] With this judgment Jörg heartily agreed, and in closing, he remarked that he had only one reservation on the book: "The author gives it the title, *The Darker Side of the North German Confederation*; we, however, search in vain for the brighter side." [9]

One aspect of the "darker side" in Prussia itself was the deepening conflict over control of the schools between 1868 and 1870. Traditionally the lower schools had been generally conducted under religious auspices, but in Prussia, as elsewhere, liberals were pressing for secularization of all education. Bismarck, to whom this problem, like so many others, was of concern only because of its political implications, hoped to keep the issue bottled up to avoid increasing the divisions in north Germany at a time when unity was of paramount importance. He succeeded only partially. During the 1868–69 session of the Prussian *Landtag*, liberals made several efforts to force measures of secularization on the government. None of them were in themselves of particular importance, and most of them in any case failed. Nevertheless, considerable public excitement resulted, and Catholics, viewing the attempts in relation to what was happening in Bavaria and Baden, saw a pattern which made them uneasy about the future.

During the debate on the budget for the *Kultusministerium* in December 1868, the *Abgeordnetenhaus* adopted a motion of the Hanoverian National Liberal, Grumbrecht, to eliminate the terms "Evangelical" and "Catholic" from official designations of *gymnasia* in the province of Hanover. A similar motion was later accepted with reference to Schleswig-Holstein. The minister of education, von Mühler, then announced that for the sake of uniformity the government would order confessional designations to be eliminated from all official documents referring to schools. During the same debate several petitions were received requesting changes in the organization of the educational system. One came from the municipal authorities of Breslau

---

[8] "Zeitläufe: Die Eröffnung des norddeutschen Reichstages . . . ," *HPB*, 65:382–90.
[9] *Ibid.*, 390.

asking for the erection of a nonconfessional *gymnasium*. This was matched by another from Catholics in the same city seeking government funds to construct a Catholic *Realschule*. The chief magistrate of Bromberg sought an order to halt construction of a Catholic *gymnasium* for which funds had already been voted, claiming that the city was much more in need of a new school for Protestants, since the existing one was too small. He reminded the *Landtag* that the proposed Catholic school was intended to replace one that had been closed on government order in 1863 because it had been "misused for antinational [*i.e.*, Polish] ends." He insisted that a new school would act in exactly the same fashion. These petitions suffered the usual fate of such missives, but their number and content are significant. Mühler himself spoke in defense of the traditional link between education and religion, and, for once, Mallinckrodt took the tribune in behalf of the government, voicing his alarm that so many people aspired to destroy that tie.[10]

These debates did not go unnoticed in south Germany. The *Historisch-politische Blätter* devoted an entire article to a discussion of their implications for the future. Jörg saw in them evidence of "a general assault of liberalism, first of all on the positive rights of the confessions, but, under this veil, also upon the foundations of the Christian community itself." He noted that Mühler had been hard pressed in the debate, and had been able to hold his ground only with the aid of such "Catholic celebrities" as Mallinckrodt and others. Even the Prussian conservatives had offered no assistance to the government on this question.[11]

To keep the record balanced, it must be pointed out that during the same period Catholics were carrying on considerable agitation for the establishment of a Catholic university on Prussian soil. Archbishop Melchers of Cologne, one of the most persistent advocates of such an institution, broached the question officially to the government early in 1869. Mühler quickly vetoed the request on the advice of Bismarck, who feared that the university would be used for ultramontane propaganda and to "sow anti-Prussian sentiments." The Chancellor knew

---

[10] "Zeitläufe: Die Schul- und Unterrichtsfrage, sowie das Recht der Confessionen in der preussischen Kammer," *HPB*, 63:268–69; *Stenographische Berichte über die Verhandlungen der . . . beiden Häuser des Landtages: Haus der Abgeordneten, Session 1868–69*, Feb. 26, 1869, 1971–73, 1978; Goyau, *L'Allemagne religieuse*, 3:320.

[11] "Zeitläufe: Die Schul- und Unterrichtsfrage . . . ," *HPB*, 63:256–57.

also that there would be vociferous objections from his liberal supporters.[12]

By the fall of 1869 the religious division in north Germany ceased to be merely a threat to Bismarck, and became a really serious problem. As described before, preparations for the Vatican Council gave rise to considerable ill-informed and often inflammatory speculation in the popular press over the infallibility dogma. Many "enlightened" individuals and their unenlightened fellows became, therefore, increasingly unfriendly toward members of the Catholic clergy. Feeling had already risen to a high pitch in some areas when, in July 1869, newspapers reported from Cracow in Austrian Poland that a nun who was obviously unbalanced had been discovered incarcerated in a convent under what were alleged to be inhuman conditions. Apparently the sister's mental condition was not understood by her mother superior, and consequently her admitted misconduct was not properly recognized to be the product of her disease. The news was certain to inflame liberals who hated monasticism on principle and who could now justifiably thunder against its inhumanity. In Viennese liberal circles, for example, the cry went up immediately for a fight to the death against cloisters of all kinds. This agitation soon was echoed in Berlin.[13]

The situation there came to a head on August 4, 1869, when a crowd staged a minor riot against a small religious settlement in the industrial suburb of Moabit. A few months earlier four Franciscan friars had established an orphanage, and they had been joined shortly by two Dominicans who proposed to undertake spiritual labors among workers in neighboring factories. The occasion for the riot was the dedication of a small church built in connection with the orphanage. The rioters, armed apparently with nothing more deadly than crowbars, were mostly workers from a near-by plant. Their purpose seems to have been not to harm the monks, but to render the establishment uninhabitable. The two Dominicans were forced to flee, and the buildings suffered minor damage before the authorities intervened.[14]

The *Moabiter Klostersturm*, as the incident came to be known, gave anticlerical extremists another excuse to demand abolition of all mo-

[12] Hansen, 1:797; Bismarck to von Mühler, Berlin, April 26, 1869, *GW*, 6b: no. 1377.

[13] Bachem, 3:38. For a detailed description of the Moabit affair and its aftermath, see Goyau, *L'Allemagne religieuse*, 3:321–24.

[14] Bachem, 3:38–39; Ludwig Bergsträsser, *Der politische Katholizismus: Dokumente seiner Entwicklung*, 2:7.

nastic establishments and other religious foundations, both Protestant and Catholic. In the following weeks a series of "spontaneous" public meetings took place in and around Berlin for the purpose of obtaining signatures to petitions asking the *Landtag* to act on the basis of a law, long in abeyance, which forbade the settlement of monastic orders in Prussia. It appears that Berlin Catholics, led by a clergyman, *Missionsvikar* Eduard Müller, had considerable success in "packing" some of these meetings in order to sabotage them. In some cases they managed to take control. Eleven petitions were finally forwarded to the *Landtag* from various groups in Berlin, and one from Elbing. The most important one bore the signature of a bookbinder, Krebs by name, as sponsor. It demanded that all existing cloisters, cathedral and other foundations maintained by either confession be closed permanently by January 1, 1870, and their property confiscated by the state. No such establishments were to be authorized in the future. The petition charged that cloisters had been for centuries "spawning grounds of superstition." Most of the other petitions contained similar demands. One insisted that cloisters had to be closed to preserve religious peace. Nearly all of them asked that Prussia's 1821 agreement with the Papacy be revoked.[15]

These petitions were duly received by the Prussian lower house, and were submitted in the regular manner to the appropriate committee. The situation was politically explosive. Catholic members of the *Landtag,* in common with the Catholic population generally, feared an attack on the independence of the Church comparable to the "reforms" of Jolly in Baden. Bismarck, although there appears to be no record of his role in what followed, obviously preferred to avoid a showdown, so that the damage already done to the cause of unity would not be made worse. The committee on petitions, which, so far as can be ascertained, had only one Catholic member, the deputy Göddertz, made its report on February 9. It is not known whether Bismarck influenced its deliberations directly or not. Its chairman, Gneist, a National Liberal, gave for the committee a circumspect account of the issues involved, concluding that the petitions went further than the facts justified. Abolition of the cloisters would, it had been

---

[15] Bachem, 3:39; Bergsträsser, *Politischer Katholizismus,* 2:7; *Stenographische Berichte über die Verhandlungen der . . . beiden Häuser des Landtages: Haus der Abgeordneten, Session 1869–70* (hereafter cited as *Stenographische Berichte Prussian Landtag, 1869–70*), Anlagen, 2:990–91.

decided, impinge upon legal rights which had long been in possession of the Church. Specifically, the demand that the Moabit institution be closed rested on claims that the committee deemed inaccurate. However, the committee did recommend enactment of a general law which would prevent future establishment of educational and eleemosynary institutions by religious orders. Moreover, "the committee recognizes that in many ways legal regulation of the entire field of religious societies equally for all provinces appears desirable." It concluded, therefore, that the government should undertake to secure enactment of such legislation by the North German Reichstag, while immediately taking steps to eliminate anomalies in the operation of existing laws.[16]

Despite the relative mildness of the committee's report, it was only to be expected that Catholics would regard its recommendations as an attack on themselves. In order to avoid the almost inevitable parliamentary wrangle, which could only further endanger Prussian and national unity, Bismarck's parliamentary spokesmen sought to table the report. On February 8 Count Bethusy-Huc made an impassioned appeal that the house not plunge the nation into a religious controversy, the end of which could not be foreseen. Catholics, however, were in no mood to see the question dropped. Apparently sensing the government's discomfiture, Reichensperger rose to insist that the report dealt with issues so fundamental that failure of the chamber to air them fully was tantamount to abdication of its responsibilities.[17]

The rules of procedure gave the president substantial control over the agenda, his rulings being subject to challenge only upon written request of thirty members. However, on his proposal — obviously intended to prevent debate — that the report be dropped altogether until the following day, when it would appear as the final item on the agenda, Catholics had no difficulty in obtaining sufficient signatures to overrule the chair. But although the report remained, therefore, on the agenda, it appeared that time would not permit the house to reach it that day. Mallinckrodt thereupon moved that the committee's report be placed at the top of the next day's order of business, but his motion was easily defeated. Thus, at the close of the session on Febru-

---

[16] *Stenographische Berichte Prussian Landtag, 1869–70,* Anlagen, 2 : 1007; Bergsträsser, *Politischer Katholizismus,* 2 : 7.

[17] *Stenographische Berichte Prussian Landtag, 1869–70,* Feb. 8, 1870, 3 : 2010–11.

ary 8 the president was still in a position to control whether or not the report would come to the floor.[18]

The next day the story was essentially the same. The report appeared at the bottom of the agenda, and the house did not reach it. Just before adjournment Mallinckrodt submitted a motion, signed by more than eighty members, requesting that the matter be taken up at the beginning of the following day's session. The altercation which followed makes clear the tense feelings which the matter had aroused in the house. Mallinckrodt insisted that full discussion was necessary if the uneasiness of Catholics was to be allayed; for, in his opinion, the report attacked basic principles of the Prussian constitution which guaranteed freedom to the Church. It was, he shouted, a *"Fehdehandschuh"* thrown down to all Catholics, and "we do not intend to let it lie." Two Free Conservatives then rose in succession to argue that the report was routine and had no claim to special treatment.[19] This, Windthorst proceeded to deny vehemently, saying, "In my long parliamentary life no document has ever been introduced which contained more provocative insults toward a large segment of the membership of the house, and toward a large part of the population of the country."[20] The chair ruled the Hanoverian out of order, and a noisy demonstration developed on the floor. When Windthorst could again make himself heard, he repeated Mallinckrodt's closing warning: "We cannot allow the glove that has been thrown at our feet to lie unregarded."[21]

The Free Conservative, Kardorff, precipitated another disturbance by announcing that the Mallinckrodt motion should be defeated, since if Windthorst favored it, that in itself was sufficient reason to vote it down. The Hanoverian, he claimed, had created more difficulties for the German nation than any other single member of the house. After the chair had again restored order, Windthorst spoke to rebut the charges made against him. Always, he insisted, he had worked for the advancement, "in the true and correct sense," of the German people. Always he would strive to do so. At length, as was certain from the beginning, Mallinckrodt's motion went down to defeat on a standing vote.[22]

[18] *Ibid.*, 2010–12.
[19] *Ibid.*, Feb. 9, 1870, 2039–40.
[20] *Ibid.*, 2040–41.
[21] *Ibid.*, 2041.
[22] *Ibid.*, 2041–42.

The report did not appear on the agenda for February 10. There was no protest. Apparently the Catholics had given up hope of forcing a debate, and thereafter no more was heard of the matter in the *Abgeordnetenhaus.*[23] A great deal more was heard of it, however, in German Catholic circles as a whole. For the Moabit affair and its aftermath were among the chief reasons why many Catholic politicians concluded that an organized political party was vitally needed once again. The reconstruction of the Prussian Center by Peter Reichensperger and others followed within a few months.

Bismarck's desire to minimize the entire affair is suggested by the fact that his diplomatic correspondence contains only one reference to it. On January 12, 1870, he wrote to Arnim — in answer to a query as to what the government contemplated — that the question, in so far as it concerned the *Landtag,* was a technical matter involving only an interpretation of existing laws. He added, obviously for communication to interested parties at Rome, that the outcome of the Council could not fail to influence whatever action the government took.[24] Bismarck could hardly have escaped the conclusion that the vehemence of Mallinckrodt and Windthorst in the debate was somehow related to the growth of political Catholicism in south Germany, and he was probably considerably shaken. Were Prussian Catholics and their clergy still Prussians first and Catholics second, as he had once believed? Or would they, in a moment of crisis, aid their fellows in the South to wreck Prussia's efforts to unite the nation? Might it not, then, be inescapably necessary to end the division at the Main before the gulf became wider and even more difficult to bridge?

Whatever fears Bismarck may have had early in February 1870, he preserved an outward calm, which is considerably more than can be said of some of his political allies. The 1870 session of the North German Reichstag opened on February 14, immediately after the *Landtag* adjourned. Since it was to be the last session of the Reichstag's first legislative period, the opening address which Bismarck had prepared for the King reviewed achievements of the previous three years, and then dealt at considerable length with relations between North and South. It mentioned specially a treaty recently concluded with Baden

[23] *Ibid.,* Feb. 10, 1870, 2045–2122, *passim.*
[24] Bismarck to Arnim, Berlin, Jan. 12, 1870, *GW,* 6b: no. 1472; Bergsträsser, *Politischer Katholizismus,* 2:7–8.

which extended the judicial comity adopted by the Reichstag in 1869 "in a national sense beyond the frontiers of the federal territory." Moreover:

All the treaties which link north Germany with the South confer the reliable guarantees of security and welfare contained in the strong and definitive organization of the northern Confederation upon the whole of the German fatherland. The trust which our south German allies place in these guarantees rests on complete reciprocity. The feeling of national solidarity, which owes its existence to the present treaties, the reciprocally pledged word of the German princes, the community of the highest interests of the fatherland confer upon our relations with south Germany a solidarity which is independent of the shifting waves of political passion.[25]

To the National Liberals, who were becoming more and more restive after a year and a half of what they called Bismarck's *"Stillstandpolitik,"* the address presaged an indefinite continuation of that policy. Their impatience and anger overflowed a few days later in what proved to be the only open revolt against Bismarck's leadership in the period of the North German Confederation. On February 24, when the treaty with Baden came up for ratification, Lasker, Bennigsen, and several others introduced the following motion:

The Reichstag resolves upon the adoption of the treaty to declare:
The Reichstag of the North German Confederation expresses with thanks its recognition of the ceaseless national efforts with which the government and people of Baden are associated;
The Reichstag recognizes in these efforts the vigorous expression of national solidarity and will take with joyous satisfaction as its goal the union of Baden with the existing Confederation as rapidly as possible.[26]

The Lasker motion, representing an outburst of pent-up dissatisfaction on the part of a group which had loyally supported Bismarck since 1866, posed a serious threat to the Chancellor. For unquestionably the leaders of the National Liberal party, in attempting to force his hand, were again seeking to inject the Reichstag into the conduct of foreign policy, a field in which he would brook no interference. A tumultuous debate ensued. During its course Bismarck castigated

---

[25] *Stenographische Berichte über die Verhandlungen des Reichstages des norddeutschen Bundes, I. Legislatur-Periode, Session 1870* (hereafter cited as *Stenographische Berichte 1870*), Eröffnungssitzung, Feb. 14, 1870, 1:1–2.
[26] *Ibid.*, Anlagen, 1:204.

Lasker for striving to extend the powers of the Reichstag beyond those granted in the constitution. The tone of his address, unusually vehement even for Bismarck, demonstrated how seriously he regarded the revolt. He was in the end forced to appeal for patience from his erstwhile supporters, and Bismarck in the guise of a suppliant, at least in public, was indeed a rare phenomenon. Lasker eventually withdrew the motion, stating that its chief purpose had been achieved, for the debate itself had demonstrated to the world the gratitude of the North German Reichstag for Baden's faith in the national cause.[27] Its other major purpose remained unmentioned, although that too had been achieved. Bismarck had been warned that if he wished to retain the support of the National Liberals, his policy of inaction had to come to an end.

Many people in Baden reacted angrily to the rude manner in which the Chancellor had rebuffed the Lasker proposal, regarding his action as completely unjustified, and as a slap in the face. So concerned was Jolly over this widespread feeling that he felt obliged to write an open letter to the *Karlsruher Zeitung,* informing the public that his government had been in no way responsible for Lasker's motion. Despite Bismarck's rudeness, he would continue, he wrote, to work for the admission of Baden into the *Nordbund,* for union with the North was in the Duchy's best interests. Since the north German Chancellor had in the past given many indications that he regarded the existing division of Germany as temporary, Jolly would continue to assume, despite the events of February 24, that his views had not changed.[28]

Bismarck himself, seeking to repair the damage that had been done, wrote a soothing letter to the Baden minister on February 28, reaffirming, however, in a more gentle fashion what he had said in the Reichstag: that the Lasker motion had been an unwelcome surprise to him, and that he could not deal properly with the issues involved for fear of complications abroad. He suggested that his own speech had at least served to let Europe know that he did not consider that Article IV of the 1866 treaty forbade the North German Confederation to

---

[27] *Ibid.,* Feb. 24, 1870, 1:58–77. Although the debate contained numerous derogatory references to the Bavarian Patriots and to the *Volkspartei* in Baden, the Catholic members, with one exception, remained aloof. That came when Kantak announced that the Poles would abstain from voting because they felt that the question of German unity was beyond their competence. See *ibid.,* 174–75.

[28] Baumgarten and Jolly, 162.

complete the unification of Germany, the position taken by both France and Austria. Further, he pointed out in extenuation of his remarks, he had been embarrassed by the possible effects of Lasker's motion on the sensitivities of the King of Bavaria and on those of the Patriot Party. Again he counseled patience.[29] Jolly in the end was not dissatisfied with the exchange, for Bismarck had been forced to take a more definite stand, both publicly and privately, than he had in the past, or would have preferred to take at the time.

Nevertheless, the anger which had given rise to the revolt remained Bamberger, writing home from Berlin in May, showed bitter resentment over Bismarck's treatment of the Lasker motion, complaining of the *"müde deutsche Stillstandpolitik"* which left Hesse "suspended in the air between North and South." What made the situation particularly intolerable for him was the increasing tendency he discerned everywhere to regard the existing state of affairs as just, right, and permanent. Bismarck's unwillingness to act had made a substantial contribution, he felt, to this disastrous situation.[30]

While national enthusiasts were raking the Chancellor over the coals for inactivity, Catholic sources saw both the address from the throne and the debate on the Lasker motion as indications that Prussian aggression against the South was imminent. Jörg's article, already cited, in addition to pointing out the constitutional instability of the Confederation, made much of the contrast between the *Thronreden* of 1869 and of 1870. The former had not even referred to south Germany, while the latter devoted nearly half its length to relations between the sections. The Bavarian concluded that the difference could be explained in one of two ways, both ominous for south Germany. Either the recent conversion of France from an authoritarian to a parliamentary régime meant that Paris would no longer oppose Prussian annexation of south Germany, or Prussia was now prepared to assume the risk of international complications. He regarded the latter as the more likely possibility, finding confirmation for this interpretation in Bismarck's speech of February 24. The address indicated to Jörg that Bismarck had abandoned the position he had so long maintained: that

[29] *Ibid.*, 162–63.

[30] Letter to His Constituents, Berlin, May 22, 1870, Bamberger, *Vertrauliche Briefe*, 142–46. In the same letter Bamberger denounced the Vatican Council for its forthcoming definition of the dogma of papal infallibility. He branded Rome as the chief ally of those in Germany who hated the North German Confederation. See *ibid.*, 145.

force would never be used to compel the south to enter the *Bund*. Now Bismarck had capitulated completely to the National Liberals.[31] The chasm which separated the judgments of Bamberger and Jörg on the significance of the Lasker motion and on Bismarck's reaction to it is a measure of the extreme divisions which existed in German public opinion only a few months before the outbreak of the Franco-Prussian War.

After the flurry at the beginning, the 1870 session of the Reichstag was unproductive either of debate or of legislation which bore directly on the German question. Most of the time was occupied by discussion of a code of criminal law, which was ultimately adopted. Reichensperger, Windthorst, and a few other Catholics participated in some highly technical debates on the code, none of which had special political significance. A budget was approved for 1871; again the debates were mostly technical.[32] Only once, early in April, did the Windthorst of former sessions appear for a moment, when the Hanoverian denied the competence of the Reichstag to expand public health activities under federal jurisdiction, as requested in a petition received by the house.[33]

The King closed the session on May 26 with an address written by Bismarck which reviewed with moderate satisfaction the legislative achievements of the four years in which the Reichstag had been in existence. It closed with the politically innocuous paragraph:

When with the help of God we win for the German nation the position in the world to which its historical importance, its strength, and its pacific tradition destines and qualifies it, Germany will not forget the share which this Reichstag has had in the task, and for that, gentlemen, I again give you my thanks.[34]

What proved to be the final session of the *Zollparlament*, held as before during a Reichstag recess between April 21 and May 7, was equally devoid of political importance. The King did not even attend the opening, and his colorless address was read for him by Bismarck's economic adviser, Rudolph Delbrück. As before, Hohenlohe was reelected vice-president, and this time the south German fraction did not even trouble to put up a candidate. Most of the important Catho-

[31] "Zeitläufe: Die Eröffnung des norddeutschen Reichstages . . . ," *HPB*, 65:377–81; "Zeitläufe: Der bismarckische Generalbericht im norddeutschen Reichstag," *ibid.*, 65:484.
[32] *Stenographische Berichte 1870*, 1 and 2: *passim*.
[33] *Ibid.*, April 6, 1870, 2:695–97.
[34] *Ibid.*, May 26, 1870, 2:1205–6.

lics from the South were back, but Lindau had resigned his seat to devote all his efforts to the *Katholische Volkspartei* in Baden. On the first day there was a behind-the-scenes move by some southern liberals to come to an agreement with their northern counterparts on the issuance of a proclamation that "reunion of the South with the North" was the common national goal, but no such proposal ever reached the floor.[35]

The only interesting debate came on a motion of Bamberger to require member states to investigate the feasibility of adopting for the entire *Zollverein* the currency reforms approved shortly before by the North German Reichstag. Becher (Württemberg) opposed the motion in the name of the south German fraction on the familiar ground that the *Zollparlament* was not competent to deal with the question, since the *Zollverein* treaties had not specifically granted it that authority. The Bamberger motion, for what it was worth, passed on a voice vote. Presumably the majority of south Germans voted against it. The only major legislation of the session was a law to reduce certain tariffs on the schedule of 1865. The south German protectionists held firm, and many north German Catholics, as on similar occasions in the past, abstained, torn between their economic and their political sympathies. The King's closing address of May 7 was as uninspiring as his opening speech. It was, however, delivered in person. During the entire session none of the important Catholics were active.[36]

As late as the end of May 1870, then, it appeared that Bismarck was bent on maintaining his cautious policy. To the public there were few indications that he was disturbed over the increasing strength of Catholic-particularist opinion in the South, over the smoldering religious conflict in Prussia, over the complex issues posed by the Council, or over the ominous signs of revolt within the ranks of his own supporters. During these months, however, Bismarck was quietly laying the basis for a solution to all these problems on his own terms. That he regarded a war with Germany's western neighbor as a prerequisite for the completion of national unity has been mentioned before in this

[35] Friedrich Kiefer to Eduard Lasker, Offenburg (Baden), April 21, 1870, Heyderhoff, *Liberalismus*, 468–69; *Stenographische Berichte über die Verhandlungen des durch die Allerhöchste Verordnung vom 8. April 1870 einberufenen deutschen Zoll-Parlaments* (hereafter abbreviated *Stenographische Berichte Zollparlament 1870*), April 21, 1870, April 25, 1870, April 27, 1870, 1–2, 10, 17.

[36] *Stenographische Berichte Zollparlament 1870*, May 5, 1870, May 7, 1870, 181–82, 229–30, 233–34.

study. Only the national passions which such a conflict would release could overcome south German antipathy toward Prussia sufficiently to make possible the entry of the four independent states into a new *Reich* at least seemingly uncoerced. However, while he hoped to make use of inflamed national sentiment as the agency of unification, he had no desire to be himself used by it.

Hence, although the many events discussed above were conspiring to force Bismarck's hand, he could not take advantage, for example, of the situation which the Lasker motion created. It is entirely possible that Lasker judged correctly, and that, as he claimed in the Reichstag, Baden's admission to the *Nordbund* would have forced the other states to follow suit sooner or later. But in that event the credit would have gone to the Reichstag and to the National Liberal party, not to the King or to Bismarck. This the Chancellor dared not permit, for the prestige of parliamentary institutions vis-à-vis the Prussian monarchy would have been strengthened far too much. Moreover, even if these moves succeeded without provoking a war with France, as Lasker predicted, Bavaria and Württemberg — their governments hostage to the Patriots and the clerical-democratic *Volkspartei,* respectively — would have entered the new Empire resentfully, and only because they felt themselves deprived of choice. In Baden itself, where the *Volkspartei,* although far from possessing a parliamentary majority, certainly spoke for a much larger segment of the population than Lasker was willing to admit, resentment would have been very great. The new *Reich* would thus have come into being with all existing tensions unallayed, if not in fact strengthened. On the other hand, supposing that war with France did result from the annexation of Baden in defiance of the spirit, if not the letter, of the Prague Treaty, Prussia would be branded as aggressor by her Catholic and other south German opponents, and by the world at large. All the denunciations of Prussian militarism which had been hurled by Catholics in Bavaria and Baden, and echoed by their friends in the North, would stand apparently proved. A war, then, could accomplish Bismarck's objective only if France were the aggressor.

It was this situation that made the Hohenzollern candidacy for the Spanish throne so perfectly adaptable to his purposes. At worst Prussia would gain a not-to-be-disdained ally on France's southwestern frontier; at best she could provoke France into declaring war. The latter alternative was, perhaps, more probable in 1870 than it seemed a year earlier. For, while the appointment of the liberal Olivier ministry on December 28, 1869, delivered France somewhat from the whims of the Emperor, it created a political situation that was even more unstable than before. Thus, considerations of prestige took on still greater importance. Bismarck, who seems to have been dealing surreptitiously with the Spanish government off and on throughout 1869, began seriously to push for acceptance of the throne by the King's nephew when the Spanish renewed their offer in February 1870. The chronological relationship between his adoption of the candidacy, the resignation of Hohenlohe in Bavaria, the campaign to cut the military budget in Württemberg, the crisis in the Prussian *Landtag* and the National Liberal revolt, all of which reached a climax the same month, is more than suggestive. Although it would probably be impossible to demonstrate conclusively the interconnections among these events, to assume that they were mere coincidence stretches the limits of credulity too far.

Bismarck's diplomacy proceeded slowly until early July, when a major crisis suddenly developed following a series of French blunders which culminated in the famous interview at Ems on July 13. During the next few days Bismarck maneuvered in such a way as to convince the public in both countries that national honor and national interest required war. The French obliged with a declaration, which was presented at Berlin on July 19.[37]

Meanwhile, on July 15, the North German Reichstag had been summoned for a special session. The consent of the Reichstag was, of course, not required for a declaration of war, but its approval of an

---

[37] The best account of the origins of the war and the diplomatic crisis is still Robert H. Lord, *The Origins of the War of 1870*. For a highly personal French account, see Émile Olivier, *The Franco-German War and Its Hidden Causes*, which is an extract from his long work, *L'Empire liberal*. The text of the declaration is in *Verhandlungen des durch die Allerhöchste Präsidial-Verordnung vom 15. Juli 1870 zu einer ausserordentlichen Session einberufenen Reichstages des norddeutschen Bundes* (hereafter cited as *Stenographische Berichte 1870, First Special Session*), Anlagen, no. 11, p. 22. For Bismarck's views on the possibility of using the Spanish question, among others, to provoke France to war, see Bismarck to Prince Reuss (St. Petersburg), Berlin, March 9, 1869, *GW*, 6b: no. 1334. The possibility of a connection between Hohenlohe's dismissal and the adoption of the Hohenzollern candidacy was first suggested to the author by Professor Lawrence D. Steefel. Professor Steefel's research on the Hohenzollern candidacy has convinced him that Bismarck did not decide definitely on war until early in July, although Bismarck could hardly have been unaware from the beginning that the denouement might be armed conflict.

extraordinary appropriation was necessary. In addition, certain other pieces of special legislation were desired by the government. The session opened on July 19, and on the following day Bismarck read to the house the news of the French declaration of war. He laid before it the protocols of the special *Bundesrath* session which had decided upon war unless France retreated, and presented a sheaf of diplomatic correspondence covering the preceding two weeks, including the edited, but not the original, version of the Ems telegram.[38] It was already clear to the members from the King's opening address that the war was to furnish the occasion for completing German unity. The address contained a minimum of references to Prussia and to north Germany, repeatedly speaking of "Germany," "the German people," and "the German fatherland." Similarly the address to the throne, drawn up by Miquel, used the phrase *"Deutsches Volk"* six times in about five hundred words. It proclaimed that "the people from the shores of the sea to the foot of the Alps have risen at the call of their princes, standing together courageously as one man," and announced that "Your Majesty and the allied governments see us, like our brothers in the south, ready." [39]

No Catholic voices were heard in opposition during the three-day session. Moreover, the names of five of them appeared as original cosponsors of the Miquel draft address, and those of three others were added before it came to a vote. Most of the eight had in the past customarily supported Bismarck.[40] But the inclusion of Reichensperger is both surprising and indicative, revealing that one of the most hardheaded Catholic politicians was as capable of being swept away by the emotion of the day as were any of the National Liberals. Conversely, the failure of such men as Mallinckrodt and Windthorst to add their signatures is equally significant. It demonstrates that even on an occasion when, because of Bismarck's skillful handling of the crisis, it appeared in Berlin that Prussia was totally innocent of any provocation, serious reservations about her policy could remain. Mallinckrodt's unwillingness is of more importance than Windthorst's, for Mallinckrodt, like Reichensperger, was a Prussian. The address was,

---

[38] *Stenographische Berichte 1870, First Special Session,* Anlagen, no. 11.

[39] *Ibid.,* July 19, 1870, 1–2; Anlagen, no. 9.

[40] The original five were Fühling, Hompesch, Künzer, Graf Münster, and Reichensperger. The later signers were Hüffer, Holzer, and Kratz. See *ibid.*

however, adopted unanimously without a record vote. Moreover, the only votes cast against a law granting extraordinary war credits were those of the Social Democrats, Bebel and Liebknecht. There was no opposition to a law extending the term of the Reichstag until the end of the war, or until December 31, 1870, whichever was earlier.[41]

Meanwhile, mobilization of the federal army had been under way since July 16, one day after it became clear that France had decided on war. Throughout north Germany the war was accepted as unavoidable; nowhere were there mobilization riots or disturbances like those which had taken place in the Rhineland in 1866. Bismarck's handling of the crisis had, for the time being at least, destroyed disunity. Likewise south of the Main, except in Bavaria, the circumstances under which the war came about brought a sense of solidarity with Prussia which long years of diplomacy had failed to achieve. For Hesse-Darmstadt there was, of course, no question, since the Hessian division had already been incorporated into the Prussian army. Rupture of diplomatic relations with France came swiftly, and on July 21 the Hessian chamber unanimously granted the extraordinary war credits asked by the government.

Dalwigk was in an unenviable position. Bound irrevocably to the Prussia he hated, he hoped vainly for a French victory which would make possible, with the cooperation of Austria, restoration of independence for the middle states. Despite Hesse's smooth transition from peace to war, the government incurred the wrath of the suspicious Bismarck when a scheduled mass meeting of nationalist enthusiasts at Darmstadt was forbidden on the grounds that public order would be endangered, since the French were allegedly already in Freiburg. The prohibition was not attributable to Dalwigk, who was otherwise engaged, but although the Hessian minister in Berlin explained that the order had been issued out of fear that antinational elements intended to take over the meeting for their own purposes, Bismarck was not convinced. There was certainly little overt opposition to the war. The Grand Duke's nephew, Prince Ludwig, feared the possible outbreak of civil strife brought on by the alleged open hostility of "ultramontanes," but his fanatical hatred for the Church and Catholics, which has been noted before, made him see dangers where none existed. Dalwigk continued for some weeks momentarily to expect news that

[41] *Ibid.*, July 20, 1870, July 21, 1870, 14, 25.

French troops had entered south Germany; only slowly and reluctantly did he abandon his dream.[42]

Württemberg, like north Germany, was swept by a wave of patriotism which brought to a sudden end the *Volkspartei*'s campaign to cut the strength of the army. The King, returning from an interrupted holiday on July 17, immediately ordered mobilization and convened the *Landtag* for the twenty-first. Generally regarded as unfriendly toward Prussia, the King unhappily realized that Swabian involvement as Prussia's ally was inevitable. Varnbüler, likewise not numbered among Bismarck's admirers, saw no course but to carry out the alliance treaty. Even Mittnacht, heretofore a particularist and a *Grossdeutsche*, made no objections. The government's request for war credits was granted on July 22 with only one negative vote, although thirty-eight members of the *Volkspartei* felt obliged to issue a declaration stating that they would have preferred to fight for the unity of *all* Germany. This war, said the declaration, was a logical outgrowth of the events of 1866, which had deprived the nation of the possibility of Austrian assistance, which would now be sorely missed.[43]

As expected, the Baden government supported the war enthusiastically. Here the *Landtag* was not even summoned. Mobilization was decreed on July 16; the Rastatt fortress was reinforced; the Rhine bridge from Kehl to Strassburg was destroyed. Of all the German states Baden was the most exposed to French invasion, and it cannot be seriously maintained that the decision would have been different had the chambers been consulted. In July 1870 not even Catholics, however fanatical their hatred of Prussia, could have preferred French occupation to fighting beside the northern Confederation. When the diplomatic crisis was brewing, Jolly had appealed through the *Karlsruher Zeitung* for a political truce until the foreign threat had been eliminated. The leaders of the *Volkspartei* had seen no alternative but to accept.[44]

While it was almost a foregone conclusion that these three southern states would carry out their treaty obligations toward Prussia, Bavaria's adherence to her alliance was far less certain, with the lower

[42] Vogt, 190–92, 191, notes 1 and 2; Prince Ludwig to Grand Duke Ludwig, Schloss Kramschstein, July 24, 1870, *Dalwigk Tagebücher*, Anlagen, 469.
[43] Sybel, 7:367–69; Eyck, *Bismarck*, 2:492.
[44] Sybel, 7:369–71; Baumgarten and Jolly, 174; "Der ausserordentliche Landtag des Grossherzogthum Badens vom 12. bis 21. Dezember, 1870," *HPB*, 67:81–82.

house in control of the Patriots. Bavaria, moreover, was the key to both the military and the political problems. A united Germany was inconceivable without the second largest German state, and the largest south of the Main. Once France was defeated, Bavarian resistance could be eliminated by force if necessary — although there were valid objections to that policy — but without the two Bavarian army corps military victory over France might well be impossible. Therefore many Germans waited breathlessly to learn whether Munich would recognize a *casus foederis* within the meaning of the alliance treaty.

The sudden onset of the war crisis early in July found the lower chamber in the midst of a virulent debate on the budget for 1871. The Patriots had been striving since the opening of the session to force Bray to seek revision of both the *Zollverein* and the alliance treaties. Specifically they hoped, as did the *Volkspartei* in Württemberg, to revoke the military reforms which had reorganized the army along Prussian lines. For the military establishment the government sought an extraordinary grant of approximately six and a half million gulden, in addition to a regular appropriation of about eight and a half million. Much of the special fund was to be spent on rearming troops with the newest model breech-loading rifle and on the construction of new barracks. The finance committee, controlled by the Patriots, had pared both requests, the first to about four million and the second to around six. To these cuts was coupled a recommendation that the term of military service be shortened to eight months as the first step toward reintroduction of the militia system.[45]

The lower chamber was on the verge of adopting these proposals when the Ems dispatch was published on July 14. From that moment the tactics of the Patriots necessarily shifted. The military bills were temporarily pushed into the background while Jörg and his associates began a campaign to keep Bavaria out of the war which was now looming. Jörg argued that the alliance treaty was not applicable in this case. If Napoleon wanted to quarrel with Prussia over the throne of Spain, how could this legitimately involve Bavaria? The *Schutz- und Trutzbündnis* certainly did not require Bavaria to support Hohenzollern dynastic policy in the Iberian peninsula. Bavarian interests required it even less.[46]

[45] Bachem, 2:242; Sybel, 7:242; Schieder, 240–51.
[46] Schieder, 252–53.

To the dismay of nationalists Bray made no effort to answer.[47] On the following day, the fifteenth, the chamber adjourned temporarily to await developments from Berlin and Paris. Even the Patriots had no desire to act until the situation had been clarified. Clarification came very rapidly. A few hours after the session closed, news arrived that France had resolved to go to war, and less than twenty-four hours later the Bavarian government ordered mobilization, thus at approximately the same time as Prussia and the other south German states. When the *Landtag* reconvened on July 18, public excitement had reached a high pitch. In Munich and other major cities sentiment appeared to favor entry into the war alongside Prussia. The viewpoint of rural Bavaria is less easily ascertained, but in some regions hostility toward participation was marked. The Catholic press, especially the *Münchener Volksbote*, echoed Jörg's speech of July 14, and some of the minor Patriot organs were temporarily suppressed by the government, allegedly to prevent riots.[48]

With the order for mobilization, debate on the peacetime military budget had become, for the time being at least, meaningless. The government now requested from the chamber an extraordinary credit of 26,700,000 gulden to defray war expenses. It thus tacitly assumed that Bavaria would fight. The chamber voted to refer the request to a special committee elected for the purpose, apparently to insure its consideration by a group with a stronger Patriot majority than existed in the finance committee. The special committee included only two nationalists and was under the chairmanship of Jörg. It met on the evening of July 18, and in the early hours of the next morning decided to recommend granting the government a credit of 5,600,000 gulden "for the maintenance of an armed neutrality." [49]

Jörg argued in the committee, and later on the floor of the chamber as he had on the fourteenth: that a war arising out of the Hohenzollern candidacy for the Spanish throne did not oblige Bavaria to recognize a *casus foederis*. The issues, he insisted, concerned solely the honor and interests of the Prussian royal house, not those of the German people. If Bavaria were to recognize this occasion as a *casus foederis*,

[47] Marquard Barth to Hermann Baumgarten, Munich, July 14, 1870, Oncken, *Bennigsen*, 2:172–73.
[48] Sybel, 7:361; Journal, July 26, 1870, Hohenlohe, *Memoirs*, 2:14; Marquard Barth to Hermann Baumgarten, Munich, Aug. 19, 1870, Oncken, *Bennigsen*, 2:175.
[49] Bachem, 2:242–43; Sybel, 7:362; Schieder, 255.

then was there any circumstance in which the treaty could not be invoked? Bavaria would inevitably become permanently subjugated to the "military despotism of Prussia."

Throughout the crucial debate on July 19, Jörg strove desperately to win a majority for the committee's resolution. In the end, however, national sentiment proved stronger, even among some of the Patriots, than party discipline, Bavarian particularism, or religious conviction. Approximately twenty Patriots, under the leadership of Dr. Sepp, a retired professor of the University of Munich and one of the founders of the party, announced that they could not in conscience support the extreme position taken by the committee. It then became possible for the national party to offer a compromise acceptable both to the government and to the dissident Patriots. A grant of 18,260,000 gulden was to be made available "in case of the unavoidability of war." In this way the issue of the *casus foederis* was technically avoided, and the government remained officially a free agent, albeit actually no less committed to fighting beside Prussia and the rest of Germany. On the final ballots the committee report was rejected, 58 to 89, and the compromise approved, 101 to 47. The *Reichsräthe* approved the bill unanimously, and Bavaria entered the war on July 20 without a formal declaration.[50]

Moltke's well-conceived campaign was already in its opening stages. The armies of all Germany, on their way to becoming the German army, moved swiftly across the Rhine. Bismarck's diplomacy had obviated for the time being a minor possibility of Austrian or Italian intervention. On August 4, the Prussian Crown Prince, in command of the south German contingent, crossed the frontier near Weissenburg, and this crossing was soon followed by others carried out by further units of Moltke's combined force. A campaign in northeastern France lasting less than a month decided the issue. One French army, commanded in person by the Emperor, surrendered at Sedan on September 2. Another, under Bazaine, allowed itself to be surrounded in Metz, and the way to Paris was open. Although it would take until the end of January 1871 to end resistance in the capital, ultimate German victory was no longer in doubt. Bismarck had achieved his first

[50] "Zeitläufe: Der Krieg und die Parteien in Süddeutschland," *HPB*, 66:475; Spielhofer, "Bayrische Zentrumspartei," *HPB*, 165:424–25; Bachem, 2:242–43; Wöhler, 24; Schieder, 255–61.

goal, a successful war against France fought by all Germany together. His next task, to reap the harvest of victory by completing the national union, he was now ready to undertake.

The latter task was in many ways more difficult than the former. The King was anything but enthusiastic over Bismarck's plans, for still to him an imperial crown was less worthy than the one he wore *gratia dei* as King of Prussia. The *Junkerthum* still resented what it felt would mean absorption of Prussia into Germany. The National Liberals, this time with the support of the Crown Prince, hoped to achieve what they had failed to accomplish in 1866–67, a parliamentary régime. And, most important, the south German states, although pushed into the war by the strength of aroused national patriotism, were still capable of putting spokes into the Prussian wheel. As early as August 19, for example, Marquard Barth, the Bavarian unionist, warned the more sanguine northern National Liberals not to attribute much importance to the split in the Patriot party. "Be convinced," he wrote, "that their every concession was wrung from them." Dissolution of the Bavarian chamber and new elections, he went on, were not being considered, nor, in his opinion, would such measures serve any useful purpose.

You are very much in error if you believe that the majority of the Bavarian people now has a different political opinion than before the last election. This is at least not yet the case, even if the real views of the so-called Patriots are not at the moment so shrilly proclaimed, . . . and with many of them, their wrath, though concealed, is thereby the greater because they cannot for the moment let it burst forth. . . . Do not overrate the decision of our chamber of July 19; we owe our victory then not to the changed convictions of the Patriots, but entirely to their bad tactics and discipline, and to the loutish chirping [*Piepmeierei*] of one of them [Jörg?].[51]

Barth's communication and others of similar import were largely responsible for the journey through south Germany undertaken by Bennigsen and Lasker in September. It was their hope to win support for the idea of completing the unification of Germany by simply expanding the North German Confederation to include the southern states. This solution, if adopted, would avoid interminable constitu-

---

[51] Barth to Baumgarten, Munich, Aug. 19, 1870, Oncken, *Bennigsen*, 2:175. Hohenlohe expressed a similar view at about the same time. See Journal, Aug. 17, 1870, Hohenlohe, *Memoirs*, 2:19.

tional wrangles. Bennigsen was of the opinion that only the Catholic extremists were beyond reach by a reasoned approach. In order to avoid the impression that the journey was simply a political maneuver of the National Liberal party, the two tried to induce men from other political groups to accompany them. This scheme collapsed, however, largely because of opposition from the conservatives, who suspected that the trip was an attempt to undermine Bismarck. Peter Reichensperger was invited to go along, but, although apparently sympathetic with the objectives, he refused. At Lasker's request he did allow the two parliamentarians to take with them a written statement of his opinion that "a Protestant Emperor would be much more desirable for the Church than a Catholic Emperor, who would, as such, interfere much more [in its affairs]." The note cited examples of the contrasting attitudes of Joseph II and Frederick the Great in the eighteenth century. Despite his willingness to permit the two National Liberals to use this note in their talks with southern leaders, Reichensperger would not authorize its publication.[52]

Bennigsen and Lasker visited Munich from September 10 to 15, where they conferred with Bray and other officials, as well as with men of their own party. They succeeded in making it clear that north Germany would demand more than a loose federal connection with Bavaria, which was as far as the government, under extreme pressure from the Patriots, was willing to go at the time. Moving on to Stuttgart and Karlsruhe, the two met a warmer reception, and when they returned to Berlin shortly after September 20, they could feel that, although nothing concrete had been accomplished, the air had been cleared somewhat. Meanwhile Delbrück had been traveling in the South on a similar mission as the direct representative of Bismarck, and he kept the Chancellor informed of the progress of his own negotiations, as well as those of the Reichstag deputies. Bismarck, though willing enough to accept the possible benefits of the Lasker-Bennigsen journey, distrusted its motives, and was particularly disturbed that it had been undertaken without his prior approval.[53]

[52] Lasker to Bennigsen, Berlin, Aug. 18, 1870, Aug. 24, 1870, Aug. 27, 1870, Aug. 28, 1870, Oncken, *Bennigsen*, 2:176–80. See also *ibid.*, 180–81; Goyau, *Bismarck*, 1:85 and note.

[53] Oncken, *Bennigsen*, 2:181–86; Barth to Baumgarten, Munich, Sept. 27, 1870, Oct. 13, 1870, *ibid.*, 186–88; Bennigsen to Lasker, Hanover, Oct. 11, 1870, *ibid.*, 188–89; Eyck, *Bismarck*, 2:543.

The difficulties faced by the national party in dealing with Bavaria can easily be understood through consideration of the attitude which Jörg's *Historisch-politische Blätter* took toward the war. His first *Zeitläufe* published after the beginning of military operations was entitled significantly "The War Between Prussia and France." Although he could hardly deny that Bavaria and other German states were taking part, it was to him still Prussia's war.

Can we . . . who have never abandoned and will never abandon the idea that a "Germany" without Austria is inconceivable [regard it otherwise]? On the contrary, the situation is such that the present war could never have come about had not the fatal attempt been made, and been to a certain degree successfully carried through; I mean the attempt to construct a Germany in which the eight million Germans in Austria have no part, and in the creation of which the Habsburg Monarchy, formerly regarded by all the world as the foremost "German" power, had to be forcefully excluded. We stand now before the chief result of that act.[54]

In his next issue Jörg described the conflict as a "war of the [National Liberal] party," and predicted that Prussia, once having subdued south Germany at the behest of that party, would not easily free herself from its grasp, "even with all . . . [her] military power."[55] With good reason were Lasker and his colleagues apprehensive over the implacable hostility of this Catholic editor, for whatever arrangement was finally concluded would have to be ratified by the Bavarian *Landtag,* whose lower chamber was controlled by his party.

By October German military headquarters was in Versailles, and Bismarck's discussions with representatives of the south German governments began. The story of those complex and difficult negotiations has been told many times and requires no detailed repetition here. As expected, Bray made demands which were completely unacceptable, either to Bismarck or to the other southern leaders. The Bavarian's proposal was one which had been recommended by the moderate wing of the Patriots at a caucus in Munich on September 26, held under the leadership of Weiss, president of the lower chamber. The group had realized that what to the Patriots was the ideal answer to the German question — dissolution of the North German Confederation and its replacement by a new loose federal union of all the states — was no

[54] "Zeitläufe: Der Krieg zwischen Preussen und Frankreich," *HPB,* 66:238–39.
[55] "Zeitläufe: Der Krieg und die Parteien in Süddeutschland," *HPB,* 66:473.

longer attainable. It decided, therefore, that Bavaria should offer to enter a restricted federal relationship with the *Nordbund,* in which the alliance and *Zollverein* treaties would be replaced by a statute covering military and commercial matters and "all [other] circumstances deemed worthwhile for common regulation." Bray had adopted this as the program of his government three days later. Bavaria's demands played into Bismarck's hands in dealing with the other states, which had long resented Bavarian pretensions to special consideration. Baden and Hesse-Darmstadt signed conventions with the North German Confederation on November 15. Bray, fearing to see Bavaria isolated, capitulated on November 23, and Württemberg, now actually isolated, followed suit on the twenty-fifth. Bismarck made a minimum of concessions to the particularism of the two kingdoms. Württemberg retained the right to control her own postal system, and Bavaria obtained that privilege plus certain additional ones, including the authority to maintain a separate army in time of peace. None of these meant very much in fact, although they served to make subjection to Prussia more palatable. For Bray, the fear that Bavaria's entry into the new *Reich* would end traditional connections between Munich and Vienna was perhaps the most difficult hurdle. Bismarck's assurances that he was willing to negotiate an alliance treaty with the Habsburg Monarchy helped smooth the path, for the Bavarian minister came, with Bismarck's help, to see himself as the agency through which that alliance might be brought about.[56]

Two days after the conclusion of the treaty with Bavaria, Bismarck began negotiations with Count Holnstein, representing King Ludwig, to arrange for the latter to offer the imperial crown to the King of Prussia in the name of the German princes. Whether Ludwig accepted a bribe out of the *Welfenfonds,* as charged by Eyck, or simply chose to make a magnanimous gesture in a situation which he was powerless to change, is probably beyond knowing. In any event, Holnstein visited the King and returned to Versailles early in December with a letter in Ludwig's handwriting which invited William I to accept the crown. The letter was an exact copy of a draft which Bismarck had furnished Holnstein. King William's aristocratic prejudices, and Bis-

[56] Michael Döberl, *Bayern und Deutschland im 19ten Jahrhundert,* 100–1, 141–42; *Stenographische Berichte über die Verhandlungen des Reichstages des norddeutschen Bundes, I. Legislaturperiode, II. ausserordentliche Session 1870* (hereafter cited as *Stenographische Berichte 1870, Second Special Session*), Anlagen, nos. 9 and 12.

marck's desire that the Empire be established through the will of the princes, not the will of the Reichstag, could now be satisfied.[57]

Nevertheless the treaties still had to be ratified both by the North German Reichstag and by the respective *Landtage* of the southern states. The key to the situation was, as before, the Bavarian Patriot party, the only organized group in Germany which had both the desire and perhaps the strength to prevent peaceful consummation of the Reich. In this context Bismarck's relations with the Papacy during the war have considerable importance, for if he could obtain papal endorsement of the *Reich,* the resistance of the Patriots might conceivably be lessened. This project, however, was made more complicated by the necessity, at least in the early stages of the war, of preventing an Italian-French alliance. Such an alliance would have altered the military picture significantly, and might not have been beyond the realm of possibility had Napoleon III abandoned Pius IX early enough. Trying to keep alive the Curia's hope that Prussia would replace Napoleon as defender of the Eternal City, Bismarck rejected in August one Italian request for his diplomatic support in acquiring the remaining papal territories. This he did as gently as possible, and although the battle of Sedan practically eliminated any danger of Italian intervention in the war, he did not even then consider it wise to make an enemy of Florence. Accordingly, faced with increasingly importunate Italian requests for a Prussian "passport" to Rome, he concluded early in September that the issue could be avoided no longer. A dispatch to Arnim on September 9 announced Prussia's refusal to intervene on the peninsula against the interests of Italy. At the same time he informed the Prussian ambassador in Florence, Brassier de St. Simon, that, in the interests of German Catholics, Prussia found it necessary to ask that Italy make reservations "in favor of a respectable and independent position for the Holy See." Brassier, who had received a copy of the dispatch to Arnim, communicated both to the foreign minister, Visconti-Venosta, and the die was cast. Rome was occupied on September 20.[58]

Although Prussia was, therefore, in a sense responsible for the unfortunate position in which the Pope found himself, the Curia, confronted with the necessity of seeking a possible refuge for Pius IX,

[57] Eyck, *Bismarck*, 2:553–56.
[58] Goyau, *Bismarck*, 1:31–34; Sybel, 7:405–7; Eyck, *Bismarck*, 3:82–85.

could not afford a break with Berlin. Nor did it particularly desire one, for Arnim, without instructions from his government, was periodically suggesting that the Pope seek asylum in Germany, somewhat to the embarrassment both of Bismarck and the Curia itself. On October 7 Antonelli inquired whether Pius IX would have Prussian support against Italian interference if he decided to quit the city. Bismarck, who would have preferred to avoid the question, told Arnim on October 8 to reply with a qualified affirmative. At the same time he asked Brassier at Florence to suggest to the foreign minister that Prussia had no fear that Italy would fail to respect the "liberty and dignity" of the Pope even if he decided to change his place of residence. Brassier was also to make clear in Florence, as Arnim had been instructed to do in Rome, that Prussia did not seek to intervene in the internal affairs of any country, but that she had certain obligations to her own Catholic subjects. In effect Bismarck would assist the Pope in the event his departure became mandatory, but he did not wish to be associated with any move to induce him to quit the Holy City.[59]

The Chancellor's attempts to avoid commitments to the Pope were further complicated when, early in November, the Archbishop of Posen, Count Ledochowski, arrived in Versailles as an emissary of the Vatican. Ledochowski had been Bismarck's choice for the post in 1865, and he was likewise on friendly terms with the King. He bore two requests. First, he asked that Prussia issue a formal protest against the Italian appropriation of Rome. Second, he sought definite information on whether, if Pius decided to abandon the Vatican in protest over the occupation, he would be received in Prussia. Bismarck was, of course, unwilling to issue such a protest, but by November he had become more than moderately sympathetic with the idea of granting asylum to the Pontiff. He recognized the difficulties that would follow, but he felt, nevertheless, that the advantages might well outweigh them. Ultramontane strength in Germany would doubtless increase. Yet with the Pope on German soil, the Catholic population, and especially the

[59] Goyau, *Bismarck*, 1:38–39; Bismarck to Brassier de St. Simon, Versailles, Oct. 8, 1870, *GW*, 6b: no. 1852. After the battle of Sedan, Bismarck's attitude toward the Papacy was almost entirely determined by his relations with German Catholics. See his remark at Ferrières on Sept. 27: "It would be possible to do more for him [the Pope] if the ultramontanes were not so much opposed to us everywhere. I am accustomed to pay people back in their own coin." Moritz Busch, *Bismarck, Some Secret Pages of His History*, 1:161.

Bavarian Patriots, might be induced more easily to accept, if not to approve, the new *Reich*. Moreover, he explained on one occasion, let German Catholics see the Pope as a man living among them, and they would cease to regard him as a supernatural symbol. As he put it, "the scales would drop from their eyes."

On this occasion Bismarck ran into the solid opposition of the King, the Crown Prince, and the Grand Duke of Baden, who was a member of the headquarters staff. The last-named protested vehemently against any dealings with the Archbishop as soon as he learned of his presence. He argued that to offer asylum to the Pope would sharpen the already dangerous confessional division within the country, and might precipitate an open struggle. King William received the prelate, but the question of asylum was not discussed. Later Bismarck informed Ledochowski that Prussia did not approve of Italy's action, but, since military force alone could effect a change, she could not render assistance. He suggested that the papal cause might be benefited if ecclesiastical influence were brought to bear on France in behalf of a swift restoration of peace. As far as a diplomatic protest was concerned, he thought that might better come from a Catholic power. Whether Prussia would second such a note was not mentioned. On the question of asylum Bismarck offered only to consult the other German bishops. He said that the King was unwilling to make a decision at that time, but he did mention vaguely the possibility of a conference on the subject of the Pope's domicile at the conclusion of the war. The impression is at best one of equivocation adding up to a firm, if polite, refusal. The whole incident is of some importance as one of the rare occasions on which Bismarck seems actually to have respected the wishes of his sovereign when they differed from his own.[60]

On November 12 a royal ordinance was issued at Versailles summoning the North German Reichstag to meet in Berlin, November 24. The possibility of a Reichstag session in Versailles itself had been discussed, but was abandoned as unsuitable. Probably the timing of the summons involved Bismarck's desire to put pressure on the south German states, none of which had yet signed treaties. In fact, on the pre-

[60] Bismarck, *Gedanken und Erinnerungen*, 2:150–51; Eyck, *Bismarck*, 3:83–84; Goyau, *Bismarck*, 1:43–45; Busch, 1:220–21; Diary of Grand Duke Friedrich I of Baden, Versailles, Nov. 9, Nov. 16, Nov. 19, 1870, Hermann Oncken, *Grossherzog Friedrich I von Baden und die deutsche Politik von 1854 bis 1871: Briefwechsel, Denkschriften, Tagebücher*, 2:163–64; 179–80; 189–91, 164, note 2.

ceding day the scheduled signing of Baden, Hesse, and Württemberg had broken down because at the last moment Württemberg refused to go ahead without Bavaria. A Reichstag session was in any case necessary very soon, for the original war appropriations expired December 31. Moreover, it was essential that the Reichstag ratify whatever agreements came out of Versailles before the end of the year when its already once-extended term came to a close. Otherwise it would be necessary either to extend the term again, or to elect another North German Reichstag solely for the purpose of ratifying the treaties. In the latter case elections for the new German Reichstag would then have to follow almost immediately. It was also desirable that the final stages of unification be carried through while the war kept public enthusiasm at a high pitch.[61]

By the time the Reichstag assembled, three of the treaties had been concluded, and the fourth with Württemberg was to be signed the following day. Bismarck, realizing that the special concessions granted Bavaria might not be accepted with good grace by the more doctrinaire National Liberals and Progressives, urged all deputies of the former party who were at headquarters to hurry back to Berlin for the opening of the session. Even so, Bennigsen, who was to lead the fight for ratification of the treaties, had serious doubts that he could get a majority for the agreement with Bavaria.[62]

Such fears were totally unnecessary. Bennigsen, the other National Liberals, and even Bismarck underestimated the force of national patriotism which had been unleashed in north Germany by the war. The most striking example can be seen in the altered attitude of Catholic spokesmen. When the question of Alsace-Lorraine first became important in early September, the *Kölnische Volkszeitung* appeared as one of the most active propagandists in favor of annexing the entire region to Germany. Loyal to its tradition of defending southern Catholic interests, it rejected any suggestion that the provinces be taken over by Prussia, unless there were compensations for the other states; but this was its sole reservation.[63] In mid-September the liberal *Kölnische*

[61] *Stenographische Berichte 1870, Second Special Session*, v; Oncken, *Bennigsen*, 2:195–96; Ernst Feder (ed.), *Bismarcks grosses Spiel: Die geheimen Tagebücher Ludwig Bambergers*, 208–9.

[62] Eyck, *Bismarck*, 2:558; Bennigsen to his wife, Berlin, Nov. 30, 1870, Oncken, *Bennigsen*, 2:201.

[63] Gustav Körner, *Die norddeutsche Publizistik und die Annexionsfragen im Jahre 1870*, 33–34.

Zeitung proposed that the city of Metz should be excluded from the territory annexed because of the unquestionably French character of its population. It suggested further that only territory necessary for the security of Germany should in any case be acquired. The *Volkszeitung* replied on September 26 with a fiery editorial entitled, "Metz and the Pedants."

One really does not know what has happened to human understanding if such scholastic sophistry is to be regarded as higher wisdom. Let us pack up our five senses and go away to the lunatics, so that the sublime minds may rule the world alone! In fact, there is nothing proper to say against this kind of wisdom, nothing to propose; it is such a compact tissue of false axioms and misleading conclusions that one is unable to know with which knots to begin unraveling this madness. Germany deserves, Germany has a right, to be saved, protected, and made secure. We rejoice that the highest directors of German policy are statesmen and not schoolmasters.[64]

A similar attitude was apparent in Reichensperger's speech to the Reichstag on November 26. Except for an appeal that centralized government of the French variety be avoided in the recovered provinces, the address could have been delivered by one of the National Liberals.[65]

None of the other Catholic members appears to have been quite so carried away by the excitement of the period as Reichensperger, but almost all of them showed some imprint. Not a single Catholic was included among the eight members who voted against further extension of war credits, although the Poles abstained *en bloc*.[66] On December 5, immediately after the prearranged announcement of Ludwig II's request to King William, Windthorst rose to voice his judgment on the new Germany. In an address from which his usual rancor was absent, the Hanoverian once more arraigned the Bismarck administration, not for its objectives, but for its methods. He lamented the fact that German unity was now to be achieved through a series of treaties and protocols which only amended the constitution of the North German Confederation, when what was desperately needed was an entirely new

[64] *Ibid.*, 71–72. The fact that the region was over eighty per cent Catholic cannot be ignored in this connection. The *Historisch-politische Blätter* published a series of articles on Alsace-Lorraine during the first half of 1870 which stressed the German character of the area, and described in glowing terms the spread of Catholic workingmen's societies there. See *HPB*, 65: *passim*, especially 109, 112–14, 241.

[65] *Stenographische Berichte 1870, Second Special Session*, Nov. 26, 1870, 8–9; Hansen, 1:800–1.

[66] *Stenographische Berichte 1870, Second Special Session*, Nov. 28, 1870, 33.

document which would remedy the faults of the old. He summarized those faults, as he had done on numerous occasions before. They included the lack of responsible government, the omission of an upper house, without which the future would inevitably bring either "absolutism or the republic," the absence of a federal supreme court, and, finally, the glaring failure to include guarantees of civil rights such as those in the Prussian constitution. Windthorst took the occasion also to appeal again for pay and allowances for members of the Reichstag. He declined to indicate whether he would finally vote for or against the treaties, and that fact, as well as the general tone of the address, probably invalidates Hohenlohe's judgment that it was an effort to incite the Bavarian Patriots against the treaty.[67]

None of the reservations which troubled Windthorst were evident in the almost lyrical speech of the Breslau Canon, Künzer, which came during the final debate on the treaties, December 9. Künzer praised them as "the last stone[s] of the structure on which the German people, on which the representatives of the German people have labored tirelessly. . . ." He had nothing but scorn for those who argued that no united Germany was possible so long as the German provinces of Austria remained outside.

It is not our fault, and we would not want to have even our German brothers in Austria at the cost that Hungary, that Czech and other elements would again take precedence in the government of the German Empire. Let those provinces once enter the German union without that non-German influence, then they will be greeted by us with the same joy as we now greet the admission of the south German states to our *Bund*.

Gentlemen, from my viewpoint I see in the reorganization of Germany everywhere the miraculous hand of God.[68]

On this occasion the only Catholic who seriously attempted to dampen the enthusiasm of the house was Mallinckrodt. He admitted that he probably constituted a minority of one, since he could not agree even with Windthorst. He recognized that the new *Reich* was better than the old *Bund*, that *Kaiser* was more satisfactory than *Bundespräsidium*, and that the changes consequent on the admission of the southern states would be beneficial in maintaining the federa-

---

[67] *Ibid.*, Dec. 5, 1870, 75–81; Hüsgen, 68–70; Journal, Berlin, Dec. 5, 1870, Hohenlohe, *Memoirs*, 2:31.

[68] *Stenographische Berichte 1870, Second Special Session*, Dec. 9, 1870, 157–58.

tive principle. Nevertheless, he felt obliged to point out the darker side. For, as Windthorst had stated four days earlier, most of the weaknesses which had marred the North German Confederation still existed. Moreover, although he agreed that this was perhaps not the most opportune moment to bring up the matter, he still felt that the military burden imposed upon individual citizen was far too heavy. He could not follow those who said "First let us establish the Empire, and then later revise its constitution." Successful revision was possible only at the moment when the new *Reich* was being born, and he added prophetically, "Let this moment be lost, and then I cannot escape the conviction that we will be forced deeper into militarism." For these reasons Mallinckrodt declined to vote for the treaties, although in his slightly pompous peroration he promised to support wholeheartedly the *Reich* and the Emperor, once the decision had been made.[69]

The treaties with Baden and Hesse were adopted together on a standing vote, with only four nays. Although no record of individual votes is, of course, available, Mallinckrodt was obviously one of the four. Two of the others were certainly the Social Democrats, Bebel and Liebknecht. The latter had almost precipitated a riot on the floor by his charges that the treaties were the product of rank militarism. It may be conjectured, although not definitely established, that the fourth was Windthorst. The Württemberg treaty was approved with the same division.[70] Only the convention with Bavaria required a roll call, since a considerable number of Progressives had announced their intention to vote against it. But even here only thirty-two negative votes were cast, including those of three Catholics, Fühling, Mallinckrodt, and Windthorst. Reichensperger and the Poles abstained.[71]

On the following day the house adopted an address to the throne drafted by Lasker, asking the King to accept the imperial crown in the name of the Reichstag. The vote was 191 to 6. No Catholics voted against it; Hüffer and Mallinckrodt were absent, the former because of illness, and the latter on account of "pressing family problems." Gommelshausen, Künzer, Reichensperger, Schorlemer-Alst, Windthorst, and the Poles abstained. A few moments earlier, however, both Windthorst and Schorlemer-Alst had voted in favor of the constitu-

[69] *Ibid.*, 151–52.
[70] *Ibid.*, 153–54, 161–62.
[71] *Ibid.*, 164.

tional changes necessary to confer the title *Deutscher Kaiser* upon the king, as well as for the adoption of the name *Deutsches Reich*. Both these proposals were approved together, 188 to 6. The votes of all other Catholics were cast as they were to be on the address, as, indeed, were those of nearly every other member of the house. The only remaining business was the choice by lot of a thirty-member delegation to present the address of the Reichstag in Versailles. The only Catholic chosen was Count Hompesch, a Free Conservative.[72]

Ratification of the respective treaties by three of the four southern *Landtage* followed before the end of the month with little difficulty. In Hesse-Darmstadt the vote was all but unanimous. Geography, and the fact that both Dalwigk and the Grand Duke knew that opposition was futile, prevented any forlorn attempt to prolong the agony. Nevertheless, the unforgiving Bismarck forced the dismissal of Dalwigk a few months later.[73] The Mittnacht-Varnbüler ministry in Württemberg, now with the reluctant support of the royal family, worked energetically to secure ratification. The government felt considerable anxiety over the strength of the *Volkspartei* in the lower chamber, and in order to capitalize on the national enthusiasm liberated by the war, it dissolved the chamber, despite some misgivings, and called new elections. The *Deutsche Partei*, hitherto hostile to Varnbüler, campaigned now as the ministerial party. The election on November 5 showed that while clerical-democratic-*grossdeutsch* sentiment still existed, its vitality was gone. The government won no overwhelming victory, but it made a considerable dent in the *Volkspartei*'s representation — certainly enough easily to insure approval of the treaty. The upper house made no difficulties.[74] The Hessian minister at Stuttgart attributed the *Volkspartei*'s declining prestige to the influence of the troops in the field. He wrote to Dalwigk, "Prussia has most cleverly done everything to win the armies of Bavaria and Württemberg; thus this spirit [of friendliness toward Prussia] penetrates even to the lowest classes of the population." [75]

The Baden *Landtag* was summoned to meet in special session on

[72] *Ibid.*, Dec. 10, 1870, 167, 181–85.

[73] Vogt, 200–3.

[74] Otto Elben to Hermann Baumgarten, Stuttgart, Nov. 8, 1870, Heyderhoff, *Liberalismus*, 483; von Breidenbach to Dalwigk, Stuttgart, Oct. 18, 1870, Vogt, Beilage V, 221–22; Goyau, *Bismarck*, 1:84.

[75] Breidenbach to Dalwigk, Stuttgart, Oct. 18, 1870, Vogt, Beilage V, 222.

December 13 to ratify the Versailles agreement. Although new elections would have been in order according to the reforms adopted by the last regular *Landtag*, the government, perhaps afraid of possible gains for the *Katholische Volkspartei*, recalled the old chamber. It need not have worried. The *grossdeutsch*-federal dream was dead, and Baden could not afford isolation. Even the Quadrilateral voted to a man for the treaty, although reluctantly. Baumstark expressed the views of the party during the key debate of December 16. The new *Reich*, he said, was the creation of diplomats, not of the people. The treaty by which Baden would enter it contained no guarantee of freedom for the Church, and Austria was permanently excluded. On all these counts the new arrangements were unsatisfactory. Nevertheless, members of the *Katholische Volkspartei* would vote to adopt them because nothing better could be hoped for at the time. The party pledged itself, however, to work unceasingly for future revision of the *Reich* constitution in order to introduce those features which it regarded as essential for the welfare of Germany. On the final ballot, later the same day, only two votes were cast against the treaty, and those by radical democrats. The upper chamber likewise, on December 21, approved the treaty with only two dissenting votes.[76]

Again, and for the last time in the nineteenth century, the eyes of Germany were turned with apprehension and anticipation on Munich. The Bavarian people in general had reacted to the war in much the same fashion as had other Germans, and by early fall the vast majority had come to accept union as the only feasible answer to the problem of Bavaria's future, however little affection they had for Prussia. But the extreme wing of the Patriots under Jörg was still determined to prevent the loss of Bavarian sovereignty at all costs. Since an organic change in the Bavarian constitution required a two-thirds majority in both houses of the *Landtag*, it was not unlikely that Jörg would prevail, despite logic and the wishes of most Bavarians.[77]

It is difficult to avoid the impression that Jörg, after the beginning of the war, was scarcely rational any longer. His impassioned appeal

[76] "Der ausserordentliche Landtag des Grossherzogthums Baden vom 12. [*sic*] bis 21. Dezember 1870," *HPB*, 67:82–83, 85–89, 94, 98; text of Baumstark's speech, *ibid.*, 90–93; Dor, 103; Baumgarten and Jolly, 203–4.

[77] Döberl, *Bayern und Deutschland*, 187; Schieder, 266–67, 285. Dissolution of the *Landtag* and a new election were not feasible because of the brief period available for action on the treaty.

in the early days of the conflict for Austria to compel peace by stepping between the belligerents is hardly the work of a man with a firm grasp on reality,[78] nor is his ferocious denunciation of the National Liberals after Sedan:

[They] believe that the moment of their complete triumph has now arrived. They present as an unavoidable consequence of the victory over the French the demand that our country must give over its independent political existence into the hands of Prussia. What was saved of our sovereignty from the defeat of 1866 shall now go down to destruction through the victory of our own weapons. For this our brave sons shall have poured out their blood, so that in the future an independent state of Bavaria will no longer exist.[79]

The only encouraging feature of the situation, from the nationalist point of view, was the fact that the Patriot party was not united. A group of its deputies, as pointed out before, had broken away in July on the issue of entry into the war, and by mid-September this faction, now associated closely with Dr. Huttler, editor of the *Augsburger Postzeitung,* had achieved a considerable degree of cohesiveness. It was this moderate wing which rejected Jörg's extreme particularism in the Munich caucus, already mentioned, of September 26, where it revived the old *"engerer und weiterer Bund"* concept of an earlier day. The emergence of the *Postzeitung* faction had given Bray for the first time a modicum of parliamentary support for his own ideas, which helped him win a few concessions from Bismarck at Versailles.[80]

The treaty which was finally signed on November 23 did not, of course, satisfy any of the groups into which Bavarian opinion was now divided. The Jörg faction, still the majority of the Patriots, began immediately to agitate for rejection of the treaty. Its leader argued that Bavaria, perhaps alone of the south German States, could still survive as an independent state. To him, therefore, the most logical outcome of the war, and the consequent elimination of the French threat, would have been dissolution of the 1866 treaties and the resumption of untrammeled Bavarian sovereignty. He denied having any objection to the Munich decision of September 26, but he insisted that the treaty which Bray had signed was in no way compatible with that resolve,

[78] "Zeitläufe: Der Krieg zwischen Preussen und Frankreich," *HPB,* 66:247.

[79] "Zeitläufe: Der Krieg und die Parteien in Süddeutschland," *HPB,* 66:478.

[80] Michael Döberl, *Bayern und die bismarckische Reichsgründung,* 76; Schieder, 268, 273.

for the proposed new *Reich* was not a federation, but a unitary state under the absolute domination of Prussia.[81]

When the news came that Ludwig II had invited the Prussian King to become German Emperor, the screams of anguish from Patriot extremists were even louder. The *Donauzeitung* announced, "*Caesarem habemus*," and described the new *Reich* as a scourge of God on the German people.[82] Sigl's *Bayrisches Vaterland*, in a similar fashion, spoke of 1870 as the year of God's punishment. To it the imperial crown was only an enlarged Prussian spiked helmet.[83]

Rejoice that the crown of Caesar, which has been thrown from the head of the man of Sedan to the satisfaction of all honorable people, will now be placed upon another precious head; . . . Prussian is Prussian, whether he is called King or Emperor.[84]

The *Vaterland* warned that Patriot deputies could never again face their voters unless they kept firmly to their pledged word and rejected this treaty, which meant final destruction of Bavarian independence. Otherwise the future offered nothing but "more war, more cripples, more lists of the dead, more tax bills." [85]

Although during these critical weeks responsible statesmen sought usually to keep the religious issue in the background, there is little doubt that the religious tensions of the preceding two years had had a not inconsiderable effect on political opinions. The north German National Liberals and their southern allies seldom referred to their opponents in private communications by any other term than "ultramontanes." Even a moderate like Bennigsen spoke of the coming "Hohenzollern, Evangelical, German Empire." On the other side the *Bayrisches Vaterland* offered its most vociferous objections to William I on the ground that he would be a Protestant Emperor. A German Emperor who was not Catholic would violate "historical and legal precedents." The paper spoke of the old "just" imperial office as the creation of Leo the Great and Charlemagne, while the new, and presumably "unjust," version descended directly from Luther and Gustavus Adolphus. The next war would, then, inevitably be a struggle be-

[81] "Zeitläufe: Bayern und seine Zukunft," *HPB*, 66:713, 715–16, 720.
[82] Döberl, *Bayern und Deutschland*, 168–69.
[83] *Ibid.*, 169.
[84] *Ibid.*, 176.
[85] *Ibid.*, 169, 176.

tween Hohenzollern and Habsburg. The approach of the *Historisch-politische Blätter* was often similar.[86]

The special session of the *Landtag* opened on December 10. There had originally been considerable sentiment among Bavarian liberals for an effort to eliminate some of the special provisions of the treaty, but the idea was abandoned so that ranks could be closed in order to meet the fanatical opposition to the treaty itself expected from the Patriots. Barth wrote to Bamberger on December 5 that the liberals would be indeed fortunate if they could merely force the agreement through the chamber. Any attempts to improve the German constitution would necessarily have to be postponed until a more propitious moment. The deputy, Stenglein, informed Bennigsen two days later that the Versailles convention would probably be approved, but only if it first received the assent of the North German Reichstag "without significant changes," and if, therefore, the breach in the Patriot ranks could be kept open.[87]

The treaty was submitted to the lower chamber on December 14, and on the following day the house again chose a special committee of fifteen members to conduct preliminary discussions. The committee included eleven Patriots, three nationalists, and one radical democrat. Jörg was named *Referent,* while his closest associate, Ruland, served as chairman. Other well-known haters of Prussia were Greil, Weis, and Hafenbrädl. The only moderate Patriot was Huttler. The mere composition of this special committee was sufficient to throw a chill into the National Liberals all over Germany. Von Schauss, a Munich banker and member of the chamber, wrote to Bennigsen pessimistically on December 15 that it had become highly improbable that the requisite two-thirds majority could be obtained.[88] Barth, one of the three liberal members of the committee, was less gloomy. As he put it: "Our current opponents in the chamber have already demonstrated in July that they certainly have a great deal of ill-will, but that they have at the critical moment little courage, and I put my hope in that." [89]

The treaty specified ratification was required before the end of December. The committee, however, made no effort to speed its labors.

[86] *Ibid.,* 169–70; Bennigsen to his wife, Berlin, Dec. 7, 1870, Oncken, *Bennigsen,* 2:202.

[87] Marquard Barth to Bennigsen, Munich, Dec. 5, 1870, Oncken, *Bennigsen,* 2:204–5; Stenglein to Bennigsen, Munich, Dec. 15, 1870, *ibid.,* 206–7.

[88] Von Schauss to Bennigsen, Munich, Dec. 15, 1870, *ibid.,* 207–9; Schieder, 281–82.

[89] Barth to Baumgarten, Munich, Dec. 23, 1870, Oncken, *Bennigsen,* 2:208, note 1.

Rather, it proceeded with sublime contempt for the wishes of Bismarck, the National Liberals, and probably the majority of the Bavarian people. Meanwhile the irreconcilables were using every possible tactic to make the treaty unpalatable to important segments of the population. With somewhat dubious logic, they seized upon War Minister von Pranckh's request for an appropriation of forty-one million gulden to pay the costs of the war, to demonstrate to the peasants what crushing financial burdens Bavarian entry into the *Reich* would entail. To avoid the defection of clerics, they planted the idea that if Bavaria joined the new Germany her people would ultimately be converted to Protestantism. They spread the rumor that the King himself hoped for rejection of the treaty. Finally, they magnified Beust's visit to Munich on December 5 — actually a vain attempt to delay what he had come to regard as inevitable — into a promise of Austrian aid.[90]

Bismarck at Versailles was also making desperate efforts to influence events in Munich. His task was complicated by the fact that here too rumor was much more readily available than news. On December 17 he sent a peremptory message to Werthern demanding immediate telegraphic information on the outlook for adoption of the treaty. He particularly wanted to know whether, as rumor in Versailles had it, the "ultramontanes and the clergy" were going to unheard-of lengths to secure its rejection.[91] Arnim at the same time was working in Rome, probably on Bismarck's instructions, to obtain the intervention of the Vatican at Munich in the hope of curbing the Patriots. The intermediary in these delicate negotiations was Bishop Franchi, Papal Nuncio at Madrid, who was a friend of Arnim. Antonelli refused to act directly. He did, however, communicate through Arnim the Pontiff's desire to send to Versailles a delegation which would offer the King of Prussia congratulations upon his elevation to the imperial rank. The papal secretary of state informed Patriot circles in Bavaria of this offer, which King William himself called "one of the most remarkable signs of the times," but Jörg and his associates saw, or professed to see, the move as a mere formality without significance.[92]

[90] "Vertrag über den Beitritt Bayerns zur Verfassung des deutschen Bundes," par. no. 26, Sec. VI, *Stenographische Berichte 1870, Second Special Session*, Anlagen, no. 12; Döberl, *Bayern und Deutschland*, 186; Vogt, 201 and note 1.

[91] Bismarck to Werthern, Versailles, Dec. 17, 1870, *GW*, 6b: no. 1978.

[92] Diary of Grand Duke Friedrich I of Baden, Dec. 25, 1870, Dec. 29, 1870, Oncken, *Friedrich I*, 271–76; Busch, 1:312; Goyau, *Bismarck*, 1:52.

Bismarck could hardly afford to let matters rest at that point. He transmitted to Arnim on December 21 a dispatch containing a threat calculated to impress upon the Papacy the necessity of taking more vigorous action. If the Patriots, Bismarck wrote, succeeded in preventing ratification of the Versailles agreement, they would not thereby stay the creation of the German *Reich*. Defeat of the treaty would only mean that the basis upon which that *Reich* was to be established would have to be altered. Although Bismarck preferred that the new Empire come into being through negotiated agreements, he was prepared, if necessary, to unleash the revolution, and to bring about German unity through the will of the people. In that event, he warned, all those elements which were hostile to the *Reich* would be shown up in their true colors, and would have to suffer the consequences of that hostility.[93] Rome was not visibly impressed, and shortly afterward Bismarck undertook a final diplomatic effort to force the Papacy into taking a hand in Bavaria. This time he sent the former Bavarian ambassador to the Holy See, Count Tauffkirchen, who was now in the Prussian service, to Rome as his special envoy. Tauffkirchen arrived on January 2, 1871, but Antonelli again, despite all the pressure put upon him, remained unmoved. All he would say was that "the Roman Curia is under no obligation to intervene in a debate which appears in any case superfluous, since those at Munich who favor union certainly ought to be persuaded, considering how far things have gone, that success will not escape them." This was not what Bismarck wanted, but it was still perhaps not without effect. Tauffkirchen made certain that Antonelli's words came to the attention of King Ludwig II, and the latter is known to have quoted them to Archbishop Scherr of Munich in justifying his own request that the prelate influence clerical deputies in behalf of the treaty.[94]

Antonelli was, of course, right. Bismarck's efforts, which in the long run served only to strengthen his own conviction of the Pope's hostility to the *Reich,* were unnecessary. Considering the misinformation which he received at Versailles, however, his behavior is not surprising. It was rumored there, for example, in the last days of December,

[93] Bismarck to Arnim, Versailles, Dec. 21, 1870, *GW*, 6b: no. 1986. Some of the Bavarian liberals also considered a solution of the problem through revolution if the treaty was defeated. See von Schauss to Bennigsen, Munich, Dec. 15, 1870, Oncken, *Bennigsen*, 2:208–9.

[94] Goyau, *Bismarck*, 1:52–53; Döberl, *Bayern und Deutschland*, 188.

that Jörg and Bray were in close contact with the Hungarian minister Eötvös, trying to devise some way to bring the Habsburg Monarchy back into the picture. It was also claimed that Jörg had recommended a separate Bavarian peace with France. Neither charge was true. Jörg had, in fact, opposed the desire of some less responsible Patriots for a separate peace, on the grounds that it would violate the treaty of alliance which had been recognized in July as binding.[95]

Even before Tauffkirchen arrived in Rome, the tide was turning. The *Kammer der Reichsräthe* approved the treaty on December 30 with only three negative votes. Included in the majority were Scherr and the Bishop of Augsburg. Shortly afterward the King sent a telegram to the president of the upper chamber expressing his satisfaction, thus counteracting claims that he hoped the treaty would be rejected. Moreover, Bishop Senestrey of Regensburg, regarded as an ultramontane, wrote to Werthern speaking favorably of the treaty. His letter was not long in finding its way into the hands of the Patriots. Gradually the arguments of Huttler and the moderates were coming more and more to sound like those of Barth and the milder National Liberals, with a slight change of emphasis. The treaty left much to be desired, they said, but what was to be gained by rejecting it?[96] The position of the moderates was neatly summarized in a pamphlet entitled *Was dann?* by the deputy, Simmel:

Alone, without allies, with only the Catholic Casinos and the *Bauernvereine* — to take up the struggle with the government, the bureaucracy, the officer class, the whole Protestant population, the opposition press, all the cities of the country, with the whole force of sham liberal public opinion in league with Prussianism and its agents in the country, is foolish and hopeless.[97]

On January 3, 1871, twenty-nine members of the Patriot party announced that they would vote for ratification. Werthern calculated that only two more "conversions" would be necessary to insure victory. Debate in the lower chamber began on January 11, following the report of Jörg for the special committee, which recommended rejection of the treaty. The *Referent* insisted that the so-called national spirit

[95] Diary of Grand Duke Friedrich I of Baden, Dec. 29, 1870, Oncken, *Friedrich I,* 276; Rovère, 73.

[96] Döberl, *Bayern und Deutschland,* 177, 188; Döberl, *Bismarckische Reichsgründung,* 76; Schieder, 282.

[97] Döberl, *Bayern und Deutschland,* 177–78.

which demanded unification of Germany was nothing more than a fig-ment of Prussian imagination. The real question was this: Should the house approve or reject the extinction of Bavarian independence? As the representative of the Bavarian people, it had no right to compro-mise that independence. Further, if Bavaria entered the *Reich,* the monarchy would be forever destroyed. The title "King of Bavaria" would become meaningless, since its bearer would be subject to the "Prussian Emperor." To ratify the treaty would violate the Bavarian — or, in fact, any — constitution, for no state could legitimately de-stroy itself. Moreover, the Catholic Church, to which a majority of the population belonged, would be subjected to mortal danger in an em-pire controlled by Prussia, which, through her predominance in the federal council, could always subject Bavaria to her will. Prussian mili-tarism would be extended to the Alps. All the alleged concessions con-tained in the treaty were thus rendered illusory. The very least that the government could do, said Jörg, was to dissolve the chamber and order new elections, so that the people might have a voice in deciding their own fate. The only positive recommendation which the commit-tee would make was that Bavaria, having rejected the treaty, should inaugurate negotiations with Prussia for an indissoluble treaty of alli-ance, and for renewal of the *Zollverein* on the pre-1866 basis.[98]

The debate, of unprecedented ferocity, lasted for eleven days, dur-ing which more than a third of the deputies were heard.[99] On January 18, Huttler read to the house a declaration of the moderate Patriots along the lines of the pamphlet *Was dann?* After enumerating the evils and weaknesses of the treaty in terms not greatly different from those of Jörg, Huttler stated:

In spite of this, we, the undersigned, have, after conscientious exam-ination and reflection, decided not to withhold our agreement, for the sake of the situation in which our Bavarian fatherland finds itself. We do not want to share responsibility for the far greater evils which must arise from rejection of the treaty.[100]

Perhaps the most critical moment came shortly thereafter when Bray successfully countered Jörg's claim that Bavaria would be re-garded as an enemy by Austria if she joined the *Reich.* He produced

[98] *Ibid.,* 183–84; Wöhler, 24; Rovère, 67–73; Bachem, 2:243.
[99] Schieder, 283.
[100] Döberl, *Bayern und Deutschland,* 190; Rovère, 74.

and read a dispatch from Beust to Bismarck, written December 14, which quoted Franz Joseph's expression of good will toward the new Empire. Although Jörg maintained that this was merely an act of politeness, the psychological effect of Bray's dramatic gesture was considerable. Finally, on January 17, it became known that King Ludwig, as mentioned above, had requested Archbishop Scherr to work for adoption of the treaty. The extremist position was obviously crumbling.[101]

Nevertheless, the crucial vote was taken on January 21 in an atmosphere of extreme tension, for no one could predict the final outcome with assurance until very nearly the last member had cast his ballot. For example, the deputy, Father Westermayer, forsook the chamber before balloting began, a matter of considerable importance in view of the narrow margin which would decide the issue one way or another. The final count gave 102 votes for, and 48 against, ratification. The treaty thus received two votes more than the required two-thirds majority. Seventy liberals and thirty-two Patriots voted in favor of joining the *Reich*; forty-seven Patriots and one democrat voted against it. Only three Patriots had shifted their position since the declaration of January 3, one more than Werthern had then correctly judged to be necessary. Had Jörg been able to hold a half dozen more votes by party discipline, all Germany might have been thrown into political chaos even at that date, three days after Wilhelm I had been proclaimed German Emperor at Versailles. This possibility in no way stretches credulity, since many of the Patriots who voted with the majority would have preferred to do otherwise. Jörg and his coterie stalked out of the chamber immediately after the result was announced, in order to avoid having to listen to the *"Hochs"* for the Empire and the Emperor. A few of them, however, let it be known later that they were secretly glad to have lost.[102]

With Bavarian ratification of the Versailles treaty, Germany had at last become again a state as well as a nation. The particularists had lost, but only by the slimmest of margins. The nationalists had won, but only with the aid of some who were in their hearts chagrined at

[101] Döberl, *Bayern und Deutschland*, 188; Schieder, 288–89; Goyau, *Bismarck*, 1:87; Rovère, 67; Bachem, 2:243.

[102] Schieder, 293; Rovère, 67, 75; Goyau, *Bismarck*, 87; Döberl, *Bayern und Deutschland*, 191.

what they had done. Neither side was likely to forgive or forget. Jörg in his New Year editorial, penned sometime before January 21, had already written *"Novus nascitur saeclorum ordo,"* [103] leaving no doubts that, in his mind, the new order would be worse than the old.

If we are now to have a German Empire — in other words, if Prussia is now to govern all the states of the former German Confederation, with the temporary exception of German Austria, as provinces — the Napoleonic idea can, if it wishes, boast that it is the real creator or founder of this German *Reich,* whose crown is offered and assumed in Versailles before besieged Paris.[104]

A few weeks later he wrote for the *Blätter* his own account of the ratification debate, beginning on a note of deepest pessimism:

Consummatum est. The French were not so badly defeated that they felt obliged to accept Prussia's peace terms unseen. But Prussia's puissant ally, which contributed so much blood and treasure to the glorious victory over the hereditary enemy, has sheathed its weapons and capitulated. Bavaria has been conquered from within by the Prussian party. . . .[105]

Or, as Zander, the editor of the *Münchener Volksbote*, put it: "Bavaria capitulates, Prussia commands; the Bavarian people must pay, pay, again pay!" [106]

Catholic opposition to the *Reichsgründung* thus came to an end throughout the length and breadth of the land only after resistance had been rendered utterly hopeless. It ended on notes as widely different as Mallinckrodt's promise to make the best of a bad situation and Jörg's angry departure from the chamber when he became certain he had lost. Throughout the country many individuals of both faiths had come to regard the war, and the future of Germany, as another stage in the centuries-old struggle between Wittenberg and Rome. The fury of Catholic opposition, particularly in Bavaria, was in part responsible for this facile oversimplification of a tremendously complex problem. The unwillingness of men like Jörg to accept defeat graciously is perhaps even more responsible. The spring of 1871 saw the Bavarian editor, as before, endeavoring to convince his readers that the

[103] "Das grosse Neujahr," *HPB*, 67:1.
[104] *Ibid.*, 6.
[105] "Zeitläufe: Die Verhandlungen in der bayrischen Kammer und das deutsche Reich," *ibid.*, 223.
[106] Döberl, *Bayern und Deutschland*, 176.

war had been largely confessional in nature, citing Protestant as well as Catholic sources as evidence.[107] But Protestants and freethinkers were also partly responsible, because of the importance, absurd in retrospect, which they attributed to the decrees of the Vatican Council. In truth, Germany, and Catholic Germany in particular, went through a shattering intellectual crisis in 1870, as well as an overwhelming political upheaval. Catholics were faced with the problem of making difficult adjustments to both, just as they had been after the debacle of 1866. The establishment of the new Empire, however, required a different sort of adjustment from the one of a few years earlier. No longer could Catholics fight the battle for their Church within the restricted frontiers of petty states, or even in the somewhat broader framework of the North German Confederation. The founding of the Empire made possible the Center party; the circumstances undei which it was founded made such a party appear necessary. For Bismarck, having successfully outmaneuvered the south German particularists, no longer had to display the "tender regard" [108] for the Papacy, the Church, or its adherents which had marked his course between 1866 and the beginning of 1871. Resistance to Bismarck would go on; the means of resistance would, of necessity, be different.

[107] See, e.g., "Das grosse Neujahr," *HPB*, 67:3–4; "Zeitläufe: Das confessionelle Moment im letzten Krieg," *ibid.*, 480–84; Bachem, 2:245–46; Rovère, 112.

[108] *Neue Freie Presse* (Vienna), June 24, 1871, quoted in "Zeitläufe: Das Reich und die Kirche," *HPB*, 68:231.

Chapter 9

Epilogue: The Center Party

S CARCELY had the last stone in the Bismarckian edifice been laid when the Imperial Chancellor found himself again confronted with the implacable opposition of German Catholics, who appeared to him bent on undermining the foundations of the new structure before the mortar holding it together had solidified. During the last six months of 1870 and the first three of 1871 all the streams which have been followed in the foregoing chapters merged; the result was the *Zentrumspartei Deutschlands*. In the first Imperial Reichstag, which convened in March 1871, its representation was second only to that of the National Liberals, the party most intimately bound to the Chancellor and his policies.

The new party originated in Prussia, actually from the rebirth of the defunct *Zentrumsfraktion* of an earlier day. It was already established in the Prussian *Landtag* before the proclamation of the Empire made possible a national organization. Many considerations went into the decision made by leading Prussian Catholics in the summer of 1870 to enter again the campaign for *Landtag* seats under clerical banners, after having refrained for four years. The alarming growth of liberal anticlericalism, the ominous increase of Protestant hostility toward the Church, the retreat of Catholics themselves from the spirit of the age, symbolized by the decrees of the Vatican Council — all contributed to the decision.[1] That the Church was in danger few Prussian Catholics could doubt after the Moabit affair and its aftermath in the *Landtag*. Many of them became convinced that Bismarck's government would no longer protect the Church even in the exercise of

[1] Hansen, 1:797–98; Hertling, 1:210; Bergsträsser, *Parteien*, 60–61.

its minimum constitutional rights. The tone of the petitions received by the *Abgeordnetenhaus,* the government's refusal to allow debate on them, and the religious passions which revealed themselves on the floor of the house foreshadowed the coming *Kulturkampf.* To Catholics, the need of organized self-defense became obvious.[2]

A second factor, more difficult to evaluate, was the long-standing opposition of Catholics in the Rhineland to the heavy military expenditures of Prussia and of the North German Confederation. It is probable that this distaste reflected more the economic and social circumstances of the area than it did the religious convictions of its inhabitants. The *Rheinprovinz* was economically the most advanced region of Germany and would benefit most from the lower taxes which cutting military expenses would make possible. The area had not yet, moreover, become dominated completely by the heavy industry which profited later so tremendously from military spending. In 1867 many Catholic deputies to the North German Reichstag had opposed the military budget to no avail. The four-year budget period would expire at the end of 1870. If any effective fight was to be made in 1871, an organization was required. By 1870 Rhineland Catholics were almost as loud in their denunciations of Prussian militarism as were their fellows in the South. Mallinckrodt, representing a Rhineland constituency in the *Landtag,* had long argued that the inevitable strengthening of militarism was the greatest danger to be feared from a union of north and south Germany. This argument has direct bearing on the preference so often expressed by north German Catholics for a loose federal union, in which Prussia's military propensities would be checked by other member states. So strong was this sentiment that the *Kölnische Volkszeitung,* as late as the middle of June 1870, regarded curtailment of military expenditures and shortening the term of military service as the chief task of the next North German Reichstag. On July 6, only a few days before the outbreak of war, the same paper announced that Catholics were "not inclined to throw blood and treasure into the jaws of the Moloch of militarism."[3]

[2] See Chapter Eight, 235–39, and the references cited there, especially Goyau, *L'Allemagne religieuse,* 321–24. See also Bergsträsser, *Parteien,* 61.

[3] Hansen, 1:801–2. It should be remembered that most of the Rhineland had belonged to Prussia only since 1815. Many Rhinelanders looked upon their cousins from the east as naïve and boorish, a feeling that had nothing to do with religion, although the religious difference made it more difficult to eliminate.

The Catholics and German Unity, 1866–1871

By 1870 the mood of black despair which had afflicted German Catholics after the disaster of 1866 was gone. Ketteler, along with Peter Reichensperger, is credited by later Catholic writers with primary responsibility for the change. The Bishop's insistence that Germany must follow Prussia was, of course, more palatable in the Rhineland and Silesia than in south Germany, but even there, except perhaps in Bavaria, an awareness of the facts of political life had slowly developed.[4] One of the major elements in the reawakening of political Catholicism was the expansion of interest on the part of many clerics in social welfare. Here again Ketteler is the central figure. His distaste for socialism had begun to crystallize shortly after the War of 1866, and in the following years the alarming growth of the socialist movement in the Rhineland became more and more difficult for other churchmen to ignore. During the winter of 1869–70 the formation of Catholic workingmen's associations, along lines suggested by Ketteler's report to the Fulda Conference the preceding September, was speeded up, and an active campaign against the Social Democrats got under way. The latter was marked by efforts of existing Catholic societies to found cooperative credit associations, to stimulate the formation of labor unions, and to secure construction of adequate housing for workers. In March 1870, delegates of Catholic *Vereine* of the Rhineland and Westphalia met at Elberfeld to coordinate these efforts. Here, as at earlier meetings of the same sort, political questions inevitably came up for discussion, and this time plans were made for petitioning the *Landtag* to enact certain legislation favorable to the working class. Although conclusive evidence is lacking, it is probable that the feasibility of reestablishing the old Prussian *Zentrum* was also discussed at Elberfeld. The fact that leading roles were played by Schorlemer-Alst, then a member of the *Landtag*, and J. P. Bachem, publisher of the *Kölnische Volkszeitung*, is significant, for both were prominent members of the new party from its inception.[5]

The first active steps toward reestablishing the party came early in June 1870, when a group of prominent Catholics from the Rhineland and Westphalia met at Münster, and agreed upon a program drawn up mostly by Mallinckrodt. Both Schorlemer-Alst and Wildrich von

[4] See, e.g., Bachem, 3:11.
[5] Vigener, *Ketteler*, 546–48; Hansen, 1:795; Bongartz, 34–36, 84–85, 96–98, 149–50.

Ketteler, brother of the bishop, took part.[6] The program began with a reference to the increasing attacks on the freedom of the Church, citing particularly the Moabit affair. It went on specifically to defend both ecclesiastical marriage and ecclesiastically controlled schools. On the German question, it advocated a federal union, and condemned all efforts to establish a centralized unitary state into which, it claimed, the North German Confederation was being converted. There was no reference to Austria. The program went on to demand decentralization of Prussian administration, and to denounce militarism. It not only opposed any increase in the military budget, but insisted on a reduction in taxes, which would be possible only if military expenditures were curtailed considerably. Mallinckrodt, politically wiser and more experienced than his associates, insisted on qualifying this statement with the phrase "in so far as this is possible without endangering national independence."[7] Finally, the document contained a paragraph on the "social question," reminiscent of Ketteler's Fulda Report, and concluded as follows:

None of the parties which have formed fractions in the *Landtag* and Reichstag support the points of view and efforts sketched above in their entirety. For that reason there is the necessity for those who are in agreement with these principles to unite, so that they, as voters, can use their strength and direct their activity toward the election of qualified and trustworthy representatives, and so that our deputies will become strong through being united, so that they may give our viewpoint not only proper expression, but also bring its influence actually to bear on the life of the state.

Unity gives strength.[8]

The first public notice of the intention of Prussian Catholics to reenter the political arena as an organized party was given on June 11, 1870, when the *Kölnische Volkszeitung* published a letter from Peter Reichensperger containing the draft of a platform for the consideration of Catholic voters. It contained five points, all of them obviously derived from the Münster declaration, but edited for popular appeal. It omitted, for example, Mallinckrodt's reservation on curtailing military expenditures mentioned above, and added a specific demand for a shorter term of military service. Inexplicably it also omitted any ref-

[6] Bachem, 2:99–100, 103–4.
[7] *Ibid.*, 100.
[8] Text, *ibid.*, 100–3.

erence to the "social question," which had occupied approximately a fourth of the space in the Mallinckrodt program.[9]

On June 29 the third annual conference of the *Katholikenvereine* of the Rhineland and Westphalia opened at Essen. In addition to the customary discussion of measures to advance the interests of Catholic workers, the delegates discussed Reichensperger's platform at length. Their resolve to act was strengthened by the reading of a letter from Archbishop Melchers, then in Rome attending the Council, which expressed hope that the assembly would clarify for the public the attitude of loyal Catholics on crucial political issues, "so that the bases of our country's constitution, so important and so beneficial, will remain in force, unimpaired." Consequently, before adjourning, the conference adopted a program of seven points, five of which are restatements of the corresponding articles in the Reichensperger platform. The other two called for a fight against the introduction of civil marriage, and for "elimination of social injustice and furtherance of the workers' interests by Christian legislation." Both of these were derived from the Münster program, although some statement on the social question would have been expected from this group in any case. At approximately the same time, Melchers withdrew the prohibition he had imposed in 1867 on clerical participation in political campaigns, because of "the special importance of this election." [10]

For Catholics, the advent of the war a few weeks later, and the swift defeat of France only made the founding of a political organization more urgent, since major questions were certain to take on added significance with the establishment of a new *Reich*. In August Melchers voiced his conviction that attacks on the Church would be renewed with increased vigor once France was defeated, and, therefore, on October 28, three weeks before the election, he issued a pastoral letter asking "the election of devout Catholics of insight and experience." Only such men, he went on, would be certain to fight to preserve both the constitutional freedom of the Church and "its rightful influence

[9] The five points were (1) maintenance of the independence of the Church as guaranteed in the Prussian constitution, (2) preservation of the confessional character of the elementary schools, (3) preservation of the federal nature of the North German Confederation, (4) decentralization of the Prussian administration, and (5) amelioration of the financial status of the country through curtailment of military expenditures. Text in Salomon, 139–40; Bachem, 2:106–7. See also Bergsträsser, *Parteien,* 61–62; Hansen, 1:798.

[10] Hüsgen, 82–84; Hansen, 1:798–99.

on the school, on marriage, and on the family." The letter made it a duty of parish priests to give political instruction to the faithful, and to use their influence in all possible ways to insure a "favorable outcome of the election." Similar pastorals were issued by prelates in Trier, Münster, and Kulm.[11]

Meanwhile, August Reichensperger, elder brother of Peter, who had abandoned politics in disgust after the catastrophe of 1866, had now concluded that he could no longer remain aloof. In his view, however, Catholics could not possibly hope to gain their objectives without aid from devout Protestants, whose interests, he felt, were as seriously threatened by Bismarck and the National Liberals as were those of Catholics. Peter wrote to him on October 22, indicating complete agreement, but pointing out the practical difficulties which were, perhaps, more apparent to him than to his brother, who had been in retirement. "I see no one inclined to join us, since we are now attacked generally as ultramontanes, and no one will want to see himself so designated."[12]

On October 28, the same day on which Melchers issued his pastoral, a group of well-known Westphalian Catholics met at Soest and agreed unanimously upon a platform which later came to be regarded as the official program of the Prussian Center. By this time the question of the future *Reich* constitution had become extremely important, and the Soest document is the first of the Prussian Catholic manifestos of 1870 to contain a definite statement on this question. Point number five read:

[We seek] for the whole German fatherland a federal state, which will give unity in the necessary matters, but which will leave untouched in all other aspects the independence, the free self-government of the member states, as well as their constitutional rights.[13]

The other eight points were taken bodily from the Münster program, the Reichensperger proposals, or the Essen platform. The authors were Hulskamp, an editor from Münster; Mallinckrodt; and Schorlemer-Alst. All three had participated in the original Münster conference. The Soest program was signed by fifty-one individuals, nineteen of whom were clergymen.[14] Two days later another set of

[11] Goyau, *Bismarck*, 1:77; Hansen, 1:799.
[12] Pastor, *Reichensperger*, 1:605–6.
[13] Text, Salomon, 140–41; Bachem, 2:113–14.
[14] Hüsgen, 84–85; Salomon, 140–41; Bachem, 2:113–14.

proposals, couched in almost the same terms, was adopted by a similar group meeting at Essen. On the constitutional question, this declaration stated:

With reference to the organization of the entire German fatherland, [we believe in] holding firm to the hope of a single, great Germany, whose constitution will secure a solid union, and will guarantee the free development, as well as the justified individuality, of its parts.[15]

The election took place on November 9 and 16, and the concerted action of these various political leaders, plus the labors of the clergy, produced results which surprised even some of those who had worked hardest to bring them about. Approximately forty-eight Catholics who had agreed in advance to support the Soest program were elected, twenty-one of them from the Rhineland, which was allotted sixty-three seats in all. Six of the twenty-one were clergymen. In the Rhineland, Catholic candidates had been asked to promise beforehand that they would join the new Catholic fraction which was shortly to be established. The liberal newspapers at one extreme and the Prussian King at the other were horrified at the outcome. The *Kölnische Volkszeitung* was naturally gratified, and attributed the results largely to resentment over attacks on the Church which had been so numerous in the years just past. Peter Reichensperger wrote a letter to his brother on November 21, crediting a large share of the victory to the latter's decision to reenter politics, on the grounds that his prestige as a man and as a scholar had counted heavily with many voters.[16] By no means all Catholics, however, were enthusiastic over the Soest program, or the candidates who stood on it. In the Rhineland many of them took the attitude that, since admittedly nowhere in Germany did the Church have a position more advantageous than in Prussia, they were obliged, as a matter of "simple gratitude," not to vote for candidates who prided themselves on hostility to the Prussian government.

Of the total of roughly one hundred Catholics elected, twenty-two eventually joined the Free Conservatives, six became members of the Conservative party, two enrolled in the National Liberals, and twenty refused to commit themselves to any group. The rest, who established the new Catholic fraction, were able from the beginning to exercise an

[15] Text, Bachem, 2:114.

[16] Hüsgen, 87; Hansen, 1:799; Pastor, *Reichensperger*, 1:606; Bergsträsser, *Parteien*, 62; Diary of Ludwig Bamberger, Versailles, Nov. 27, 1870, Feder, *Bismarcks grosses Spiel*, 232.

influence scarcely warranted by their numbers, by virtue of the fact that the chamber was otherwise divided almost equally between conservatives and liberals.[17]

The initial steps toward reconstituting the Center were taken during the special session of the North German Reichstag early in December, when Peter Reichensperger, Mallinckrodt, Windthorst, Künzer, and others discussed the problem during a dinner at the home of Savigny. They found that the most serious impediment was the fact that Catholics who had been elected on the Soest program were, as Peter Reichensperger put it, "devilishly heterogeneous." Savigny, representing the views of a considerable number of them, wanted to reestablish the Catholic fraction as it had existed before 1866, *i.e.*, as a purely confessional party to defend the Church. Mallinckrodt, on the other hand, impressed by the development of Catholic parties in Baden and Bavaria, aimed at creating a Catholic *Volkspartei* in Prussia. Reichensperger insisted strongly that the designation "Catholic" not be used, for he was afraid that fuel would thereby be added to the fires of religious controversy. Late at night, after Windthorst and Künzer had already gone home, it was decided tentatively to proceed with the organization of "a political fraction along Christian-conservative lines." Peter Reichensperger, Savigny, and von Kehler were appointed as a committee to make further arrangements. On December 11, these three issued invitations to those Catholic members of the *Landtag* who were not yet committed to other parties for a meeting to be held at the *Englisches Haus,* a Berlin hotel, on the evening of the thirteenth. This gathering, and a similar one on the following evening, brought together most of those to whom invitations had gone, but three of the most important individuals were absent from both. Peter Reichensperger became ill at the last moment, Mallinckrodt was unavoidably out of the city, and Windthorst seems to have feared that his presence would be compromising in view of his past association with the King of Hanover.[18]

Upon the recommendation of Savigny, who had been converted, and August Reichensperger, it was decided to minimize the confessional issue and simply to call the new organization *Zentrumsfraktion (Ver-*

---

[17] Hansen, 1:799.

[18] Pastor, *Reichensperger,* 2:1, 3, 6, 9; Bergsträsser, *Parteien,* 62; Hüsgen, 87–88; Bergsträsser, *Politischer Katholizismus,* 2:9.

fassungspartei). It was hoped thereby that conservative Protestants could be induced to join in a common struggle against secular liberalism. In order to give the new group as wide an appeal as possible, a program much simpler and less specific than the Soest platform was adopted. Its two paragraphs read:

The fraction takes as its special task to work for the maintenance and organic development of constitutional rights in general, and especially for the freedom and independence of the Church and its foundations.

Its members will seek to achieve this goal by means of free understanding, and the freedom of each individual member to vote as he likes will suffer no limitation.[19]

To the original forty-eight members of the Prussian *Zentrum* were added, during the next four years, six others, most of whom, like Windthorst, joined within a matter of a few weeks or months. Although Bishop von Ketteler had no direct connection with the organization of the new fraction, his influence pervaded it then and later. Not all Prussian Catholics were pleased with the decision to soft-pedal confessionalism. In the Rhineland, where the election had been fought very largely on those lines, there was widespread objection to the efforts to enlist Protestants. The *Kölnische Volkszeitung* had warned on November 26 that such an alliance was unlikely to succeed because Protestants inevitably felt that their interests were basically in harmony with those of the state, while Catholics could only conceive of their Church as within the state, but not part of it. In the east, and even in Westphalia, where Catholics and Protestants were more evenly divided, the policy had more appeal. The Rhinelanders need not have worried, however. Protestants, conservative or otherwise, did not rush to join the fraction. Despite repeated denials that it was a confessional party, and announcements that membership was open to all sincerely religious individuals, it never attracted any appreciable non-Catholic membership. Religious feeling was too high, even in relatively tolerant Prussia.[20]

Meanwhile, preliminary labors were already well advanced toward the creation of a parallel and interlocking party on a national basis. Progress in this direction was symbolized by the incorporation, early in

[19] Hansen, 1:799; Hüsgen, 88; text, Salomon, 141; Bachem, 3:128.
[20] Hüsgen, 90; Hansen, 1:796, 799–800; Pastor, *Reichensperger,* 2:6 (note 1), 9; Vigener, *Ketteler,* 616.

December, of a new Berlin daily, *Germania,* soon to become the official organ for both the Prussian and German parties. *Germania* was not, properly speaking, founded by the Prussian fraction *per se,* since only one member of the triumvirate which established the paper, von Kehler, was politically prominent at the time. However, from the first issue, which appeared on December 17, *Germania* noticeably mirrored the viewpoint of leading Prussian Catholic politicians. Its verdict on the new *Reich,* for example, was moderately favorable; it adopted the thesis of Ketteler and Peter Reichensperger that the Church's constitutional position in Prussia was so advantageous that a Germany controlled from Berlin would be more satisfactory than one strongly influenced by Catholic Austria.[21]

This point of view was valid, however, only to the extent that those constitutional rights became part of the *Reichsverfassung* as well. In the fall of 1870, Ketteler apparently believed that this would follow as a matter of course. On October 1 he wrote to Bismarck at Versailles asking him to sponsor the inclusion of these Prussian guarantees in the imperial constitution. At that time Bismarck was involved in the preliminary stages of his negotiations with the south German states, and did not wish further to complicate his problem by injecting a controversial religious issue into the discussions. Moreover, his increasing anger at the tactics of the Bavarian Patriots was not likely to make him sympathetic with the Bishop's plea. He ignored the communication. Two weeks later, on October 15, Ketteler, probably at least partially in answer to this snub, published one of his most belligerent pastoral letters. Ostensibly, it was a protest against the occupation of Rome, but it did not overlook the opportunity to denounce Bismarck's government for its failure to prevent Italy's action. Prussia, Ketteler warned, by refusing to defend the interests of the Church either in Germany or in Italy, was following a path which could lead only to the complete triumph of secular liberalism in the new Empire. So long as the Hohenzollern Monarchy pursued what the Bishop called "French policies," internal peace in Germany would be impossible.[22] Ketteler's pastoral is of more significance than appears immediately. It contains, in embryonic form, a statement of what was soon to become the pro-

[21] Löffler, 52–53; Hansen, 1:800–2.
[22] Ketteler to Bismarck, Mainz, Oct. 1, 1870, *Ketteler Briefe,* 422–26; Vigener, *Ketteler,* 612–15; Goyau, *Bismarck,* 1:81–82.

gram of the *Zentrumspartei Deutschlands*: acceptance of the *Reich*, but unfaltering opposition to the secularism and liberalism upon which Bismarck was apparently going to base his régime.

By the time the Prussian *Zentrum* was founded in December, the Bishop's propaganda in favor of a national Catholic party had become much more specific and insistent. In the last week of 1870, he suggested that the chief task of the new newspaper, *Germania*, would be "to make easier the now necessary union of all German Catholics into a single great party." Shortly after the new year, he took occasion, in a pamphlet on the infallibility dogma, to denounce the National Liberals as "the party of injustice and untruth," and to express again his hope that a strong party embracing Catholics from North and South would be formed to fight for the liberties of the Church in the first Imperial Reichstag.[23]

The first official appeal to Catholic voters came in the *Aufruf zu den Reichstagswahlen*, issued on January 11, 1871, over the signatures of the entire Prussian *Zentrum*. This short statement, in which the word "Catholic" does not once appear, represented again, this time on a national scale, an effort to find a basis broader than membership in the Catholic Church for the new party. It asked for the election of "men of firm character who have in their hearts the moral and material welfare of all classes of the population and of all the *Stämme* which compose the German *Reich*, . . . who . . . want to see upheld not only political, but also religious freedom, and the rights of religious organizations against all potential attacks of hostile parties." [24]

One twentieth-century writer has called this declaration "the mobilization of political Catholicism." [25] At best the charge is an exaggeration, for the *Aufruf* was no more than an expression of hope. German Catholics were far from united. As has been pointed out before, Peter Reichensperger had, in the fall of 1870, lent the prestige of his name privately to the efforts of Bennigsen and Lasker to soften anti-Prussian feeling in south Germany. During the same months, Windthorst had visited Bavaria and discussed with several members of the aristocracy associated with the Patriots the feasibility of trying to create an all-German Catholic-conservative party.[26] None of these efforts had pro-

[23] Vigener, *Ketteler*, 616–18.
[24] Text, Salomon, 141; Bachem, 3:136–37. See also Hansen, 1:802.
[25] Hansen, 1:802.
[26] Spielhofer, "Bayrische Zentrumspartei," *HPB*, 165:425.

duced any encouraging results. At the time the *Aufruf* was issued, not only had Bavaria not entered the *Reich,* but it appeared eminently possible that she would not do so. In south Germany only the *Katholische Volkspartei* of Baden had yet given definite signs of willingness to cooperate in the founding of a national Catholic party. Immediately following the close of the extraordinary *Landtag* on December 21, 1870, the members of the Quadrilateral had issued a declaration explaining to their constituents why they had voted for ratification of the treaty of Versailles. After making the obvious point that Baden could not stand alone, they stated that "from now on it must be the task of the Catholic People's party of Baden to uphold and to contribute to the realization of its principles through a loyal union with the great all-German Catholic party, within the framework of the new *Reichsverfassung.*" [27] This declaration is extremely remarkable, since it came only a few days after the organization of the Prussian *Zentrum.* It was an expression of Lindau's often expressed belief that the defense of the Church's interests could no longer be successful solely within state boundaries.

The first German Reichstag was elected on March 3, 1871, by universal, direct, equal, manhood suffrage. It was the first election since 1848 in which all Germany participated. Catholics campaigned under various banners, for only in Prussia did the *Zentrum* enter the race as such. In Baden, the *Volkspartei* preserved its identity, although its candidates promised in advance to join the proposed new parliamentary fraction. The Patriots in Bavaria, still only grudgingly accepting their defeat of January, made no such promise, although, in fact, the deputies they sent to Berlin did join. In all, fifty-seven Catholics who were willing to cooperate in the establishment of a *Zentrumspartei Deutschlands* were elected. More than seven hundred thousand votes, or roughly eighteen and a half per cent of the total, were cast for them. Although far weaker than the National Liberals, who held 120 seats, they did form, unexpectedly, as mentioned before, the second largest bloc.[28]

[27] Dor, 104–5; text in "Der ausserordentliche Landtag des Grossherzogthums Baden, vom 12. bis 21. Dezember 1870," *HPB,* 67:99–100.

[28] Bachem, 2:137, 139, 244–45, 247; Bergsträsser, *Parteien,* 62; Pastor, *Reichensperger,* 2:20. Bachem says (2:139) that the commonly quoted figure of sixty-seven for the *Zentrum*'s strength in the first Reichstag is probably due to a typographical error in an early publication which has been repeated again and again.

Over a third of them came from the Rhineland, which returned men who had campaigned on the basis of the January 11 declaration from twenty-one of the thirty-five electoral districts. As in the earlier *Landtag* election, the clergy exercised considerable influence upon the vote in the Rhineland. Striking evidence of the effectiveness of clerical intervention, and of that of the various workingmen's organizations sponsored by the Church, can be seen in the fact that the industrial Rhineland did not elect a single Social Democrat in 1871, and only one in 1874. From Westphalia were elected eight deputies who joined the Center; from Silesia, two. The north German states, other than Prussia, contributed together only a handful.[29]

In the Reichstag election the Bavarian Patriots suffered the penalty for their efforts to defeat the Versailles treaty, winning only nineteen of the forty-eight seats allotted to the kingdom. Many Bavarians who had voted for the Patriots in 1869 could see little point in electing particularists, now that Bavaria was part of the *Reich*. Others were simply swept away by the national enthusiasm of the day. The Patriots did succeed in capturing practically all the conservative vote, and thus destroyed the possibility of establishing an alliance of northern and southern conservatives on a nonconfessional basis.[30]

Although the *Katholische Volkspartei* now had the direct suffrage it had fought for, at least in national elections, it won but two seats out of fourteen. Lindau was the only Badener who took part in the founding of the Reichstag *Zentrumsfraktion* in March. From Württemberg came Probst and a few comparatively unknown men. Hesse-Darmstadt returned Bishop von Ketteler and Canon Moufang. The latter was elected as a *Christlich-soziale*, although he soon joined the Center after he arrived in Berlin. Ketteler intervened indirectly in one Hessian district against a Catholic candidate, out of fear that the few votes he was likely to poll would be sufficient only to insure the defeat of the Protestant conservative, Gagern, and the election of his chief rival, a *Fortschrittler*.[31]

It is probable that the relatively poor showing made by Catholic candidates in south Germany is to be explained largely by the apathy

[29] Hansen, 1: 795, 803–4.
[30] Bachem, 2: 244; Hohenlohe to Count Münster, no place, March 10, 1871, Hohenlohe, *Memoirs*, 2: 39–40.
[31] Baumgarten and Jolly, 220; Nitti, 137; Bachem, 2: 138, 149; *Dalwigk Tagebücher*, Feb. 25, 1871, 483.

of voters who, viewing the new *Reich* with little enthusiasm, stayed away from the polls. Much later Count Hertling reminisced that he had not been particularly interested in the events of 1870, except for the "natural" patriotic enthusiasm which the military victories had aroused. A man who was later to be Chancellor of the *Reich* admitted having taken no part in the Reichstag election of 1871.[32] As a scholar, Hertling is perhaps not typical, but doubtless many individuals of more mundane callings shared his indifference.

The Reichstag convened on March 21, and on the same day the *Zentrumspartei Deutschlands* was formally organized. A few days later it published its first official program. The document was headed by a quotation from Mallinckrodt's famous Reichstag speech of 1867, *"Justitia fundamenta regnorum,"* and listed three objectives of the party, all reminiscent of the earlier platforms already cited. The Center, it stated, would strive to preserve the federal character of the Empire; it would seek "civil and religious freedom for all citizens of the *Reich*"; and it would not attempt to compel its members to vote in accordance with any official party viewpoint, which viewpoint, however, would always be arrived at through free discussion.[33]

Although the program made no mention of the Roman Question, it was upon this that the imperial *Zentrum* chose to make its first parliamentary fight. On February 18 the Prussian Center had moved in the *Landtag* an address to the throne protesting Italy's appropriation of Rome. The motion was, of course, voted down. During the first days of the Reichstag, the National Liberals, under Bennigsen's leadership, in order to forestall a similar move there, moved an address to the Kaiser declaring the unwillingness of the Reichstag to see Germany intervene in the internal affairs of any country, *i.e.*, in this case, Italy. Immediately, August Reichensperger introduced an amendment which would have substituted a request that the government take action to secure the Pontiff's traditional rights. The lines were clearly drawn, and practically the entire membership, other than that of the *Zentrum*,

[32] Hertling, 1:227.

[33] Text, Salomon, 142; Bachem, 3:137–38. The program was signed "Vorstand der Fraktion des Zentrums, von Savigny, Dr. Windthorst, Probst, P. Reichensperger, Karl Fürst zu Löwenstein, Freytag." Bachem, 3:138. The main lines of the program were elaborated in Ketteler's *Die Katholiken im deutschen Reich: Entwurf zu einem Programm*, completed in February 1871 and circulated confidentially among leaders of the party, but for tactical reasons not published until 1873. See Bowen, 88–89; Vigener, *Ketteler*, 618.

combined to defeat the Reichensperger amendment. The house then proceeded to adopt the original draft by the overwhelming majority of 243 to 63.[34] Thus the *Zentrum* began its parliamentary career with a crushing defeat. This was followed only a few days later by an equally impressive rejection of Peter Reichensperger's motion to include the Prussian guarantees of religious freedom in the *Reich* constitution. These two debates form the prelude to the *Kulturkampf*. The *Kölnische Volkszeitung*, which had called Peter Reichensperger's motion "an excellent test for judging the prevailing spirit within the other parties," [35] had its answer. Windthorst predicted darkly that "in the new Germany the legal rights of Catholic citizens will be crushed." [36] The National Liberal, Miquel, expressed the view of a large part of the Reichstag: "Germany has come into existence against the will of these gentlemen; they are now the defeated party." [37] Bismarck regarded the Center's proposals as a declaration of war against himself.[38]

To him they appeared an attempt to secure by parliamentary maneuver what Ketteler's letter of October 1, 1870, and Ledochowski's November mission to Versailles had failed to achieve by negotiation. Moreover, Ketteler had repeated his demands when he called on Bismarck in Berlin on March 9, shortly after the latter's return from Versailles. This time Bismarck had courteously refused.[39] Both projects of the *Zentrum* impinged upon areas in which Bismarck was inordinately sensitive to interference. His general dislike of parliamentary intervention in foreign policy has been remarked upon before. In this case, having just completed a great war which seriously upset the European balance of power, he had no wish to involve Germany in avoidable difficulties with any country, particularly over an issue so complex as the Roman Question.

Furthermore, Bismarck was understandably annoyed that north German Catholics, who in the past had fought savagely any effort to widen the competence of the federal authority, and their southern friends, who had in some cases been willing to defend state sovereignty

[34] Hansen, 1:802–3; Goyau, *Bismarck*, 1:104–8; Eyck, *Bismarck*, 3:86; Oncken, *Bennigsen*, 2:220–29.
[35] Hansen, 1:802.
[36] *Ibid.*, 803.
[37] Eyck, *Bismarck*, 3:86.
[38] Bergsträsser, *Parteien*, 62.
[39] Goyau, *Bismarck*, 1:100–2; Bismarck, *Gedanken und Erinnerungen*, 2:151–53.

literally to the death, were now demanding exactly what they had always opposed: a significant extension of the area of federal jurisdiction. Beyond that, the *Zentrum*'s proposals for altering the constitution could hardly have been accepted without opening up again the whole question of the Reichstag's functions in all its aspects.[40] It is not impossible that he suspected this to be the real purpose behind the moves.

In addition to these specific grounds, Bismarck had many other reasons to hate and fear the *Zentrum*. Its membership was a patchwork of discordant elements. It included *hochkonservative* aristocrats from Prussia and Bavaria, moderately liberal bourgeois from the Rhineland, and radical democrats like Krebs of Cologne, who, had he not been a Roman Catholic, would doubtless have joined Bebel and Liebknecht. Among its leaders were intimates of the old deposed dynasties, such as the Hanoverian, Windthorst. The Polish fraction, although it retained its own individuality, likewise supported the party on many occasions. Finally, on the national level the *Zentrum* absorbed the Bavarian Patriot party, though the Patriots for a long time remained a powerful force in state politics, where they persisted in their extreme particularism.[41] These widely divergent elements were held together by a single principle. As defined by the *Zentrum* itself, this principle was merely the desire to prevent individual states and the Catholic Church from being crushed by an omnipotent central government. As defined by Bismarck and his National Liberal allies, it was *Reichsfeindlichkeit,* not significantly different in the Chancellor's eyes from hostility to him personally.

These two viewpoints, one merely the converse of the other, posed a dilemma which was incapable of peaceful resolution in the political and intellectual frame of reference which dominated Germany in 1871. Thus the *Kulturkampf,* covertly under way since 1866, broke into the open. It was apparent in the increasingly fanatical tone of the press on both sides during the spring of 1871,[42] and it acquired official status when, on July 8, 1871, Bismarck, in his capacity as Prussian minister-president, abolished the Catholic section of the Prussian *Kultusministerium,* after his renewed efforts to secure papal intervention, in the

[40] Bergsträsser, *Parteien,* 62.

[41] *Ibid.,* 62–63; Spielhofer, "Bayrische Zentrumspartei," *HPB,* 165:425.

[42] Catholics were now reasonably well armed in this sphere of activity. By 1871 there were 126 Catholic dailies in Germany, printing more than 300,000 separate copies. See Bornkamm, "Staatsidee im Kulturkampf," *Historische Zeitschrift,* 170:54.

hope of forcing moderation upon the Center, had failed.[43] A new era in his relations with German Catholics opened.

This new era, which was to be dominated by the *Kulturkampf,* grew directly out of the old. The foregoing pages have sought to demonstrate that religious and politico-ecclesiastical issues played a role in the *Reichsgründung* far larger than has been conventionally recognized by historians.[44] Bismarck's struggle with south German particularism has been explored many times, but few writers have even attempted to show to what degree that particularism was motivated by allegiance to the Catholic faith. Conversely, the conviction held by many north German liberals that Protestants, or at least non-Catholics, had a near monopoly on progressive, enlightened, and national sentiments has usually been underestimated as a political force. In this so-called age of realism, romantic political notions had by no means died out.

During the period covered by this study much of the hostility of Catholics toward Bismarck is attributable to their attachment to intellectual, political, and ecclesiastical traditions which were alien to the main streams of middle and late nineteenth-century culture. They distrusted secular education, liberty of conscience, separation of Church and state, and all these they saw advocated, if not by Bismarck himself, at least by his allies, the National Liberals. In south Germany Catholics were, in many cases, also convinced that a Germany united under Prussia would mean ultimate strangulation of the Church itself. These fears appeared all the more justified when so many northern, and especially Prussian, liberals persisted in identifying Protestantism as the true German religion and Catholicism as the symbol of reaction and foreign domination.

The tendency of political opinion to polarize around confessional viewpoints had unfortunate, even disastrous, results. Persons who should have been natural allies found themselves in opposite camps. In retrospect, at least, the basic cleavage of the age appears to have been between a traditional, morally and religiously oriented *Weltanschauung,* shared historically by both confessions, and the secularistic, realistic, amoral outlook typified in Germany most spectacularly by

[43] Hansen, 1:805; Goyau, *Bismarck,* 1:124–31.
[44] Cf. Jörg after the War of 1866: "We know well the truth of the old maxim, that every political complication in Germany is in its innermost core a confessional question." "Zeitläufe: Confessionelle Leidenschaften im Ruine Deutschlands," *HPB,* 58:782.

Bismarck. The gulf between the confessions, which had narrowed considerably during the first half of the century, was now artificially widened by political maneuvers on both sides. This helped to push the majority of people south of the Main into a sterile particularism, and thereby indirectly forced nationalists of all varieties, in both North and South, willy-nilly into the arms of Bismarck.

To Catholic writers, of whom the Bavarian, Jörg, is the outstanding example, Bismarck after 1866 stood as the embodiment of the revolution in Germany. In this judgment they were not far from the mark. Where they erred disastrously was in their constant efforts to identify him with liberalism. Whatever else the great Prussian may have been, he was not a liberal, and Catholics, in so trying to label him, betrayed a striking lack of understanding of either the man or the movement. Rarely did they show any appreciation of his honest sympathy for federalism, in which they, too, generally professed a belief. Their federalism, of course, was quite incompatible with their constantly reiterated demands that the central government undertake to guarantee the freedom of the Catholic Church from interference by state governments. Such inconsistencies were products of the political immaturity of most German Catholics. Had their leaders possessed a better understanding of Bismarck's true purposes, much of the bitterness of the late sixties, as well as the *Kulturkampf* of the seventies, might have been avoided. Moreover, it is not beyond the realm of possibility that, under such circumstances, a working alliance between the Chancellor and Catholic political leaders might have developed before 1870, instead of a decade later.

That Bismarck would have welcomed such an alliance in 1868 and after is clear from his correspondence.[45] The unexpected victory of the hostile clerical-particularists in the *Zollparlament* elections in Bavaria and Württemberg, and their near victory in Baden, both angered and frightened him, for it brought to a sudden halt the slow but consistent progress toward a *kleindeutsch* union which had begun with the War of 1866. The south German fraction was able, for the most part, to prevent any action on the problem of national unity at the *Zollparlament* sessions of 1868 through 1870. In the two latter sessions the question was scarcely mentioned. Between the middle of 1868 and early 1870 control over the political situation in Germany gradually

---

[45] See Chapter Seven.

slipped out of Bismarck's hands. That period of a year and a half was marked by the rise of the Patriot party in Bavaria, its victory at the polls, and the ensuing overthrow of Hohenlohe; by the founding· of the *Volkspartei* in Baden; by the beginnings of a revolt against Bismarck's military policy in these states and in Württemberg; and by an open revolt of the National Liberals in the North German Reichstag. Together, these ominous developments, all of which culminated in February 1870, spelled potential catastrophe for Bismarck, for they destroyed his long-cherished belief that time was on his side. The necessity of counteracting these multiplying disasters is primarily what induced him to press the Hohenzollern candidacy when it was taken up by the Spaniards for the second time in February 1870.[46] That he was able to use the candidacy to bring about a solution for his many problems satisfactory to himself is a measure of his political genius. It is, moreover, in no way uncomplimentary to that genius to underline the fact that he was in a sense grasping for a straw, and that it was the inexcusable French blunders of July 1870 which insured the success of his almost desperate stratagem.

Bismarck's relations with German Catholics were intimately bound up not only with the origins of the Franco-Prussian War, but also with the constitutional arrangements for the German *Reich* which emerged from it. The concessions to Bavarian particularism, made necessary because of the Patriots' control of the Bavarian lower house, satisfied no one. Many National Liberals on both sides of the Main were outraged at what they considered a betrayal of the national principle. But even more important was the fact that among liberals in both areas there was in 1870 a strong sentiment in favor of making another attempt to force parliamentary government and ministerial responsibility upon Bismarck, in order to remedy the defects of the 1867 constitution. It is clear, however, from correspondence between National Liberal politicians during the fall of 1870 that the feeling *"Etwas muss zustande kommen"* gradually forced these ideas into the background, once it became certain that Bavaria would accept nothing beyond what Bismarck offered — if, indeed, that much. Had it not been for the particularism so strongly entrenched in Bavaria, Württemberg, and even Baden, the fight would doubtless have been undertaken, and

[46] Cf. Bismarck to King Wilhelm, Nov. 20, 1869, *GW*, 6b: no. 1449; Bismarck to Prince Reuss (St. Petersburg), Berlin, March 9, 1869, *ibid.*, no. 1334.

the *Reichsverfassung* might well have emerged a much-modified document. Actually, the constitution came a good deal closer to what the Catholic federalists desired, however unwilling they were to admit it, than it did to the wishes of the liberals.

The *Reich* was thus a compromise, but a compromise which did not eliminate, or really allay, the basic conflicts which had plagued the German people for half a century or more. Germany was no longer a geographical expression; a nation had become a state as well. But achievement of a real unity remained a task for the future.

Appendix, Bibliography and Index

Appendix

RELIGIOUS CENSUS OF THE GERMAN EMPIRE, 1871*

State	Church Affiliation			Percentage		
	Lutheran	Catholic	Other	Luth.	Cath.	Other
Prussia	16,040,750	8,268,206	380,296	65.0	33.5	1.5
Bavaria	1,342,592	3,464,364	56,494	27.6	71.2	1.2
Saxony	2,493,556	53,642	9,046	97.6	2.1	0.3
Württemberg	1,248,860	553,542	16,137	68.7	30.4	0.9
Baden	491,008	942,560	27,994	33.6	64.5	1.9
Hesse-Darmstadt	584,391	239,088	29,315	68.5	28.0	3.5
Mecklenburg-Schwerin	553,492	1,336	3,069	99.2	0.7	0.1
Saxe-Weimar	275,492	9,404	1,287	96.3	3.3	0.4
Mecklenburg-Strelitz	96,329	167	486	99.3	0.2	0.5
Oldenburg	242,945	71,205	2,490	76.7	22.5	0.8
Brunswick	302,989	7,030	1,745	97.2	2.3	0.5
Saxe-Meiningen	181,964	1,564	4,429	96.8	0.8	2.4
Saxe-Altenburg	141,901	193	28	99.8	0.1	0.1
Saxe-Coburg-Gotha	172,786	1,263	290	99.1	0.7	0.2
Anhalt	198,107	3,378	1,952	97.4	1.7	0.9
Schwarzburg-Rudolstadt	75,294	104	125	99.7	0.1	0.2
Schwarzburg-Sondershausen	66,824	176	191	99.5	0.3	0.2
Waldeck	54,055	1,305	864	96.1	2.3	1.6
Reuss, ältere Linie	44,898	150	46	99.6	0.3	0.1
Reuss, jüngere Linie	88,782	187	63	99.7	0.2	0.1
Schaumburg-Lippe	31,216	386	457	97.4	1.2	1.4
Lippe-Detmold	107,462	2,638	1,035	96.7	2.4	0.9
Lübeck	51,085	400	673	97.9	0.8	1.3
Bremen	118,103	3,550	749	96.5	2.9	0.6
Hamburg	306,553	7,748	24,673	90.4	2.3	7.3
Alsace-Lorraine	270,251	1,235,706	48,781	17.4	79.7	2.9
Total for German Empire	25,581,685	14,869,292	607,815	62.3	36.2	1.5

* *Statistisches Jahrbuch für das deutsche Reich, 1880: 13.*

Bibliography

1. Collected Documents

Andreas, Willy; Thimme, Friedrich; and Petersdorff, Hermann von (editors). *Bismarck. Die gesammelten Werke.* 2. Auflage. 15 vols. Berlin, 1924–35.

Bergsträsser, Ludwig. *Der politische Katholizismus: Dokumente seiner Entwicklung.* 2 vols. München, 1921–23.

Brandenburg, Erich; Hoetzsch, Otto; and Oncken, Hermann (editors). *Die auswärtige Politik Preussens, 1858–1871: Diplomatische Aktenstücke.* 12 vols. (Vols. 11 and 12 have not yet appeared.) Oldenburg, 1932ff.

Döllinger, Johann Joseph Ignaz von. *Briefe und Erklärungen über die vatikanischen Dekrete, 1869–1887.* München, 1890.

—————. *Letters from Rome on the Council by "Quirinus."* London, 1870. Published also as *Römische Briefe vom Konzil.* München, 1870.

—————. *The Pope and the Council (Janus Letters).* London, 1869. Published also as *Der Papst und das Konzil.* München, 1869.

Hahn, Ludwig. *Geschichte des "Kulturkampfes" in Preussen; in Aktenstücken dargestellt.* Berlin, 1881.

Salomon, Felix. *Die deutschen Parteiprogramme.* 2 vols. Leipzig, 1912.

2. Legislative Materials

[German Zollverein]. *Stenographische Berichte über die Verhandlungen des . . . deutschen Zollparlaments.* Sessions 1868, 1869, 1870. 3 vols. Berlin, 1868–70.

[North German Confederation]. *Stenographische Berichte über die Verhandlungen des Reichstages des norddeutschen Bundes. Konstituierender Reichstag.* 2 vols. Berlin, 1867.

[—————]. *Stenographische Berichte über die Verhandlungen des Reichstages des norddeutschen Bundes. I. Legislatur-Periode.* Sessions 1867, 1868, 1869, 1870. 11 vols. Berlin, 1867–70.

[—————]. *Verhandlungen des durch die Allerhöchste Präsidial-Verordnung vom 15. Juli 1870 zu einer ausserordentlichen Session einberufenen Reichstages des norddeutschen Bundes, vom 19. bis 21. Juli 1870.* Berlin, 1870.

[—————]. *Stenographische Berichte über die Verhandlungen des Reichstages des norddeutschen Bundes. I. Legislatur-Periode (II. Ausserordentliche Session 1870).* Berlin, 1870.

[Prussia. Landtag. Haus der Abgeordneten]. *Stenographische Berichte über die Verhandlungen der . . . beiden Häuser des Landtages. Haus der Abgeordneten.* Sessions 1866–67, 1867, 1867–68, 1868–69, 1869–70, 1870–71. 13 vols. Berlin, 1866–71.

[—————]. *Anlagen zu den stenographischen Berichten über die Verhandlungen des Hauses der Abgeordneten.* Sessions 1866–67, 1867–68, 1868–69, 1869–70, 1870–71. 12 vols. Berlin, 1866–71.

Bibliography

3. Miscellaneous Contemporary Publications

Allgemeine Zeitung. January–December 1866. Augsburg.

Bongartz, Arnold. *Das katholisch-soziale Vereinswesen in Deutschland.* Würzburg, 1879.

Jörg, Joseph Edmund, and Binder, Franz (editors). *Historisch-politische Blätter für das katholische Deutschland.* Vols. 58–68 (January 1866–December 1871). München.

Ketteler, Wilhelm Emanuel Freiherr von. *Deutschland nach dem Kriege von 1866.* Mainz, 1867.

Meyer, Rudolph. *Der Emancipationskampf des vierten Standes.* Berlin, 1874.

4. Memoirs and Correspondence

Bachem, Julius. *Erinnerungen eines alten Publizisten und Politikers.* Köln, 1913.

Bamberger, Ludwig. *Vertrauliche Briefe aus dem Zollparlament (1868–1869–1870).* Breslau, 1870.

Beust, Friedrich Ferdinand Graf von. *Aus drei-viertel Jahrhunderten, 1809–1885. Erinnerungen und Aufzeichnungen von Friedrich Ferdinand, Graf von Beust.* 2 vols. Stuttgart, 1887.

Bismarck-Schönhausen, Otto Fürst von. *Gedanken und Erinnerungen.* Volksaugabe. 2 vols. Stuttgart and Berlin, 1922.

Busch, Moritz. *Bismarck, Some Secret Pages of His History.* 2 vols. New York, 1898.

Feder, Ernst (editor). *Bismarcks grosses Spiel: Die geheimen Tagebücher Ludwig Bambergers.* Frankfurt-am-Main, 1932.

Friedrich, Johann. *Tagebuch während des vatikanischen Concils.* Nördlingen, 1871.

Fröbel, Julius. *Ein Lebenslauf. Aufzeichnungen, Erinnerungen und Bekentnisse.* 2 vols. Stuttgart, 1891.

Hertling, Georg von. *Erinnerungen aus meinem Leben.* 2 vols. Kempten and München, 1919.

Heyderhoff, Julius (editor). *Deutscher Liberalismus im Zeitalter Bismarcks.* 2 vols. Bonn and Leipzig, 1925.

——————. *Im Ring der Gegner Bismarcks. Denkschriften und politischer Briefwechsel Franz von Roggenbachs mit Kaiserin Augusta und Albrecht von Stosch.* Second edition. Leipzig, 1943.

Hohenlohe-Schillingsfürst, Chlodwig Karl Viktor Fürst von. *Memoirs of Prince Chlodwig of Hohenlohe-Schillingsfuerst, authorized by Prince Alexander of Hohenlohe-Schillingsfuerst and edited by Friedrich Curtius.* English edition supervised by George W. Chrystal. 2 vols. New York, 1906.

Holborn, Hajo (editor). *Aufzeichnungen und Erinnerungen aus dem Leben des Botschafters Joseph Maria von Radowitz.* 2 vols. Berlin, 1925.

Hübner, Rudolph (editor). *Johann Gustav Droysen. Briefwechsel.* 2 vols. Berlin and Leipzig, 1929.

Mittnacht, Hermann Freiherr von. *Rückblicke.* Stuttgart and Berlin, 1909.

Olivier, Émile. *The Franco-German War and Its Hidden Causes.* Translated by George Burnham Ives. London, 1913.

Oncken, Hermann. *Grossherzog Friedrich I. von Baden und die deutsche Politik von 1854 bis 1871. Briefwechsel, Denkschriften, Tagebücher.* 2 vols. Stuttgart, 1927.

——————. *Rudolf von Bennigsen, ein deutscher liberaler Politiker; nach seinen Briefen und hinterlassenen Papieren.* 2 vols. Stuttgart, 1910.

Poschinger, Heinrich von (editor). *Conversations with Prince Bismarck.* English edition edited by Sidney Whitman. New York, 1900.

Raich, J. M. (editor). *Briefe von und zu Wilhelm Emanuel Freiherrn von Ketteler, Bischof von Mainz.* Mainz, 1879.

Schäffle, Albert Eberhard Friedrich. *Aus meinem Leben.* 2 vols. Berlin, 1905.

Schüssler, Wilhelm (editor). *Die Tagebücher des Freiherrn Reinhard von Dalwigk zu Lichtenfels aus den Jahren 1860–71.* Stuttgart and Berlin, 1920.

5. Biographical Materials

Allgemeine deutsche Biographie. 56 vols. München and Leipzig, 1875–1912.

Baumgarten, Hermann, and Jolly, Ludwig. *Staatsminister Jolly, ein Lebensbild.* Tübingen, 1897.

Dor, Franz. *Jakob Lindau, ein badischer Politiker und Volksmann in seinem Leben und Wirken geschildert.* Freiburg-im-Breisgau, 1909.

Eyck, Erich. *Bismarck. Leben und Werk.* 3 vols. Erlenbach-Zurich, 1942–44.

——. *Bismarck and the German Empire.* Translation and condensation of the above. London, 1950.

Friedrich, Johann. *Ignaz von Döllinger. Sein Leben auf Grund seines schriftlichen Nachlasses.* 3 vols. München, 1901.

Herzfeld, Hans. *Johannes von Miquel. Sein Anteil am Ausbau des deutschen Reiches bis zur Jahrhundertwende.* Detmold, 1938.

Hüsgen, Eduard. *Ludwig Windthorst. Sein Leben, sein Wirken.* Köln, 1907.

Meyer, Arnold Oskar. *Bismarck, der Mensch und der Staatsmann.* Stuttgart, 1949.

Michael, Emil. *Ignaz von Döllinger, eine Charakteristik.* Second enlarged edition. Innsbrück, 1892.

Newman, Ernest. *The Life of Richard Wagner.* 4 vols. New York, 1937–46.

Pastor, Ludwig. *August Reichensperger, 1808–1895. Sein Leben und sein Wirken auf dem Gebiet der Politik, der Kunst und der Wissenschaft.* 2 vols. Freiburg-im-Breisgau, 1899.

Pfülf, Otto. *Bischof von Ketteler.* 3 vols. Mainz, 1899.

Vigener, Fritz. *Drei Gestalten aus dem modernen Katholizismus: Möhler, Diepenbrock, Döllinger.* Beiheft no. 7 of the *Historische Zeitschrift.* München and Oldenburg, 1926.

——. *Ketteler, ein deutsches Bischofsleben des 19ten Jahrhunderts.* München and Berlin, 1924.

6. Monographs and Special Studies

Allmann, Ludwig. *Die Wahlbewegung zum ersten deutschen Zollparlament in der Reinpfalz.* Leipzig, 1913.

Bandmann, Otto. *Die deutsche Presse und die nationale Frage, 1864–66.* Leipzig, 1909.

Bergstrásser, Ludwig. *Geschichte der politischen Parteien in Deutschland.* Berlin and Leipzig, 1926.

Bornkamm, Heinrich. "Die Staatsidee im Kulturkampf." *Historische Zeitschrift.* 170(1950):41–72, 273–306.

Bowen, Ralph H. *German Theories of the Corporative State.* New York, 1947.

Clark, Chester W. *Franz Joseph and Bismarck. The Diplomacy of Austria before the War of 1866.* Cambridge, Mass., 1934.

Döberl, Michael. *Bayern und die bismarckische Reichsgründung.* München and Berlin, 1925.

——. *Bayern und Deutschland im 19ten Jahrhundert.* München, 1917.

Doeberl, Anton. "Graf Konrad Preysing und das Erwachen der katholisch-konservativen Partei in Bayern." *Gelbe Hefte,* 2:843–55.

Friedjung, Heinrich. *Der Kampf um die Vorherrschaft in Deutschland, 1859 bis 1866.* 2 vols. Stuttgart, 1900.

Goyau, Georges. *Bismarck et l'église: le culturkampf, 1870–78.* 2 vols. Paris, 1911.

Hüffer, H. "Die Soester Konferenzen." *Festschrift Felix Porsch zum siebzigsten Geburtstag, dargebracht von der Görres-Gesellschaft.* Paderborn, 1923.

Körner, Gustav. *Die norddeutsche Publizistik und die Annexionsfragen im Jahre 1870: vom 15. Juli bis 24. November.* Hannover, 1907.

Krache, Enno E. A History of the German Confederation, 1851–66. Unpublished doctoral dissertation. University of Minnesota, Minneapolis, 1948.

Laux, John J. (pseudonym, George Metlake). *Christian Social Reform. Program Outlined by Its Pioneer William Emanuel Baron von Ketteler, Bishop of Mainz.* Philadelphia, 1923.

Bibliography

Lempp, Richard. *Die Frage der Trennung von Kirche und Staat im Frankfurter Parlament.* Tübingen, 1913.

Löffler, Klemens. *Geschichte der katholischen Presse Deutschlands.* München-Gladbach, 1924.

Lord, Robert H. *The Origins of the War of 1870.* Cambridge, Mass., 1924.

Martin, Hans. "Die Stellung der 'Historisch-politischen Blätter' zur Reichsgründung, 1870–71" *Zeitschrift für bayrische Landesgeschichte,* 6(1933):60–84, 217–45.

Müller, Karl Alexander von. *Bayern im Jahre 1866 und die Berufung des Fürsten Hohenlohe.* München and Berlin, 1909.

Mundwiller, Johannes. *Bischof von Ketteler als Vorkämpfer der Christlichen Sozialreform. Seine soziale Arbeit und sein soziales Programm.* München, 1911.

Nitti, Francesco Saverio. *Catholic Socialism.* Translated from the Second Italian edition by Mary Mackintosh. New York, 1908.

Oncken, Hermann. *Napoleon III and the Rhine: The Origin of the War of 1870–71.* Translated by Edwin H. Zeydel. New York, 1928.

Rachfall, Felix. "Windthorst und der Kulturkampf." *Preussische Jahrbücher,* 135(1909): 213–53, 460–90; 136:56–73.

Rapp, Adolph. *Die öffentliche Meinung in Württemberg von 1866 bis zu den Zollparlamentswahlen, März, 1868.* Tübingen, 1907.

————. *Die Württemberger und die nationale Frage, 1863–1871.* Stuttgart, 1910.

Rovère, Julien. *La Bavière et l'empire allemand. Histoire d'un particularisme.* Paris, 1920.

Salzer, E. "Fürst Chlodwig zu Hohenlohe-Schillingsfürst und die deutsche Frage." *Historische Vierteljahrschrift,* 11(1908):40–74.

Schieder, Theodor. *Die kleindeutsche Partei in Bayern in den Kämpfen um die nationale Einheit, 1863–1871.* München, 1936.

Schübelin, Walter. *Das Zollparlament und die Politik von Baden, Bayern, und Württemberg, 1866–70.* Berlin, 1935.

Schüssler, Wilhelm. *Bismarcks Kampf um Süddeutschland, 1867.* Berlin, 1929.

Spielhofer, Hans. "Bayrische Parteien und Parteipublizistik in ihrer Stellung zur deutschen Frage, 1866–70." *Oberbayrisches Archiv für vaterländische Geschichte,* 63:143–233.

————. "Zur Vorgeschichte der bayrischen Zentrumspartei." *Historisch-politische Blätter für das katholische Deutschland,* 165(1920):346–58, 418–25.

Vogt, Ernst. *Die hessische Politik in der Zeit der Reichsgründung, 1863–71.* München and Berlin, 1914.

Weber, Josef. *Die katholische Presse Südwestdeutschlands und die Begründung des deutschen Reiches, 1866–72.* Strassburg, 1918.

Wendorf, Hermann. *Die Fraktion des Zentrums im preussischen Abgeordnetenhause, 1859–67.* Leipzig, 1916.

Wöhler, Fritz. *Joseph Edmund Jörg und die sozial-politische Richtung im deutschen Katholizismus.* Leipzig, 1929.

Zuchhardt, H. K. *Die Finanzpolitik Bismarcks und die Parteien im norddeutschen Bunde.* Leipzig, 1910.

7. General Works

Bachem, Karl. *Vorgeschichte, Geschichte und Politik der Zentrumspartei, 1815–1914.* 7 vols. Köln, 1927–30.

Binkley, Robert C. *Realism and Nationalism, 1852–1871.* New York, 1935.

Brandenburg, Erich. *Die Reichsgründung.* Second edition. 2 vols. Leipzig, 1922.

Darmstaedter, Friedrich. *Bismarck and the Creation of the Second Reich.* London, 1948.

Dawson, William Harbutt. *The German Empire, 1867–1914, and the Unity Movement.* 2 vols. New York, 1919.

Gorce, Pierre de la. *Histoire du second empire.* 7 vols. Paris, 1904.

Goyau, Georges. *L'Allemagne religieuse: Le catholicisme, 1800–1870.* Paris, 1909.

Hansen, Joseph, *et al. Die Rheinprovinz, 1815–1915. Hundert Jahre preussischer Herr-schaft am Rhein.* 2 vols. Bonn, 1917.

Marcks, Erich. *Der Aufstieg des Reiches. Deutsche Geschichte von 1807–1871/78.* Stuttgart and Berlin, 1936.

Mourret, Fernand. *Histoire générale de l'église.* 9 vols. Paris, 1928.

Nippold, Friedrich. *The Papacy in the 19th Century.* Translated by Laurence Henry Schwab. New York, 1900.

Rosenberg, Hans. *Die nationalpolitische Publizistik Deutschlands vom Eintritt der neuen Ära in Preussen bis zum Ausbruch des deutschen Krieges: Eine kritische Biblio-graphie.* 2 vols. München and Berlin, 1935.

Schnabel, Franz. *Deutsche Geschichte im neunzehnten Jahrhundert.* 4 vols. Second and third edition variously. Freiburg-im-Breisgau, 1947–50.

Schulthess, H. *Europäischer Geschichtskalender.* Vol. 9 (1868). Nördlingen, 1869.

Srbik, Heinrich Ritter von. *Deutsche Einheit: Idee und Wirklichkeit vom Heiligen Reich bis Königgrätz.* 4 vols. München, 1940–45.

Stern, Alfred. *Geschichte Europas seit den Verträgen von 1815 bis zum Frankfurter Frieden von 1871.* 10 vols. Stuttgart and Berlin, 1894–1924.

Sybel, Heinrich von. *Die Begründung des deutschen Reiches durch Wilhelm I. Vornehm-lich nach den preussischen Staatsakten.* 7 vols. München and Leipzig, 1894.

Ward, Sir Adolphus W. *Germany, 1815–1890.* 3 vols. Cambridge, 1916–1918.

Ziegler, Theobald. *Die geistigen und socialen Strömungen des neunzehnten Jahrhunderts.* Berlin, 1899.

Ziekursch, Johannes. *Politische Geschichte des neuen deutschen Kaiserreiches.* 3 vols. Frankfurt-am-Main, 1925.

8. Statistical Material

[Germany, Imperial Statistical Office]. *Statistisches Jahrbuch für das deutsche Reich.* Vol. 1 (1880). Berlin, 1880.

Index

Aegidi, Ludwig Karl, 120
Agricultural societies, 32, 35, 182, 183, 185, 271
Alliances; *see* Treaties
Alsace-Lorraine, 6, 260–61
Andlaw-Birseck, Franz X., Reichsfreiherr von, 130n, 169
Anti-Catholicism, 25, 97–98, 109–10, 162–64, 197–200, 229, 234–39, 276
Anti-Protestantism, 6
Antonelli, Giacomo Cardinal, 201, 224, 258, 269, 270
Arco-Zinneberg, Ludwig, Graf von, 179
Arnim, Harry, Graf, 59–60, 194, 200, 211, 221, 223, 239, 257, 269, 270
Arnim-Heinrichsdorff (Conserv. Reichstag deputy), 73
Army, North German Confederation: expenditures, 74–75, 112, 277, 279, 280n; military bishop, 197, 217; military service, 74–75, 89, 120, 129; mobilization riots, 248; Prussian system, 104, 150; *see also* Prussia: army
Auer, Ludwig, 176
Aufruf zu den Reichstagswahlen (1871), 286
Augsburg, 271
Augsburger Postzeitung, 50, 180, 266
Augusta (of Weimar, Queen of Prussia), 18, 19, 157
Austria, 6, 7, 10, 29, 57, 91, 93, 96, 141, 149n, 171

Bachem, Julius P., 34, 44, 278
Bachem, Karl, 7n, 27, 51
Baden: army, 173; Church-state relations, 17–20, 109; democrats, 148; education, 20–21; elections, 128, 129–31, 287; *Landtag*, 20n, 171, 173, 265, 287;

liberals, 8n–9n, 18–22, 167; press, 48–49, 170, 174; Prussian military alliance, 57, 84–85, 106–7; treaty with N. G. C. (judicial comity), 239–40; union with N. G. C., 111–12, 129, 173, 240–41, 245, 256; Versailles treaty, 263–64; *Volkspartei*, 287, 294; War of *1870*, 249, 260, 264; *see also* Political Catholicism
Badischer Beobachter, 49, 91
Ballot, secret, 58, 70, 128
Bamberg, 185
Bamberger, Ludwig, 137, 142, 151, 157, 243, 244, 268
Barth, Marquard, 186, 251n, 253, 268, 271
Bauernvereine, 32–35, 182, 183, 185, 271
Baumstark, Reinhold, 19n, 170, 171, 174, 265
Bavaria: army, 99, 104, 250–52; Catholic Church, 11, 109–10; Catholic lay groups, 35, 182; conservatives, 17, 98–99, 125, 148; elections, 16, 127, 156, 183, 186–87, 230–31, 287, 288; federalism, 147; French alliance, 106; holy orders, 28n; *Landtag*, 196–97; liberals, 8n–9n, 16, 97–99; press, 41–44, 47, 49–51, 98, 183; Prussian military alliance, 57, 104–6, 113–15, 189–90, 250; relations with Prussia, 91–92, 94, 96, 125; union with N. G. C., 91–92, 94, 256; Versailles treaty, 262, 266–75; War of *1870*, 249–52, 255, 260; *see also* *Bauernvereine*, Political Catholicism
Bayrische Fortschrittspartei, 16, 96, 100
Bayrische Patriotenpartei: democratic faction, 179–80; founded, 175–76; French sympathies, 180; majority, 294; *see also* *Bauernvereine*

Index

Index

Thüngen, Wilhelm, Freiherr von, 99, 123, 136, 138, 146, 156
Tobias (Cath. Reichstag deputy), 153n
Treaties: Austrian trade, 141; Prussian military, 84–85, 103–9, 111–12, 122–23, 193; Versailles, 261–75
Twesten, Karl, 119, 153

Ujest, Hugo, Fürst von Hohenlohe-Öhringen, Herzog von, 76
Union of the Left (Bavarian *Landtag*), 96–97
Unions; *see* Labor
Usedom, Guido, Graf, 59, 195, 210

Varnbüler, Friedrich Gottlob Karl, Freiherr von, 132, 135, 137, 147, 161, 211, 231, 249
Vatican Council (*1869–70*), 187, 203–4, 209–29, 275; *see also* Hohenlohe Circular
Vicari, Hermann von (Archbishop of Freiburg), 18, 21, 165
Visconti-Venosta, Emilio, Marchese, 257
Vogel von Falckenstein, Gen. Eduard, 63n, 74–75, 117n
Volkmuth, Peter, 102
Volkspartei: Baden, 169–70, 172, 175, 230, 287, 294; Württemberg, 160–61, 231, 249; *see also Bayrische Patrioten-partei*

Wagner, Richard, 50
Wagner, Rudolf, Freiherr von, 161
Waldeck, Franz Leo Benedikt, 74, 139, 141, 153
War of *1866*, 26, 55
War of *1870*: Baden, 249, 260, 264; Bavaria, 240, 249–52, 255, 260; campaigns, 227, 252; credits, 261; Hesse-Darmstadt, 248, 260; treaties, 255–57, 259–75; Württemberg, 249
Wegner, Father (Reichstag deputy), 72
Weis (Bavarian *Landtag* deputy), 268
Weiss (Bavarian *Landtag* deputy), 186, 188, 255
Welfare; *see* Social Catholicism
Welfenfonds, 158–59, 256
Werthern, Georg, Freiherr von, 126, 127, 190, 210, 269, 271

Westermayer, Father (Bavarian *Landtag* deputy), 273
Westfälischer Bauernverein, 32–34
Wick, Dr. Joseph, 34
Wiest, von (Württemberg *Landtag* deputy), 88–89
Wiggers, Moritz, 155
Wilhelm I, German Emperor, 3, 59–60, 144, 200, 210, 211, 243, 253, 256, 259, 267, 269, 273
Wimpffen, Felix, Graf, 223
Windthorst, Ludwig, 7n, 56, 61–62, 67, 68, 70–73, 75–79, 81, 82, 116, 117, 121, 122, 124, 136, 137, 139, 143, 151–59, 193, 205, 214, 238, 239, 243, 247, 261–63, 283, 286, 289n, 291
Wolanski, Monsignor, 202
Württemberg: church and state, 161; crisis of *1866*, 23–24; democrats, 49, 148, 160–61; elections, 131–35, 264; federalism, 147; hostility to N. G. C., 88–89; military system, 161, 231, 246; press, 49; Prussian military alliance, 57, 106–7, 112–13; union with N. G. C., 88, 256; Versailles treaty, 264; *Volkspartei*, 160–61, 231, 249; War of *1870*, 249, 260; *see also* Political Catholicism
Würzburg: declaration of *1848*, 10, 18

Zander, Ernst, 50, 98, 180, 274
Zentrumsfraktion: (*1851–66*), 5, 10–14, 54–56, 58, 59, 66–68; (*1870–*), 276, 278–86; *see also Bundesstaatlich-konstitutioneller Verein*
Zentrumspartei Deutschlands, 7n, 23–24, 67–68, 276–95; *see also Bundesstaatlich-konstitutioneller Verein*
Zimmermann, Karl (Lutheran Bishop of Hesse-Darmstadt), 163
Zollparlament: elections, 124–33, 160, 177, 197–98, 201, 293; extension of competence, 133–35, 137–38, 143–47, 150, 160, 244; sessions, 134–47, 156–57, 293; tariff, 129, 141, 157; trade treaties, 140–41
Zollverein: extension of competence, 85, 90, 96, 110–12, 122–24, 132, 137–40; *1867* treaties, 110
Zu Rhein, Freiherr von, 140

DATE DUE